$8.95

An outstanding contribution

to the history of our time

Herbert Hoover continues the story of his remarkable career, begun in the fine first volume of his reminiscences, *Years of Adventure.* The years 1920 to 1933 were equally full of adventure, but adventure of a different kind. For him they were "The Political Years," when he held public office. As his record, personal and public, of a memorable era this volume will take a place of first importance in the historical literature of our time.

Mr. Hoover discusses, first, his part in solving the problems which followed World War I — feeding Europe, an international league for the preservation of peace, disarmament, and reconstruction. He then tells of his work, during the Harding and Coolidge administrations as Secretary of Commerce. Before he took charge the chief function of that Department had seemed to be "putting the fish to bed at night and turning on the lights around the coast." Mr. Hoover soon made it one of the foremost agencies in the government.

His election to the Presidency enabled him to carry out an even broader program of constructive policies for national development, including such activities as eliminating industrial waste, promoting foreign trade, conserving and developing the country's resources, child

(Continued on back flap)

Jacket design by Riki Levinson

THE MEMOIRS OF HERBERT HOOVER

The Cabinet and the Presidency
1920–1933

THE MACMILLAN COMPANY
NEW YORK · CHICAGO
DALLAS · ATLANTA · SAN FRANCISCO
LONDON · MANILA

IN CANADA
BRETT-MACMILLAN LTD.
GALT, ONTARIO

HERBERT HOOVER
A pencil sketch by Clarence R. Mattei, 1933

THE MEMOIRS

OF

Herbert Hoover

―――――❧❧❧❧――――

The Cabinet and the Presidency
1920-1933

THE MACMILLAN COMPANY: NEW YORK

PREFACE

Four of the thirty-two Presidents of the United States have ventured into the field of autobiography. They were John Quincy Adams, Ulysses S. Grant, Theodore Roosevelt, and Calvin Coolidge. The diaries of James K. Polk also possibly belong in this category. Voluminous state papers and correspondence of all Presidents have been published, but they cannot be considered as autobiographical in the usual sense.

Every autobiography has a major justification. It presents the participation of an individual among forces and events which, if recorded, contribute pieces of mosaic to the historian. From these pieces he creates great murals of human experience—with the hope that they will illuminate the way of human progress.

I returned in 1919 from several years abroad (including most of the years of World War I) steeped with two ideas: first, that through three hundred years America had developed something new in a way of life of a people, which transcended all others of history; and second, that out of the boiling social and economic caldron of Europe, with its hates and fears, rose miasmic infections which might greatly harm or even destroy what seemed to me to be the hope of the world. Therefore, soon after my return I began public speaking, writing articles for magazines, and even published a small book of diagnosis and warnings.

After some hesitation I came to believe that through public service I could contribute something to ward off the evils; something to the reconstruction of the United States from the damage of the war; something to advance the reforms which discoveries in science, invention, and new ideas had imposed. And I believed that I could contribute to

[v]

strengthen the principles and ideals which had given us such an abundance.

These impulses caused me to spend practically all of the next fourteen years in public service; and I may remind doubting cynics that for money, mental satisfaction, physical comfort and reputation for myself and my family, my profession was a far more enticing field.

Many of my hopes in public life were interrupted by the Great Depression—a product of some misdeeds of our own, but in the main the penalty of a great war and its impacts upon Europe. The European economic hurricane, when it reached our shores, compelled me to turn part of my attention from national development and needed reforms to the defense of our economic and social life. Moreover, the wounds of the Depression opened our flesh deeply to collectivist infections from Europe.

Herein are the major reasons for the laborious task of preparing these volumes, with its denials of relaxation and normal recreation to an otherwise busy life. The effort is to support the American people in their own true philosophy of life—and to present the consequences of turning away from it.

I have divided the subject matter into seven parts.

Part I deals with activities between 1920 and 1921.

Part II describes the Reconstruction and Development of the United States during my period as Secretary of Commerce from 1921 to 1928.

Part III is concerned with my nomination and election as President.

Part IV deals with that segment of Presidential activities, during 1929 to 1933, which bore on Development and Reform.

Part V takes up Foreign Affairs from 1929 to 1933, including the Japanese invasion of Manchuria in 1931.

At this point I have divided my account of the political years into a second volume which will be issued at a later date, as follows:

Part VI relates to the Great Depression, 1929 to 1933. I am well aware that uninformed persons recollect my term as President solely as the period of the Great Depression. That was indeed the nightmare of my years in the White House. It forms so important an economic and social experience that I have believed a full analysis of its origins and events should be set out in some detail.

Part VII reviews the Presidential campaign of 1932, a hot debate which throws light on the economic, social, and governmental problems of the times.

Part VIII is a short account of the eight years of aftermath from the abrupt change in our governmental, social, and economic direction. Without this latter account the lessons of the period would be incomplete or lost, for herein an ideological discussion was transformed into realities.

In these memoirs I have adopted the practice of treating subjects topically within rough chronological order. It involves some overlapping of time but, I believe, will be of more use to students.

The text of the period from 1919 to 1921 was written about 1925 or 1926. The text covering 1921 to 1933 was written in the years 1933 to 1936 and has been changed only by condensation and some clarification. The Aftermath was written in the years 1942 and 1943 with a concluding paragraph added as of 1947. I have given a minimum of quotations from my own statements during these periods. Their full texts can be found elsewhere.[1]

[1] The full text of all public statements and addresses from 1919 to 1928 may be found in the War Library at Stanford University. Those from 1928 to 1933 may be found in *The State Papers and Other Public Writings of Herbert Hoover,* collected and edited by William Starr Myers (Doubleday, Doran & Co., 2 vols., New York, 1934). Public statements and addresses after 1933 may be found in six volumes of *Addresses upon the American Road,* by Herbert Hoover, 1933–1938, 1938–1940, and 1940–1941 (Charles Scribner's Sons, New York); 1941–1945 and 1945–1948 (D. Van Nostrand Company, Inc., New York); 1948–1951 (Stanford University Press, Stanford, California).

Three books about my administration add information to my own narrative. They are *The Hoover Administration,* by William Starr Myers and Walter H. Newton (Charles Scribner's Sons, New York, 1936), *The Hoover Policies,* by Ray Lyman Wilbur and Arthur M. Hyde (Charles Scribner's Sons, New York, 1937); *The Foreign Policies of Herbert Hoover, 1929–1933,* by William Starr Myers (Charles Scribner's Sons, New York, 1940).

CONTENTS

Chapter		Page
	Preface	v

ACTIVITIES—1920-1921

1	Final Return to the United States	2
2	An Interlude	6
3	The League of Nations	10
4	Winding Up American War Agencies	15
5	Relief Again: Continued Feeding of European Children, Further Relief by the American Government, Relief in Communist Russia	18
6	Postwar Need of the United States for Reconstruction: A Survey of Waste in Industry, The Industrial Conference of 1920, Child Protection in America	27
7	In the Political Field	33

RECONSTRUCTION AND DEVELOPMENT
OF THE UNITED STATES—1921-1929

8	Reorganizing the Department of Commerce: The Economic Conference of September, 1921	40
9	Some Public Men of the Administration: President Coolidge, A Note on Secretary Hughes, A Note on Secretary Mellon	47
10	Reconstruction Measures: The Elimination of Waste, Elimination of Wastes in the Railways, Expansion in Electrical	

Chapter   *Page*

   Power, Simplification and Standardization, Specifications,
   Elimination of Waste by Reducing Seasonal Operation of
   Industry, Elimination of Waste by Arbitration of Trade
   Disputes, Waste of Oil, Waste and Trouble in the Coal
   Industry, Waste in the Federal Bureaucracy, Elimination
   of Human Waste in Accidents, Research in Pure and
   Applied Science, The Stanford Food Research Institute,
   The Opposition to Increased Efficiency   68
11 Foreign Trade: Foreign Trade Combinations Against the
   United States, A New Balance Sheet of International Trade   79
12 Foreign Loans   85
13 Better Homes: Municipal Relations to Home Building   92
14 Better Children   97
15 Labor Relations: Unemployment Insurance, Child Labor,
   Abolishing the Twelve-Hour Day, Industrial Conflicts, The
   Railway Labor Board   101
16 Commercial Help for Agriculture   109
17 Putting Our Water to Work: The Colorado River Commission, The Great Valley of California, Columbia River
   Basin, Waterway Development, The Mississippi System,
   The Great Lakes and St. Lawrence System, Mississippi
   Flood Control   112
18 An Interlude—Relief in the Mississippi Flood of 1927   125
19 Development of Aviation and Merchant Marine   132
20 Development and Control of Radio Broadcasting: The First
   International Radio Conference, The Assets and Liabilities
   in Radio   139
21 Development of the Fisheries: Chesapeake Crab Fisheries   149
22 An Interlude—Fishing   156
23 Curing Bad Business Practices—and the Business Cycle   167
24 Some Part in Foreign Affairs: World War Debt Commission, The Washington Conference of 1921–1922, The
   Dawes Commission, Recognition of the Soviet Government   17̃

Chapter   *Page*

25   Eight Years of Economic Progress   183

26   Living in Washington as a Cabinet Officer   186

NOMINATION, ELECTION, AND PRESIDENT-ELECT—1929–1933

27   The Republican Nomination   190

28   The Presidential Campaign of 1928: My Declaration of Broad
Principles, Prohibition, Some Color of Collectivism, Campaign Dirt, Religious Bigotry   197

29   Election and President-Elect   210

30   Organization of the Administration   216

DEVELOPMENT AND REFORM

31   Water Resources: Putting Our Water Resources to Work,
Water Storage (The Colorado River Dam, The Grand
Coulee Dam, The Central Valley of California, The Ten-
nessee River, The Misissippi System, The St. Lawrence
Waterway)   226

32   Conservation: Oil Reserves, The Western Ranges, Forests,
National Parks   237

33   Development of Aviation, Radio, and Merchant Marine:
Pan-American Air Policies, Radio, Merchant Marine   243

34   Public Buildings—San Francisco Bay Bridge—Highways   249

35   Development of Agriculture   253

36   Development of Better Homes   256

37   Development of Child Welfare   259

38   Reform in Law Enforcement: Appointments to the Bench,
and the Senators, Reforms in Judicial Procedure, Reform
of the Bankruptcy Laws, Reorganization of the Federal
Bureau of Investigation, Lindbergh Kidnaping Law, Prison
Reform, Prohibition, The Wickersham Commission   267

39   Reforms in the Executive Branch: Commissions and Comit-
tees, Reorganization of the Executive Departments   279

40   Reform of Veterans' Affairs   285

Chapter   *Page*
41 Reform of the Tariff   291
42 Reforms in Regulation of Business: The Anti-Trust Laws,
     Creation of Federal Power Commission, Railroads and
     Their Reorganization, Reforms in Banking and Stock
     Exchanges   300
43 Development of Social Reforms: Old-Age Assistance, Unem-
     ployment Insurance, Education, The Indians   312
44 An Interlude—Living in the White House   320

FOREIGN AFFAIRS—1929–1933

45 General Peace Policies: Latin America, Latin American and
     Other Foreign Loans, Reorganization of Our Foreign Serv-
     ice, The Kellogg-Briand Pact, Advancement of Other
     Pacific Methods for Settling Controversies, Cooperation
     with the League of Nations in Non-Force Fields   330
46 National Defense and World Disarmament: Limitation of
     World Navies, The MacDonald Visit, Reduction of Land
     Armies, Trade in Arms   338
47 Policies as to Our Island Possessions   359
48 The Japanese Aggression in China in 1931–1932—and a
     Summary of My Foreign Policies: An Exercise in Power
     Politics, League Action, Origin of the Doctrine of Non-
     recognition, Implementing the Nonrecognition Doctrine,
     Summary of Foreign Policies—1929–1933   361
Appendix   380
Index   391

ILLUSTRATIONS

HERBERT HOOVER   *Frontispiece*

THE BELGIAN INTERLUDE   *Facing page* 8

MR. HOOVER AS SECRETARY OF COMMERCE   42

MR. COOLIDGE AND MR. HOOVER   50

POLITICS ASIDE   158

PRESIDENT COOLIDGE'S CABINET   212

PRESIDENT HOOVER'S CABINET   212

INAUGURATION, 1929   220

MRS. HOOVER, IN THE WHITE HOUSE   322

Activities
1920–1921

CHAPTER 1

FINAL RETURN TO THE UNITED STATES

In September, 1919, Mrs. Hoover, Allan, and I boarded the *Aquitania* en route home. I was sure of two things: I wanted relief from European duty. I understood fully why our ancestors had moved away from it.[1]

After five years concerned with the World War, we looked only in one direction—to get home to the West. I had not been in California for nearly six years. Our family had been together for only a few scattered and fitful months. I saw them only at meals. And always at these meals, even sometimes including breakfast, we had for guests men with whom I was working. But now we promised ourselves we would take the first train for the West, get out the fishing rods, motor into the mountains, and live again.

This program sustained a jolt when word came to the steamer that the engineers of America were going to give me a great reception and a public dinner in New York. And they demanded a speech. Speeches were not a part of my treasured occasions of life, and the preparation of "some remarks" cast a gloom over the rest of the voyage. The speech turned out to be only a sort of review of what we had done and the forces of social disruption still current in the world.

With the reception and speech over, we went West—hoping that I had served my turn in public life and might now devote myself to a reasonable existence. And, of more importance, I hoped to renew association with a great lady and two highly satisfactory boys.

I was not quite forty-five years of age and was confident I had time

[1] As a matter of fact, I did not go near Europe again for nearly twenty years.

to reestablish myself in my profession, even though all my clients had scattered to the four winds. I opened offices in San Francisco and New York and hinted that I would undertake engineering work again. We resumed housekeeping in our cottage on the Stanford campus. Mrs. Hoover, the boys and I went camping, motoring, and fishing in the mountains just as we had so often dreamed and planned.

However, soon after the return to California, I made discoveries which disturbed my ideas of blissful living. I had come out of the seething social and political movements and economic chaos of Europe. I quickly found that America was not a quiet pool either. The country was in the midst of the inevitable after-war economic headache. Troubles rising from war demobilization brought general unrest and need for many readjustments. And the natural slump from the high wartime level of altruism and idealism complicated all Americans' thinking. We were also faced with gigantic tasks of physical reconstruction from the war. I had expected that.

In addition, the bitter conflict over the Treaty and the League of Nations cut across all issues.

Another disturbance was a personal matter. Hundreds of letters a day followed me about. Cables, telegrams, and telephone calls tracked me down in the forests and on the streams. Every day the press demanded statements on something or other. The magazines asked for articles, and, above all, it seemed to me that the American appetite for speeches had been unduly expanded by war exercises of that art. Every national gathering and every lunch club wanted speeches. Leaders of national movements bombarded me with requests to lend my name to their lists of sponsors.

With a desire for a little respite, I stated in answer to this clamor and demands from the press, as to what I was going to do:

I plan to adhere to the following rules for one month:
I will reply to no telephone calls, I am spending a month with two vigorous small boys. I do not want to be tied to the end of a telephone all day.
I do not myself read any communication which exceeds more than one page. These rules are solely for my own good.
I must decline the honor of speaking at sixty-four public meetings to which I have received invitations. I am satisfied that the American people will be

gratified to find a citizen who wants to keep still. This rule is for the public good.

All this is subject to the reservation that nothing turns up to irritate my conscience or peace of mind.

I offer this intimate disclosure of private affairs so that it may be seen that I contemplate no mischief against this Commonwealth.

A third hindrance to escape was the imperative obligation to finance and administer the Children's Relief in Europe for another year; and a fourth was to wind up speedily the business and the accounts of the various war organizations with which I had been associated.

All of which required that we move to New York and Washington again. And back we went, to live in an apartment most of the next eighteen months, with offices and a staff at 42 Broadway.

I now found myself in a burst of popularity. The newspapers dubbed me, falsely, a "leading American." In fact, the *New York Times'* poll to select the ten most important living Americans placed my name on the list. I could establish by contemporaneous documents that I was not fooled by all this adulation.[2] I knew that if a man engaged in public life he was bound to create opposition every time he took a stand on a public question; that he was fated to accumulate enemies; that in the United States the laws of libel and slander had little potency, and that the customary form of reply to sober argument was proof of guilt by association or assumption of corrupt motives. It was the bitter experience of all public men from George Washington down that democracies are at least contemporarily fickle and heartless.

In any event, during the seventeen months from October, 1919, to March, 1921—the date when I went into the Cabinet—I had a busy and variegated time. My records show that I gave out thirty-one press statements, wrote twenty-eight magazine articles, made forty-six pub-

---

[2] My period of popularity lasted nearly fourteen years, which seems about the average. When the ultimate bump came, I was well fortified to accept it philosophically and, in fact, to welcome it, for democracy is a harsh employer.

In the ensuing period, also of fourteen years, I succeeded in reaching fairly deep unpopularity in consequence of the depression, fighting the New Deal, opposing World War II and its subsequent political policies. But after this second term of fourteen years some people began to think I had been right, and life was more complimentary.

lic addresses, presided over fifteen public meetings, gave evidence at nine Congressional hearings, and made four extensive reports on various subjects. I was presented with more gold medals by national bodies and received more honorary degrees from universities. It seemed to me that I had adopted a Pullman berth as my eternal home.

A primary right of every American family is the right to build a new house of its heart's desire at least once. Moreover, there is the instinct to own one's own home with one's own arrangement of gadgets, rooms, and surroundings. It is also an instinct to have a spot to which the youngsters can always come back. Mrs. Hoover had long dreamed of building a house upon a near-by campus hill where the glorious views of the mountains and bay came into sight. It was to be a Hopi house (not Spanish) with flat roofs, and all modern inside. She had leased the lot some years before, and, upon our return to California, she resurrected her preliminary architectural drawings and began to build. The house was all her own making, but the dreams which she built into it had a rude awakening. I again had to be away at intervals over many years and she, in loyalty and service, had to make more new and temporary homes. The house, however, reflected well her excellent sense of taste and form in arrangement and workmanship. It was her own blend of fine living and the new spirit of native western architecture to modern America. With outdoor living, its terraces, its foreground of the University, its magnificent views of the mountains and bay, it was an expression of herself. The house was two years in the building and was not completed when we migrated for another thirteen-year period—except to return sometimes for a few days in the summer.

CHAPTER 2

AN INTERLUDE

While we were temporarily at home on the Stanford campus in October, 1919, the King and Queen of the Belgians paid a visit to the United States as guests of the United States Government. They were the first official national guests by Congressional invitation since Lafayette, nearly a hundred years before, came to lay the cornerstone of the Bunker Hill Monument. They were scheduled to visit the principal cities from the Atlantic to the Pacific.

About four o'clock one morning my telephone began to ring furiously. The operator said that the King's secretary wished to speak to me from New York. Apparently the secretary did not know the difference between Eastern and Pacific time.

The royal party, he explained, had been notified of President Wilson's sudden illness, and had called off their week's visit at Washington. This disorganized their whole schedule. The State Department thought it a good idea for them to spend this extra week in California and to undertake their receptions by American cities from that starting point. Could I put the King and Queen up on my "estate"? I asked how many there were in the royal party. "Forty," he replied. I was at least awake enough to realize that I could not pack them all into the one spare bedroom of our cottage. The Belgians evidently thought that I owned a ducal domain. As gracefully as I could, I side-stepped the honor, but told him to bring along the party; I would find accommodations somewhere.

Later that morning I called up Harry Webb at Santa Barbara. He was a former engineering colleague who knew the ways of Europe. I asked if he could borrow for ten days two big places that would

[6]

accommodate twenty people each with all the servants thrown in. He promptly asked, "Will there be any buttons?"—that being current slang among Americans for kingly decorations. Knowing the habits of kings in dealing with innkeepers, mayors, and hospitable people generally, I assured him there would be "buttons." With the good will of the owners, and with this assurance to one of them, he secured two houses some miles apart. The King and his party duly arrived. At that time, Santa Barbara still maintained a Hollywood sheriff with a ten-gallon hat, high boots, and two revolvers. Although there were plenty of uniformed police, the Sheriff considered that his responsibilities extended to guarding the gate of the King's residence, mounted and with deputies. When on the first morning the King went for a horseback ride, he met this keeper at the gate. The Sheriff fell in behind. Promptly the King and the Sheriff became devoted to each other. The Sheriff addressed him as "O King" until someone corrected him. The next morning the Sheriff used the formal address of "Your Majesty." The King objected to this change and assured the Sheriff that his former salutation was the correct form—and so he remained "O King" for the week.

When the party was about to leave Santa Barbara, I called up the King's secretary about the "buttons." He cheerfully agreed to fill the bill by giving out the Order of the Crown—the Belgian decoration that was customarily bestowed on worthy and useful civilians.

In the meantime Mayor Rolph of San Francisco had called upon me to reveal a personal difficulty. He was up for reelection in a few days, and he was worried over the effect that consorting with Kings and Queens might have on the South of Market Street vote. I offered to take over the chairmanship of the reception in San Francisco and let him play as large or as small a part as he thought advisable. This was arranged by getting the Governor to appoint me official host. I worked up the program and presided.

We decided to have a parade escorting the King and Queen up Market Street from the Ferry Building to the City Hall, where the Mayor could make a short address of welcome. When we consulted the Chief of Police about our arrangements he offered the surprising question: "How big a crowd do you want?" I did not quite see what influence he could have in that matter, but he explained that, while San Francisco was a checkerboard city, it had the unique feature of Market Street cutting diagonally across the other streets. If he stopped the public from crossing Market Street they would pile up on the sidewalks; if he held them for five minutes we should have a fair crowd, and ten minutes would produce a big crowd. We took ten minutes.

The party duly arrived in San Francisco to begin their transcontinental series of public receptions. Just as I arrived at the Ferry Building to meet them, Mrs. Hoover called up to say she would not be able to be there as Allan had fallen out of a tree and broken something in his insides.

With the help of Army and Navy contingents and their bands, we made a good showing in the parade and, in time, arrived at the City Hall with plaudits from great crowds. I duly presented the King to the Mayor, who stood on a little platform under the dome of the City Hall. Mr. Rolph at once noticed that all the galleries around the dome were crowded—an opportunity that no good politician would overlook. After a few words of welcome he delivered a few minutes of well chosen remarks upon our municipal issues and the virtues of the common man. A good time was had by all. I managed to get in a telephone call home and found Allan's insides were all right but his arm was broken.

From the City Hall we went to the Palace Hotel, where we had engaged rooms for the King's use prior to a public luncheon in his honor. At this point an agitated Webb called me up from Santa Barbara. He said that the King had bestowed the Order of the Crown, second class, on the Sheriff, and only the third class on the one of his hosts. That one had read up in advance on Belgian decorations, and was now in an explosive state of disappointment. I found the King's secretary and laid our trouble before him. Immediately he pulled an Order of the Crown, second class, out of the bag. I informed Webb by telegraph that it was coming, and that the secretary did not mind in the least taking the blame for the mistake.

I had no sooner returned to the King's rooms than the Mayor descended upon me with the Order of the Crown, second class—glittering star, red ribbon, and all—in his hand, and a troubled look. The

THE BELGIAN INTERLUDE
Crown Prince Leopold, Mr. Hoover, Queen Elizabeth,
and King Albert

King had just put it on him. And the very next day, he was coming up for reelection. He felt certain that if he faced over a thousand people and reporters at the luncheon with this display of feudalism on his breast, he would lose thousands of votes. It was an emergency that called for quick action. I suggested to His Honor that certain European cities had been decorated for valor; Verdun, for example, had received the Croix de Guerre. Why should he not speak at the luncheon, refer to this precedent, and go on to grow eloquent over the great honor conferred on the City of San Francisco? The Mayor thought this a stroke of genius. When he rose to speak, he held up the Order for all to see and in most eloquent terms accepted it on behalf of the city of which he had the honor to be chief magistrate. I sat next to the King, who turned to me and said, sotto voce, in the colloquialism of his youthful period as an American railroad man:

"What in blank is he talking about?"

"Pay no attention to the Mayor," I replied. "He has his troubles. I'll explain later on." Which I did. The King was so interested that he asked me to telegraph him the result of the election. I was happy to inform him next night that the Mayor had been retained in office by an unusually handsome majority.

I had forgotten this episode when later I was called on to serve as pallbearer at Mr. Rolph's funeral—he died Governor of California. On his breast was the button of the Belgian Order of the Crown.

CHAPTER 3

THE LEAGUE OF NATIONS

A few weeks after my return I was plunged into the controversy over ratifying the Treaty of Versailles, then under debate by the Senate. I was fully aware of the weaknesses of the treaties, as distinguished from the League Covenant, perhaps more aware than most Americans. Nevertheless, I had concluded that they should be ratified in order to save what was left of the European structure. I hoped that the League might later revise and modify the destructive parts of the treaties. I also felt that, if the League did not work, we could get out on a year's notice and, since our consent as a member of the council was necessary to any action, no harm could come to us.

The American people mainly concentrated their criticisms on the provisions concerning the League. The text of the treaties outside the League Covenant required nearly six hundred paragraphs. The Covenant comprised only something over twenty. It was not the League that brought calamity on the world, nor was it the failure of America to join the League. It was the failure of many of the twenty-five "points" and of the nations which, through the Treaty of Versailles, took over the domination of Europe, and of their interpretation of the League as the enforcement agency of the treaties. Our military intervention had destroyed German militarism and aggression. It resulted in placing the British, French, and Italians in domination of Europe. Their domination was better than German domination; but it was "balance of power," not "collective security."

I supported the League in an address on October 2, 1919, at Stanford University which was widely republished. In it I stated that the Treaty of Versailles was far indeed from perfect. I stated that the League was an experiment in the concept of collective action against aggressions which should be tried out. I stated that an era of peace was essential, and that the Treaty should be ratified by the Senate.

On October 15 I spoke again on the League and related subjects at San Francisco. Here I elaborated the idea that the hope of peace lay in sustaining the new representative governments in Europe. I emphasized that the best protection from radical infections in the United States was the preservation of these new governments and the consequent disinfection of the cesspools at the source.

The fight on the League in the Senate, so far as it had important merit, revolved around Article 10 of the Covenant, which provided:

The Members of the League undertake to respect and preserve as against external aggression the territorial integrity and existing political independence of all Members of the League.

This amounted to a practical guarantee of all the boundaries and settlements made in the Treaty and all the European empires. It was a practical freezing of the world into a mold of Versailles cast in the heats of war—and was a stifling of progress and all righting of wrongs. Moreover, I knew this article had been forced into the League by the French as a part of their demand for an indirect military alliance of the principal Allies. Article 10 was troublesome enough, but the separate Allied Military Alliance signed by the President also stood in the background. Fortunately, Mr. Wilson did not press the latter upon the Senate.

When asked into conference with some of the more reasonable Senators, it was evident that the Treaty could not be ratified without some reservation on Article 10. I advised them of my sympathies for a reservation, but insisted upon the great value of the League otherwise. They, as well as I, resented the destructive attacks on President Wilson then being made by Senators Lodge, Johnson and others.

As I wanted the President to know my views, I wrote him on the 19th of November, 1919, urging that to secure the ratification he accept the reservations "as on the whole they do not imperil the great principle of the League"; and I added that, as the League gained experience in a venture unprecedented in history, it would have to change anyway. The President had already been stricken, and I expected no reply, but I did not wish even to appear to be going behind his back. Later on, at Senator Hitchcock's request I sent the same text to all the members of the Foreign Relations Committee. Hitchcock was a supporter of the President but had a leaning to the reservations in order to secure ratification.

The Senate had divided into three groups. One group was for rejection of the whole business including the Treaty; a second was for rather drastic reservations; and a third group favored "mild" reservations. The second and third groups were at one time in large majority.

In a Commencement address at Johns Hopkins University on February 23, 1920, I urged again that the President accept the reservations, and that the Senate ratify the Treaty. On March 18, May 8, and May 13, I gave out statements to the press urging ratification with the reservation on Article 10.

Mr. Wilson was himself somewhat responsible for the failure of ratification. There were two occasions in the Senate in which the necessary two-thirds could have been had for "mild" reservations. But he declared he would not change "the crossing of a *t* or the dotting of an *i*." However, he was already an ill and exhausted man.

The misrepresentations and demagoguery of the League's opponents were driving public opinion steadily against it and the Treaty. More important than the domestic enemies of the Treaty were the blazing headlines depicting the frictions and quarrels in Europe and the obvious practices of old diplomacy in the resurrection of power politics, balance of power, and military alliances. These incidents daily helped the opposition. Also, it gradually became clear to the American people that the Treaty, as distinguished from the League Covenant, retained little substance of Wilson's Fourteen Points, plus the eleven points in his "subsequent addresses." Beyond this, two million returning soldiers were, in the majority, very anti-European. They had little experience with the peoples of Europe and regarded them as "just foreigners." They generally opposed the League on the ground that they never wanted to be sent out of the United States again.

On September 6, 1920, I made an address at West Point almost wholly devoted to the League. I followed it with press statements on the 9th and 15th of the month. On October 9 in an address to a Republican meeting in Indianapolis again I urged that we join the League with the reservations.

During his campaign for the Presidency, Mr. Harding carried water on both shoulders. I joined with former President Taft, former Republican candidate for President, Charles E. Hughes, Senator Elihu Root, and other important Republicans in a statement expressing confidence in the League, with the reservations. This was issued in consequence of personal assurances from Mr. Harding.

CREDITS TO EUROPE

In the fall of 1919 propagandists from Britain, aided by some of our own people, began a campaign to obtain more billions of credits from our government for European nations. I took a sharp slap at this propaganda in a public statement on January 7, 1920, insisting that Europe must now rely on private credits and that our business people should provide such credits on a business basis, and saying: "The world needs to get away from the notion of governmental help, both internally and externally, and get back to work and to business."

In a statement on January 19 and again in April, I insisted that private credit was needed, but that our government should not mix with the affair, and that our system for extending private credit should be better organized to prevent fraud, waste, and loss.

A committee of the American Bankers Association consulted me on the subject and finally called a meeting in Chicago on December 10, 1920, to consider the problem. I was the principal speaker. The purpose was to organize a corporation through which these credits could flow, with proper checks against speculative, wasteful, and bad loans. Congress, some years before, had authorized such corporations. By an organization of this kind a larger volume of credit for constructive purposes could be provided. I said in part:

It is far better that these problems be solved by the process of business and individual initiative than that they be attempted by our government. The resort to direct loans by our government to foreign governments to promote commerce can lead only to a dozen vicious ends. . . . Our government would be subject to every political pressure that desperate foreign statesmen can invent and their groups of nationals in our borders would clamor at the hall of Congress for special favors to their mother countries. Our experience in war shows that foreign governments which are borrowing our money on easy terms cannot expend it with the economy of private individuals and it results in vast waste. Our government cannot higgle in the market to exact the securities and returns appropriate to varied risk that merchants and banks can and will exact. Finally, the collection of a debt to our Treasury from a foreign government sets afoot propaganda against our officials, against our government. There is no court to which a government can appeal for collection of debt except a battleship. The whole process is involved in inflation, in waste, and in intrigue. The only direct loans of our government should be humane loans to prevent starvation. . . .

The world must stop this orgy of expenditure on armament. European Governments must cease to balance their budgets by publishing paper money if exchange is ever to be righted. . . .

The world is not alone in need of credit machinery. It is in need of economic statesmanship. . . .

I spoke on the subject again to the Merchants' Association of New York on January 24, 1921. But after a promising start the movement fell apart. As Secretary of Commerce I took up the question again.

CHAPTER 4

WINDING UP AMERICAN WAR AGENCIES

After my return, I was confronted with the accounting, settlement, and final liquidation of the large financial operations which I had directed during the previous five years. It involved much more time and work than we had anticipated. I had held many official appointments. At this time I sent to President Wilson a cordially expressed resignation from each of these offices; but he never acknowledged it. So far as I know the ghosts of the United States Food Administrator, the Chairman of the Export Council, and a dozen other offices have never been laid. Moreover, the President never acted upon the resignations of many other members of our staff. This oversight was no doubt because he was so deeply engrossed in the fight for the League, and because of his illness.[1]

The Treasury advances for relief, the direct Congressional appropriations for relief, the business of the Belgian Relief, the Grain Corporation, the Sugar Equalization Board, and the Food Administration operations at home and abroad involved some seven billion dollars of transactions. They had to be settled in such manner as to leave no loopholes of any kind. Because of shipping losses, insurance litigation, and a hundred other things, some of these liquidations lasted for years. But those are details tiresome to recollect. In each case we had from the beginning insisted upon such records, independent audits, and final auditors' certificates as would serve to answer any possible criticism. Owing to the ability and scrupulous integrity of the men in charge of

---

[1] Perhaps the endurance of our wallboard Food Administration Building over the next thirty years was due to its spiritual obligation to house those unlaid ghosts of public jobs—or new ones.

this work, particularly Julius Barnes, Edgar Rickard, Edward Flesh, John B. White, George Zabriskie, Robert Taft, Theodore Whitmarsh, Edwin Shattuck, and Lewis Strauss, ours was the one administrative branch of the war that was never "investigated" by Congress. We were, of course, subjected to the usual slanderous attacks which follow every large official activity in a representative government. But we were able, all of us, to prove instantly that we had never taken a dollar of salary; that we had not stolen a dollar; that we mostly had paid our own expenses; and that we had lost much because we had to neglect our own professions.

Before the planting of winter wheat in August, 1918, while the war was still on, I had had to decide whether to guarantee to wheat farmers a minimum price on the harvest of 1919. As we could not take risks on war ending before that time, I established that guarantee. This necessitated keeping the Grain Corporation alive to market the wheat harvest of 1919, and the job thus extended to the summer of 1920. I had arranged that Julius Barnes be given full authority, but I had a continuing moral responsibility to see that the work was properly done. Mr. Barnes did a most effective job, and we ended the organization on June 1, 1920.

The Sugar Equalization Board also lived on for a time. In the spring of 1919 before the peace was signed, we had to decide whether we would continue the corporation and again purchase the sugar crops of various countries. I recommended to President Wilson that the Board should again purchase and distribute all West Indian, American, Hawaiian, and Philippine sugar from the 1919 crop. Sugar production could not be resumed in Europe for another year, and there was obviously a great shortage in the world. Through our control of supply, we were holding the retail price in the United States to between 8 and 9 cents a pound without rationing and were insuring a just division among the American and Allied peoples. I advised the President that unless the sugar control continued for at least another twelve months, until the world crops were recovered, there would be speculation, profiteering, and a great rise in prices to the consumer. The majority of the Board approved this course. However, my friend Professor Taussig, who was a member, got the President's ear, and Mr. Wilson ordered the Board to cease operations. Professor Taussig was an indomitable devotee of freedom. The price of sugar subsequently rose to 25 cents a pound; profiteering ran rampant, and speculators made huge fortunes. Finally the sugar boom collapsed with great losses to thousands of retailers, wholesalers, and other innocent distributors. Although all this occurred long after the Food Administration was liquidated, unkind critics have often laid the sugar orgy to my administration.

Winding up the Belgian Relief Commission also involved problems, chiefly shipping and insurance claims, which hung around for many years. I have already related our contributions to Belgian education from our residual funds.

CHAPTER 5

RELIEF AGAIN

When I sailed for home at the end of September, 1919, I was not to be free from relief and reconstruction in Europe. Some of these activities stretched into my term as Secretary of Commerce after March, 1921, but I include them all here in order to wind up the subject.

CONTINUED FEEDING OF EUROPEAN CHILDREN

In the previous volume I have described our arrangements for relief to millions of European waifs, orphans, and undernourished children. We had established the work during the Armistice period as a charity with a contribution from the $100,000,000 relief appropriation of the Congress. In addition, we had currently received a large number of charitable gifts.

In order to keep the accounting of the Congressional appropriation of $100,000,000 clear from the other and much larger credits furnished by the United States Treasury to European governments for the purchase of food from the Food Administration, we set the $100,000,000 fund up as a separate legal entity under the title "The American Relief Administration." Its legal life expired on June 30, 1919. It had become evident that the service to children must be continued another year. As this work had become so well known under the name "A.R.A." we decided, with the approval of the President, to transform the public organization into a private one which would continue the work under the same title.

On July 7, 1919, I asked the principal officers of the old Food Administration if they would join with me, and we set up the organization under a Board of Directors comprising Julius H. Barnes, Edgar

Rickard, James F. Bell, Lewis Strauss, Perrin C. Galpin, R. W. Boyden, Robert A. Taft, Edward M. Flesh, William A. Glasgow, John W. Hallowell, Gertrude Lane, Howard Heinz, Dr. Vernon L. Kellogg, Dr. Alonzo E. Taylor, John B. White, Colonel James A. Logan, Colonel Alvin B. Barber, and Theodore Whitmarsh, with myself as Chairman.

We at once created committees in each state mostly comprising former Food Administration and Relief Officers. Their purpose was to encourage gifts to us.

We had some supplies in stock from the government organization and some cargoes en route when the official life of the American Relief Administration ended. With the President's approval, we turned these over to our private A.R.A. as liquidator.

We had some further resources aside from gifts. They came from the liquidation of our accounts in the general relief of the eighteen liberated and enemy nations. As explained in the narrative of that work, we had declared the United States Government would take no profits between purchases and sales of food for the relief of the famine. It was necessary, for simplification of the accounting of these enormous transactions with their purchases at a multitude of prices, to set uniform prices of sale and to put them high enough to make sure that the Food Administration agencies suffered no losses. An accounting contract with all the governments, made in February, 1919, provided that any profits as certified by our auditors would be used for children's relief. On June 12, 1919, we addressed all the governments concerned and secured their confirmation to use these funds in our new child-feeding organization.

We established another source of considerable income through what we called a "food draft." I addressed a letter to every American bank describing it and asking for its cooperation. Some 5,000 banks undertook to help out. The idea was to sell drafts in multiples of $10 which carried on their face the undertaking to deliver at any of our many American Relief Administration warehouses in Europe a specific number of pounds of flour, bacon, milk, etc., to a designated individual. This device enabled hundreds of thousands of American families with relatives in Europe to send them food. The chaos in European exchange made this a safer and more economical action than remitting cash—and moreover in many parts of Europe food beyond the continuing government rations could not be had at any price.

The bankers undertook to issue the drafts without any charge. We sold them on such terms that they returned a profit for the Children's Relief. During the following year we sold drafts to a total of $8,000,000. We had scarcely a complaint as to quality of the food or failure to deliver. The profits, all of which went to the Children's Relief, amounted to more than $600,000.

At the time of our new organization in the summer of 1919 I had expected to wind up the Children's Relief activities with the completion of the August, 1920, harvest in Europe and believed the above sources would pay our way to that termination. But it was soon obvious that some governments were not organized strongly enough to take on the task of feeding some six or seven million children still on our hands. Therefore, in May, 1920, a year after the peace, we determined to continue the work over the third winter (1921).

As we required new sources of income, we determined to make a more systematically organized public appeal.

On June 23, 1920, I called all of the relief organizations interested in Europe to a preliminary meeting and laid the foundation for a "European Relief Council" to join in a drive for funds. The organization was set in its final form at a meeting on September 27 with me as Chairman, Franklin K. Lane as Treasurer and Christian A. Herter as Secretary. Our public relation embraced Raymond S. Mayer and James Rosenberg. The Council comprised the American Relief Administration, the Red Cross, the Friends Service Committee, the Jewish Joint Distribution Committee, the Federal Council of Churches, the Knights of Columbus, the Y.M.C.A. and the Y.W.C.A., with their representatives on its directorate.

Examination of the needs in Europe seemed to show that we must raise about $33,000,000 to continue our programs for another year. In addition to joint action at home we made arrangements to prevent any overlap of the work of our various American organizations in Europe. The American Relief Administration undertook to feed and clothe several million children directly and to continue contributions to the American Friends Service Committee's work in Germany. The Red

Cross undertook to provide the medical supplies. Some religious organizations provided for adults as well as children. The American Relief
Administration undertook to issue food and clothing from its warehouses in Europe to all the other organizations; and thus all buying
and shipping became our burden. The organizations worked together
without friction.

In order to have full state and local cooperation between all the
organizations, it was agreed that the American Relief Administration
state committees should manage the coordination of local fund-raising.
We arranged for the initial appeal by President Wilson on December
13, 1920, together with proclamations by the Governors of the states.

We dramatized the drive by banquets to the "Invisible Guest." The
visible guests entered the room to find rows of rough board tables set
with tin dishes. At the center of the head table, in the place of honor,
stood an empty high chair with a lighted candle before it, symbolizing
the Invisible Guest. When the company sat down, Red Cross nurses or
college girls served them with the same food that we gave as an extra
meal to the undernourished children in Europe—but with second
helpings.

The most profitable of these dinners was in New York on December
29, 1920. We had secured a thousand guests, at $1,000 a plate. General
Pershing and I, flanking the Invisible Guest, made short addresses, and
leading artists filled the rest of the program. Suddenly a gentleman
whose name I never learned rose and suggested that I ask for more
money on the spot. "There is a million dollars here for the asking," he
said. In our invitations, we had stated that we would solicit no contributions beyond the $1,000 charged for the "banquet." I recalled this to
the audience, and refused as politely as I could. Whereupon the stranger
rose again and himself put to the house a motion that I proceed with a
collection. It was carried, unanimously and enthusiastically. This
brought, as he predicted, another million dollars. Later on, John D.
Rockefeller, Jr., asked me to announce that he would give another
million. So this one dinner brought in $3,000,000.

Our joint committees put on similar dinners all over the country at
an admission price of $100 to $500 a plate. I spoke in several cities and
wrote many press releases and magazine articles in support.

We closed the drive in March, 1921, to get out of the way of appeals for funds by domestic charitable organizations. The total receipts were $29,068,504.73, of which $10,000,000 went to the Red Cross, $2,200,000 to the Jewish Joint Distribution Committee, and $753,086 to the Friends Service Committee. The remaining $16,115,418.73 was assigned to some smaller organizations but mainly to the American Relief Administration. Later the Red Cross ceded a large part of its allotment to the A.R.A. and we undertook the medical side.

Thus, we provided for a great mass of children in eighteen nations over the years 1919, 1920, and until the autumn of 1921. No accurate estimate of the number of individual children cared for is possible. As fast as they recovered health, we took on others. Probably from the beginning fifteen to twenty million children were built back to strength. Our programs included not only food but also a vast amount of used clothing and new cloth, shoes, fixings, and medical supplies.

During this work for children after the peace we found acute destitution in the intellectual groups of many countries as a continuing aftermath of the war. I enlisted the support of the Commonwealth Fund, the Jewish Joint Distribution Committee, the Laura Spelman Rockefeller Memorial. With their help, combined with our own resources and those of other organizations, and the food drafts, we were enabled to supply more than 200,000 lawyers, doctors, scholars, teachers, journalists, and artists with food and clothing. The special funds raised and expended for this purpose amounted to $3,511,457.55.

Statistics can give only the bare bones of this service. No statistical table can portray the hunger, disease, recuperation, and the chattering glee of health-restored children.

FURTHER RELIEF BY THE AMERICAN GOVERNMENT

I had hoped that Europe could get through the winter of 1920 without any more governmental relief from the United States. But as the winter approached it was certain Armenia, Austria, Czechoslovakia, Hungary, and Poland must have some help in breadstuffs for adults in addition to our work for children. It seemed impossible to meet this need by funds from private sources. Therefore I took part in arranging Congressional authority for the Food Administration Grain Corporation to sell some of its surplus grain on credit. In this operation, we shipped 481,944 tons of grain of a value of $75,994,592 to five countries. As they repaid but little of the credits, this was also charity.

In July, 1921, just as we were preparing to wind up our activities in the rest of Europe, Maxim Gorky, the Russian author, addressed an appeal to me and the American people for aid in the stupendous famine among Russian people in the Ukraine and the valley of the Volga. This had been due partly to freaks of the weather, but mostly to a halt in agricultural production while the Soviets were communizing the Russian peasants. At that time we had a few million dollars left over in the American Relief Administration.

Ten days later I replied to Gorky, stating: "I have read with great feeling your appeal to Americans for charitable assistance to the starving and sick people of Russia, more particularly the children." I then outlined certain minimum conditions upon which we would undertake the task, particularly for children. They included freedom of all American prisoners in Russia; full liberty to Americans to administer the relief, to travel without interference; the power to organize local committees; distribution on a nonpolitical basis; free storage, free transportation, and free offices.

Commissar of Foreign Affairs Kamenev replied, suggesting a meeting with a representative of our organization. We designated Walter L. Brown, who was at that time in Riga. He and Maxim Litvinov, representing the Commissariat of Foreign Affairs, after tedious negotiations reached an agreement on August 20, 1921. More than a hundred American prisoners in Russian dungeons were released on September 1. The number was a surprise, as our Government knew the names of fewer than 20. We served the first meals from imported food in Kazan on September 21—just one month later.

I dispatched Dr. Vernon Kellogg and former Governor James P. Goodrich of Indiana to examine the situation. Their report disclosed an appalling condition in which some fifteen to twenty million adults and children must perish unless we undertook a far wider operation than was first contemplated of simple relief to children.

The Soviet Government had been subsidizing revolution over the world with Czarist gold. I demanded that they place a substantial amount of the remainder in our hands for expenditure upon food. They raised many difficulties, and at one time I threatened to abandon the whole project unless they complied. I finally got together $78,000,000 of which about $18,000,000 came from this gold. Part of our resources came also from an appropriation by the Congress of $20,000,000 profits remaining in the Grain Corporation and some $8,000,000 in medical supplies from Army surplus. We raised the rest from public charity.

The American people were not too enthusiastic over saving people who were starving because of their Communist Government. To make it more difficult the Communists in the United States promptly organized their own relief committee and appealed for funds. The drive was inspired by a Communist agent sent from Moscow, named Dubrowsky (or Ivanoff at times), and the director was Walter W. Liggett. As usual, they secured some respectable and well-meaning people such as Senator Arthur Capper on their letterheads. There was no assurance of honest expenditure, and I advised Senator Capper and later the public to support either us or some one of the religious bodies cooperating with us. At once I came under the usual rain of left-wing abuse. My critics, if I may use so mild a word, included many "liberals." Years afterwards, the Dies Committee unearthed the fact that the funds raised by this Communist drive, amounting to more than a million dollars, was with the approval of the Soviet Government largely spent on Communist propaganda in the United States—again demonstrating the ethics of the left wing and its devotion to the common man.[1]

I appointed Colonel William N. Haskell, who had administered the Armenian relief for me in 1919, to take charge in Russia and assembled for him a staff of some 200 experienced and loyal Americans. In the acute period of the spring we were giving food to 18,000,000 persons.

Our limited resources drove me to reduce the dietary regime of these people to the lowest common denominator. As we could get twice the

---

[1] This fraud on the American people was also subsequently exposed in the memoirs of a recanted Communist, Benjamin Gitlow (*The Whole of Their Lives,* Charles Scribner's Sons, New York, 1948, pp. 85, 87, 221). Liggett was subsequently murdered.

nutritive food value for a dollar from American shelled corn that we could from any other foodstuff, we relied upon it for our major food. The Russians knew little of Indian corn, but they possessed village mills and starving people quickly accommodate themselves to any kind of food. At the most difficult period we issued a bushel per month (50 pounds) to each person, costing about 70 cents delivered. In addition we gave a ration of something over a pound of fats, costing about 30 cents per month. That is, we were preserving human lives at a cost of about $1.00 a month. We fed the children an extra meal daily of condensed milk, stew, and wheat bread. It was a ghastly task, but our men carried it through with an estimated loss of fewer than a million lives.

We shipped a considerable quantity of seed wheat, and the acute crisis ended with the harvest in 1922. We found, however, that we must continue to care for millions of undernourished and waif children over the winter of 1923; which we did.

I received the following letter from Gorky:

. . . Permit me to express my feelings of gratitude . . . and complete satisfaction with the humanitarian work of the American Relief Administration, of which you are chairman. In the past year you have saved from death three and one-half million children, five and one-half million adults, fifteen thousand students, and have now added two hundred or more Russians of the learned professions. . . .

In all the history of human suffering I know of . . . no accomplishment which in terms of magnitude and generosity can be compared to the relief that you have actually accomplished. . . . It is not only the physical help which is valuable but the spiritual succor to the minds of mankind which are tormented by the events of the past years and sick, due to cruelty and hate.

. . . Your help will be inscribed in history as a unique, gigantic accomplishment worthy of the greatest glory and will long remain in the memory of millions of Russians . . . whom you saved from death. . . .

In the end I received an elaborate scroll of thanks from the Soviet Government signed by the President of the Council of People's Commissars, July 10, 1923, stating:

. . . in the name of the millions of people who have been saved, as well as in the name of the whole working people of Soviet Russia and of the Con-federated Republics, and before the whole world, to this organization, to its leader, Mr. Herbert Hoover, . . . and to all the workers of the organization, to express the most deeply felt sentiments of gratitude, and to state, that all the people inhabiting the Union of Soviet Socialist Republics never will forget the aid rendered to them by the American people, through the agency of the American Relief Administration, holding it to be a pledge of the future friendship of the two nations.

Kamenev.

Coincidentally, a notice appeared in the Moscow papers that I had carried on the relief hoping that "his mines in the Urals would be returned to him." As this appeared in some of the American papers, I had to explain that I had not even the remotest interest in these mines, and that if they were restored to their rightful owners, it would not benefit me one dime.

As a matter of fact no Communist ever doubted that we had some sinister purpose in all this activity. Many of the Russians who entered the employ of the Relief, often for no wages but their daily bread, were imprisoned when our staff withdrew; and our men have never since been able to get any news of them.

My reward was that for years the Communists employed their press and paid speakers to travel over the United States for the special purpose of defaming me.[2]

[2] Full confessions of this by recanting Communists appear in Benjamin Gitlow's *The Whole of Their Lives*. See also John T. Pace's statement, *Congressional Record*, Aug. 31, 1949.

CHAPTER 6

POSTWAR NEED OF THE UNITED STATES
FOR RECONSTRUCTION

Coincident with these many activities, it was apparent that the United States had its own job of reconstruction from the war and its aftermaths. Having come out of a gigantic laboratory of fierce ideas and clamor for change, I could not fail to observe many of the same fires in my own country.

Among our problems was the beginning of infections from European ideologies. They appeared not only as the long-agitated socialism, but as Communist fifth columns and a new mixture later known under the name of Fascism. This latter was a mere continuation of wartime economic controls wrapped in new clothes and a police state.

We had a large sprinkling of intellectuals who, stimulated by the fumes from the caldrons of Europe, were promulgating the idea that there was merit in a mixture of these new systems. Certain industrial, farm, labor organizations gave innocent support to the Fascist ideas, as they had rather enjoyed government assurances of prices and wages. The Marxist groups were clamorous for continued government operation of railways, ships, and factories which had been undertaken during the war.

I had come out of the European laboratory more convinced than ever that in the centuries of our separation from the Old World we had developed something which, for lack of a better term, I called the American System, which was alone the promise of human progress and the force which had led our nation to greatness. I well knew its faults. But these faults were marginal. I wrote a small book about it, entitled *American Individualism.*[1]

[1] Doubleday, Page & Company, New York, 1922.

[27]

It was apparent that from war, inflation, overexpanded agriculture, great national debt, delayed housing and postponed modernization of industry, demoralization of our foreign trade, high taxes and swollen bureaucracy, we were, as I have said, faced with need for reconstruction at home. Moreover, not only were there these difficulties arising from the war but there was the letdown from the nation's high idealism to the realistic problems that must be confronted. Deeper still was a vague unrest in great masses of the people.

Our marginal faults badly needed correction. We were neglecting the primary obligations of health and education of our children over large backward areas. Most of our employers were concertedly fighting the legitimate development of trade unions, and thereby stimulating the emergence of radical leaders and, at the same time, class cleavage. The twelve-hour day and eighty-four-hour week were still extant in many industries.

During my whole European experience I had been trying to formulate some orderly definition of the American System. After my return I began a series of articles and addresses to sum up its excellent points and its marginal weaknesses.

Constantly I insisted that spiritual and intellectual freedom could not continue to exist without economic freedom. If one died, all would die. I wove this philosophy, sometimes with European contrasts, into the background of my addresses and magazine articles on problems of the day. Along with these ideas, I elaborated a basis of economic recovery and progress. I did not claim that it was original.[2]

It involved increasing national efficiency through certain fundamental principles. They were (a) that reconstruction and economic progress and therefore most social progress required, as a first step, lowering the costs of production and distribution by scientific research and transformation of its discoveries into labor-saving devices and new articles of use; (b) that we must constantly eliminate industrial waste; (c) that we must increase the skill of our workers and managers; (d) that we must assure that these reductions in cost were passed on to consumers in lower prices; (e) that to do this we must maintain a competitive system; (f) that with lower prices the people could buy

---

[2] Twenty years later an economic institution in Washington, with loud trumpet-blasts of publicity, announced this as a new economic discovery.

more goods, and thereby create more jobs at higher real wages, more new enterprises, and constantly higher standards of living. I insisted that we must push machines and not men and provide every safeguard of health and proper leisure.

I listed the great wastes: failure to conserve properly our national resources; strikes and lockouts; failure to keep machines up to date; the undue intermittent employment in seasonal trades; the trade-union limitation on effort by workers under the illusion that it would provide more jobs; waste in transportation; waste in unnecessary variety of articles used in manufacture; lack of standard in commodities; lack of cooperation between employers and labor; failure to develop our water resources; and a dozen other factors. I insisted that these improvements could be effected without governmental control, but that the government should cooperate by research, intellectual leadership, and prohibitions upon the abuse of power.

I contended that within these concepts we could overcome the losses of the war.

Aside from the better living to all that might come from such an invigorated national economy, I emphasized the need to thaw out frozen and inactive capital and the inherited control of the tools of production by increased inheritance taxes. We had long since recognized this danger, by the laws against primogeniture. On the other hand, I proposed that to increase initiative we should lower the income taxes, and make the tax on earned income much lower than that on incomes from interest, dividends, and rent.

I declared that we should have governmental regulation of the public markets to eliminate vicious speculation, and that we must more rigidly control blue sky stock promotion.

I proposed that, as a part of eliminating waste and aiding recovery, we must have better organization and planning of our use of water resources, and that to this purpose all Federal public works should be concentrated in the Department of the Interior or in a special department created for it. I proposed the building of dams to conserve our water, the development of our waterways, including the St. Lawrence Waterway.

I used up much breath in expounding the folly of Socialism. I strongly advocated the return of the railways to private ownership and

the liquidation of the government ownership and operation of shipping
and the ending of war controls on prices and wages.

At that time these ideas were denounced by some elements as
"radical."

THE INDUSTRIAL CONFERENCE OF 1920

In the fall of 1919, President Wilson called a conference representing
industry, labor, and the general public to find some remedy for the
growing conflict between management and labor. The conference
broke up in a general row and got nowhere. Later in November he
announced, without consulting any of his appointees in advance, another conference to meet in Washington on December 1. The members
received their first notice of appointment through the newspapers.
They were unusually able and thoughtful men, obviously chosen for
their wide public backgrounds and broad interests. At the first meeting
the Secretary of Labor was elected chairman. But when he stated that
he could give but little time to the work they asked me to serve as Vice
Chairman. I presided at most of the meetings and superintended the
making of the report.[3]

We sat almost continuously, except during the holidays, from December 1, 1919, to March 4, 1920, when our report was completed. At
that time there was comparatively little collective bargaining in industry. Fewer than 10 per cent of the workers of the country were organized
in unions—and probably fewer than 5 per cent of the factory workers.
The first independent body to do so, we flatly recommended collective
bargaining by agents of labor's own choosing. As a step toward
progress in collective bargaining, and remedy of grievances, we recommended the extension of what later were improperly called "company
unions," who were to engage non-employee agents. We supported the

---

[3] The group comprised William B. Wilson, Secretary of Labor; Martin H. Glynn,
former Governor of New York; Thomas W. Gregory, former Attorney General; Richard
Hooker, Editor of the *Springfield Republican*; Stanley King, industrialist, subsequently
President of Amherst; Samuel W. McCall, formerly Governor of Massachusetts; Henry
M. Robinson, banker; Julius Rosenwald, merchant; Oscar S. Straus, former Secretary
of Commerce and Labor; Henry C. Stuart, former Governor of Virginia; Frank W.
Taussig, economist; William O. Thompson, President of Ohio State University; Henry J.
Waters, agriculturist; George W. Wickersham, former Attorney General; and Owen D.
Young, industrialist.

right to strike, except in the case of government and public utility employees. We set up a plan for adjustment of disputes which, while overelaborate, yet contained the germs of all constructive development since. We made strong recommendations opposing child labor, supporting decreased hours of labor, better housing, and advocating national investigation and development of plans for old-age insurance. Other recommendations included measures for the control of inflation.

The report was not well received by either the extreme left or the extreme right wingers. On March 24, 1920, the Boston Chamber of Commerce invited me to speak on the report. I accepted only on the urging of my colleagues of the Commission, as I knew it would be a very frosty audience. When I sat down from this address, the applause would not have waked a nervous baby.

Nevertheless I continued to advocate these ideas.

A SURVEY OF WASTE IN INDUSTRY

On November 19, 1920, I was elected President of the American Engineering Council. This was a joint body of all the leading engineering societies, designed to give my profession an outlet for its views on public questions. I suggested at once that we make an exhaustive inquiry into elimination of industrial waste as a basis for increased national efficiency, productivity and thus for both reconstruction and progress. I named for this investigation a committee of seventeen leading engineers whose experience covered the whole field of major industry, and secured gifts of $50,000 for incidental expenses.

The survey determined that 25 per cent of the cost of production could be eliminated without reduction in wages, increase in hours or strain on workmen. Published in 1921,[4] it attracted wide attention. Later, I put this plan into voluntary action on a nation-wide scale through the Department of Commerce.

CHILD PROTECTION IN AMERICA

My vivid experience with millions of children in Europe naturally turned my mind to examine our own American house.

Our army draft experience during the war had brought to the surface

[4] *Waste in Industry,* McGraw-Hill Book Co., Inc., New York, 1921.

appalling defects in health and education. There had been over 30 per
cent of rejects in the draft for these reasons. It had proved that our
vaunted national progress had some very black spots. And black spots
too often originated in the childhood surroundings of the rejects. As
a nation we had never really accepted the national relationship of these
mass questions of undernutrition and health in children to national
progress. My experience with mass problems of child health seemed to
me to carry some lessons for America. There were already devoted
sporadic efforts and numbers of isolated groups struggling to direct
public attention to these questions. On December 29, 1919, I opened the
subject in its national aspects in an address to the Associated Charities
of San Francisco.

In order to express my views more fully I accepted an invitation to
deliver the principal address before the annual meeting of the American Child Hygiene Association at St. Louis on October 11, 1920. This
was a struggling association of small influence, kept alive by the devotion of physicians who were specialists in children's diseases.

In this address, I proposed a program for national action. It had a
fine reception. I stated that 40 per cent of our children required organized action by health inspection in the schools; feeding a noonday
school meal in certain areas; more general compulsory education; and
prohibition of child labor.

My immediate purpose at this meeting was to obtain the support
of these devoted men for a plan to consolidate the half-dozen other
scattered associations dealing with child problems into a strong national
organization. To this they enthusiastically agreed. With this beginning,
we ultimately succeeded in creating the potent American Child Health
Association with adequate private funds and staffs. I shall have more
to say as to its accomplishments.[5]

[5] I discussed the various themes referred to in this chapter publicly in a number of
addresses and articles listed in the Appendix, under the heading Chapter 6.

CHAPTER 7

IN THE POLITICAL FIELD

Soon after I returned from Europe in September, 1919, a host of politically amateur friends began to work for my nomination as President for the election of 1920.

I had been so nonpartisan during the war, both in word and in deed, that I had no standing in either political party. In serving under a Democratic President, I had given him the full loyalties which he deserved in his gigantic task. Some thought, because of this service, I had a Democratic complexion. They felt more so because of a letter I had written during the Congressional campaign of 1918, urging the election of Congressmen and Senators who would support the President irrespective of political party. I was convinced then that if a majority opposed to his foreign policies were elected his position would be weakened in the impending peace negotiations. This happened, and his influence was weakened.

I believed in two-party government in peacetime. I had two generations of Republican blood in my veins. I was a registered Republican from my twenty-first birthday. In the Presidential campaign of 1912, I had enlisted under the standard of Theodore Roosevelt. That same year, I joined the National Republican Club, all of which was known to my Democratic colleagues in Washington.

My work in Washington had given me intimate opportunity to observe the Democratic party in its political aspects, all of which reenforced my Republicanism. It was obvious that the Democratic party at that time was composed of three widely divergent elements: First, an ultraconservative Southern group whose actions were often dominated by the black specter of the Reconstruction period after the Civil

War; second, a set of plundering political machines in many of the large cities; third, in the North generally the party embraced the whole lunatic fringe of greenback, "free silver" agrarian fanatics and near-Socialists. These latter elements had grown into a large voice in the party through Bryanesque demagoguery. In order to maintain "white ascendancy" and political office, the Southern Democrats were prepared to cater to these Northern groups.

There were in the Democratic party men of the highest purpose and ideals. Woodrow Wilson had been a beneficent accident due to a last-minute compromise in the Democratic Convention and a split in the Republican party. With fine exceptions, such as Houston, Baker, Lane, Baruch, and McCormick, the leaders in Washington expressed this chaotic combination.

I also disliked such Republican phenomena as Senators Penrose, Watson, Knox, Lodge, and their followers. But the rank and file membership of the Republican party in the North and West comprised the majority of skilled workmen, farmers, professional and small-business men. They gave it cohesion in ideas whose American aspirations I greatly preferred.

Despite my protest a committee of engineers and my former colleagues in public service broke out with a measles of Hoover Clubs and were insistent that I announce myself as a candidate. It was obvious enough that I could not be nominated by either party, even if I wanted the honor. Discouraged by the failure of personal protestations, I issued a flat statement on February 9, 1920, asking them to stop. I had to repeat it several times. However, this did not entirely quench their ardor.

My name was placed in the primaries of some scattered districts, both Republican and Democratic. Wherever I had any authority to prevent it I did so except in one case.

In California, at this time a strong Republican state, Senator Hiram Johnson, a candidate for the nomination for President, was running on a violent anti-League platform. His nomination as President would have pledged the Republican party to abandon the League altogether. None of the other Republican candidates, General Leonard Wood,

Governor Frank Lowden, Senator Warren Harding, all of whom at that time took a more moderate view of the League, would oppose Johnson in the California primaries. My friends urged me not to disavow their placing my name in the primaries, so as to allow an expression on the issue of the League. As I was not a real candidate, and as Senator Johnson controlled the state organization, there was no possibility that he could be defeated. However, a reasonably large vote for me might show enough protest in the Republican party of that state to prevent the Republican Convention from out-and-out opposition to the League. I did not make a single political speech or statement in the primary.

Johnson joined the isolationist newspapers in an orgy of personal abuse and slander directed at me. Their general line was that I was an Englishman and even a British citizen; that I was possessed of untold millions, and so on.

The California returns showed 370,000 votes for Johnson and 210,000 for me. This was extremely good, considering all the circumstances. The amount of support I received had a major effect upon Republican leaders in respect to Johnson's availability.

Without any organized campaign over the country, there were a few scattered delegates in the Convention. However, Nathan Miller of New York put my name in nomination in order to bring out the support in the galleries. He wanted the League, and he wanted me in the Cabinet. The galleries seemed to impress the Republican leaders.

After Harding's nomination, I took some part in the Republican campaign, making two poorish speeches. Will Hays, the Republican Chairman, complained that they were "too objective."

The deeper issues were badly confused. Harding's main appeal was to get back to "normalcy." It was just what the people wanted to do after all the emotional and other strains of the war. It was a sort of "leave-me-alone" feeling after a fever.

My concern was that Harding should not desert his original position as a Senator, of being for the League with reservations. He, however, wobbled a good deal. He privately assured me and others that he favored it. Many of us protested to him whenever he leaned the wrong way on this issue. On the other side, Senators Borah, Norris, and Johnson, opponents of the League, bombarded him likewise every time he leaned toward it.

Mr. Harding, soon after the election, sent me word he would like me to join his Cabinet and suggested the Secretaryship of the Interior or of Commerce. I replied that, as in my mind our major problems were reconstruction and national development, I preferred Commerce although it was considered less important than the Interior.

I heard nothing more for nearly three months and assumed there was nothing in it. The long delay in announcement was due to the opposition of Senators Penrose and Lodge. They were urging Andrew Mellon for Secretary of the Treasury. Harding subsequently informed me that he had told them, "Mellon and Hoover or no Mellon."

Mr. Harding formally tendered me the appointment on February 24, 1921. I told him there were some ideas in my mind that he should consider before the matter was finally settled. I stated I was interested in the job of reconstruction and development in front of us; that for the Department to be of real service, I must have a voice on all important economic policies of the administration. I stated this would involve business, agriculture, labor, finance, and foreign affairs so far as they related to these problems. I stated that, if I accepted, I wanted it made clear to the other departments from the very beginning. He said that this was what he wanted and he would make it clear to all the other Cabinet members. He subsequently informed me he had done so except to Mr. Hughes, who was to be Secretary of State. He said he did not know how Mr. Hughes would take to this idea. He seemed a little afraid of his stiff Secretary of State. I replied that I would see Mr. Hughes about it myself. Mr. Hughes was enthusiastic over both the idea and my entry into the government.

On this occasion we had an extensive discussion as to the Versailles and other war treaties. We were both concerned that the new administration make good the ratification of the treaties with reservations, according to the declaration which he and I had signed together with former Senator Elihu Root, former President Taft, and others during the campaign.

Hughes agreed with me that the treaty, as distinguished from the

League Covenant, was not satisfactory. Particularly was this the case in respect to reparations, mandates, and the boundaries of the newly liberated states, disarmament, etc. The decisive arguments for our support of the treaty were that we should be more effective for remedy by sitting inside, instead of outside, and that peace was urgent in a world shaking with political and economic instabilities. Hughes was a warm advocate of the League, and he had great enthusiasm for the World Court as an outgrowth of years of effort by statesmen of good will, including himself.

We had some discussion as to President Wilson and the "fourteen" and "eleven subsequent points." We were in agreement that the "points" had proved unfitted to the European mind in its present stage of enlightenment and political ideals. Hughes had been defeated for the Presidency by Wilson in 1916. He stated that he believed Wilson's "Kept Us Out of War" slogan had given the margin which defeated him in 1916, but he showed no bitterness toward Wilson.

Subsequently, Hughes made an earnest effort to mobilize Senate support for the ratification. But public opinion had so crystallized that not even a majority—much less two-thirds—of the Senate could be rallied to it. The Secretary finally had to end the state of war by a series of separate treaties.

He postponed presentation of the World Court statute to the Senate until after ratification of his great accomplishment in the Disarmament, the Nine Power and the Four Power treaties of 1922. He then made a valiant effort to secure the Senate approval of the Court but failed amid a torrent of destructive reservations.

On the occasion of this discussion we laid the foundation for action on two comparatively minor questions. There were poor relations between the State and Commerce departments over their foreign services. We agreed that this was petty stuff, and in fact we straightened it out by a formula which I presented soon after we were seated in Washington.

I suggested he investigate our outdated commercial treaties. Some were a century old. Later we set up a joint committee of the Commerce and State departments which worked out their revision. Mr. Hughes in the ensuing years brought about important improvements in them.

Reconstruction and Development of the United States

1921–1929

CHAPTER 8

REORGANIZING THE DEPARTMENT OF COMMERCE

I was confirmed by the Senate as Secretary of Commerce on March 4, 1921, and served more than seven years, until mid-1928. That Department in the Washington social scale was next to the bottom at the dinner table.

The Enabling Act founding the Department contained one sentence of major importance to me:

It shall be the province and duty of the said Department to foster, promote, and develop the foreign and domestic commerce, the mining, manufacturing, shipping and fishery industries, the labor interests and the transportation facilities of the United States.

Our primary problems being development and reconstruction from the war, it was a wide-open charter.

The other members of the initial Cabinet were Charles E. Hughes, Secretary of State; Andrew W. Mellon, Secretary of the Treasury; Harry M. Daugherty, Attorney General; John W. Weeks, Secretary of War; Edwin Denby, Secretary of the Navy; Will H. Hays, Postmaster General; Albert B. Fall, Secretary of the Interior; Henry C. Wallace, Secretary of Agriculture; and James J. Davis, Secretary of Labor.

Hughes, Mellon, Weeks, Denby, and Hays stood above the others. These five went out of their way on many occasions to further my work. Changes in the Cabinet during my seven years saw Frank B. Kellogg, Secretary of State; Harlan F. Stone, Attorney General; Hubert Work and Harry S. New, Postmaster General; Curtis D. Wilbur, Secretary of the Navy; Dwight F. Davis, Secretary of War; William M.

Jardine, Secretary of Agriculture; and a change of Hubert Work, to the office of Secretary of the Interior. Of these new members, Harlan Stone, Frank Kellogg, Curtis Wilbur, and Hubert Work were unusual and superior public servants. Mellon, Davis, and I were the only members of the initial Cabinet who remained in office almost the eight years.

Very little had been done by the Democratic administration in reconstruction from the war, and development had been suspended during that time. Even important reconversion matters had been neglected because of President Wilson's illness. Many of the problems required fundamental solutions which would take time. But we soon had to face an emergency in the shape of the postwar depression of 1921–22 and general economic demoralization with rising unemployment.

The people were demanding a return to ways of prewar living—Harding's "normalcy." But in reality, after such a convulsion, there could be no complete return to the past. Moreover, the social sense of our people, livened by the war, was demanding change in many directions.

Fifteen days after taking office (March 19) I invited twenty-five leaders in business, labor, and agriculture to serve as an advisory committee on policies and undertakings of the Department. At our meeting we determined upon the broad direction we should follow. We also decided that we should at a later date summon an extensive national conference on reconstruction and development problems, but that before so doing we should grant subcommittees some months to prepare a program for the larger meeting, which was set for September.

After this preliminary meeting I issued a short statement of "problems":

. . . The great-economic difficulties that we inherit from the war . . . emphasize the necessity of better governmental machinery to assist in their solutions. Their final remedy must rest on the initiative of our own people but the rate of recovery can be expedited by greater co-operation in the community, and with the community by the government. This Department . . . wishes to assist wherever it can to stimulate and assist this co-operation.

We have many idle men walking the streets, and at the same time we are short more than a million homes; our railways are far below their need in equipment; our power plants, waterways, and highways are all far behind our national needs in normal commerce. To apply this idle labor to our capital equipment is one of the first problems of the country.

Some of the economic difficulties arising from the war will no doubt solve themselves with time, but an infinite amount of misery could be saved if we had the same spirit of spontaneous co-operation in every community for reconstruction that we had in war.

The Department of Commerce was a congeries of independent bureaus left behind when the labor activities were separated into the Labor Department some years before. It consisted of the Bureaus of Foreign and Domestic Commerce, Lighthouses, Navigation, Coast and Geodetic Survey, Census, Standards, and Fisheries and the Steamboat Inspection Service. They were all old establishments created prior to the Department itself. Each was an inbred bureaucracy of its own. There was little departmental spirit, or *esprit de corps*. Some of the bureaus even placed their own names on their letterheads without mentioning the Department. This lack of cohesion was emphasized by the fact that the Bureaus were housed in fifteen different buildings, mostly rented, and some of them condemned by the District of Columbia fire and health departments.

Oscar Straus, who was one of my predecessors, told me that my job would not require more than two hours of work a day. Indeed, that was all the time that the former Secretaries devoted to it. Putting the fish to bed at night and turning on the lights around the coast were possibly the major concepts of the office.

In order to free myself from routine administration, I divided the direction of the Bureaus between the Assistant Secretary, Claudius H. Huston, and the Solicitor, Stephen B. Davis, except Foreign and Domestic Commerce and Standards, which I took under my own wing. Most of the Bureaus in the Department were of technical character and should have been free from politics. However, we found that the directorships of five of them had been filled with politicians, strangers to the real problems. These we promptly removed, promoting men from the technical staffs. I never inquired into their politics.

The employees were practically all under Civil Service. However, the previous Democratic administration had removed certain branches

SECRETARY OF COMMERCE

from Civil Service by Presidential order and, after having appointed good Democrats, then had blanketed them back under the Civil Service again by another Presidential order. I got President Harding to remove them again from the Civil Service and had the Civil Service Commission select their successors. Many of the previous staff failed even to pass the examinations.

There were some badly neglected services, particularly the aids to navigation. Some salaries after thirty years' service were only $60 a month with no pensions. Ultimately we secured from Congress a minimum of $1,200 per annum with gradual increases for length of service and pensions on retirement.

I established a weekly meeting of all important Department officers where we discussed departmental and general questions off the record. Gradually we built up a fine departmental spirit. In 1925 we secured the transfer of the Bureau of Mines and the Patent Office from the Department of the Interior, as these bureaus were directly concerned with commerce and industry, the general motif of the Department. In 1922 Congress added a Housing Division, and in 1926 an Aeronautics Division, and in 1927 a Radio Division.

Beyond routine reorganizations to make the Department function, I devoted myself wholly to reconstruction and development problems.

I had little difficulty in obtaining good young men, as service with us became a steppingstone to a job outside the government. Their subsequent success in life is proof both of their capacity and of their opportunity. However, the Congressional committees had some fixed ideas on staff. While giving us generous support for our new activities, they refused to add to my personal staff. Therefore, I employed two secretaries and three assistants at my own expense—a very much larger amount than my salary as a Cabinet officer. They were not government officials but my private assistants. This was, however, living up to my determination never to take a cent from public service for my own use. Among those young men who served as my personal assistants or secretaries were: Harold Stokes, Christian Herter, William Mullendore, Richard Emmett, Paul Clapp and George Akerson. Their characters are amply demonstrated by the high positions to which they subsequently rose in American life.

Although it is ahead of my story, I may summarize the development of the Department over my own seven and a half years as Secretary.

When we took over, the total number of employees of the Department was 13,005. The total annual appropriations for the Department at that time were about $24,500,000. The total number of employees eight years later was 15,850, and the appropriations, $37,600,000. Of the 2,800 increase in employees, 2,400 were due to the addition of bureaus to the Department. Therefore, the increase of employees over eight years in the original bureaus was about 400. Of the increased appropriations, $7,400,000 was for the agencies added to the Department. Of the remaining expansion, $1,300,000 was for scientific research, $2,200,000 for increased foreign trade service and $2,000,000 for additional construction aids to navigation.[1]

In 1924, when the new building program for the Departments was authorized by Congress, I secured that the first of these buildings should be for the Commerce Department. The building was not completed during my term as Secretary, so that for eight years I occupied a corner room of a rented apartment building on Nineteenth Street, especially superheated for summer.

THE ECONOMIC CONFERENCE OF SEPTEMBER, 1921

In cooperation with the Departmental Advisory Committee, we assembled the general Economic Conference in September, 1921. We had selected some three hundred leaders from production, distribution, banking, construction, labor, and agriculture. In the meantime the postwar slump had deepened, and unemployment had seriously increased. The original purpose of the Conference to deal with long-view reconstruction and development was overshadowed by the need to deal with the immediate crisis.

Our advisory committees presented ideas upon: (1) the alleviation of the unemployment situation over the winter 1921–1922; (2) the development of industrial efficiency and elimination of waste; (3) the stimulation of foreign trade, including the provision of credits to foreigners;

---

[1] The mispresentation by the opposition party as to my extravagance was demonstrated by the fact that after eight years of the New Deal the number of employees in the same divisions was 28,300 and the appropriations were more than $50,000,000.

(4) a long-view study of the business cycle of booms and slumps and their alleviation.

In view of the increased unemployment, I emphasized this immediate problem in opening the Conference:

Obviously our unemployment arises from the aftermath of the great World War. We have been plunged into a period of violent readjustment and one of the bitter fruits of this readjustment is large unemployment. This period of depression . . . has been continuous since the fall of last year, but our working population was able to carry over during the past winter upon its savings. There can be no question that we are on the upgrade, but economic progress can not under any expectation come with sufficient rapidity to prevent much unemployment over the coming winter. Great numbers will have exhausted their savings, and must be subjects of great concern to the entire public. There is no economic failure so terrible in its import as that of a country possessing a surplus of every necessity of life in which numbers, willing and anxious to work, are deprived of these necessities. It simply cannot be if our moral and economic system is to survive. . . .

. . . We need a determination of what emergency measures should be undertaken to provide employment and to mitigate the suffering that may arise during the next winter, and the method of organization for their application.

We need a consideration and a statement of what measures must be taken to restore our commerce and employment to normal or, to put it in another way, what obstacles need to be removed to promote business recovery, for the only real and lasting remedy for unemployment is employment.

It seems to me we can on this occasion well give consideration to an expression of the measures that would tend to prevent the acute reaction of economic tides in the future. A crystallization of much valuable public thought in this matter would have lasting value. . . .

The remedies for these matters must in the largest degree lie outside of the range of legislation. It is not consonant with the spirit of institutions of the American people that a demand should be made upon the public treasury for the solution of every difficulty. The Administration has felt that a large degree of solution could be expected through the mobilization of co-operative action of our manufacturers and employers, of our public bodies and local authorities, and that if solution could be found in these directions we would have accomplished even more than the care of our unemployed. We will have again demonstrated that independence and ability of action amongst our own people that saves our government from that ultimate paternalism which would undermine our whole political system. . . .

What our people wish is the opportunity to earn their daily bread, and surely in a country with its warehouses bursting with surpluses of food, of clothing, with its mines capable of indefinite production of metal and fuel, and given sufficient housing for comfort and health, we possess the intelligence to find solution. Without it our whole system is open to serious charges of failure.

The unemployment had increased over the summer to more than 5,000,000. Under the committee on unemployment, we set up a vigorous organization with headquarters in the Department. I gave it personal direction. We expanded the Conference committee by establishing a branch in each state where there was serious unemployment, and the state branches in turn created subcommittees in cities or counties. They had the responsibility to look after the destitute, and we undertook national and local drives for money for their use. We developed cooperation between the Federal, state, and municipal governments to increase public works. We persuaded employers to "divide" time among their employees so that as many as possible would have some income. We organized the industries to undertake renovation, repair, and, where possible, expansion construction.

Our committee on credits to expand exports had, in cooperation with the Department, already secured results which we now developed as an unemployment relief measure. Our other committees, now expanded, undertook exhaustive research into broad policies of reconstruction and development. Their reports over the years became landmarks in the progress of economic thought.

These measures were singularly helpful and aided the natural recuperative power of the country. By the spring of 1922 economic forces had begun to recover, and we were soon over the unemployment hump.

CHAPTER 9

SOME PUBLIC MEN OF THE ADMINISTRATION

I may well interrupt the description of our reconstruction measures with some notes on the administration leaders during these eight years.

President Harding died in August, 1923, after two and one-half years in office. He was a kind of dual personality. The responsibilities of the White House gave him a real spiritual lift. He deeply wanted to make a name as President. He had real quality in geniality, in good will and in ability for pleasing address. He was not a man with either the experience or the intellectual quality that the position needed. But he was neither a "reactionary" nor a "radical." For instance, I relate later on how he opposed the leading bankers by demanding supervision of their foreign loans. Likewise he stood up against the whole steel industry when he backed the abolition of the twelve-hour day and the seven-day week. He vetoed the so-called McNary-Haugen bill, which provided a regimentation of farmers.

On one occasion Attorney General Daugherty had got out an injunction against railway employees then on strike. The morning papers brought me the news. I was outraged by its obvious transgression of the most rudimentary rights of the men. Walking over to the Cabinet meeting that morning, I met Secretary Hughes. He said that it was outrageous in law as well as morals. I suggested that he raise the question in Cabinet. He replied that it scarcely came within his function as Secretary of State to challenge the actions of the Attorney General, and suggested that as Secretary of Commerce, interested in the economic consequences, I had the right to do this. He stated he would support me if I spoke out. When the Cabinet convened, I expressed myself fully

and called on Hughes to verify the legal points of my protest. He did
it vigorously. Daugherty was obviously flabbergasted, and when Harding turned upon him demanding explanation of this illegal action
could only mumble that the objectionable passages were approved by
the lawyers as being within the constitutional rights of the government.
Harding very abruptly instructed him to withdraw those sections of
the injunction at once. Daugherty dropped the whole action as quickly
as possible.

He had another side which was not good. His political associates had
been men of the type of Albert B. Fall, whom he appointed Secretary
of the Interior; Daugherty, whom he appointed Attorney General;
Forbes, whom he appointed Director of the Veterans' Bureau; Thomas
W. Miller, whom he appointed Alien Property Custodian, and Jesse
Smith, who had office room in the Department of Justice.

He enjoyed the company of these men and his old Ohio associates
in and out of the government. Weekly White House poker parties were
his greatest relaxation. The stakes were not large, but the play lasted
most of the night. On one of these evenings Hughes and I were invited.
We went, not knowing that a poker party was in prospect. A collection
of Harding's playmates were the other guests. After dinner we went
to the President's study where a large poker table was laid out. I had
lived too long on the frontiers of the world to have strong emotions
against people playing poker for money if they liked it, but it irked
me to see it in the White House. Hughes and I found some excuse to
remain out of the game. Some time afterward Harding remarked that
I did not seem to like poker; and, as I agreed, I was not troubled with
more invitations.

In June of 1923 I was in the West on an inspection trip. One day I
received a telegram from the President saying that he had decided to
change the personnel which had been announced as accompanying
him on his forthcoming trip to Alaska, and asking if Mrs. Hoover and
I would join the party. He added that the other guests would be
Speaker Gillett of the House, Secretary of Agriculture Wallace, Secre-

tary of the Interior Work, Admiral Rodman, and a respectable gentleman from Ohio named Malcolm Jennings, with their wives. I was naturally surprised, as it had been announced that Daugherty, Jesse Smith, and others of his cronies were to be the guests. Mrs. Hoover and I joined the party at Tacoma on July 3.

Some three months before, a Senate Investigation of the Veterans' Bureau had developed some ugly facts and one of its officials—Cramer —had committed suicide. Just before the President's departure from Washington the press announced that Jesse Smith of the Department of Justice had committed suicide. I found Harding exceedingly nervous and distraught. As soon as we were aboard ship he insisted on playing bridge, beginning every day immediately after breakfast and continuing except for mealtime often until after midnight. There were only four other bridge players in the party, and we soon set up shifts so that one at a time had some relief. For some reason I developed a distaste for bridge on this journey and never played it again.

One day after lunch when we were a few days out, Harding asked me to come to his cabin. He plumped at me the question: "If you knew of a great scandal in our administration, would you for the good of the country and the party expose it publicly or would you bury it?" My natural reply was, "Publish it, and at least get credit for integrity on your side." He remarked that this method might be politically dangerous. I asked for more particulars. He said that he had received some rumors of irregularities, centering around Smith, in connection with cases in the Department of Justice. He had followed the matter up and finally sent for Smith. After a painful session he told Smith that he would be arrested in the morning. Smith went home, burned all his papers, and committed suicide. Harding gave me no information about what Smith had been up to. I asked what Daugherty's relations to the affair were. He abruptly dried up and never raised the question again.

The President grew more nervous as the trip continued. Despite his natural genius for geniality, he was now obviously forcing gaiety. He sought for excitement from the receptions, parades, and speeches at every port, and all along the railway to Fairbanks. To the rest of us, these events were at least some relief from the everlasting bridge game. On the return trip, he asked me to draft him a speech upon the admin-

istration policies in relation to Alaska, to be delivered when we reached
Seattle. I did so, and he introduced into it his usual three-dollar words
and sonorous phrases.

On the return trip we first stopped at Vancouver on an exceptionally
hot day in July. There were great crowds, long parades, and many
receptions. The President rode through the city bareheaded in the heat.
He was called upon for five different speeches. His speeches said little,
but his fine faculty for extemporaneous friendly phrasing pleased
people. That night he appeared very worn and tired, but he had
to face another day of receptions, parades, and speeches in Seattle on
July 27. Again the crowds were enthusiastic. But Daugherty turned up
and had an hour with him. In the afternoon we went to the Stadium,
where the President was to deliver the speech on Alaska. There were
sixty thousand cheering people. I sat directly behind him. When he was
about half through his address he began to falter, dropped the manuscript, and grasped the desk. I picked up the scattered pages from the
floor, gave him the next few quickly, and, knowing the text, sorted out
the rest while he was speaking. He managed to get through the speech.
As soon as he finished, Speaker Gillett, Secretary Work, the White
House physician, Dr. Sawyer, and I hustled him to the special train,
put him to bed, and canceled the engagements for the evening.

It was intended that we should start late that night for Portland,
San Francisco, and Los Angeles, and he had arranged to speak at each
city. The major speeches had been prepared by his White House staff
and reached him at Vancouver. He had asked me to look over and
revise the one to be delivered in San Francisco, which made important
announcements on foreign policies. En route from Vancouver to Seattle
I had snatched an opportunity to make, with his approval, some
changes pledging his administration to the World Court and to a larger
degree of world cooperation in maintaining peace which I knew
Secretary Hughes would approve.

After a report from Dr. Sawyer that the President was suffering
from some bad sea food and that he would require two days to recover,
we announced it to the press and canceled the engagements in Portland
and directed the train to run through to San Francisco.

The next morning we were somewhere in southern Oregon when
Dr. Joel Boone, a very competent young naval surgeon who had accom-

panied the party to look after the guests and crew, came to me and stated that he believed that the President was suffering from something worse than digestive upset, but that Dr. Sawyer would not have it otherwise. Boone was much alarmed, so I took him to Secretary Work, who had been a physician in his younger days. Work insisted on going into the President's room and soon sent for Boone. They came out and asked me to arrange that some heart specialists should meet the train in San Francisco. I telegraphed at once to Dr. Ray Lyman Wilbur, who arranged it.

We got the President to the Palace Hotel where he insisted that Work and I take rooms close by. The doctors, despite Sawyer, at once diagnosed the case as a heart attack. In their view, it was most serious; and I therefore called Secretary Hughes and told him it might be desirable for him to keep in touch with Vice President Coolidge.

Under treatment the President seemed to improve. The doctors insisted that he must have two months of absolute rest. Through friends I arranged to take a private residence for him on the California coast. In the meantime, the date for the San Francisco speech (July 31) had arrived, and the President authorized me to release it to the press, although it was not delivered. I did so, as I wanted to establish that much of a broader foreign policy. Senator Hiram Johnson and the isolationist press were greatly irritated and attacked me for some days as being the author.

By the next afternoon it appeared that the President's condition had so much improved that I called Secretary Hughes and told him the worst seemed to be over.

That evening, however, while Mrs. Harding was reading him a magazine article, the nurse saw he had broken out with perspiration. Throwing back the blankets, she began to bathe his chest, when she perceived that he was dying. Dr. Sawyer was in the room, but Mrs. Harding ran out and summoned Dr. Boone, who sent for Dr. Wilbur also. The doctors could do nothing—in a few minutes he was dead. The cause was undoubtedly a heart attack. Dr. Wilbur en route to the sick room had said to me that something had gone wrong, and I accompanied him within a few moments after the President was dead. People do not die from a broken heart, but people with bad hearts may reach the end much sooner from great worries.

I at once telephoned a message to Secretary Hughes, who arranged for Vice President Coolidge to be sworn in that same night. We appointed Captain Adolphus Andrews to take charge of arrangements, transformed the special train into a funeral train and started a long, slow four-day journey to Washington.

Uncovered crowds came silently at every crossroads and filled every station day and night. There was real and touching grief everywhere. The newspapers announced from Ohio that Mr. Harding's favorite hymn was "My Redeemer Liveth." Soon at every station and every crossroads the people sang it as we passed. At the many places where we stopped a moment to give the people a chance for expression, bands and orchestras played it. My chief memory of that journey is of listening to this hymn over and over again all day and long into the night.

At that moment, the affection of the people for Mr. Harding was complete. Had it not been for the continuous exposure of terrible corruption by his playmates, he would have passed into memory with the same aura of affection and respect that attaches to Garfield and McKinley.

A very large fund was instantly subscribed—with thousands of small subscriptions—to build for him a magnificent tomb. Today Mr. Harding's monument is more impressive than that of any other President except Washington, Lincoln, and Jefferson.

When the authorities at Marion, Ohio, completed the tomb a few years later, they asked President Coolidge to dedicate it. To do this, everyone believed, would be to assume a great political liability. When the Marion people brought pressure to bear on him, Coolidge expressed a furious distaste and avoided it. When I became President, I felt that I should return Harding's kindness to me and do it. I eulogized his good qualities and took a slap at the friends who had betrayed him. None of them came to the dedication.

I said in part:

I was one who accompanied the late President on his fateful trip. . . . Those who were his companions on that journey . . . came to know that here was a man whose soul was being seared by a great disillusionment. We saw him weakened not only from physical exhaustion, but from great mental anxiety.

Warren Harding had a dim realization that he had been betrayed by a few of the men whom he had trusted, by men who he had believed were his devoted friends. It was later proved in the courts of the land that these men had betrayed not alone the friendship and trust of their staunch and loyal friend but they had betrayed their country. That was the tragedy of the life of Warren Harding.

There are disloyalties and there are crimes which shock our sensibilities, which may bring suffering upon those who are touched by their immediate results. But there is no disloyalty and no crime in all the category of human weaknesses which compares with the failure of probity in the conduct of public trust. Monetary loss or even the shock to moral sensibilities is perhaps a passing thing, but the breaking down of the faith of a people in the honesty of their government and in the integrity of their institutions, the lowering of respect for the standards of honor which prevail in high places, are crimes for which punishment can never atone.

But these acts never touched Warren Harding. . . . He was a man of delicate sense of honor, of sympathetic heart, of transcendent gentleness of soul . . . who reached out for friendship . . . who gave of it loyally and generously . . . a man of passionate patriotism.

But any objective weighing of Mr. Harding's Presidential contribution in the balances of time must show that his playmates tipped the scales from his very considerable accomplishments in national progress toward national degeneration.

PRESIDENT COOLIDGE

After the Harding funeral ceremonies in Washington, President Coolidge and all the Harding Cabinet accompanied the body to burial at Marion. Secretary Fall had resigned six months previously and been replaced by Hubert Work. On the return journey, President Coolidge sent word to me that he proposed to make no Cabinet changes. Had he known what bugs crawled about under the paving stones of the Harding regime, he would not have been so inclusive.

Quickly the scandals of Teapot Dome and the California Naval Reserve oil, and misfeasance in the Office of the Alien Property Custodian, the Veterans' Bureau, and the Attorney General's office came to light.

Coolidge was loath to believe that such things were possible. He greatly delayed the removal of Daugherty from the Cabinet. From this man's long-time character, he should never have been in any government. Finally Hughes and I went to the President and urged Daugherty's removal. Coolidge had a high sense of justice and asserted that he had no definite knowledge of wrongdoings by Daugherty and could not remove him on rumors. We urged that Daugherty had lost the confidence of the whole country and himself should be willing to retire for the good of public service.

A little later the President asked me who would be a good man for Attorney General. I suggested Governor Nathan L. Miller of New York. He asked me to ring up the Governor and find out if he would accept. Mr. Miller told me that he had agreed to become chief counsel for a large business and could not, with his large family, afford to make the sacrifice. Dwight Morrow recommended Harlan F. Stone, who accepted. It was indeed a good appointment. Stone cleaned up the department at once and proceeded to the rapid prosecution, by special counsel and otherwise, of the cases involving Harding's so-called friends.

Under the hail of exposures, the country passed into a mood of despair through fear that there was no integrity left in the government. This state of mind was well stimulated by Frank A. Vanderlip, a retired and highly regarded New York banker, who moved into Washington with a publicity staff to save the country by newspaper releases. But Coolidge's calm New England make-up and obvious rugged honesty served well to stabilize the public mind.

Among the cruelties of the times were the attacks made upon Edwin Denby, the Secretary of the Navy. He was charged with negligence in allowing Fall to sell the Naval Reserve oil. He had no authority in the matter, and did not participate in the deal. Denby was a good and able man; and he was driven from the Cabinet by political persecution and public hysteria.

Under the vigorous action of the administration, all the malefactors were indicted. Fall, Forbes, Miller, and Sinclair were sent to prison. Daugherty escaped by a twice-hung jury, and three others, Jess Smith, John T. King, and Charles F. Cramer, had committed suicide.

Charges were made by our political opponents that the other members of the Cabinet must have been aware of these transactions. It would have seemed unnecessary to deny that such conspiracies were ever so communicated. But the statements were so persistent that Secretary Hughes, my other colleagues, and I found it necessary to denounce them. As a matter of fact, Secretary Fall had resigned in March, 1923, six months before any hint of wrongdoing had been exposed.

An incident in connection with Attorney General Stone was an inquiry from him as to who might be a good man to head the Federal Bureau of Investigation. Lawrence Richey, one of my secretaries who had one time been in the Bureau, suggested that he consider J. Edgar Hoover (no relation), who was an able young lawyer already in the Department of Justice. He was later appointed.

Before Mr. Coolidge came to the Presidency, I had only a secondary acquaintance with him—such as one gets by dinner contacts. He was reputed to be a most taciturn man. This was true in his relations with the general run of people and with the press. With his associates there was little of taciturnity. Many times over the five years he sent for men to come to the White House after dinner just to talk an hour or two. He had a fund of New England stories and a fine, dry wit. After my election in 1928, he undertook to give me some fatherly advice as to how to run the White House. He said: "You have to stand every day three or four hours of visitors. Nine-tenths of them want something they ought not to have. If you keep dead-still they will run down in three or four minutes. If you even cough or smile they will start up all over again."

Mr. Coolidge was well equipped by education, experience, and moral courage for the Presidency. He was the incarnation of New England horse sense and was endowed with certain Puritan rigidities that served the nation well. He possessed New England thrift to the ultimate degree, and his tight hold on government expenditures and his constant reduction of public debt were its fine expression.

He was most reluctant to take any action in advance of the actual explosion of trouble. One of his sayings was, "If you see ten troubles coming down the road, you can be sure that nine will run into the ditch before they reach you and you have to battle with only one of them." It was a philosophy that served well while the nation was making a rapid convalescence from its war wounds. The trouble with this philosophy was that when the tenth trouble reached him he was wholly unprepared, and it had by that time acquired such momentum that it spelled disaster. The outstanding instance was the rising boom and orgy of mad speculation which began in 1927, in respect to which he rejected or sidestepped all our anxious urgings and warnings to take action. The country was prosperous and I suspect that he enjoyed the phrase "Coolidge prosperity" more than any other tag which the newspapers and the public pinned on him.

Mr. Coolidge was a real conservative, probably the equal of Benjamin Harrison. He quickly dissolved our controls over foreign loans. He was a fundamentalist in religion, in the economic and social order, and in fishing. On one of his summer vacations, when he started in that art to which he was a stranger, he fished with worms to the horror of all fly fishermen.

I soon found that he had no liking for many of my water development projects, because they might involve money. In 1926 I was going about the country making speeches on water conservation. After such an address in Seattle, I received a sharp telegram from him objecting on the ground that my proposals would improperly increase expenditures. I succeeded in convincing him that at least the advance engineering planning would not be expensive; but he consented to put only part of my development plans up to the Congress. Dr. Work and I had some difficulty, because of its great cost, in persuading him to recommend the construction of a dam across the Colorado River in Boulder Canyon.

During the Presidential Campaign of 1924, Mr. Coolidge asked me to take charge for him of the Presidential primary in California where Hiram Johnson was running against him. I secured the creation of a strong committee under Mark Requa; and through its efforts Johnson, by losing the California primary, was eliminated from consideration as an opponent to Coolidge at the National Convention.

During that campaign against the Democratic candidate John W. Davis, Mr. Coolidge requested that I make a number of addresses in the Middle and Far West. I did so. I learned that political campaigning consisted of (*a*) sitting about with local committees, (*b*) a little speech at a public luncheon, (*c*) another at a dinner and a third to a large audience at night. This happened almost every day, with a night journey in between. And I discovered that the universal and exclusive campaign food was fried chicken and peas.

The western radio had been engaged for a half-hour for me to make a supposedly important speech in the Mountain states. The chairman, who had never had such an opportunity to address the whole West before, used a large part of the radio time. During his ecstasy, the others on the platform pulled his coattail repeatedly. Finally he launched out a backward, random mule kick which reached the shin-bones of the lady chairman, who sat immediately behind him. She did not applaud.

I was reminded of a debate between Congressman Cole and Senator Brookhart, both of Iowa, each of whom was to have fifteen minutes on the radio. It was an outdoor audience with some two thousand automobiles parked about. Brookhart took twenty-seven minutes to prophesy the impending doom and the yawning poorhouse. When Cole arose, he threw down his manuscript and remarked that he had only three minutes to answer, but it was time enough. "If what the Senator says of the poverty and doom of this state is true, we will at least all go over the hill to the poorhouse each in his own automobile." And he sat down. I was not able to think up so good a retort for my occasion—until the next day.

Overshadowing all Coolidge's friends was the figure of Dwight W. Morrow, a college mate who had been the leader in Mr. Coolidge's campaign for nomination as Vice President in 1920. Later, as Mr. Coolidge's Ambassador to Mexico, Morrow proved to have great public abilities and independence of mind. He was subsequently elected to the Senate, where he bid fair to become its ablest and most conscientious member. I felt his death deeply, for he was not only a most likable man but a stanch helper in time of trouble.

Any summation of Mr. Coolidge's services to the country must conclude that America is a better place for his having lived in it.

A NOTE ON SECRETARY HUGHES

I had met Mr. Hughes a number of times before we found ourselves associated in the Harding and Coolidge cabinets. I was not really acquainted with him before Cabinet days, but we built up a warm friendship out of four years of constantly working together. In his previous gubernatorial and Presidential campaigns, he had been reputed to be cold and indifferent in personal relations. In fact, he was a man of great reserve who did not reach out for friends; but when he gave his friendship it was deep and lasting.

He was the most self-contained man in my acquaintance, but it was not selfishness. If he had possessed more capacity for reciprocal friendliness he would probably have been President. He was the soul of courtesy, fair dealing, and devotion to his family. His abilities in law, his sense of justice were transcendent. He had a mental and a moral stature that commanded my unceasing admiration. When I came to the White House, I appointed him Chief Justice. He distinguished the position above the great majority of his predecessors. He held the respect and esteem of the whole American people. Mr. Hughes must be credited with having added to the moral and spiritual wealth of the nation.

A NOTE ON SECRETARY MELLON

It is not inappropriate at this point to say something as to Mr. Mellon. He was in every instinct a country banker. His idea and practice had been to build up men of character in his community and to participate in their prosperity. He had no use for certain varieties of New York banking, which he deemed were too often devoted to tearing men down and picking their bones. When the boom broke he said, "They deserved it."

One day he remarked that he had always been puzzled over the distinction some church or other charity seekers made between "good" money and what was "tainted." He said that when his grandfather came from Northern Ireland he brought a modest fortune and divided it into three parts. With one part he opened a private bank in Pittsburgh, with another part he bought common stock in the Pennsylvania

Railroad, and with the third part he bought real estate in St. Louis. He recounted that the portion invested in the railroad never brought the family more than $6,000 a year, but that was apparently "tainted." Likewise was the money made from building up the great steel and aluminum industries which gave jobs to hundreds of thousands of men. However, the part invested in St. Louis real estate, which brought the family several million dollars without any effort at all, was apparently "good money," appropriate for gifts.

Some years later I received an insight into Mr. Mellon as a banker from one of the officials of the Aluminum Company of America. This gentleman told me the original inventor of the process had gone to Mr. Mellon, hoping he could sell an interest in his idea so that he could continue his laboratory experiments. Mr. Mellon listened to the notion of converting a metal curiosity into a great industrial material and then explained that his bank only loaned money, against security. The inventor had nothing but an idea and a small laboratory and was also near to hunger. As he was about to turn away, Mr. Mellon said to him: "I sometimes personally loan money on the security of character, and if you want to take $10,000 on that basis you can have it." The inventor was fearful that he would be frozen out by foreclosure of the loan any time, but was desperate and took the money. His work progressed slowly, he needed more money, and Mr. Mellon increased his loan. Finally, the pilot plant was a success and promised millions in profits. Mr. Mellon sent for the inventor and suggested that the concern should now have a real working capital to build a plant and asked what the inventor thought would be a fair proportion of the business if the Mellons provided the several hundred thousands of dollars needed. He accepted the inventor's own proposal of a 50-50 interest without quibble. As the inventor was leaving he said to Mr. Mellon: "You could have foreclosed upon me any time in the last three years and taken the whole business." The reply was, "The Mellons never did business that way." The founders of that industry, including the inventor, realized scores of millions of dollars from it. The story may be apocryphal, but it accords with my knowledge of Mr. Mellon's character.

Later on, while Mr. Mellon was in my Cabinet the question of a certain site for a public building came up. After the Cabinet meeting he came to me and asked that that particular site be kept vacant. He disclosed to me his purpose to build a great national art gallery in Washington, to present to it his own collection which was to include the large number of old masters which he was then purchasing from the Soviet Government. He said he would amply endow it and thought it might altogether amount to $75,000,000. I urged that he announce it at once, and have the pleasure of seeing it built in his lifetime. He was a shy and modest man. The only reason he told me at all was that he wanted that site reserved. He asked me to keep it in confidence. Had he made this magnificent benefaction public at that time, public opinion would have protected him from the scandalous persecution under the New Deal. He was accused of having evaded income taxes. I knew that in the years he was supposed to be robbing the government he was spending several times the amount charged against him in support of public institutions and upon the unemployed in his state.

While every agency acquitted him, he felt the wound to a lifetime of integrity and many years of single-minded public service. The whole was an ugly blot on the decencies of democracy.

On the balance sheet of national welfare Andrew Mellon should be credited with having added to both the material and spiritual assets of America.

There were many other able men in the administration during the Harding-Coolidge terms, and I comment upon them as this account proceeds.

RECONSTRUCTION MEASURES

My studies of recuperation from previous great wars had led me to the conclusion that recovery and ability to carry the burdens left by a great war depended upon an increased per capita productivity in the people. The British had come out of the Napoleonic Wars with debts and losses that seemed unsupportable. But the development of the steam engine and the consequent factory expansion had so increased their productivity that the burden was negligible. Again, the United States had come out of the Civil War with such national debt, inflation, burden of veterans and destruction, particularly in the South, that it seemed a generation would be required for recovery. But the expansion of the vast fertile area of the Midwest and Far West by rapidly expanded railway development so increased our productivity that, with some intermediate readjustment, the seemingly enormous economic burden of the war was hardly noticed. I therefore believed that if we could secure a rapid increase in productivity we again could shoulder our burdens.

There was no special outstanding industrial revolution in sight. We had to make one. The obvious opportunity to increase the per capita production was by recovery from war deterioration, elimination of waste and increasing the efficiency of our commercial and industrial system all along the line.

THE ELIMINATION OF WASTE

I determined that the practical approach to the elimination of the waste problem by the Department of Commerce was to take up some area where progress was manifestly possible, thoroughly to investigate its technology, and then to convene a preliminary meeting of representatives of that particular segment of industry, business and labor. If the preliminary meeting developed a program, a committee was appointed to cooperate with us in its advancement. There was no dictation or force of law. During my term as Secretary of Commerce more than three thousand such conferences or committees were brought into action, with most surprising results. In April, 1921, I asked the Congress for a few hundred thousand dollars special appropriations to advance these activities. We made so good a case that the Congress, in June, gave me double what we had asked.

I can describe the whole purpose and method no better than to reproduce pertinent paragraphs based upon my reports to the Congress of 1925 and 1926, prior to which we had been well organized under the able direction of Dr. S. W. Stratton and Frederick M. Feiker of the Bureau of Standards and the specialists of the Bureau of Foreign and Domestic Commerce under Dr. Julius Klein.

Those reports said:

. . . It must be borne in mind that the whole program is one fundamentally to stimulate action among industries, trades, and consumers themselves. It is obviously not the function of government to manage business, but for it to recruit and distribute economic information; to investigate economic and scientific problems; to point out the remedy for economic failure or the road to progress; to inspire and assist in co-operative action.

The term "elimination of waste" is subject to some objection as carrying the implication of individual or willful waste. In the sense used in these discussions elimination of waste refers wholly to those wastes which can be eliminated by co-operative action in the community. It does not refer to any single producer, for in the matters here discussed he is individually helpless to effect the remedy. Nor does the elimination of such wastes imply any lessening of fair competition or any infringement of the restraint of trade laws. In fact, the most casual investigation of the work in progress will show that its accomplishment establishes more healthy competition. It protects and preserves the smaller units in the business world. Its results are an asset alike to worker, farmer, consumer, and businessman.

. . . The major directions for national effort as they were outlined by the department at the beginning of the undertaking five years ago are:

1. Elimination of the waste imposed by inadequate railway transportation,

through improved equipment and methods, and the establishment of better co-operation between shippers and the railroads.

2. Vigorous utilization of our water resources for cheaper transportation of bulk commodities, flood control, reclamation, and power.

3. Enlarged electrification of the country for the saving of fuel and labor.

4. Reduction of the great waste of booms and slumps of the "business cycle" with their intermittent waves of unemployment and bankruptcy.

5. Reduction of seasonal variations in employment in construction and other industries.

6. Reduction of waste in manufacture and distribution through the establishment of standards of quality, simplification of grades, dimensions, and performance in nonstyle articles of commerce; through the reduction of unnecessary varieties; through more uniform business documents such as specifications, bills of lading, warehouse receipts, etc.

7. Development of pure and applied scientific research as the foundation of genuine labor-saving devices, better processes, and sounder methods.

8. Development of co-operative marketing and better terminal facilities for agricultural products in order to reduce the waste in agricultural distribution.

9. Stimulation of commercial arbitration in order to eliminate the wastes of litigation.

10. Reduction of the waste arising from industrial strife between employers and employees.

What the country as a whole has accomplished during the past five years in increased national efficiency in these directions is beyond any possibility of measurement. Nor does the Department of Commerce lay claim to credit for the great progress that has been made, save as we may have helped to organize it into a definite movement. That movement is the result of a realization by every group—businessmen, industrial leaders, engineers, and workers—of the fundamental importance of this business of waste elimination. In support of this movement we have had the benefit of notable advances in science, many inventions, much increased economic understanding, and prohibition.

ELIMINATION OF WASTES IN THE RAILWAYS

The railways were one of our first problems. They had been thoroughly demoralized by the war and government operation, so that in

1920, when they were returned by the Congress to private operation, the lack of replacements and repairs during the war left them short of rolling stock. Their car shortages and delays in delivery were demoralizing the whole economic system.

I had given support, prior to becoming Secretary of Commerce, to their return to private operation. We made and published many studies of the detailed economic effect of transportation failures. Through the Railway Association we gave aid to better organized supply and to interchange of cars and equipment. We set up regional joint committees of shippers and railway operators for better handling of traffic. We set up committees for simplification and standardization of equipment. We set up a new system of handling perishable consignments, and improvement in methods of packing which reduced damage claims by $100,000,000 per annum for this item alone. We created a score of other activities, among which was a major contribution to passage of the Railway Mediation Act (described later on), which prevented railway strikes for many years afterwards.

Again I make no claims that the Department was responsible for the revolutions that followed, but it did help. The tremendous improvement is indicated by comparing 1919, the last full year of government operation, with 1926:

Calendar year	Number of cars loaded	Million ton-miles of freight	Average number of employees	Revenue freight ton-miles handled per employee	Revenue per ton-mile
1919.....	41,832,536	364,293	1,960,000	185,000	$0.987
1926.....	53,635,807	443,746	1,822,000	243,500	1.096

It is an interesting commentary upon government operation of the railroads that their employees in that period had risen to a maximum of nearly 2,000,000. By 1926, about 8 per cent fewer employees were handling a 20 to 30 per cent greater volume of traffic.

The result of this great reorganization upon the whole economic fabric of the country was far-reaching. Rapid dispatch greatly reduced the inventories of the country, contributed to stabilization of production and employment, and increased the efficiency of all production and distribution.

EXPANSION IN ELECTRICAL POWER

The discoveries in long-distance transmission had now opened a new vista in the production and use of electrical power which had not yet been much availed of. The problem was to bring about the development of central generating plants interconnected so as to secure maximum load factors. We urged the possibilities of larger use of water power in such interconnected systems. The Department made many regional and national surveys of the technical problems involved, issued many reports and much propaganda. I attended many conventions urging more development in these directions. We issued many studies as to advantageous conversions of factories to electric power. Again these urgings should not be credited with the gigantic accomplishment, but they helped. Our report to Congress stated:

. . . In five years after we took office in 1921 the electrical generating capacity in the country has increased from 14,280,000 to 23,840,000 kilowatts, an increase of 67 per cent. Although 66 per cent of our energy output is from fuel, the development of water power has been most active. Of the total of 8,300,000 water horsepower now developed and connected into the systems 2,500,000 horsepower, or some 43 per cent, has been set to work in the last five years. The enormous savings that have been made in fuel consumption are indicated by the fact that while the electrical output of fuel-burning central stations increased 67 per cent in five years the total fuel used increased less than 15 per cent. The average consumption of coal or its equivalent . . . decreased from 3 pounds per kilowatt hour in 1920 to 2.1 pounds during 1925, a saving at the average rate of 11,500,000 tons per annum; new water power effected a further annual saving equivalent to 3,100,000 tons.

. . . While there has been an increase during this period of between five and six million horsepower used in factory production, there has been no increase in boilers and engines installed within these plants, the increase having been made almost entirely by electrical motors operated through purchased power. . . . Apparently 70 per cent of factory power is now delivered to the machines electrically.

The application of electrical power to home use has received enormous expansion. The number of homes served has increased in six years from 5,700,000 to over 15,000,000. The number of farms served is expanding

rapidly, . . . the average price of power throughout the country is now somewhat less than before the war. . . .

This transformation, it may be said at once, has increased the productivity
of our workmen beyond those of any other country; it contributes to our
maintenance of high real wages and to the reduction of human sweat; it
relieves the homemakers of many irksome tasks and adds immeasurably
to home comforts.

There is still further promise of great progress. . . .

SIMPLIFICATION AND STANDARDIZATION

One of our early attacks upon the problem of elimination of industrial waste was to organize what we called "standardization" and
"simplification." They were different in approach but complementary
to each other. The activities of the Department were confined to staple
products, style of articles being excluded as being matters of personal
taste. In all this we had the constant co-operation of the Standards Committee appointed by the Engineering Societies.

My 1925 report to Congress described the simplification idea:

By simplification we secure . . . elimination of the least necessary varieties,
dimension, or grades of materials and products. The usefulness . . . is not
limited in the application to materials and machines but extends . . . to
business practices such as specifications, and . . . other documents. Uniformity in such specifications reinforces the demand for standardized and simplified products.

For instance, by simplification our automotive committee brought
about the reduction of the number of sizes of automobile wheels from
eight to three, and tires correspondingly. As an instance of standardization, the thread for bolts, nuts, pipes, and nipples had been agreed upon
and adopted by all manufacturers. Previously, each manufacturer had
his own standards, and any replacement must be made from him. The
consequence of this cooperative action was of the utmost importance.
Manufacturers were able to engage more fully in mass production, as
they could produce for stocks instead of filling specific orders; the
amount of inventories which must be carried by consumers was greatly
reduced, and competition was enhanced in such articles.

Our method in this field, as in others, was a study of the particular subject, and a preliminary meeting of the trades concerned. If they were interested, committees were created which developed recommendations. A circular was sent out by the Department on behalf of the committees to all members of the trade, both producers and consumers, giving the recommendations and asking for acceptance. When acceptances were sufficient to warrant action, the recommendations were promulgated by the Department as the desirable simplification or standard for the trade. The interaction of consumers and producers upon each other secured rapid adoption. The committees were maintained to aid in adoption of any necessary revisions.

In addition to such articles as I have mentioned, we covered building materials (bricks, lumber, cement, doors, windows, and hardware); containers (wood, steel, and paper); bedsprings, mattresses; hospital linen and blankets; office furniture; tools and general hardware, plumbing fixtures, electric light sockets and electric bulbs; railway equipment and ship construction parts; ball bearings, brake linings, spark plugs, and scores of others. In all, probably three thousand articles were covered.

SPECIFICATIONS

Allied with these actions was the general advancement of uniform specifications. Our 1925 report stated:

. . . One of the great unnecessary wastes of public funds arose from faulty specifications. Four years ago a division was established in the Bureau of Standards to develop standard specifications, and already . . . it has covered over 300 groups of items purchased by the government. . . . Specifications in every case have been submitted to co-operating representatives of industry in order that they may be certain of their practical character. Many state and public institutional purchasing agencies are now using Federal specifications, together with a considerable number of industrial buyers. The work has already resulted in large economies in government and industrial purchases.

A specification directory containing references to 27,000 items relating to 6,600 commodities was published, which served the buying agencies of the country as a guide in securing the best developed specifications.

These specifications not only were used by the government and

public institutions, but came into large use by consumers. As they
called for the simplified or standardized articles, they reenforced that
whole program.

Another phase of these activities was simplification and standardization of commercial documents, such as invoices, shippers' documents,
and warehouse receipts. Still another phase was contractors' agreements. The 1925 report mentions that:

> Through the committee sponsored by the Secretary of Commerce, repre-
> senting contractors' associations, architects, engineers, railways, public offi-
> cials, and other large construction users, standard construction contract forms
> have been drawn up and are in wide and growing use, which afford better
> assurance to both contractor and owner, and which should eliminate much
> of the area of possible dispute and create a more uniform basis for com-
> petitive action.

ELIMINATION OF WASTE BY REDUCING SEASONAL OPERATION OF INDUSTRY

The 1926 report stated:

> In June, 1923, the Secretary appointed a committee of leading business and
> labor representatives upon "seasonal operation in the construction industries."
> This committee, after exhaustive investigation, made most important rec-
> ommendations. The better understanding of the problem brought about by
> the committee's report and the co-operative activities established in "fol-
> low-up" in the most important localities have had a marked effect. The
> annually enlarged building program of the country has been handled in
> large part by extension of the building season into the winter months; this
> has had a stabilizing effect upon prices and given increased annual earnings
> to workers, not only in construction but in the construction-material indus-
> tries. The price of most building materials has, in fact, decreased despite the
> large increased demand.
>
> . . . The practical results are shown by the fact that . . . the average
> monthly variation from the previous yearly mean has decreased from 11.4
> per cent to 8.2 per cent in five years. . . .

ELIMINATION OF WASTE BY ARBITRATION OF TRADE DISPUTES

Our 1926 report stated:

> We took up actively the settlement of business disputes by arbitration
> instead of litigation. We made important progress, particularly marked in

the past fiscal year. The Department has held that commercial arbitration eliminates waste by removing ill will, by saving costs of litigation, by preventing undue delays in business transactions, and by strengthening contractual relations. We actively advocated national and state legislation facilitating and legalizing such settlement in co-operation with the Bar Association, the Chambers of Commerce and other voluntary leaders interested. These efforts began to bear fruit in 1925-26 when New York, New Jersey, Massachusetts and Oregon adopted commercial arbitration laws. On January 1, 1926, the Federal arbitration law was finally passed. By this act the Federal courts are given jurisdiction to enforce such agreements. . . . An information service has since been set up in the Bureau of Foreign and Domestic Commerce to report future progress in arbitration practice.[1]

WASTE OF OIL

As our United States oil reserves were estimated by the Geological Survey at only twelve years and new discoveries seemed to be diminishing, the subject came up in Cabinet. President Harding asked me to see what could be done. Mr. Hughes supported a suggestion of mine that the practical thing was to urge our oil companies to acquire oil territory in South America and elsewhere before the European companies preempted all of it. As a result, a conference of the leading oil producers was called, and such action taken that most of the available oil lands in South America were acquired by Americans.

President Coolidge in 1924 appointed four Cabinet members, including me, to an Oil Conservation Board. The purpose was primarily to assure naval and military petroleum supplies from domestic sources. It involved a study of the entire question of oil conservation. Again we employed experts, held hearings, assembled all the facts. We for the first time pointed out in a vigorous and scientific manner the waste in American oil production and our faulty methods of conservation.

The Board, in a preliminary report issued in 1926, outlined the conservation remedies needed and recommended that the oil on all free Federal public lands should be reserved. Again in 1928, we made systematic recommendation as to methods for reducing waste from

[1] A list of my more important statements and reports on matters discussed in this chapter may be found in the Appendix, heading Chapter 10.

overdrilling and through the irrecoverable loss of oil due to wasteful release of gas pressures mainly during the flush flow of new pools. We recommended that states should enact rigid laws to prevent such waste.

This activity carried over into my Presidential administration, where I will resume the subject.

WASTE AND TROUBLE IN THE COAL INDUSTRY

The coal industry was filled with grief, woe and waste. The war had resulted in great overexpansion. Not only did demand for coal shrink with peace, but improvements in electrical power, increased supplies of fuel oil, and natural gas, steadily cut down its use.

There were too many mines and too many men in the industry. Prices at this time were below cost, work was intermittent, and yearly earnings of workers were insufficient to maintain a decent standard of living.

President Harding appointed a Coal Commission, with John Hays Hammond as Chairman, to search for a remedy. I urged Hammond to work out a plan for a transition period by which an excise tax would be temporarily imposed on every ton produced, and an amount equivalent to this furnished by the government to liquidate the surplus high-cost mines. It seemed to me that the overexpansion for war purposes placed a responsibility on the Federal government. I proposed that an allowance be made to the men thus displaced out of this same fund so as to carry them over the period of readjustment. The normal labor turnover would gradually decrease the dependent staff. The Commission rejected the idea.

John L. Lewis, the head of the miners' union, periodically projected his own remedy. It was simple. He demanded a larger daily wage so as to furnish a living, despite intermittent amount of work. Strikes took place to enforce the demand, and by periodic suspension of production had the indirect effect of forcing up prices of coal by famine. He usually got his wage increase. The operators certainly sympathized with suspension, as they reaped a temporary harvest in prices for some months after work was resumed.

In 1922 I was compelled to deal with the public effect of one of these nation-wide strikes, as the shortage of coal brought great hardship to the householder and began to stop the public utilities, the railways, and industries generally. I organized a voluntary limit on prices of the coal produced outside the strike area and secured the effective distribution of what coal there was. The details are of no importance except as representing months of worry.[2]

On fundamental remedies, Mr. Coolidge was sure the industry would readjust itself if left alone. He temporarily proved right, for it did recover in the boom of 1928–1929.

WASTE IN THE FEDERAL BUREAUCRACY

In my service in Washington during the war I had observed the amazing duplication, overlap, waste, red tape, tyranny, and incompetence of the government bureaucracy. So, being zealous to make a better world, I took a dash at this windmill, beginning in 1921. My most exhaustive crack at it was in a public address in May, 1925.

The sum of the speech was:

What we need is three primary reforms: first to group together all agencies having the same predominant major purpose under the same administrative supervision; second, to separate the semijudicial and the semilegislative and advisory functions from the administrative functions placing the former under joint minds, the latter under single responsibility; and third, we should relieve the President of a vast amount of direct administrative labor. . . .

But practically every single item in such a program has invariably met with opposition of some vested official, or it has disturbed some vested habit, and offended some organized minority. It has aroused paid propagandists. All these vested officials, vested habits, organized propaganda groups, are in favor of every item of reorganization except that which affects the bureau or the activity in which they are specially interested. . . . In the aggregate, these directors of vested habits surround Congress with a confusing fog of opposition. Meantime the inchoate voice of the public gets nowhere but to swear at "bureaucracy."

Nor will we ever attain this until Congress will authorize the President or some board, if you will, or a committee of its own members to take the time to do it. . . .

[2] My important statements on oil and coal are listed in the Appendix (heading, Chapter 10).

I do not expect that the Federal government will ever be a model of organization, but I have aspirations to see it improve. Some have said that the first ten years in any needed reform are the hardest. The first ten years are up.[3]

ELIMINATION OF HUMAN WASTE IN ACCIDENTS

The Department of Commerce, with its Bureaus of Mines, Navigation and Aviation, was working to reduce accidents in mines, at sea, and in the air. I undertook to extend this work by means of voluntary organizations in quarters where the Federal government had no authority—and wanted none.

In the spring of 1924 I organized the first National Conference on Street and Highway Safety and called it into session at the Department. It has flourished ever since with the support of the state highway authorities, the automobile and railway industries.

In my address to the first meeting of this Conference I said:

There could be no doubt of the need. In the year preceding the Conference 23,900 persons were killed, approximately 600,000 suffered serious personal injury accidents, while the total economic loss due to the destruction of property, congestion, and other causes incident to inadequate traffic facilities is estimated to be not less than $2,000,000,000 annually.

Out of this meeting came a proposed uniform code covering motor vehicle registration, motor operators' and drivers' licenses and regulation of speed on highways. These codes, with some amendments, were rapidly adopted in practically every state and municipality. In our work to promote its adoption we sent an automobile from New York to San Francisco and another from San Francisco to New York. The driver of each car had orders to follow scrupulously the laws of his own state and municipality. One of them was arrested eighteen times, the other twenty-two times, for violation of laws which differed from their own. The two together met with sixteen actual accidents and

[3] My more important statements on reorganization of the Federal government are listed in the Appendix (heading, Chapter 10). It was not until thirteen years later, in 1947, that any substantial progress was made in this direction. At this time Congress created a bipartisan Commission over which I presided. The Congress adopted many of our recommendations.

avoided scores of potential ones only because of their driving skill (and quick breaks from home-state laws).

Street and highway accidents have increased slightly each year since then, despite all efforts, but in the meantime the volume of auto traffic has increased several thousand per cent. At least it can be said that if nothing had been done by the Association the list of dead and injured would have been enormously greater.[4]

RESEARCH IN PURE AND APPLIED SCIENCE

As a part of the whole program for eliminating waste and increasing national efficiency, I sought to stimulate research in pure and applied science. During the period when I was Secretary of Commerce, I greatly enlarged the research work of the Bureau of Standards, the Bureau of Fisheries, the Radio and Aviation divisions.

The Bureau of Standards had hitherto been devoted mostly to formal administration of weights and measures. We secured such support from Congress that we were able to devote more than $1,500,000 per annum to scientific research, making ours one of the largest physics laboratories in the world. Its scientists made notable contributions, not only to abstract knowledge but to its application in industry. Notable among hundreds of accomplishments in the applied field were those in electrical transmission and interconnection, radio, aviation, strength of materials, alloys, and techniques in pottery.

Our research in the Bureau of Fisheries not only cast light on biological problems but also resulted in a material increase in the number of fish.

As an aid to research in abstract science, I created in 1926 a committee under my chairmanship to seek financial support from industry to be given to the universities and other centers of pure research. The committee included such men as Elihu Root, Charles E. Hughes, Henry M. Robinson, Robert A. Millikan, Gano Dunn, and Cameron Forbes. We obtained annual contributions from the industries for a ten-year period amounting to about $1,000,000 per annum. Its distribution was administered by the National Research Council, a branch of

[4] My more important statements on street and highway safety are listed in the Appendix under the heading Chapter 10.

the National Academy of Sciences. The depression checked further contributions, which we had hoped to build up to $5,000,000 per annum.[5]

In furtherance of this project I made a number of public addresses, one of which, on December 28, 1926, contains the following pertinent paragraphs:

I should like to discuss . . . certain relationships of pure and applied science research to public policies. . . .

Huxley . . . was the most forceful in his demand that preliminary to all understanding and development of thought was a definition of terms. . . .

For the practical purposes of this discussion we may make this definition—that pure science research is the search for new fundamental natural law and substance—while applied science . . . is the application of these discoveries to practical use. Pure science is the raw material of applied science.

I should like to emphasize this differentiation a little more to my non-scientific audience. Faraday in the pursuit of fundamental law discovered that energy could be transformed into electricity through induction. It remained for Edison, Thomson, Bell, Siemens, and many score of others to bring forth the great line of inventions which applied this discovery from dynamo to electric light, the electric railway, the telegraph, telephone and a thousand other uses which have brought such blessings to all humanity. It was Hertz who made the fundamental discovery that electric waves may traverse the ether. It was Marconi and De Forest who transformed this discovery into the radio industry. It was Becquerel who discovered the radio-activity of certain substances and Madame Curie who discovered and isolated radium. It was Dr. Kelly who applied these discoveries to the healing art and to industrial service. It was Perkins who discovered the colors in coal-tar by-products. It was German industrial chemists who made the inventions which developed our modern dye industry. It was Pasteur who discovered that by the use of aniline dyes he could secure differentiation in colors of different cells, and this led to the discovery of bacilli and germs, and it was Koch and Ehrlich who developed from this fundamental discovery the treatment of disease by antitoxins.

I could traverse at great length these examples. . . .

[5] When the New Deal came in, the fund was dissolved as being a dangerous activity of "big business."

Business and industry have realized the vivid values of the application of scientific discoveries . . . in twelve years our individual industries have increased their research laboratories from less than 100 to over 500. . . . Our Federal and State governments today support great laboratories, research departments, and experimental stations, all devoted to applications of science to the many problems of industry and agriculture. . . . The results are magnificent. . . . But all these laboratories and experiment stations are devoted to the application of science, few to fundamental research. Yet the raw material for these laboratories comes alone from the ranks of our men of pure science whose efforts are supported almost wholly in our universities, colleges and a few scientific institutions.

We are spending in industry, in government, national and local, probably $200,000,000 a year in search for applications of scientific knowledge—with perhaps 30,000 men engaged in the work.

For all the support of pure-science research we have depended upon universities to carry it as a by-product of education, and that our men of great benevolence would occasionally endow a Smithsonian or a Carnegie Institution or a Rockefeller Institute. Yet the whole sum which we have available to support pure-science research is less than $10,000,000 a year, with probably less than 4,000 men engaged in it, most of them dividing their time between it and teaching.

.   .   .   .

Some scientific discoveries and inventions have in the past been the result of the genius struggling in poverty. But poverty does not clarify thought, nor furnish laboratory equipment. Discovery was easier when the continent was new. Discovery nowadays must be builded upon a vast background of scientific knowledge. It is stifled where there is lack of staff to do the routine—and where valuable time must be devoted to tending the baby or peeling potatoes, or teaching your and my boys. The greatest discoveries of today and of the future will be the product of organized research free from the calamity of such distraction.

The day of the genius in the garret has passed, if it ever existed. The advance of science today is by the process of accretion. Like the growth of a plant, cell by cell, the adding of fact to fact some day brings forth a blossom of discovery, of illuminating hypothesis or of great generalization. He who enunciates the hypothesis, makes the discovery or formulates the generalization, and thus brings forth the fine blossoms of thought, is indeed a genius; but his product is the result of the toil of thousands of men before him. . . . The genius in science is the most precious of all our citizens. We cannot invent him; we can, however, give him a chance to to serve.

. . . .

And there is something beyond monetary returns in all this. The progress of civilization depends in large degree upon "the increase and diffusion of knowledge among men." We must add to knowledge, both for the intellectual and for the spiritual satisfaction that comes from widening the range of human understanding. If we would command the advance of our material and, to a considerable degree, of our spiritual life, we must maintain this earnest and organized search for truth. I could base this appeal wholly upon moral and spiritual grounds; the unfolding of beauty, the aspiration after knowledge, the ever-widening penetration into the unknown, the discovery of truth, and finally, as Huxley says, "the inculcation of veracity of thought."

THE STANFORD FOOD RESEARCH INSTITUTE

My experience in the Food Administration, and in the reconstruction of Europe after the Armistice, had demonstrated a woeful lack of scientific approach to our national food problems in the mass. Therefore in 1920 I proposed to the Carnegie Corporation that a research institute, devoted exclusively to this subject, should be established at Stanford University. I proposed that its work should be with products after they left the farmer. It was to study processing and distribution with a view to eliminating waste and improving standards and quality and preventing fraud; to study nutritional questions in different groups and areas; and also to study existing regulatory methods and the legislative proposals for price-fixing, etc.

Statistics and questions of production were already well taken care of by the various governmental agencies and the agricultural colleges.

The idea appealed strongly to Mr. Elihu Root, then Chairman of the Carnegie Board. That institution granted us $70,000 a year for ten years, and subsequently an endowment of about $750,000 was given to the Institute. Dr. Alonzo E. Taylor was made the Director. The Institute has been fruitful in results.

Over the years I made several addresses and statements on the subject of research.[6]

THE OPPOSITION TO INCREASED EFFICIENCY

These methods of reconstruction and increasing the efficiency did not gain universal acceptance. The opposition did not come from either employers or labor but from the conglomeration of professors and intellectuals tainted with mixed socialist, fascist, and antique ideas. They produced only one effective attack: "It would produce vast and constant technological unemployment." The Department and I personally answered these arguments over and over. We insisted that science and the machine had lifted more burdens from men and women than all governmental action in history, and that "technological unemployment" was in fact a ghost. The ghost has been periodically summoned from its closet ever since Eli Whitney invented the cotton gin. We cited that for every man in the livery stable of yesterday there are twenty in the garage today, at double real wages.

A study by the Department of new inventions showed that two-thirds of them produced new articles and new jobs, which absorbed the men whom labor-saving devices threw out of work on the older articles. We confirmed this in the national census conducted by the Department. It showed that the decline of jobs in older industries was paralleled by three times the number of new jobs in new occupations.

Gradually this thesis of greater efficiency, lower costs, and development of resources gained acceptance. The American Federation of Labor and the United States Chamber of Commerce both passed resolutions endorsing the whole program.

A committee of economists whom I appointed, "the Committee on Economic Trends," reported in 1928 that our per capita productivity had increased in eight years by the unprecedented amount of over 35 per cent. I do not claim the credit for this, but certainly the Department helped.

Thanks to elimination of waste and these other contributing factors, we could as a nation show one of the most astonishing transformations in economic history, the epitome of which lies in the following table

[6] Listed separately in the Appendix, under the heading Chapter 10.

compiled from the Department of Labor statistics. This does not include my whole seven years as Secretary of Commerce, as it was compiled only to mid-1926, but it is indicative:

MOVEMENT OF WAGES AND PRICES, 1921–1926
[1913 = 100]

Year	Union Wage Rates	Wholesale Prices
1921	205	147
1922	193	149
1923	211	154
1924	228	150
1925	238	159
August, 1926	238	150

These figures demonstrate one positive thing—the rapid increase of
real wages.

A comparison with similar British indexes gives evidences that these
results are peculiar to the United States, for in Britain there was a
decrease instead of an increase in real wages.

INDEX NUMBERS OF WAGES AND PRICES,
GREAT BRITAIN, 1921–1925
[1913 = 100]

Year	Wage Rates	Wholesale Prices
1921	239	181
1922	185	159
1923	171	162
1924	173	174
1925	175	166

Our work attracted the attention of European governments. Britain,
France, and Germany sent commissions to study the methods of our
department, and their reports were more eulogistic than our modesty
permitted to our own. An official of the British Board of Trade published in England a notable book on my ideas concerning these problems and my efforts to solve them. This resulted in the establishment
of similar activities by the British Board of Trade.[7]

[7] I made great numbers of addresses and statements on these subjects and a great
literature upon them grew up in the country, all of which can be consulted at the War
Library.

CHAPTER 11

FOREIGN TRADE

There was no quarter from which reconstruction and employment could come faster and more effectively than in the restoration of our foreign trade from the slump which followed the ending of exports for war purposes

There was a feeble agency in the Department—the Bureau of Foreign and Domestic Commerce—presided over by an ineffective appointee. I at once appointed a new director—Dr. Julius Klein. Dr. Klein was not only a most able economist but a great administrator—a perfect public servant. By careful nonpolitical selection through combined Civil Service and personal examinations, we built up a staff of trade experts whom we sent into every principal country abroad and into the principal cities at home. We established divisions in the Bureau under expert direction to deal with our principal commodities. Older divisions were expanded to deal better with foreign tariffs, foreign commercial laws, trade intelligence—which meant constant reports from abroad as to trade opportunities. We expanded economic research, transportation, information on credit rating of foreign firms, and a score of other activities.

The actual increases in sales abroad, brought about through personal service or information we provided, ran into hundreds of millions of dollars annually. Not only were our foreign agents hounds for possible American sales, but they made themselves welcome abroad by helping the merchants of the countries to which they were assigned. They sought out raw materials and commodities which were less competitive with American industry, and stimulated their export to the United States.

[79]

Our campaign to eliminate waste which I have already related gave rise to important contributions to our foreign trade. I have mentioned as an example that we induced the automobile manufacturers to reduce the varieties and dimensions of wheels on export cars to a small number, uniform for all makes, and the tire manufacturers similarly to reduce the number of their sizes and coordinate them with the wheels. The tire manufacturers were induced to appoint an agency in every center of the world so that all American cars could always be serviced. In addition, we aided the manufacturers to establish convenient supplies of spare parts of all American cars. The double effect of these simplifications and availabilities to the consumer was greatly to increase the foreign sales of both cars and tires. Our action helped to raise the American car to its dominant position in world trade.

Another example was the effect of screw-thread uniformity. Ultimately any American bolt, nipple, or pipe would screw together with any other of the same caliber by any other American manufacturer. Every British or German manufacturer had his own dimensions, and foreign customers could not use those of any other manufacturer. In consequence, the foreigners "bought American." As another example of these efforts, through our committees American electric light bulbs had been standardized so that any size bulb would fit the same socket. This at once gave American equipment and bulbs an advantage abroad. The group of ingenious young men in the Department invented a thousand other devices and stratagems.

As a partial confirmation of the service of the Bureau of Foreign and Domestic Commerce, I may quote from the report to the Congress in 1929:

On nearly 3,000,000 occasions last year the Bureau rendered some specific service to the American export and import public. This was five and one-half times as many as it performed . . . seven years ago. The foreign offices now number 57 as against 27 then. American domestic offices are 23 instead of 9, in addition to which there are 43 co-operative offices which cost us nothing.

I do not claim the credit, but it is of interest that our total exports expanded from $3,771,286,428 in 1922 to $4,880,000,000 in 1928. Our imports increased from $2,608,079,008 to $4,147,000,000.

FOREIGN TRADE COMBINATIONS AGAINST THE UNITED STATES

There were a number of raw materials which we did not produce in the United States, and therefore our supplies had to come by imports. In 1922, it became evident that foreign producers of many such commodities were organizing aggressive controls of price and distribution. These took the form of foreign government-fostered combinations, cartels, or trade agreements, directed against American and other consumers. The British erected a control of rubber; the Dutch, of quinine; the Germans, of potash; the Chileans, of nitrates; the Mexicans, of sisal (hemp); the Brazilians, of coffee; the Spanish and Italians, of mercury; the Egyptians, of long-staple cotton; and various countries, of tanning extracts. In 1922, before these combinations got to work on prices, we were paying about one billion dollars a year for our needs. Three years later they held us up for about two billion dollars annually for the same quantities.

In March, 1923, we obtained a substantial appropriation from Congress to investigate these activities and to conduct a battle against them.

In my report to Congress in 1926 I reviewed these actions of foreign governments, saying:

The object of these controls is universally asserted to be to stabilize prices to both producers and consumers at "fair rates"; and we would probably not be considering the question today if all these combinations had been content with "fair rates," no matter how much we might object to them as fundamentally a restraint of industrial progress.

The economic objection to these controls is the stifling of production through forced restriction combined with price fixing, which entirely deflects the producer's objective from decreasing costs of production—under competitive pressure—to arbitrary high prices. Thus there is a suspension of fundamental progress of industry which can come only in increased volume of consumption and decreased costs of production. The high prices artificially imposed stifle consumption, lead to use of inferior substitutes, stimulate production in areas of inferior economic adaptation and higher costs, and thus place the commodity on an entirely fictitious basis of both production and consumption. Furthermore, in most cases the controls have resulted in periodic speculative operations by which large sums are abstracted from industry and consumers without any service rendered. Every manufacturer and distributor of these raw materials must carry large quantities in transit and in stock for his operations. His investment in materials becomes so great at these artificial price levels that if he is to be subjected to changing policies, with any ill wind or any shift in the views of their governmental officials, then the savings invested in his business are in constant peril.

The public relations resulting from governmental controls are even more objectionable than the economic losses. Our consumers, instead of trading with fellow merchants in the open market, bargaining with their respective views of supply and demand, find themselves confronted by governments whose whole course is in disregard of the economics of production and trade, and whose policies are often enough determined by matters entirely foreign to the industry. No industrial consumer of these commodities can rely upon his own judgment as to the conduct of his business when the policies of government officials in some foreign land dictate his destinies.

The result has been, and always will be, that the just complaint of consumers drags our Government into relations which should be left to the higgling of the market. This injection of the Government inevitably results in the arousing of national feeling. It may safely be said that if governments were not involved and the prices rose equally high, there would be no national feeling aroused, because under such conditions the consumer realizes that high prices are stimulating production and that relief is sure to come; but with governmentally restricted production these forces do not operate or operate but feebly and slowly. It is equally safe to say that if the conduct of industry is left in the hands of private individuals they will not cut the throats of their consumers. . . .

The worst example was the British rubber control originated by the energetic Secretary of State for the Colonies, Winston Churchill. It was organized in 1922 to reduce rubber production and steadily advance the prices. The prices were forced up from 13 cents per pound to $1.21 a pound by 1925. Rubber at 20 cents a pound was highly profitable to the growers and the extra dollar was mulcting the United States at the rate of $900,000,000 per annum, as we imported 900,000,000 pounds of rubber yearly.

Mr. Churchill is not subject to criticism for serving the interests of the British Empire, but we likewise had a duty to serve the United

States. To do so, we organized a nation-wide campaign to reduce imports by conservation and by substitution of reclaimed rubber. We urged the Dutch Government that to maintain reasonable prices from their Far Eastern rubber industry was to their long-view interest. They remained out of the combination and proceeded to expand their production. We encouraged American rubber manufacturers to plant rubber in non-British territory, which they did on an extensive scale.

This campaign, beginning in the summer of 1925, had by March, 1926, broken the price from the top of $1.21 a pound to 59 cents and by June the price was 40 cents with a corresponding reduction in prices of tires and other rubber goods. Making allowance for the increased number of cars, we reduced the rate of consumption during this drive by about 20 per cent. The purpose of all this was not only to get relief from such action but to demonstrate our ability to defend ourselves against all such attempts to hold us up. The conservation and stimulated production outside the British Empire ultimately brought the price of rubber back under 20 cents per pound.

We undertook action against the other combinations by different tactics. Working with the Bureau of Mines, I secured appropriations to drill for geologically suspected potash in Texas and New Mexico. We struck pay dirt and ultimately relieved American consumers from the oppression of the German potash cartel. In the end, we not only destroyed German exports to the United States but exported to the cartel's previous markets.

We stopped American credits to the Brazilian Coffee Valorization. We started an agitation for the use of coffee from other sources by American consumers.

The high prices of nitrates stimulated our chemical companies to build great synthetic plants.

In order to relieve the oppression of the Mexican sisal control, we persuaded Cuba to begin producing that commodity.

American chemists, stimulated to action through the Bureau of Standards, had already succeeded in making synthetic camphor and broke the Japanese control of that drug.

The Department of Agriculture succeeded in production of a longer staple cotton in Arizona and California, which took the edge off the Egyptian cartel.

One result stood out after the years of battle were over. The price hold-ups of these organizations so stimulated production in other countries, and new substitutes at home, that in five years' time all controlled materials except one were overproduced and sold at a loss by the producer. While such low prices were not in world interest, they at least demonstrated the United States could protect itself. The library of the Department of Commerce contains a large literature on this battle.

A NEW BALANCE SHEET OF INTERNATIONAL TRADE

Soon after taking office I started a study of the real volume of our international trade. The "invisible items," which embraced the movement of capital and interest, tourist expenditures, emigrant remittances, ocean freights, and other items had not been calculable by statisticians, for lack of information. These items had become so important as to determine what was known as the "favorable" or "unfavorable" balance of trade. We developed methods of computing the amount of the items which enabled us to present a fairly accurate picture of the national situation each year, helping economists and businessmen—for the first time—to reach sound conclusions as to trade movements and their effect on our credit structure and exchange rates. Thereafter we published an annual balance sheet. Gradually other nations developed the same sort of balance sheet, but we inaugurated it.[1]

---

[1] For a list of my principal public statements and articles on foreign trade, see the Appendix, under the heading Chapter 11.

CHAPTER 12

FOREIGN LOANS

A part of the whole program of export expansion revolved around the provision of loans or credit to foreign enterprises and governments with which to buy American products. I have discussed in Chapter 3 my insistence that such credits should be private and not governmental.

In 1920 and 1921 the foreign governments and business were slow to realize that our era of taxpayers' largess was over; but by 1922 they came to understand it, and the whole problem took another complexion. A boom began in foreign loans with the offer by foreign countries of extravagant interest to private lenders, from 5 to 8 per cent per annum.

These loans soon began to raise disturbing questions as to their security, their reproductive character, and the methods of promotion. To serve any good purpose, such loans had to be adequately secured and should increase the productivity of the country of their destination. Out of such increase alone could they be repaid. Loans used for military purposes, for balancing budgets, and for nonproductive purposes generally would be distastrous.

The situation became so alarming that in February, 1922, President Harding, at my suggestion, called a conference at the White House of Secretaries Hughes, Mellon, and myself with representatives of the bond-issuing houses and banks, to discuss the problem. It was finally agreed that all proposals for new foreign loans should be submitted to the State Department for its opinion, and a public notice to that effect was issued on March 3, 1922. The State Department in turn was to submit these proposals to Commerce and Treasury. The Commerce Department gave advice to the promoters, as to security and reproductive character. The State Department advised upon political desirability and undesirability. We made no pretense of authority, but relied upon cooperative action.

The New York banks soon developed a dislike for this program, and in April, 1922, Governor Benjamin Strong of the New York Federal Reserve Bank filed with the State Department a vigorous protest and a demand that we take our hands off.

I replied, on April 29, 1922, to the Secretary of State. My unpublished letter amplifies our grounds of action, and has some economic importance:

My dear Mr. Secretary:

I am in receipt of the very able memorandum prepared by Governor Strong upon the subject of foreign loans. I do not think anyone disputes Governor Strong's economic premise that foreign loans made in the American market will be represented by the ultimate export of goods or gold to some destination—either to the borrowing country or otherwise. It can at once be agreed that in principle foreign loans are vital in the present situation of the world and of our commerce.

I am not, however, prepared to accept Governor Strong's implied conclusion that no standards should be set up in the placing of foreign loans in the American market. I believe these standards can be developed in the banking community itself. I am convinced that, unless they are so developed, Congress will, sooner or later, impose controls on the placing of such obligations, as there are other and larger considerations than those enumerated by Governor Strong. It appears to me that the Federal Government has certain unavoidable governmental and moral responsibilities toward these operations, and that our bankers have certain internal responsibilities to our commerce.

Governmental Responsibilities. In the public category it may be stated that credits from our citizens to foreign governments or municipalities have a different complexion from either internal credit operations or even of credits to private persons abroad, in that there is no method by which failure in payment of such loans can be prosecuted, except by the diplomatic intervention of our government. There rests upon the Federal Government, whether desired or not, an implication that it will assist our citizens in relation to such transactions. To impose such lines of conduct on defaulting governmental creditors as will recover to our citizens their due is a path which has led to infinite complexities in international relations. It is perfectly possible to carry an argument against foreign loans to an extreme, but even a moderate view should certainly go to the extent of creating some concern in the Federal Government that the security and form of these loans should, at the outset, involve a fair hope that the Federal Government will not be required to enter. . . .

A further governmental interest lies in finance which lends itself directly or indirectly to war or to the maintenance of political and economic instability. We are morally and selfishly interested in the economic and political recovery of all the world. America is practically the final reservoir of international capital. Unless this capital is to be employed for reproductive purposes there is little hope of economic recovery. The expenditure of American capital, whether represented by goods or gold in the maintenance of unbalanced budgets or the support of armies, is destructive use of capital. It is piling up dangers for the future of the world. While it may bring temporary values to the lender of the money, or the exporter of goods, it makes no contribution to the increase of economic stability and in fact contributes directly toward the continuation of instability, and thus indirectly robs both the lender and the exporter of goods of the real benefit that would otherwise accrue.

Broadly, the reproductive use of export gold or goods means an increased standard of living, increased demand for further goods, and increased social stability, whereas the unproductive use is the negation of these ends.

The most pertinent fact with regard to Europe today is that the whole political and economic life is enveloped in an atmosphere of war and not of peace. Restrictions on loans made from the United States to reproductive purposes will at least give the tendency to render impossible that form of statesmanship which would maintain such an atmosphere.

Moral Responsibilities. In the second category, that of moral responsibilities, the problem is also much involved, and argument can be carried to extremes; but again some middle ground does exist. Our citizens have had but little experience in international investment. They are not possessed of the information with regard to the security of many of these offerings which is possessed by the Government, or such offerings would not be entertained. A serious question arises in my mind as to whether the Federal Government has the moral right to withhold this information from its citizens.

For instance . . . foreign currencies, and securities in foreign currencies, have been sold to the American investor, which have resulted in a national loss of probably upwards of five hundred millions of dollars in the last three years. It may be contended that it is the duty of the different state governments to protect their citizens from such frauds, but in the international field it seems to me improbable that any action of the state governments would be practical, and if once undertaken under the various investment control laws of the different states, might lead to a large amount of international complication.

Even in the field of more respectable finance, the loan history of some of the nations who are borrowing freely in these markets for the first time could not be familiar to the American investor, or there would be less ease in placing these loans. . . .

Another instance of . . . moral responsibilities lies in loans to countries already indebted to the United States Government in large sums, who from every apparent prospect will not be able to meet these obligations. . . . Our Federal authorities must have some responsibility to inform our citizens (or the promoters of them) that these nations will probably have to confess inability to meet their creditors. Unless some such action is taken, the citizens from whom such information has been withheld would seem to me to have the moral right to insist that the Federal Government should not press its governmental claims to the prejudice of their investment.

The only justification for allowing loans to proceed to countries already unable to meet their liabilities would be that the resources obtained from such loans would be applied to reproductive purposes which would increase the assets of such borrowing nation in such manner as to strengthen its ability to meet its obligations to the United States Treasury. Therefore, the Federal Government must from this reason alone be at once interested in the purpose to which such loans are applied.

The whole of these problems or moral responsibilities are perfectly capable of dialectics in ethics to their total obliteration, but the test of action of the Federal Government in these particulars should at least be the standard that would be expected of a reputable business man dealing with his own customers. . . .

However, President Harding and Secretary Mellon insisted upon a retreat from our original standards, and President Coolidge reduced the authority of the committee of the three Cabinet members to the limited duty of passing upon the effect which any particular loan might have directly on our foreign political relations.

Nevertheless, I sought to educate the public to look hard into the security and reproductive possibilities of the foreign bonds they were buying. In an address at Washington on May 16, 1922, I said:

. . . It is essential that these loans should be confined to reproductive purposes. All loans to foreign nations which are not employed for reproductive work are a destruction of the capital. Furnishing of raw materials, construction of transportation facilities, public utilities, factories, and production throughout the world, are uses for American capital that bless both the borrower and the lender. . . .

But loans that are dissipated . . . in military expenditure or in unbalanced budgets, or in the bolstering up of inflated currencies, are a double loss to the world. . . . They add nothing to increased productivity, they . . . entail the postponement of measures which are vital for the economic rehabilitation of the world.

Again, speaking to a bankers' convention on October 30, 1923, I said:

. . . There are responsibilities which come to you . . . to develop an understanding of the difference between speculation and investments at home, but of even more importance, to safeguard our country in the . . . investments abroad. In the case of loans . . . to foreign countries our people are even less able to judge of the security than they are in the case of domestic issues. Thus where foreign loans are involved even more depends upon the character of the bankers. . . .

. . . Such loans of surplus capital . . . promote our exports, increase the productivity of foreign lands, increase their standard of living, and increase their buying power. . . . But it is essential . . . that these loans should be used for reproductive purposes. . . . but loans . . . for military expenditures . . . or . . . deficient budgets . . . are a destruction of capital.

In addressing the Pan-American Commercial Conference in 1927, I returned to this subject again:

. . . One essential principle dominates the character of these transactions. That is, that no nation as a government should borrow or no government lend and nations should discourage their citizens from borrowing or lending unless this money is to be devoted to productive enterprise.

Out of the wealth . . . created from enterprise itself must come the ability

to repay. . . . Any other course of action creates obligations impossible of
repayment except by a direct subtraction from the standards of living of the
borrowing country and the impoverishment of its people. . . .

If this body . . . is able to develop the firm conviction . . . that financial
transactions between nations must be built on the primary foundation that
money transferred is for reproductive purposes, it will have contributed to the
future of the Western Hemisphere in a degree seldom open to a conference
of this character.

Despite our hobbles the Department of Commerce did service in this
field. We gave public warning that German municipal and other bond
issues would rank after reparations and therefore were most doubtful
of repayment. In the latter part of 1925 I publicly protested at certain
loans to the Brazilian Coffee Valorization and European Potash cartels.
The real purpose of this financing was to extend the monopolies so as
to advance prices to the American consumer. A press statement of
January 4, 1926, explains itself:

I note that the *Wall Street Journal* scolds me for the suggestion . . . to
American bankers that they should not make loans to the foreign monopolies
which control the price of import products to American consumers.

. . . No mention is made of the importance of the consumer.

These foreign loans were used as an attack upon my Administration
later on. What we had feared as to the quality and methods of some
part of the private loans was realized; but the evil was exaggerated out
of all proportion in the Presidential campaign of 1932. Nevertheless,
even with failure to stop a margin of rotten loans, the private credits
extended proved an inexpensive relief measure if one ignored the hardship of individual losses of purchases of these securities. In the ten years
of the 1920's, we made net private loans to foreigners of about seven
billions. In 1936—six years after that decade—two billions of these particular loans had been paid in full, while three billions were not yet due
but amortization and interest were being paid regularly. Two billions were in default but were partly salvaged. At most the whole
period of eight years represented a loss of about one billion dollars.
That loss would never have happened had more care been used in

making loans. However, if we assume the loss was a billion, it certainly was a cheap method of unemployment and agricultural relief. We were the only large nation engaged in the World War which did not have continuous unemployment and constant drains on the Treasury for relief of the unemployed some time during the decade.

CHAPTER 13

BETTER HOMES

Two concerns which were of more stimulating and more satisfying interest than these tense economic activities were Better Homes and Better Children.

When I came to the Department I was convinced that a great contribution to reconstruction and a large expansion in employment could be achieved by supplying the greatest social need of the country—more and better housing.

Adequate housing for people of lesser incomes had fallen behind because of restrictions on construction during the war; but even without this setback fully 30 per cent of our housing was below American ideals of decent family life. The cost of construction was excessive, the designs were wretched, and the sentiment, "Own your own home," was losing force. At that time I did not believe that governmental financial subsidy to home building was either desirable or necessary.

At the outset I set up a Division of Building and Housing under Dr. John M. Gries to stimulate and to better guide home building. We secured a small appropriation from the Congress for its support. At the same time, together with Mrs. William Brown Meloney, I created a volunteer organization called Better Homes in America, of which I was the president or chairman for twelve years. I raised from $75,000 to $150,000 per annum from private sources to support the Better Homes movement.

The purposes of the Commerce Department Building and Housing Division were stated to be: economic research; publication of information concerning house plans, choice of locality, and methods of purchase and financing; organization and encouragement of zoning to protect homes; reduction of costs by simplifying or removing cumbersome and unnecessary municipal and state building regulations; simplification and standardization of building materials to reduce costs; organization of the building trades to extend the seasonal period of building and thus fundamentally reduce costs; encouragement of reasonable credits both for homes and for slum improvement; creation of public interest in home ownership.

The purpose of the Better Homes organization was to support the Departmental ideas. Under Better Homes we organized more than 9,000 active committees in as many centers. The members—more than 30,000—were mostly women. They carried on campaigns to stimulate home ownership. They gave much instruction as to what constituted good housing. Better Homes organized an annual contest for the best small house erected during the year in the thousands of communities. They gave prizes up to $5,000 for the best exhibits and awarded thousands of distinctive plaques to the owners, architects, and contractors for good examples.

In the Department we prepared under skilled hands several simple pamphlets telling how to locate, acquire, finance, and build a home. As a result of the propaganda of Better Homes, the Public Printer sold millions of them.

I had for years been greatly depressed by the early Long Island and late *Ladies' Home Journal* type of small-house architecture. To help remedy this unhappiness, we persuaded the National Association of Architects to make Better Homes a gift of one hundred modern and attractive designs, chosen by competition, for houses costing from $3,000 to $9,000. At our request, that Association established a small bureau in Pittsburgh, where complete specifications for these houses could be purchased for nominal sums. The designs and specifications were such that any contractor could build them without further assistance from an architect. Better Homes made illustrated catalogues of these designs available in every town.

MUNICIPAL RELATIONS TO HOME BUILDING

There were great indirect problems involved in home building. Our Commerce Report of 1922 said:

The enormous losses in human happiness and in money, which have resulted from lack of city plans which take into account the conditions of modern life, need little proof. The lack of adequate open spaces, of play-grounds and parks, the congestion of streets, the misery of tenement life and its repercussions upon each new generation, are an untold charge against our American life. Our cities do not produce their full contribution to the sinews of American life and national character. The moral and social issues can only be solved by a new conception of city building.

The building codes in our towns and cities had been largely domi-nated by contractors and labor organizations who greatly and un-necessarily increased costs. We called a national conference of public officials and technical experts to consider the question. In my Annual Report to Congress for 1922 I indicated the beginnings of this work:

> Systematic measures of co-operation have been set in motion by the ap-pointment of a committee to formulate a standard building code . . . as varying regulations in force in hundreds of different municipalities . . . imposed an unnecessary cost upon building of from 10 to 20 per cent. . . . A tentative draft was submitted to some 975 engineers, architects, municipal officials, and representatives of the building industry, whose useful criticisms were incorporated.

Finally, a standard code was formulated. We put on a campaign for its adoption and secured its acceptance in several hundred munici-palities.

We inaugurated nation-wide zoning to protect home owners from business and factory encroachment into residential areas. We called a national conference of experts who drafted sample municipal codes for this purpose. When we started, there were only 48 municipalities with zoning laws; by 1928 there were 640.

The Department Report for 1928 said:

> . . . Most gratifying results have come from the department's co-operation with business, civic, and labor groups, and local government officials toward solving various outstanding homebuilding problems. . . .
>
> . . . At least 120 municipalities . . . have now made use of the recom-mendations prepared by the department's building code committee. . . .

Savings up to 20 per cent of the cost are . . . made by the revision of obsolete requirements. . . .

. . . Campaigns to put construction more nearly on a year-round basis were inaugurated in a number of cities during the past year. . . . These voluntary efforts have helped to stabilize employment among more than 1,000,000 men engaged in construction, and several times as many engaged in the manufacture and transportation of building materials. . . .

Now more than 640 cities and towns [have adopted] zoning ordinances. . . . These communities . . . now number ten times more than when the . . . committee . . . was created in the department seven years ago. . . .

We organized committees in the building trades, which included representatives of manufacturers, contractors, architects, and labor, to standardize and simplify building materials. I discuss this subject elsewhere in connection with waste elimination.

We gave wide encouragement to mutual building and loan associations in order to lower financial charges on the home builder.

One of the obstructions to home building was the rates of interest on second mortgages, of 15 to 25 per cent per annum. I interested Julius Rosenwald of Chicago in an experiment in loaning second mortgage money to steadily employed people at 6 per cent. He applied $1,000,000 to this project and, over the years, proved it could make a profit over bank interest. With this proof a number of financial institutions followed Mr. Rosenwald.

The period of 1922–1928 showed an increase in detached homes and in better apartments unparalleled in American history prior to that time. I am far from claiming this was due to our various campaigns. They, however, helped.[1]

The following table shows how the housing of the nation was improving during this period.[2]

The normal minimum need of the country to replace worn-out or destroyed dwellings and to provide for increased population was estimated by the Department at 400,000–500,000 dwelling units per annum.

[1] For a list of my statements on housing, see the Appendix, under the heading Chapter 13.

[2] F. W. Dodge Corporation reports.

	Dwelling Units Constructed
1921	449,000
1922	716,000
1923	817,000
1924	893,000
1925	937,000
1926	849,000
1927	810,000
1928	753,000
1929	509,000

By 1929, the housing delayed by the war had been completed, and we had obviously replaced considerable bad housing. But during the depression, after 1929, dwelling construction fell below normal need. There was, therefore, again a great deficit in housing by 1935. Under the New Deal a vast Planned Economy program of government aid was inaugurated to stimulate house construction; but the effect was far below our voluntary program, as is shown by the following table:

	Dwelling Units Constructed
1934	126,000
1935	221,000
1936	319,000
1937	336,000
1938	406,000
1939	515,000
1940	war impulses

Thus with a minimum need of 450,000 units the average under voluntary organization in a free and confident economy was nearly 750,000 per annum and under these years of "planned economy" the average was 320,000 per annum.

CHAPTER 14

BETTER CHILDREN

In 1920 I had undertaken the consolidation of a number of organizations devoted to health and welfare of children into the American Child Health Association, of which I was the president. Dr. S. J. Crumbine was director with Courtenay Dinwiddie and Dr. George Palmer as his assistants. Our Board of Directors included such devoted souls as Doctors Philip Van Ingen, Samuel Hamill, Thomas Wood, Linsly Williams, together with Grace Abbott, Mrs. William B. Meloney, Clinton Crane, Edgar Rickard, Edward Flesh, and Aida de Costa Root.

We carried this work forward during my whole term as Secretary of Commerce, during my term in the White House, and on to the year 1935—a total of thirteen years. Securing the money to support the work proved a great burden. The income of the old associations which we consolidated did not exceed $50,000 per annum and was precarious at that. We succeeded in raising the available funds as high as $600,000 per annum—a total of fully $5,000,000 in the thirteen years during which I directed the Association. All this would have been impossible without the steadfast zeal of Edgar Rickard, who also saw to it that the money was well and properly spent.

We held our first great national convention in October, 1923, at Detroit, where we had a thousand delegates from the official and non-official organizations all over the nation. In opening this meeting I said:

The growth of the American Child Health Association is the direct result of a national realization of the sad deficiency in the protection of child health.

The disclosures in the army draft, under which 30 per cent were defective in face of the fact that more than 90 per cent of our children are born with normal physical possibilities, gave to many of us a resolution that . . . we

would make further effort toward the determination of these causes and
their remedy. Military service is not the purpose of a nation—but it provides a cross-section that must give us national concern, for the physical and
moral well-being of the nation marches forward on the feet of healthy
children. . . .

I am able to report . . . the inauguration of the most important project
that has yet been undertaken in the field . . . the systematic determination
of the shortcomings in child health protection, community by community
. . . and the demonstration of remedy. . . .

There were thousands of devoted workers, hundreds of local organizations, many well developed community services for children in
existence throughout the country. Our major purpose was to support
and spread them. Our activities developed along four lines: expert
assistance; stimulating public demand for better care of children;
educating the children on health, and educating their parents on
certain fundamentals of nutrition and public health service. On the
nutritional side, the major problem was not poverty but ignorance.
Probably 30 per cent of the American children were improperly nour-
ished—malnutrition rather than undernutrition.

We made an exhaustive survey of eighty-six cities of 40,000 to 70,000
population, in thirty-one states, and published in 1925 an appraisal of
the findings. The report produced a spectacular explosion. The survey
showed that forty-one of the cities had no full-time health official and
that half of the part-time officials they had were without a medical degree. Sixteen cities had not even a nominal board of health, and forty-
one had fewer than three sanitary inspectors. Half of the cities had no
reliable birth or death records on children. Twenty-eight different pro-
cedures were in use for release from quarantine of diphtheria and
scarlet fever patients. In thirty-seven cities vaccination was not compulsory, and 44 per cent of the children were not protected against
smallpox. Eighteen cities had no facilities to hospitalize contagious
diseases. Twenty-one did not even have clinics for diagnosis and treatment of venereal disease. Fifteen were without clinics to diagnose
tuberculosis. A large majority had no maternity hospitals. Seventeen
had no medical inspection in the schools, and in thirty-five the inspectors devoted less than two minutes to each child. Scarcely any of

the cities had a "follow up" system to correct defects. In twenty-one there was no health instruction in the schools. Four had an unsafe water supply. Only eight cities pasteurized their whole milk supply. Forty-seven pasteurized less than half of it. Four cities had no playgrounds outside the school yards. In forty others the play facilities were wholly inadequate.

We set up a standard for city conduct based upon the best work in the eighty-six cities. Then we published in the press the ratings of each city. There were heated mayors and town councilmen in the delinquent communities, but their press rubbed it in hard. The report became an issue in the elections of many towns. Our published plan for ideal community organization became a bible for many a belligerent mothers' society.

We joined in securing the funds to set up the ideal health activities for children in three typical rural counties and ran them for three years as a test. This experience proved that without Federal or state aid, or both, backward rural counties did not have the economic strength to attain the standard which we had set. Some years later I translated this conclusion into legislative proposals to Congress.

One of our dramatic measures was the establishment of May Day as Child Health Day. Beginning in 1924 and continuing through the next decade, we organized parades of children. They carried banners demanding protection for their health. Each year saw an increase in the number of communities observing this celebration. I secured Presidential proclamation of the day, and finally the passage through Congress of a bill legalizing it. The Communists had previously appropriated the ancient festival of May Day for their demonstrations; and I took special satisfaction in giving them this particular competition.

For many years we supported a radio program—"Cheerio," by Charles K. Field—for the benefit of shut-ins.

We of course opposed child labor and advocated a constitutional amendment to stop it. We advocated better school facilities in backward areas. We published volumes of expert studies for the benefit of social workers and health officials, and millions of pamphlets for the inspiration of the public. Among the latter was my "Child's Bill of

Rights" which had very wide circulation. In 1931, I expanded and revised this document, and I embody the full text in a later chapter.

When I entered the White House I continued and expanded these activities. But after my term expired, I was no longer in a position to secure the funds to keep the Child Health Association running, and in 1935 it went out of existence.[1]

[1] For a list of my statements on child problems see the Appendix, under the heading Chapter 14.

CHAPTER 15

LABOR RELATIONS

From a technical point of view labor problems were in the hands of the Secretary of Labor, James J. Davis. He was a most amiable man who through his natural abilities had climbed from the ranks on the ladder of labor union politics. He was skillful in handling industrial disturbances—"keeping labor quiet," as Mr. Coolidge remarked. He proved to be good at repair of cracks. He had a genuine genius for friendship and associational activities. If all the members of all the organizations to which he belonged had voted for him, he could have been elected to anything, any time, anywhere.

When I accepted membership in the Harding Cabinet I had stipulated that I must have a voice on major policies involving labor, since I had no belief that commerce and industry could make progress unless labor advanced with them. Secretary Davis was very cooperative. I have already related my part in the Economic Conference of 1921, which bears upon these activities.

My views on labor relations in general rested on two propositions which I ceaselessly stated in one form or another:

First, I held that there are great areas of mutual interest between employee and employer which must be discovered and cultivated, and that it is hopeless to attempt progress if management and labor are to be set up as separate "classes" fighting each other. They are both producers, they are not classes.

And, second, I supported continuously the organization of labor and collective bargaining by representatives of labor's own choosing. I insisted that labor was not a "commodity." I opposed the closed shop and "feather bedding" as denials of fundamental human freedom.

I held that the government could be an influence in bringing better relations about, not by compulsory laws nor by fanning class hate, but by leadership.

The labor unions in that period were wholly anti-Socialist and anti-Communist. On September 5, 1925, I stated:

> It is my opinion that our nation is very fortunate in having the American Federation of Labor. It has exercised a powerful influence in stabilizing industry, and in maintaining an American standard of citizenship. Those forces of the old world that would destroy our institutions and our civilization have been met in the front-line trenches by the Federation of Labor and routed at every turn.[1]

UNEMPLOYMENT INSURANCE

One result of the Industrial Conference of 1919 was an attempt on my part to convince the private insurance companies that it was to their advantage as well as that of the people at large to work out a method of unemployment insurance. I spoke on the subject at the Metropolitan Life Insurance Company managers' conference on January 27, 1923, stating my belief that in some industries, such as the railways and the utilities, the fluctuations in employment were not widespread, and that there was in them actuarial experience which would give a foundation and a start to such an insurance. However, the companies did not wish even to experiment with it.

CHILD LABOR

The Federal statutory prohibition of child labor had been declared unconstitutional by the Supreme Court. I had joined during 1920 in several efforts to secure a new Constitutional prohibition. Soon after I entered the Cabinet Senator Lenroot consulted me about the text of a new Constitutional amendment which he proposed to introduce into the Congress. I objected to his draft, as he had placed the age limit— eighteen—so high as to generate great public opposition. I agreed that this standard was ultimately desirable, but I feared that the lunatic fringe was demanding two years more than was attainable. The

[1] The C.I.O., with its socialist and Communist control in its early stages, was not organized until several years later.

Senator, however, refused to change it and passed the amendment through the Congress. I was proved right as to the strength of the opposition. I spoke several times in support of the amendment, for instance, in April and December, 1921, and June, 1922.

When I became President I urged the adoption of the amendment by the states, but some of them, particularly the Democratic-controlled ones, would not ratify it. Roosevelt during his four years as governor of New York did not give more than lip service to its passage.

In the meantime, the agitation, particularly of the American Child Health Association, drove many of the Republican states to pass better laws prohibiting child labor. By the end of my administration in 1932 this evil was largely confined to the backward states.

ABOLISHING THE TWELVE-HOUR DAY

For the practical improvement of working conditions I undertook a campaign to reduce the work hours in certain industries. This black spot on American industry had long been the subject of public concern and agitation. Early in 1922 I instituted an investigation by the Department of Commerce into the twelve-hour day and the eighty-four hour week. It was barbaric, and we were able to demonstrate that it was uneconomic. With my facts in hand I opened the battle by inducing President Harding to call a dinner conference of steel manufacturers at the White House on May 18, 1922.

All the principal "steel men" attended. I presented the case as I saw it. A number of the manufacturers, such as Charles M. Schwab and Judge Elbert H. Gary, resented my statement, asserting that it was "unsocial and uneconomic." We had some bitter discussion. I was supported by Alexander Legge and Charles R. Hook, whose concerns had already installed the eight-hour day and six-day week. However, we were verbally overwhelmed. The President, to bring the acrid debate to an end, finally persuaded the group to set up a committee to "investigate," under the chairmanship of Judge Gary.

I left the dinner much disheartened, in less than a good humor, resolved to lay the matter before the public. The press representatives were waiting on the portico of the White House to find out what this meeting of "reactionaries" was about. I startled them with the information that the President was trying to persuade the steel industry to adopt the eight-hour shift and the forty-eight-hour week, in place of the twelve-hour day and eighty-four-hour week. At once a great public discussion ensued. I stirred up my friends in the engineering societies, and on November 1, 1922, they issued a report which endorsed the eight-hour day. I wrote an introduction to this report, eulogizing its conclusions, and got the President to sign it. We kept the pot boiling in the press.

Judge Gary's committee delayed making a report for a year—until June, 1923—although it was frequently promised. They said that the industry "was going to do something." When their report came out, it was full of humane sentiments, but amounted merely to a stall for more time. I drafted a letter from Mr. Harding to Judge Gary, expressing great disappointment, and gave it to the press. The public reaction was so severe against the industry that Judge Gary called another meeting of the committee and backed down entirely.

On July 3 he telegraphed to the President, saying that they would accede. I was then with Mr. Harding at Tacoma en route to Alaska. He had requested me to give him some paragraphs for his Fourth of July speech. I did so, and made the announcement of the abolition of the twelve-hour day in the steel industry a most important part of the address. He did not have time to look over my part of his manuscript before he took the platform. When he had finished with the American Eagle and arrived at my paragraphs, he stumbled badly over my entirely different vocabulary and diction. During a period of applause which followed my segment, he turned to me and said: "Why don't you learn to write the same English that I do?" That would have required a special vocabulary for embellishment purposes. Anyway, owing to public opinion and some pushing on our part, the twelve-hour day was on the way out in American industry—and also the ten-hour day and the seven-day week.

When I became Secretary of Commerce, the working hours of 27 per cent of American industry were sixty or more per week, and those of nearly 75 per cent were fifty-four or more per week. When I left the White House only 4.6 per cent were working sixty hours or more, while only 13.5 per cent worked fifty-four hours or more. This progress was accomplished by the influence of public opinion and the efforts of the workers in a free democracy, without the aid of a single law —except in the railways.

During the years of my service in the Department we had comparatively little labor disturbance. Because of general prosperity and increasing efficiency, wages were increasing steadily in unorganized as well as organized industries—in the former to some degree because employers stood off organization by paying wages at least as high as those in the organized industries. But, in the main, employers willingly shared their larger profits with employees. We had only two bad conflicts.

In 1922, the railway shopmen and the organized bituminous coal miners went on strike at the same time. President Harding assigned the coal strike to Secretary Davis and requested me to negotiate a settlement of the railway strike. I was to learn some bitter lessons. I had arranged that the railway employees' leaders see the President and disclose confidentially to him their minimum demands, which were as usual considerably below the demands which they announced publicly. Through President Daniel Willard of the Baltimore & Ohio Railroad, the chairman of the Railway Managers' Committee, I secured a confidential statement of their maximum concessions. I found that the two antagonists were not far apart and suggested some modifications which seemed to me to be fair. The Employees' Committee believed they could carry the settlement. Mr. Willard's committee agreed to support the settlement on this basis. The railway presidents called a meeting in New York to consider the proposal. Mr. Willard asked me to attend the meeting and give him support. I secured a message from President Harding to open my statement. I was kept waiting outside the meeting for some time and was finally ushered in and introduced by the chairman with an attitude which seemed to convey, "Well, what have *you* got to say here?" Most of the two hundred men present were very antagonistic. I learned afterwards they had already re-

pudiated Willard and his committee. Anyway, I certainly had a freezing reception. Paradoxically, my temperature rose somewhat and my
preachment upon social relations raised their temperatures and made
my exit more welcome.

The railway executives now refused every concession. The men
continued the strike until the roads represented by Willard's committee fell away from the rest and gave the men even better terms
than the original formula. Then they all gave way.

While thenceforth I was not devotedly loved by certain railway
magnates, their lack of affection was more than offset by friendship
of others. Especially among these friends was Daniel Willard, who
remained unwavering during the quarter-century before his death. He
was respected by the whole American people and beloved by every
B. & O. man. There were many fine citizens among the railway presidents. At that time and in later years I had many devoted friends
among them, such as Sargent, Gorman, Budd, Crawford, Shoup, Gray,
Storey, Downs, Scandrett, and Gurley, mostly western railway presidents. It was a suggestive thing that the railway presidents who led
the opposition had their offices in New York City. They have mostly
gone to their rest in graves unknown to all the public except the sexton,
or they still dodder around their clubs, quavering that "labor must be
disciplined."

A by-product of this incident gave me deep pain. An editor of the
New York Tribune came to see me after the meeting in New York.
He was a man with a fine conception of public right; he was greatly
outraged at the whole action of the majority of railway presidents.
The following morning the *Tribune's* leading editorial gave them a
deserved blistering. The next day the editor informed me that Mrs.
Whitelaw Reid, Sr., who dominated the paper, had ordered his instant
dismissal after many years of service. The dear old lady was a righteous
and generous woman, but a partial misfit with the changing times.
In the science of social relations she was the true daughter of a great
western pioneer, Darius O. Mills. When the editor came to see me
in Washington, while he had no regrets, it was easy to see that he
was wholly unstrung by his tragedy and distracted by anxieties over

growing family obligations and lack of resources. At once we gave him an economic mission in Europe, during which he somewhat recovered his spirits and was able to keep his family going. But he never really regained his grip.

It is a safe generalization for the period to say that where industrial leaders were undominated by New York promoter-bankers, they were progressive and constructive in outlook. Some of the so-called bankers in New York were not bankers at all. They were stock promoters. They manipulated the voting control of many of the railway, industrial, and distributing corporations, and appointed such officials as would insure to themselves the banking and finance. They were not simply providing credit to business in order to lubricate production. Their social instinct belonged to an early Egyptian period. Wherever industrial, transportation, and distribution concerns were free from such banker domination, we had little trouble in getting cooperation.

Others of the Department's services to labor sprang from its broad economic programs. However, our emphasis on the needs and rights of organized labor and our constant insistence on cooperation of employers and employees as the means of reducing the areas of friction brought no little change in public attitudes.

THE RAILWAY LABOR BOARD

It was obvious that we must find some other solution to railway labor conflict than strikes, with their terrible penalties upon the innocent public. Therefore, early in 1926, I began separate conferences with the major railway brotherhoods on one hand, and the more constructive railway presidents, under Daniel Willard, on the other. I discarded compulsory measures but developed the idea of a Railway Labor Mediation Board, which would investigate, mediate, and, if necessary, publish its conclusions as to a fair settlement, with stays in strike action pending these processes. Having found support in both groups, I called a private dinner at my home of some ten leaders, half from each side—and I omitted extremists of both ends from the meeting. We agreed upon support of this idea and appointed a committee to draft a law. We presented it to the Congress, and with some secondary modifications it was passed on May 20, 1926. This machinery, with some later improvements, preserved peace in the railways during the entire period of my service in Washington.[2]

Commenting upon the progress of labor relations I was able to say in an address on May 12, 1926:

There is a marked change . . . in the attitude of employers and employees. . . . It is not so many years ago that the employer considered it was in his interest to use the opportunities of unemployment and immigration to lower wages irrespective of other considerations. The lowest wages and longest hours were then conceived as the means to attain lowest production costs and largest profits. Nor is it many years ago that our labor unions considered that the maximum of jobs and the greatest security in a job were to be attained by restricting individual effort.

But we are a long way on the road to new conceptions. The very essence of great production is high wages and low prices, because it depends upon a widening range of consumption only to be obtained from the purchasing power of high real wages and increasing standards of living. . . .

Parallel with this conception there has been an equal revolution in the views of labor.

No one will doubt that labor has always accepted the dictum of the high wage, but labor has only gradually come to the view that unrestricted individual effort, driving of machinery to its utmost, and elimination of every waste in production, are the only secure foundations upon which a high real wage can be builded, because the greater the production the greater will be the quantity to divide.

The acceptance of these ideas is obviously not universal. Not all employers . . . nor has every union abandoned the fallacy of restricted effort. . . . But . . . for both employer and employee to think in terms of the mutual interest of increased production has gained greatly in strength. It is a long cry from the conceptions of the old economics.[3]

[2] Indeed, it preserved peace until the presidents failed to give moral support to the Board's recommendations and its potency was largely destroyed.

[3] A list of my more important statements upon labor as Secretary of Commerce appears in the Appendix, under the heading Chapter 15.

CHAPTER 16

COMMERCIAL HELP FOR AGRICULTURE

The welfare of farmers being an essential part of reconstruction and of general economic welfare of the country, their problems could not be crammed into a compartment called Department of Agriculture without spilling over. As already related, when I took office I stipulated to President Harding that I wanted a free hand to concern myself with the commercial interests of farmers—that is, outside the field of production; and, knowing the departmental jealousies of Washington, I asked him to inform the Secretary of Agriculture to that effect before he took office. It was easier to define these lines of division at that time than it would be today with the Department's gigantic economic operations. However, when the Department of Commerce began to be active for the farmers, in promoting exports, and in solving problems of processing and distribution, the Secretary of Agriculture objected, as is the way of all bureaucratic flesh. At once he began to duplicate our work by establishing and expanding the same economic activities.

Before Mr. Harding selected the Secretary of Agriculture, he asked what I thought of Henry C. Wallace (the elder). I commended him because of his wide acquaintance with agriculture, although he had been a bitter critic of the Food Administration. He was a dour Scotsman with a temperament inherited from some ancestor who had been touched by exposure to infant damnation and predestination. He made much trouble for the Department of Commerce. He was still more troublesome to the President by his promotion in Congress, without the President's approval, of the McNary-Haugen bill. This was a plan for governmental price-fixing of farm products in peacetime. He wanted, in fact, two kinds of fixed prices: one, domestic; the other, for export. The export prices were to be much lower than the domestic. Mr. Coolidge later had to veto his own Cabinet member's legislation.[1]

However, the Department of Commerce went about its own business in relation to agriculture. Our first interest was to find an export market for the farmer's surplus. Our activities in this direction are indicated by the number of requests for assistance to the Department from farm organizations and agricultural commodity exporters, which increased from 42,000 in 1922 to 210,000 in 1924 and 400,000 by 1927.

We aided in better marketing of perishables by systematic cooperation between the railways, the Department of Commerce, the farm organizations, and the city markets, eliminating many wastes and cross-shipments, and protecting consignees who were the farmers or their agents. This saved millions especially for the farmers.

We supported the cooperative movement among farmers. The movement was still young and was stubbornly opposed by the commercial distributors. I believed it to be one of the most hopeful undertakings, for according to my social theories any organization by citizens for their own welfare is preferable to the same action by the government. The Department helped out with research and with action to solve their marketing problems. I made many addresses on their behalf, supporting them against the activities of certain food trades which considered them an unmitigated evil.[2]

Our other great service to the farmers was indirect, through the development of waterways, the elimination of waste in industry, the support of tariffs on agricultural imports, and the expansion of the merchant marine.

One trouble with agriculture was that it had been overexpanded during the war by turning marginal lands from pastures to ground crops. It had thus become wholly unbalanced in our peace economic setting by overproduction. As we paid the manufacturer to reduce his war-expanded plant, I advocated some device for return of the mar-

[1] Not even the New Dealers would stand for this plan when they came to power, and his own son as New Deal Secretary of Agriculture publicly condemned it.

[2] For a list of my addresses and statements on our agricultural activities, see the Appendix, under the heading Chapter 16.

ginal lands to pastures; but the Department of Agriculture offered no solution except price fixing.

Upon the death of Secretary Wallace three years after his appointment several farm organizations pressed President Coolidge to transfer me to the Department of Agriculture. Mr. Coolidge offered me the position. I declined, on the ground that I could do more for the farmers as Secretary of Commerce and was not a technologist on agricultural production.

The President appointed William M. Jardine, one of whose first acts was to pay a public tribute to the Department of Commerce for its service to the farmers. He established at once full cooperation with us.

CHAPTER 17

PUTTING OUR WATER TO WORK

Early in my administration of the Department I took up the better utilization of water resources as an essential part of the program of eliminating waste and promoting reconstruction. Probably the best summation of my views as to government policies is in an address I made at Seattle on August 21, 1926:

The time has come when we must take an enlarged vision of the future . . . We have need that we formulate a new and broad national program for the full utilization of our streams, our rivers, and our lakes.

Water today is our greatest undeveloped resource. Our streams and rivers offer us a possible total of 55,000,000 horsepower, and of this less than 11,000,000 has been developed. Of our 25,000 miles of possible inland waterways, probably less than 7,000 are really modernized, and the utility of much of these 7,000 miles is minimized by isolation into segments of what should be connected transportation systems. We still have 30,000,000 acres of possible reclaimable and irrigable lands. . . .

True conservation of water is not the prevention of use. Every drop of water that runs to the sea without yielding its full commercial returns to the nation is an economic waste.

We have for a century and a half concentrated upon development of our land and our mineral resources; we have conserved our forests and developed our rail and highway transportation. Our Government has done some effective work with water, but we have wasted vast sums of public money under political pressures; and we have now skimmed off the easy jobs. Today it is the major engineering jobs and the opportunity of great national design which lie before us.

We must broaden our sights and determine great policies and programs . . . The problem is a program of each great drainage. We must no longer think in terms of single power sites or single storage dams or single land projects or single navigation improvements; we must think . . . in terms of the coordinated long-view development of each river system to its maximum utilization.

If we study each of our great systems, we shall find that their possibilities lie in navigation, flood control, reclamation, irrigation, or electrical power. On some drainages all these uses are available, in others but part of them. But, in any event, each system must be considered as a whole and organized to the maximum results.

The question at once arises as to who is to finance and own these great developments. . . .

Navigation should be improved at the direct cost of the Federal Government, but with contributions from local governments . . . The Federal Government has long since contributed directly to flood control in support of local and state action. The Federal Government has given assistance to irrigation and reclamation works, but with the presumed provision that the cost should be recovered from the land.

Other forms of finance lie in the undertakings of . . . municipalities in the procurement of their domestic water supplies; . . . and in the great undertakings of our hydroelectric companies. . . .

Our problems become more complex when electrical power is involved. It is my own view the Federal Government should not go into the business of either generating or distributing electrical power. There may be some special cases, but our general policy should be against it. Where power is a by-product of dams for other major public purposes such as navigation, then the Federal Government should lease the power rights so as to recover as much of its total investment as can be . . . It should be leased under provisions of the Federal Water Power Acts, which amply provide for control [of the rates] by the government. . . .

. . . In most of these [various water development] projects there is involved . . . the Federal Government, often several state governments, municipalities, irrigation, reclamation, and flood-control districts, and power companies. Some of these projects involve international relationships with Mexico and Canada.

There are quarrels, litigation, and political obstructions in progress with respect to many of these projects. . . . There are four independent Federal administrative departments concerned; there are two or three different administrative departments in each state, and there is conflict of opinion between representatives of counties, municipalities, and districts. Congress and committees thereof, the governments and legislatures of several states are also concerned, not to mention town councils and district boards. The hydroelectric companies also are involved.

Nor am I about to propose any extension of Federal bureaucracy. I want to see more local responsibility. Moreover, we are a democracy and must proceed by persuasion.

. . . I should like to see a commission set up separately on each of these great drainages, on which not only the Federal Government but also state governments concerned could be represented, and which would also include independent technical members. I would not give these commissions the power and task of spending money, of construction or administration. We have efficient engineering corps in our Federal and local governments for technical determinations, and the execution of construction can be administered through existing agencies of the Government or by way of Federal contributions to the states or districts.

The job of these commissions should be to consider the engineering data, to think, to plan, to devise, to advise, co-ordinate, negotiate, persuade, and set upon the obstreperous. They should determine major lines of policy to be undertaken; they should organize the financial support and recommend what administrative bodies—national, state or local—should undertake execution (if they are governmental works) and they should make recommendations to Congress or state legislatures for action.

I reviewed these efforts in utilization of our water resources in my annual report to the Congress in 1926. I said in part:

There are imperative reasons for the execution of a comprehensive plan for the coordinated long-view development of each river system to its maximum utilization. The necessary advances in rail rates from the war, together with the completion of the Panama Canal, have distorted the economic relationship of mid-west agriculture and mid-west industry to the rest of the country and to the world markets. This relationship can be restored by conversion of our inland waterways into real connected transportation systems for cheaper movement of bulk commodities and raw materials.

In its visualization of a policy of water development, the department has indicated seven great projects of major importance: (1) Mississippi system; (2) Columbia River system; (3) Colorado River; (4) Great Lakes system; (5) the Great Valley of California; (6) intracoastal waterways; (7) other important developments including the Rio Grande and Hudson River. . . .

President Coolidge was not very enthusiastic over some of these ideas, because they would be costly. However, in certain cases he was most cooperative in preparatory work. We were able to advance the development on the Colorado, the Mississippi, the St. Lawrence, and to create interest in the Columbia and the Great Valley of California.[1]

THE COLORADO RIVER COMMISSION

The development of the Colorado River basin comprising parts of California, Arizona, New Mexico, Nevada, Utah, Colorado, and Wyoming promised great assets to these states.

The first was the protection of the Imperial Valley of California from dangerous floods which constantly threatened its destruction. The valley being below sea-level, the river had at one time broken into it and it was only saved from being turned into a salt sea by the most expensive and strenuous efforts.

The second was the expansion of irrigation in all seven states.

The third was a full water supply to the Los Angeles area.

The fourth was the creation of huge hydroelectric power as a by-product to pay for its cost.

On the legal side, however, there were great obstructions to development arising from the bitter quarrels between the seven states in the basin as to their respective water rights—and conflicts with Mexico, whose lands were also large users of Colorado water. The many actions in the courts between the states had held up all development for years.

The beginning of immense benefits could be accomplished by a great dam at Boulder Canyon, subsequently to be reenforced by other dams. I had visited the site before the war, and soon after I became Secretary of Commerce I designated it as one of the first of great multiple-purpose water conservation works to be undertaken.

A meeting of the governors and other representatives of the seven states in 1921 agreed to try to reach an interstate compact to settle these rights, stop litigation, and make a program of development. The Constitution authorizes such treaties between states, subject to Congres-

---

[1] A list of my statements on the utilization of water resources will be found in the Appendix, under the heading Chapter 17.

sional approval. Congress approved the creation of the commission, and President Harding, at the request of the governors, appointed me chairman, representing the Federal government. The governors of the seven states each appointed a member.

The members of the Commission were W. S. Norviel, Arizona; W. F. McClure, California; Delph E. Carpenter, Colorado; J. G. Scrugham, Nevada; Stephen B. Davis, Jr., New Mexico; R. E. Caldwell, Utah; and Frank C. Emerson, Wyoming.[2] I assembled the Commission at Washington in January, 1922. It held sessions at Phoenix, March 15; Los Angeles, March 20; Salt Lake City, March 27; Denver, March 31; and Cheyenne, April 2. We held hearings, public meetings and banquets, and delivered speeches trying to build up a spirit of conciliation.

Finally we met at Santa Fe on November 9, 1922, and sat ten hours daily for two weeks. It seemed impossible to get an agreement. If the Boulder Canyon dam was built and water stored, the states below the dam—California, Arizona, and New Mexico—being the most fertile, would be the first to develop their lands. The states above—Nevada, Colorado, Utah, and Wyoming—feared that the lower basin states would thus establish a priority of water rights by "beneficial use" over their own more slowly developing agriculture.

One night I awoke with a start repeating in my mind a formula. I scribbled it on a piece of paper and carried it into the conference next morning. It was a proposal to divide the basin into two parts, the "upper basin states" and the "lower basin states," and to draw up the Compact so as to divide the water forever between these two divisions. If the lower basin should develop so much land that they used more than their share of the water, then the most recently developed land would be without any right as to water. We agreed to apportion only part of the water for the time being and defer the apportionment of the remainder. We settled the Compact along these lines in a few hours. To give it more solemnity and more emphasis, we signed it in the three-hundred-year-old Governor's Palace at Santa Fe.

---

[2] An extensive account of the negotiations and subsequent agreements and legislation will be found in *The Hoover Dam Documents,* by Ray Lyman Wilbur and Northcutt Ely (Government Printing Office, Washington, 1948).

The Compact had to be ratified by the legislatures of all seven states and by the Congress. At once opposition arose from various sources. A blunderbuss of a governor in Arizona, who knew nothing of engineering, bellowed that it would "rob Arizona of its birthright." Arizona seemed hopeless. We then amended the Compact to provide that it was to be effective as to any six states which did ratify it. I visited the legislatures of all the states and urged them to ratify it again—which they did. Then suddenly Senator Hiram Johnson, having an election coming on and wanting an issue, demanded that the Compact be amended to become effective only when the Boulder dam was authorized by Congress. There was no reason for this, as the construction of the dam was inevitable once the Compact was ratified. He induced the California Legislature to repudiate the ratification unless the other six states accepted his useless and demagogic amendment. Again I had to go the rounds of all the legislatures. It took four years, but my colleagues and I finally persuaded the other five state legislatures to accept Johnson's foolishness in order to break the jam.

Johnson had introduced a bill authorizing the Federal construction of the dam, but in such socialist terms that it could not pass the Congress. Finally, when the Compact had been ratified, Dr. Work, who had become Secretary of the Interior, and I rewrote the whole of Johnson's bill. We provided that the power must be sold to the municipalities and utilities upon a fifty-year contract which would pay for the cost of the dam and the interest. We provided that the power be sold as falling water measured at the "bus bar" and retailed at state-regulated rates. Thus we avoided Government operation. With Mr. Coolidge's support we got it through Congress in 1928, for all of which Johnson claimed the credit—which was immaterial.

Prior to this, however, a dangerous opposition to the construction of the dam grew up in other quarters. Certain engineers declared that this, the highest dam conceived in all history, was infeasible, unsafe, would be subject to earthquakes and might, on bursting, drown a million people. Congress took great alarm. To answer them, Dr. Work and I selected a commission of outstanding engineers to examine the project again. They pronounced these assertions nonsense. As one remarked, "It will stick as long as the mountains around it stick."

In my annual report as Secretary of Commerce, I reviewed the successful making of the Compact, saying:

The major purposes of the Compact are to provide for the equitable division and apportionment of the use of the waters of the Colorado River.

The Compact provides a basis for the carrying out of one of the greatest of our national developments. The land under irrigation in 1920 from the river and its tributaries amounted to about 2,464,000 acres. . . . It is estimated that the irrigated land can be increased to over 5,000,000 acres. Development of 5,000,000 horsepower is a possibility . . .

The successful negotiation of an interstate compact in settlement of so important and complex a problem is significant in that it marks the first time that so large a number of states have been able to settle fundamental interstate rights by process of treaty.

I will continue this story in the account of my period in the White House.[3]

THE GREAT VALLEY OF CALIFORNIA

Ever since serving as a boy on government surveys of California I had had a profound interest in the development of the Great Valley of the San Joaquin and Sacramento. I made a number of addresses on this project, saying on June 27, 1925:

In the Sacramento and San Joaquin valleys we have about 14,000,000 acres of arable land of which about 4,000,000 are under irrigation. Of the remainder perhaps 6,000,000 can be brought quickly into intensive cultivation. We have from these river systems an average of some 37,000,000 acre feet of annual water supply—enough water for all the 14,000,000 acres, if its engineering application can be solved. . . . That means storage. We have mountain and hill storage sites of at least 30,000,000 acre feet capacity . . . as against our present constructed storage of 2,500,000 acre feet. . . . Beyond storage we have the possibilities of pumping by the cheapest power supply in the world, which is itself the by-product of our storage. . . .

We require coordination in forming plans. Which brings me to my major proposition—that is, how to definitely organize effective action. . . .

It is the essence of self-government that these problems must be solved under state leadership, not by absentee Federal control. : . . .

[3] For a list of my more important public statements on the Colorado project, see the Appendix, under the heading Chapter 17.

Therefore, the time has come when the state should move upon this problem by setting up a preliminary commission with the state engineer as the chairman. The Railway Commission and the Division of Water Rights should be given a membership; the reclamation and irrigation districts should nominate some engineer members; the Federal departments, that is, the War Department, Interior Department, Federal Power Commission, should be asked to instruct their engineers in this region to become members. I am never particular over names or details; what we want is an organism that will function. . . .

All these works—the dams and reservoirs, the power plants, the irrigation canals, the pumps, the levees, and the orchards—are not an end in themselves. They are but the means with which we may create happy homes, and under God better men and women. . . .

Mr. Coolidge was cold to this development because of its great cost, and I was not able to advance the project while I was Secretary of Commerce. I was able, however, to help in securing appropriation for the deep seaway to Stockton and the flood control of the Sacramento. And when I came to the White House, I at once joined the Governor of California in appointment of the Commission I had recommended three years before, while Secretary of Commerce.[4]

COLUMBIA RIVER BASIN

Our surveys of water development proved the Columbia River of outstanding importance. Speaking as early as August, 1926, I said:

The Columbia River system should be embraced in a national program of major water improvement. This is one of our greatest drainages, rich in possibilities for irrigation, power, and navigation. In the drainage of this river there are three and one-half million idle horsepower. Within it there is an abundance of water to bring into cultivation not only 1,800,000 acres of fertile land in the Columbia Basin but many hundreds of thousands of acres in other important projects. Its great tributaries, including the Snake River, are capable of great development. The future expansion of the states of Oregon, Washington, and Idaho is involved in its undertaking. The full utilization of the waters of the Columbia drainage will double the population and wealth of these states.

[4] For my more important statements on the Great Valley project and the Columbia River development, see the Appendix, under the heading Chapter 17.

A program of development involves the creation of large storage, the regulation of the flow of the river, the proper and systematic location of dams for reservoirs and power, together with sound plans for extensive irrigation. There are involved today interstate questions affecting the interests of all of these three states. There must be a coordinated program definitely determined which can be hewn to over a term of years.

The largest of the projects in this drainage, the "Grand Coulee," has been long since pronounced of engineering feasibility. Its ultimate construction is inevitable. The sole problem is as to the time when it should be undertaken.

I advocated a joint commission of the states and the Federal government to develop the plans and advise Congress. But Mr. Coolidge could not bear the high outlay of public money that its construction implied. He even refused to allow any substantial engineering work in preparation for it. When I went to the White House I at once ordered the necessary engineering studies to be made and the plans drawn. They were ready in 1932, and I set it as one of the first projects to be undertaken in that second term which did not come off.

WATERWAY DEVELOPMENT

A part of the whole concept of better use of our water resources was the sensible development of our interior waterways for transportation. In planning this improvement, I divided it for discussion and our reports into four major parts: (a) the Mississippi system, (b) the Great-Lakes-to-the-sea, (c) the intercoastal canals, (d) the improvement of harbors and connections with such inland points as their extensions could reach. I urged and wrote extensively upon this whole subject.

THE MISSISSIPPI SYSTEM

Speaking at St. Louis on November 22, 1926, I said:

The Midwest is primarily interested in the development of the Mississippi system, in navigation problems on the Great Lakes themselves, and in the shipway from the Lakes to the sea—a transportation system 12,000 miles in length. Better distribution of population, relief from burdensome freight rates imposed by the War, aid to agriculture and to industry will result from the development of these resources in the heart of the country. . . .

The whole interior waterways system is a problem of greater depth—a six- or nine-foot channel in all of our rivers, stabilization of the depths of the Great Lakes, deepening their channels, and the construction of the great shipway.

A unified connected system, with interconnection of the great Mississippi system and the Lakes, is essential. Disconnected though improved segments are of no avail. The whole chain is only as useful as the weakest link. . . .

A unified program for completing the whole Mississippi system is necessary. The capital cost will not exceed $120,000,000 beyond present appropriations and not more than five years in time. . . .

On our rivers the romantic three-foot packet boats with their few tons of burden were the pioneers of Western transportation. Their teeming life faded before the more economical transportation of the railways. In the meantime, engineering has given to us the prosaic trains of tugs pushing 500- to 2,000-ton steel barges, the box-cars of inland waterways—if we but deepen our rivers by six or nine feet. . . .

Our Government has worked at deepening these channels in spots and isolated projects for many years, but in our national policies what we have missed is the idea that to make a really successful transportation system requires large interconnected systems of trunk lines from seaboard with great feeders from our lateral rivers and its consequent widespread and diversified traffic. We have begun important works at the outer ends and worked back. We would not build a great railway system begun at the outer ends and building back toward the terminals and expect traffic to develop in the meantime.

Moreover, we have wasted vast sums of money in interrupted execution and sporadic and irresolute policies, until today we find ourselves with a mass of disconnected segments of a transportation system, the peacefulness of some of which from the noise of commerce furnished constant munitions of criticism to our opponents. . . .

We gradually put over this enlarged vision of unified systems. The Congressmen found outlets to their desires for a home improvement which was not labeled "pork barrel." The Army Engineers who had to do the job sighed in relief at something which could be finished some day.

THE GREAT LAKES AND ST. LAWRENCE SYSTEM

The problem here was to deepen the existing barge canal from the Lakes to the sea, so as to permit the passage of ocean-going vessels. Incidentally it would develop some 5,000,000 electrical horsepower from the dams which the improvements in navigation would require. The project had been agitated for many years, but Canada had not been willing to come to definite decision.

Mr. Harding approved this project in a general way. In 1922 I requested the Secretary of State to open negotiations with Canada to ascertain whether they were inclined to discuss a joint development. They responded evasively that the time was not yet ripe and proposed further engineering studies. In the meantime we had our Midwest business organizations open discussions with like organizations in Canada. Finally, in 1924, the Canadians being responsive, I suggested to Mr. Coolidge the appointment of an American St. Lawrence Commission to bring matters to a head with a like commission of the Canadian Government. I was designated chairman on March 14, 1924. We agreed with the Canadians upon further engineering and economic studies, which were quickly completed. We reported our conclusions to Mr. Coolidge, as follows:

First: The construction of the shipway from the Great Lakes to the sea is imperative both for the relief and for the future development of a vast area in the interior of the continent.

Second: The shipway should be constructed on the St. Lawrence route, provided suitable agreement can be made for its joint undertaking with the Dominion of Canada.

Third: That the development of the power resources of the St. Lawrence should be undertaken by appropriate agencies.

Fourth: That negotiations should be entered into with Canada in an endeavor to arrive at agreement upon all these subjects. In such negotiations the United States should recognize the proper relations of New York to the power development in the International Section.

The construction of a shipway of sufficient depth to admit ocean shipping from the Atlantic to the Great Lakes will lessen the economic handicaps of adverse transportation costs to a vast area . . . of more than 40,000,000 inhabitants.

I outlined the consequences of increased railway rates since the war and their incidence on our economy, the rectification of which was only possible by waterway development, saying:

If we take as a unit of measurement the cost in cents of carrying a ton of staple goods at present rate, taking the cheapest route in each case, we find that Chicago has moved 336 cents away from the Pacific coast, while New York has moved 224 cents closer . . . Chicago has moved 594 cents away from the markets of the Atlantic seaboard and South America. The same ratios apply to the other midwest points. The increased transportation costs to world markets from the mid-continent have had serious results to agriculture. This development will stabilize lake levels and save much expense in maintenance of navigation on the Great Lakes.

The report discussed the alternative routes for the seaway and rejected upon many grounds all but that of the St. Lawrence River. It estimated the cost, after disposal of the electrical power, as $148,000,000 (at the purchasing value of the dollar of that day).

I spoke many times upon this subject, seeking to enlist public support and to lessen opposition of the eastern railways and seaboard cities.

In an address in 1928 I said:

This means more than the mere saving upon the actual goods shipped over these routes. If part of our crops can move to market at a seven- to ten-cent saving per bushel, the buyers' competitive bidding for this portion of the crop will force upward the price of the whole crop.

This development concerns not alone agriculture, but every industry and business in the Midwest. . . . This development should tend to increase manufacturing industry in the Midwest and thereby create a larger diversity of employment and a greater local market for agricultural products.

I was able to further this project when I became President, and I continue the subject in that part of my narrative.[5]

MISSISSIPPI FLOOD CONTROL

In the next chapter I relate my experience in relief of the Mississippi Flood of 1927. On July 20, 1927, after the completion of that work, I

[5] For a list of my more important statements as to the St. Lawrence Waterway as Secretary of Commerce, see the Appendix, under the heading Chapter 17.

reported to President Coolidge upon the necessity for a complete revision of the government flood control measures. From my observa-
tions and opinions of the Federal and state engineers along the river,
I pointed out the major directions of this revision, saying:

It seems clear that the control must embrace the following principles:

a) Higher and consequently wider levees and the extension of Federal
responsibility for levees on some of the tributaries.

b) A safety valve upon the levees system by the provision of a "spillway"
to the Gulf to protect New Orleans.

c) A "by-pass" to protect southern Louisiana—most probably using the
Atchafalaya River.

d) A great by-pass on the east side of the flood plane from the Arkansas
River to the Atchafalaya River.

e) . . . The erection of emergency flood basins and of storage in the
tributaries.

There is no question that the Mississippi River can be controlled if a bold
and proper engineering plan is developed. It is not possible for the country
to contemplate the constant jeopardy which now exists to 1,500,000 of its citizens or the stupendous losses which the lack of adequate control periodically
brings about. Furthermore, flood control means the secure development of
some 20,000,000 acres of land capable of supporting five to ten millions of
Americans. The cost of such work if spread over ten years would be an
inconsiderable burden upon the country. It is not incompatible with national
economy to prevent $10 of economic waste by the expenditure of $1 Federal
outlay.

Mr. Coolidge, after consultation with General Jadwin, Chief of the
Army Engineers, ordered the work undertaken. General Jadwin paid
me the compliment of often consulting me. The Congress authorized
the project during Mr. Coolidge's administration, and its construction
was completed before I left the White House.[6]

[6] A second major flood ten years later, in 1937, did considerable damage along the
Ohio, yet the Mississippi from Cairo down to New Orleans carried the burden without
a break—impossible without these engineering works.

CHAPTER 18

AN INTERLUDE—RELIEF IN THE
MISSISSIPPI FLOOD OF 1927

The cause of the unprecedented flood on the lower Mississippi River in 1927 was the coincidence of floods on the Ohio, the Missouri, and the upper Mississippi which brought down more water than the lower Mississippi could carry tranquilly to the sea between its thousand miles of levees. The levees broke in scores of places. The area ultimately flooded was, in places, as much as 150 miles wide and stretched down the river 1,000 miles, from Cairo to the Gulf.

The Governors of the six endangered states asked for Federal co-operation, and suggested that I should be placed in charge of the emergency. President Coolidge complied. I went at once to Memphis and took hold. We quickly mobilized the state and local authorities and their militias, the Army Engineers, the Coast Guard, a naval air contingent, the Weather Bureau, and the Red Cross.

It took some two months for the crest of the flood to traverse the 1,000 miles, and after the first rush we were able to keep our organization up with it, and where needed in advance of it. Some 1,500,000 people were driven from their homes; some 2,000,000 acres of crops and thousands of animals were lost and hundreds of millions of dollars in property destroyed. But only three lives—one of them that of an overcurious sightseer—were lost after we took charge. There were many fatalities during the few days before that.

For rescue work we took over some forty river steamers and attached to each of them a flotilla of small boats under the direction of Coast Guardsmen. As the motorboats we could assemble proved insufficient, the sawmills up and down the river made me 1,000 rough boats in ten days. I rented 1,000 outboard motors from the manufacturers, which we were to return. (But after it was all over we could find only 120 motors. Undoubtedly every fisherman in the territory motorized his transportation.) We established great towns of tents on the high ground. We built wooden platforms for the tents, laid sewers, put in electric lights, and installed huge kitchens and feeding halls. And each tent-town had a hospital.

As the flood receded we rehabilitated the people on their farms and homes, providing tents to the needy and building material, tools, seed, animals, furniture, and what not to start them going again. We established sanitary measures to put down malaria, typhoid, pellagra and generally prevention of contagious disease, all of which we continued after the flood.

As at this time we all believed in self-help, I financed the operation by three actions. We put on a Red Cross drive by radio from the flood area, and raised $15,000,000. I secured $1,000,000 from the Rockefeller Foundation to finance the after-flood campaign of sanitation to be matched by equal contributions from the counties. We organized a nonprofit organization through the United States Chamber of Commerce to provide $10,000,000 of loans at low rates, for rehabilitation, every cent of which was paid back. But those were days when citizens expected to take care of one another in time of disaster and it had not occurred to them that the Federal Government should do it.

The railways furnished for my immediate staff and myself a free, special train of Pullmans and a dining car. There we lived when not on our "mother" steamers. We directed the train to points as near as possible to any special emergency and often went round and round east and west of the flood area from Cairo to New Orleans. We usually traveled only by day, as many sections of the tracks were under shallow water. Wherever we stopped the railway officials connected our train with the telephone. The three months spent in this residence were not particularly comfortable, for the ordinary heat of the season was lifted by the superheaters of railway yards and iron Pullmans.

But there was a lighter side to this job.

Of the people we had to move, about half were white small farmers and villagers, and half were colored. There was little hardship, as they were fed well, cared for medically, and entertained by movies and concerts. In fact, for many of them, this was the first real holiday they had ever known. There was little of tragedy and a wealth of good humor and human nature.

One morning our train came into Opelousas, Louisiana. On the platform I was greeted by the benevolent old priest whom we had placed on the staff to direct the hospital in a camp of some 30,000 colored people. The conversation went about as follows:

"Well, Father, is there any trouble or excitement in the camp?"

"No trouble, but some excitement," the Father said. "We had an event in the maternity ward last night. One of the colored sisters gave birth to triplets. She named the first Highwater, the second Flood, and the third Inundation."

An elderly colored sister was sitting on the bank at one of the landing places. She had been brought in by the Coast Guard from a night in a tree. As she remained immovable for some time, I said to her, "Missus, why don't you go on up to the camp and get something to eat?"

"Mister, I jest wants to set and set on real ground."

One night a Coast Guardsman came on to my steamer with this inquiry: "How many times am I supposed to rescue the same feller?" He explained that a certain white farmer's garret stuck out of the water; that he had moved his possessions up there and, climbing on the roof, signaled our patrol airplanes for rescue. A boat was sent out and brought him in. But filled with anxiety for his goods and possessions, he left the camp the next morning, got a boat and returned to the garret to guard his possessions. Then, becoming panicky, he asked by signals to be rescued again. He repeated this performance three times. I asked the Coast Guardsman what he suggested my doing.

"Ship him down the river and put him to work on the levees. And let me take him!" That, he persuaded "him" to do.

We had many experiences with the Acadian French settlements (the Cajuns) in southern Louisiana. Our engineers had learned to time the advance of the flood accurately and to determine within a few feet the height that the water would reach at any point. That was a simple problem in hydraulics. In the routine work in advance of the flood we ran our train into a Cajun town and, assembling the Mayor, the town council, and the principal residents, informed them that the town would go under water about a certain date, and that this would rise to certain levels in relation to the depot platform but would probably not reach to the second floor or the roofs of most houses and stores. Therefore they should move all possessions upstairs to correspond with the levels we gave them and should build a reserve of rough boats so as to move all the people to the high ground some ten miles distant if the waters came up suddenly.

Further, we instructed them how to build a camp with the lumber, tents, and other materials which we would send, and be prepared for a two months' stay. We advised the Mayor to organize a police force to stay behind and guard the town. Except for the intelligent Mayor, the audience was incredulous. Finally a gentleman arose in the back of the room and said to me:

"You are a Wall Streeter. You intend to rob us. I am a surveyor in this parish. My father was a surveyor before me. There never has been a flood here, there never will be a flood here!"

That was what the inhabitants wanted to hear. They followed this false prophet—all but the Mayor. He educated himself by visiting some of our camps farther north and did his job in building the camp for the 15,000 inhabitants. Also he followed directions and built a cement wall around the electric light plant in the town, which he connected with the camp.

A few weeks later, I was rung up on our train in the middle of the night by the Mayor.

"The water is rushing over the town!"

"Yes, we told you it would. Are your people moving? Have you had your boats built? Have all the furniture and goods been taken upstairs or onto the roofs?"

"Not any boats, not any goods moved. That surveyor persuaded the people not to do anything in spite of everything I could say. But the camp is all ready."

I knew that, for our engineers had seen to it.

I told the Mayor that we would run our train down at once and would arrive early in the morning; that we would bring a trainload of boats; that he should get all the people on to the roofs. The railway station was the highest point in town. We ran into it just at daylight with the water up to the axles of the train. On the platform a mob of terror-stricken people were standing as thick as bristles up to their ankles in steadily rising water. As our engineer feared that the mob would climb onto the train, he ran us past the station. From the rear platform I called out that the water would probably rise more but to be patient, for we had a trainload of flatcars with boats following us. I called for the Mayor, who soon appeared in rubber boots, grinning broadly. I asked him:

"Why so cheerful, Mayor?"

"Well, we had only two motorboats in town. A few minutes ago I saw that surveyor grab one and go due east. He said that he was leaving for good!"

At St. Martinville, in routine discussion of protection measures with the town council, I said that by our calculations the water would rise to a certain number of feet above the main street and that cement walls should be built around the waterworks and the electric light plant; and I added the usual directions as to moving upstairs, building camp, boats, and the like. One of the councilmen spoke up:

"How about Evangeline? Should we move her coffin?"

I was bewildered, until someone told me that Longfellow's Evangeline was buried in the churchyard and that her grave was the most precious possession of the town. I advised building a high cement wall around Evangeline to keep the water out. When I related the incident to Mrs. Hoover later on, she informed me that there might have been such a person but her name was probably not Evangeline. She said that Longfellow, seeking rhythm, had changed the name of the heroine once or twice before he settled on Evangeline. It was lucky that they did not disinter the lady. She might have been named Gwendoline.

The 100,000 Cajun farmers were difficult to deal with. They had never been flooded. They would not believe that the water was coming, and most of them would not move either themselves or their livestock to high ground in advance. On one occasion I directed the militia to move them in army trucks. But the commanding officer soon found that this meant a fight with every one of them, and rather than cause bloodshed we abandoned that idea. I concluded a Cajun would only move when the water came up under the bed.

We arranged for the Navy air patrol to be ready, and upon their reports the rescue boats would be sent out. Jean Baptiste had a worrying time. The water reached most of them during the night. Then a frantic gathering of a few things, and a few animals, and a climb for life. A plane flew over him in the morning and, seeing him on the roof, waved to him. A few hours more of worry, and a motorboat took him off from the porch or the roof, with his calf, his mule, his dog, his wife, her canary bird, and their collection of children. When they landed he was given one ticket for the dog, another one for the calf, another one for the mule, and one each was tied onto the wife and each child. He was parted from all but his kin and the canary bird and put onto a train. Arriving in camp he and his family were given shots of antityphoid serum, and another ticket was tied onto each one to prove it. Each was vaccinated, and another ticket was tied on, to prove that. He was given a ticket that entitled him to a tent; others separately entitled him and his brood to meals, beds, and blankets. Thus, the great experience of his life became an education in tickets.

When time for the evacuation of the camps neared, Jean Baptiste had more tickets coming—tickets that entitled him to a railway fare, and to a tent if his house was gone, tickets that gave him lumber, seeds, implements, and a mule or cow. If he presented his original ticket he got his dog (or a dog), his calf (or a calf). From all of which Jean acquired great confidence in the potency of tickets.

Some months afterwards a letter came from a village priest. "Dear Mr. Hoover: The people here would like you to send them some more tickets." And he enumerated what they wanted the tickets to specify.

One permanent and benevolent result came from the flood. The Rockefeller Foundation gift enabled us to establish a health unit for one year in each of the 100 flooded counties. Each unit comprised a physician, a trained nurse, and a sanitary engineer, the counties finding half the cost. It was they who stamped out malaria, pellagra, and typhoid. They improved the health and raised the self-respect of the people generally. The statistics of the diseases against which these "units" applied protective measures showed that they dropped even below pre-flood averages.

This beneficent experience lent much weight to my subsequent proposals of Federal and state aid for permanent establishment of such units in rural counties when I came to the White House.[1]

I received a lasting impression from this experience. I had organized relief among many peoples in Europe. One of our difficulties there had been to find sufficient intelligence, organizational ability and leadership in the many villages and towns to carry on the local work. But in this organization among Americans the merest suggestion sparked efficient and devoted organization—indeed often in advance of specific request. The reasons for this reach to the very base of our American system of life. In this there also lies a special tribute to the peoples of these States.

[1] A list of my more important statements on waterway development and Mississippi flood control may be found in the Appendix, under the heading Chapter 18.

CHAPTER 19

DEVELOPMENT OF AVIATION AND MERCHANT MARINE

On taking over the Department of Commerce I found that no one in the government was interested in developing commercial aviation. Military flying had received a great impulse from the war, and the Army was continuing development for war purposes. The Post Office had carried some experimental mail, using made-over war planes. There were no regular transport services, no developed air lanes, no regulation to insure safety, few and poor commercial landing fields and little organized research in aeronautics. The commercial air activities consisted largely of stunt flying at county fairs. The fatal accidents which marked these "stunts" delayed public acceptance of the new form of transportation. And all this in the country that had given the airplane to the world.

It seemed to me that the first necessity was a Federal service of the same kind of aids as we had for years given to navigation. That parallel implied development of airways, airports, examination of pilots, inspection of planes, weather service, and aeronautical research.

Therefore in 1922 I called a conference of manufacturers, engineering societies, and experienced pilots and urged these necessities. A committee of the conference, in cooperation with our Department's legal staff, drafted the necessary laws, and I submitted them to the Congressional committees.

In 1923 I was still urging action, and stated that we were falling behind foreign development "that means so much to our economic and social progress." Congress is always overburdened with legislative demands, and only those having large public support can get attention.

Therefore we carried the matter to the country as best we could; but the subject, being highly technical, had little emotional appeal.

In 1925 General William Mitchell was waging a violent agitation for the unification and development of the military air services. Taking advantage of this, I recommended to President Coolidge the appointment of an outstanding national board to consider not only the military but also all the commercial phases, and suggested Mr. Dwight Morrow for chairman. I urged that the foundation for military aviation was a strong commercial service with all its collaterals.

On September 23 the President's Aircraft Board assembled. I presented my case in a long memorandum in which, after saying the essential was "the creation of a Bureau of Civil Aviation through which the government should undertake to give services to commercial aviation comparable with those which the government has over a century given to commercial navigation," I outlined the services and regulations which should parallel navigation, and continued:

Without such services . . . aviation can only develop in a primitive way. We can no more expect the individual aviator or the individual aviation company to provide these services on land than we could expect the individual navigator or the individual shipping company to provide them on the sea.

I emphasized the defense importance of commercial aviation and manufacture, and summarized my recommendations:

First. The establishment of an Aviation Bureau, so as to provide the services I have mentioned.

Second. We should contract out the carriage of the mail. . . . This income, together with the promise of additional revenue that could be obtained from express and passengers, appears to be sufficient to induce substantial concerns to undertake these ventures.

Third. The establishment of airports by the important municipalities.

With this minimum extension of governmental activity we can secure a commercial aviation in the United States without subsidy.

The Morrow commission adopted my recommendations in full. By dint of this constant work which had extended over four years, we secured enactment by the Congress of our recommendations on May 20, 1926.

In the four years during which we were agitating for this legislation —from 1922 to 1926—there had grown up only a puny 369 miles of regular air services operated by private enterprise and about 3,000 miles of mail lines, operated by the Post Office. The latter carried neither passengers nor express.

As soon as the law passed Congress, I organized the Aviation division in the Department under the able direction of William P. MacCracken, Jr. We went at it with great zest. I know of no satisfaction equal to the growth under one's own hand of a great economic and human agency. We arranged that the Post Office should let contracts for carrying the mail to private concerns and launched a campaign for municipal development of airports. We began building airways with radio beacons, lights, emergency landing fields, and weather services.

I felt a personal triumph with every mile of service we added. Within a year after the establishment of the Aviation division we had 4,000 miles of fully equipped airways; 10,000 miles more in preparatory stages; 864 airports in operation, and 144 more cities stirred up to the point of letting contracts for such facilities. Our research laboratories established in the Bureau of Standards were daily improving construction of planes and the ground aids to aerial navigation. Of twenty-five airplane accidents where persons were killed or injured in the last half of 1927, only three had occurred on our regulated airways. Public confidence in air travel began to grow. Under the impulse of commercial development at home our exports of airplanes rose 400 per cent over 1922, and our commercial planes were destined to lead the world.

The next three years showed enormous development. In a message to the Congress in 1929 I reviewed the progress of the industry under the guidance of the Department of Commerce. By that time there were 25,000 miles of government-improved airways of which 14,000 were lighted and beaconed; there were 1,000 well developed airports and another 1,200 in development, 6,400 planes licensed and in regular flights of over 25,000,000 miles per annum. Our manufacturing output had risen to 7,500 planes yearly.

We had no control over the finances of air transport companies on our routes. Difficulties soon began to develop. These could have been resolved through the Post Office contracts, but the Postmaster General in the Coolidge administration took the attitude that under the law he was interested in mail only. Because of this difficulty the development during the first three years took on some dangerous distortions. Scores of transport companies sprang up, operating shorter or longer segments on the airways. We were threatened with a permanent muddle such as had resulted from our chaotic railway development with all its separation into short and long lines, duplication and waste.

The next steps were taken under my direction while I was President and are recounted later.[1]

MERCHANT MARINE

The Secretary of Commerce not only was instructed to look after water transportation by the terms of the organic act creating the Department, he also presided over five Bureaus administering such matters. But the Department had no control of government shipping.

The First World War left us with a mass of jerry-built government cargo ships, useless in foreign trade. They were mostly too slow and too costly to operate in competition with either the foreign or the better domestic ships. And, worse still, we were left with government operation and an impossible setup—a Shipping Board appointed on a dual, bipartisan and regional basis which generated such internal dissensions that it was even less capable than boards in general. And no government board can properly administer a commercial business.

The hope of a competent merchant marine lay in reducing the Board to a body regulating rates only; getting rid of government operation, building good ships, and establishing definite regular cargo transport on definite trade routes under private enterprise subsidized by the government to the extent necessary to compensate for cheaper foreign building costs and cheaper labor.

The stumbling-block was the southern Democratic Senators who dominated the Board and insisted upon its continuance and independ-

[1] For a list of my more important statements on aviation during my term as Secretary of Commerce, see the Appendix, under the heading Chapter 19.

ence. The Senators were bent on maintaining three times too many shipping lines, all operated by the government and radiating from certain southern ports which had no adequate export or import background. For years they blocked every effort to reorganize the Board or to handle the problem constructively.

I set forth this situation innumerable times and served on endless conferences and commissions. A few extracts from my statements will indicate my position.

In a public address in New York on February 17, 1920, I said:

If the government continues in the shipping business . . . we shall be faced with the ability of private enterprise the world over to make profits from the margins of higher cost of government operation alone. . . . The largest successfully managed cargo fleet in the world comprises about 120 ships, and yet we are attempting to manage 1,900 ships at the hands of a government bureau. . . . The . . . profit or loss in a ship is measured by a few hundred tons of coal wasted, . . . a little extravagance in repairs, or by the four or five days on a round trip. . . . Lest fault be found, our government officials are unable to enter upon the detailed higgling in . . . rates required by every cargo. . . . They must take refuge . . . in fixed rates. In result, their competitors underbid by the smallest margins necessary to get the cargoes. . . . Our large fleet in the world's markets is thus to hold up rates. . . . Increasing numbers of our ships will be idle.

Speaking in November, 1923, I said:

It is simply a truism to say that we must have an American Merchant Overseas Marine. . . . We must have our own ships for the protection of our foreign trade; we must have ships if we would expand our exports on sound lines, and we must have them as an auxiliary to our national defense.

President Harding appointed me chairman of a Cabinet committee to inquire into the merchant marine. The committee stated on December 29, 1924, "The government can never operate commercial shipping as economically as private capital." We recommended that government operations be continued on certain trade routes temporarily until private enterprise could be established. We recommended the abolition of the Shipping Board and the appointment of a single administrator.

On November 4, 1925, I gave evidence before the House Committee on Merchant Marine Fisheries covering all of the above points, and added:

There are about twenty overseas trade routes which are the connecting links between our inland trade routes and foreign countries upon which our foreign trade is dependent.

For the protection of our commerce from discrimination and from combinations which would impose onerous freight rates, we must maintain upon each of these routes the operation of very substantial shipping under the American flag.

Commerce cannot operate upon uncertainty of transportation; it requires regular ferrylike sailings over essential routes.

The type of ship which is best adapted to such regular service and at the same time is the most profitable to operate is the cargo liner of from 10,000 to 18,000 gross tons, speed 12 to 18 knots, preferably Diesel-propelled, and having up to, say, 20 per cent of passenger space. . . .

The national defense requires an American merchant marine and it also largely requires the cargo-liner type.

. . . We must get out of government operation. . . .

Some of the lines of those trade routes are today successfully operated by American flag private enterprise. Some of the government lines which are losing money today would pay private enterprise, and they could be disposed of under proper guarantee of continuance if private firms could be sure of future government policies. . . . No section of the country has a right to call upon the government perpetually to operate ships at a loss. . . .

. . . Each member (of the Shipping Board) has a four-way independent responsibility. He is responsible for every act of the Board to the country as a whole, to his particular constituency, to his political party, and, finally, to Congress. Responsibility to the President, the one responsibility which every administrative officer of the government should acknowledge under the spirit of the Constitution, is denied by the Board. . . .

Finally as the result of our preaching and urging, the Congress passed the White-Jones Merchant Marine Act of 1928. However, this was the usual attempt to avoid the term "subsidy" by giving extravagant mail contracts and loose credits for shipbuilding instead of direct financial support based upon service. It did not cure the Shipping Board, who proceeded to sell old ships to feeble corporations and to bolster up unprofitable southern lines by giving them huge mail con-

tracts, thus continuing the southern port scandal. The contracts produced only a few new and better ships and did not establish them on
the most necessary trade routes.

When I came to the White House I reorganized the whole business
and started on the right track, all of which will appear later on.[2]

[2] A list of my more important statements on the merchant marine while Secretary
of Commerce is to be found in the Appendix, under the heading Chapter 19.

CHAPTER 20

DEVELOPMENT AND CONTROL OF
RADIO BROADCASTING

When I became head of the Department I found that one of its duties was to develop and regulate the use of radio. At that time radio was still little more than a ship-to-shore telegraph system. Broadcasting the human voice was only experimental—we called it the radio telephone then—but it was quickly to emerge from this stage to a new and universal art profoundly modifying every aspect of human life. In this creation the Department was destined to play a part.

Only the Westinghouse Electric & Manufacturing Company at Pittsburgh and the General Electric Company at Schenectady had erected experimental voice broadcasting stations. There were at this time probably fewer than 50,000 receiving sets, and they were not too good. The American boy, however, had taken enthusiastically to radio and, with his crystal set and earphones, was spreading interest widely over the country. Suddenly a great public interest awoke, and in six months there were 320 broadcasting stations, most of them of low power and short range.

The law authorizing the Secretary of Commerce to regulate radio had been enacted prior to voice broadcasting. It was a very weak rudder to steer so powerful a development. I was early impressed with three things: first, the immense importance of the spoken radio; second, the urgency of placing the new channels of communication under public control; and, third, the difficulty of devising such control in a new art. Radio men were eager for regulation to prevent interference with one another's wave lengths, but many of them were insisting on a right of permanent preemption of the channels through the air as private property—a monopoly of enormous financial value. Their argument was that the necessary capital could not be provided without permanent tenure. It was in a fashion comparable to private ownership of a water navigation channel.

Therefore in our usual fashion of solving problems wherever possible by cooperation rather than by law, I called a conference of representatives of the industry and various government agencies on February 27, 1922. A few paragraphs from my opening address to the conference will illustrate the situation at that time:

It is the purpose of this conference to inquire into the critical situation that has now arisen through the astonishing development of the wireless telephone; to advise the Department of Commerce as to the application of its present powers of regulation, and further to formulate such recommendations to Congress as to the legislation necessary.

We have witnessed in the last four or five months one of the most astounding things that have come under my observation of American life. This Department estimates that today over 600,000 persons (one estimate being 1,000,000) possess receiving sets, whereas there were fewer than 50,000 such sets a year ago. We are indeed today upon the threshold of a new means of widespread communication of intelligence that has the most profound importance from the point of view of public education and public welfare. The comparative cheapness . . . of receiving sets . . . bids fair to make them almost universal in the American home.

I think that it will be agreed at the outset that the use of the radio telephone for communication between single individuals as in the case of the ordinary telephone is a perfectly hopeless notion. Obviously if ten million telephone subscribers are crying through the air for their mates they will never make a junction. . . . The wireless spoken word has one definite field, and that is for broadcast of certain predetermined material of public interest from central stations. This material must be limited to news, to education, and to entertainment, and the communication of such commercial matters as are of importance to large groups of the community at the same time.

It is therefore primarily a question of broadcasting, and it becomes of primary public interest to say who is to do the broadcasting, under what circumstances, and with what type of material. It is inconceivable that we should allow so great a possibility for service to be drowned in advertising chatter.

Congress some few years ago authorized the Secretary of Commerce to . . . impose certain conditions . . . designed to prevent interference between the stations . . . This legislation was drawn before the development of the wireless telephone. . . . The time has arrived . . . when there must be measures to stop the interferences . . . between even the limited number of sending stations. . . .

The problem is one of most intensely technical character . . . Even if we use all the ingenuity possible I do not believe there are enough permutations to allow unlimited numbers of sending stations.

One of the problems . . . is who is to support the sending stations. In certain countries, the government has prohibited the use of receiving instruments except upon payment of a fee, out of which are supported government-sending stations. I believe that such a plan would most seriously limit the development of the art and its social possibilities. . . .

This is a problem of regulation . . . Regulations will need to be policed . . . and thus the celestial system—at least the ether part of it—comes within the province of the policeman. Fortunately the art permits such a policeman by listening in to detect those ether hogs that are endangering the traffic.

There is in all of this the necessity to establish public right over the ether roads. . . . There must be no national regret that we have parted with a great national asset.

The Conference agreed, irrespective of the legal authority of the Department, to abide by my decisions as umpire until we could devise needed legislation.

We set aside certain parts of the wave bands for public broadcasting, certain parts for the Army and Navy and public services. We assigned a definite wave band for boys. Because there were, as far as the art had developed, insufficient wave lengths for all the purposes then known, we forbade the use of person-to-person telephone except in restricted instances. Then with the skillful help of Stephen Davis we set about the picture puzzle of so allotting the wave lengths that the broadcasting stations would not interfere with one another. Fortunately, the weak sending power at that time enabled the same wave lengths to be used in different cities at some distance from one another, and so we were able to accommodate everybody for a while.

To sustain this cooperative action I called a second conference of the industry in March, 1923, a third in October, 1924, the fourth in November, 1925. The delegates—more than 1,000 at each session—took a most constructive attitude, and the majority of them supported our legislative proposals. Their cooperative spirit contributed enormously to the development of methods for handling the difficult technical problems.

From 1921 to 1923 we felt we should have more experience before drafting legislation. With the approval of the Congressional committees we carried on until 1924. At that time we proposed a draft bill but soon found that Congress, overburdened with more urgent work, was loath to take up such a complex subject, especially since we should have to resist pressure from some interests which still hoped for private rights in broadcast frequency channels. One of our troubles in getting legislation was the very success of the voluntary system we had created. Members of the Congressional committees kept saying, "It is working well, so why bother?" A long period of delay ensued. One bill died in transit between the House and Senate in 1925. Finally a Chicago station broke away from our voluntary regulation, preempted a wave length for itself, and established its contention in the courts against the weak legal authority of the Secretary of Commerce. Then Congress woke up and finally, in February, 1927, passed the law which we recommended, and which established the public ownership and regulation of the wave channels.

A vivid experience in the early days of radio was with Evangelist Aimee Semple McPherson of Los Angeles. One of the earliest to appreciate the possibilities in radio, she had established a small broadcasting station in her Temple. This station, however, roamed all over the wave band, causing interference and arousing bitter complaints from the other stations. She was repeatedly warned to stick to her assigned wave length. As warnings did no good, our inspector sealed up her station and stopped it. The next day I received from her a telegram in these words:

Please order your minions of Satan to leave my station alone. You cannot expect the Almighty to abide by your wavelength nonsense. When I offer my prayers to Him I must fit into His wave reception. Open this station at once.   AIMEE SEMPLE McPHERSON

Finally our tactful inspector persuaded her to employ a radio manager of his own selection, who kept her upon her wave length.

I made many public addresses and statements during a period of six years in the course of advocating legislation and obtaining public support for it, both abjuring and defending broadcasters. Some paragraphs from these expressions indicate the growth of the art, of the industry—and of the problems:

(March 10, 1924) . . . I can state emphatically that it would be most unfortunate for the people of this country, to whom broadcasting has become an important incident of life, if its control should come into the hands of any single corporation, individual, or combination.

It would be in principle the same as though the entire press of the country were so controlled. The effect would be identical whether this control arose under a patent monopoly or under any form of combination or over a wave channel. . . . In the licensing system put in force by this Department the life of broadcasting licenses is limited to three months, so that no vested right can be obtained either in a wave length or in a license.

I believe, however, that everybody should be permitted to send out anything they like. The very moment that the government begins to determine what can be sent, it establishes a censorship through the whole field of clashing ideas. . . .

(March 26, 1924) The amateurs, as you all know, have a certain wave band assigned to them, but within this band they do much of their own policing. In discussing with one of their leaders—a youngster of about sixteen—the method of preventing interference between them, he stated with some assurance that there would be no difficulties about enforcement if left to them. I pressed him as to the method they would employ. He showed a good deal of diffidence but finally came through with the statement, "If you leave it to us and if anybody amongst the amateurs does not stick to the rules, we will see that somebody beats him up." So far I have heard of no cases of such assault.

(November 9, 1925) We have great reason to be proud of the results of these conferences. From them have been established principles upon which our country has led the world in the development of this service. We have accomplished this by a large measure of self-government in an art and industry of unheard-of complexity, not only in its technical phases, but in its relations both to the government and to the public. Four years ago we were dealing with a scientific toy; today we are dealing with a vital force in American life. We are, I believe, bringing this lusty child out of its swaddling clothes without any infant diseases. . . .

Some of our major decisions of policy have been of far-reaching importance and have justified themselves a thousandfold. . . .

We hear a great deal about the freedom of the air, but there are two parties to freedom of the air, and to freedom of speech for that matter. There is the speechmaker and the listener. Certainly in radio I believe in freedom for the listener. He has much less option upon what he can reject, for the other fellow is occupying his receiving set. The listener's only option is to abandon his right to use his receiver. Freedom cannot mean a license to every person or corporation who wishes to broadcast his name or his wares, and thus monopolize the listener's set. . . .

So far as opportunity goes to explain one's political, religious, or social views, it would seem that 578 independent stations might give ample latitude in remarks; and in any event, without trying out all this question, we can surely agree that no one can raise a cry of deprivation of free speech if he is compelled to prove that there is something more than naked commercial selfishness in his purpose.

The ether is a public medium, and its use must be for public benefit. The use of a radio channel is justified only if there is public benefit. The dominant element for consideration in the radio field is, and always will be, the great body of the listening public. . . .

We have in this development of governmental relations two distinct problems. First is the question of traffic control. This must be a Federal responsibility. . . .

The second question is the determination of who shall use the traffic channels and under what conditions. This is a very large discretionary or quasijudicial function which should not devolve entirely upon any single official. . . .

Today there are nearly six hundred stations and about twenty-five million listeners.

(October 21, 1925) Four million of our families have radio receiving sets . . .; one-half of the nation can now receive the inspiration of a speech from our President and a score of millions throb with the joys and sorrows of the dramatic presentation of minute-to-minute events in the last World Series. They have knowledge . . . more quickly than some people in the grandstands. . . .

Incidentally I wish our engineers and inventors would invent another knob on our receiving sets by which we could express our feelings to the fellow who is broadcasting. Tuning out in disgust is an uncompleted mental reaction.

(December 26, 1925) A statement in one of this morning's newspapers seems to indicate a lack of information as to the basis I have proposed for radio control. The implication is that I have sought to have the job placed in my hands. Far to the contrary. I have both before Congressional Committees and in at least a half-dozen public addresses stated that no one official should dictate who is to use the radio wave lengths, and I have for years advocated that this, as a quasijudicial function, should be placed in the hands of an independent commission.

Moreover, for five years I have reiterated that these wave lengths are public property to be used by assignment of public authority. This view has been enforced by the Department of Commerce for the past five years. It was again reaffirmed by the last Radio Conference. This principle, together with a provision for a commission to control assignments, was incorporated into bills introduced to Congress . . . and approved by me. Somebody needs to find out what has already taken place before he starts something.

The legislation finally enacted required the appointment of a quasijudicial commission to administer the act. President Coolidge asked me to select its members, which I did. They were all men of technical and legal experience in the art, and none of them were politicians. The act worked very well except in one particular, to remedy which I secured its amendment in 1929.

THE FIRST INTERNATIONAL RADIO CONFERENCE

It had become evident over the years that much radio interference rose from beyond our own borders and that there must be international regulation. Through the State Department we called an international conference which assembled in Washington, October 4, 1927, attended by the delegates of seventy-six nations. I presided at these meetings.

The task proved so difficult that it required sessions extending over several months. We finally signed the treaties which established world order, certain principles, and the assignment of wave lengths. They have lasted except in the Communist states until this day in spite of all wars and murrain.

THE ASSETS AND LIABILITIES IN RADIO

With the background of interest in radio I had also the experience of making addresses by the hundred on various subjects and observing their effect upon the listeners. They do not hesitate to express themselves pro or con. I have also listened to thousands of other people's speeches and programs. With this experience, I have naturally often tried to weigh the social, political, and economic effect of this new instrument. It has not been an unmixed good.

On the good side it has been a powerful educational force. It has stimulated the appreciation of good music, despite the fact that it gives tenfold time to the worst of music. It has made science, the arts, the professions, the daily lives of other men and women familiar to all the people. It has vastly enriched the lives of shut-ins and residents of remote places. It has made transmission of news instantaneous. It has brought into every household the voice and views of the men who create thought and command action.

But truth is far less carefully safeguarded on the radio than in the press. The control of slander, libel, malice, and smearing is far more difficult. The newspaper editor has a chance to see a statement before it goes to the press. But on the radio it is often out before the station can stop it. A misstatement in the press can be corrected within twenty-four hours, and it reaches approximately the same people who read the original item and is open to all who have a grievance.

There is little adequate answer to a lying microphone. The audience is never the same on any two days or hours, and it takes days to arrange time for an answer even when the station consents. At that, no matter how grave the injustice, the broadcasting companies will seldom sacrifice time for this privilege. Action under American law as to slander is doubly futile against the radio.

Also radio lends itself to propaganda far more easily than the press.

And propaganda is seldom the whole truth. The officials currently in office have preponderant time at the microphone, and theirs becomes the dominant voice. Propaganda, even when it sticks to fact, is often slanted by the magic in the human voice. And propaganda over the air raises emotion at the expense of reason far more than the printed word. Often enough, no one is much interested in providing a counter-propaganda; or at least few are able to organize it. Not only is domestic propaganda poured on us, but it has become a special function of foreign governments and persons. Crooked propaganda has become an insidious instrument of international politics.

In the debate over going into World War II British speakers deluged our radio with their propaganda. When some of us who were opposed wished to present our views, we were refused time by the British authorities.

Some of the evils of libel and slander could be corrected by a revision of our laws in those matters. They are not adapted to the radio and they have been watered down from the original English common law by American court decisions, until they provide little protection. Unlike the British, they seldom give moral damages for misrepresentation and wrongful injury to reputation.

As I pointed out in my first statement in 1922, broadcasting, then just beginning its use of advertising, could go wild in this direction. It has often done so. The dignified presentation of the sponsor has too often been abandoned for hucksters' tattle, interlarded into the middle of programs and tiresomely continued at the end. Sensitive people refuse to buy an article because of the inept persistence of the announcer. Yet advertisers, paying $500 a minute, seemingly cannot bear to hear any minute lost in the barking of their wares or names.

The danger is that some day the public will revolt against all these misuses of radio and put programs into the hands of a government agency. That is a sorry thing to contemplate. With all its faults the private ownership has proved far superior in its enterprise, its enter-tainment, and its use in public debate and in public service to the government-owned systems of Europe.

Some of these evils could be cured by the industry itself. Many radio directors deplore them. No one station or chain can alone stamp them out. They might be much reduced by resuming the annual conferences of the early twenties and by making an effort to develop codes of ethics to apply not only to stations, but to speakers.[1]

[1] A list of my more important statements on radio while Secretary of Commerce is given in the Appendix, under the heading Chapter 20.

CHAPTER 21

DEVELOPMENT OF THE FISHERIES

Having been a fisherman in stream and lake ever since I was eight years old, and in oceans later in life, I was naturally interested in the Bureau of Fisheries. Moreover it contained a large area for accomplishment in the elimination of waste and thus the further growth of standards of living.

One of my first acts was to change the Director of the Bureau by appointing Henry O'Malley, who had spent twenty-five years as an expert in that service. Mr. O'Malley at once poured out to me his grief over the steady degeneration in American commercial fisheries through public neglect. The salmon and halibut fisheries in the Northwest and Alaska were slowly dying out. The shad and bluefish fisheries on the Atlantic coast were going. The great salmon and sturgeon fisheries on the Atlantic side had completely gone. The salmon, herring, and other fisheries on the Pacific coast were on their way out. The crab fisheries of the Chesapeake Bay were being ruined. Game fish were getting scarcer and scarcer all over the country.

The first of our jobs was to strengthen the scientific staff of the Bureau and begin a searching examination into the problem of every important species. These researches, first into pure science and second into application through cooperative and governmental action, are an entrancing story in themselves. All this is related in twelve years of Mr. O'Malley's reports. But to the general public such reports lack the touch of romance and adventure which mark the story of exploration in new fields of knowledge and their application to human welfare.

The coastal fisheries in the continental United States were under the separate control of each state. Alaska being a territory, its salmon, halibut, herring, and cod fisheries could be controlled by the Federal government. Owing to the degeneration of state coastal fisheries, the Alaskan fisheries were then furnishing nearly half of the national commercial supply of fish and being rapidly exhausted.

I appointed Dr. Charles Gilbert, a fish expert of Stanford University, and a staff of assistants, to study the Alaska problem. He soon reported that not enough salmon were allowed to get by the fishermen into the streams where they spawned. Of equal importance was his discovery that salmon will spawn only in the stream where they were hatched, and that several streams were already fished out and dead. Gilbert also emphasized the definite overfishing of halibut and cod in the open seas of the Northwest and the probable disappearance of these fishes.

I proposed to Congress that it pass stringent regulatory laws as to these fisheries. The canners and commercial fishermen, with the aid of the trade press, fought this bitterly. They offered instead a system of voluntary restraint. I accepted the proposal, but at the end of one season we found that about a quarter of the fishermen had violated their agreement. Therefore in 1922 I requested President Harding to use his executive authority over the Territory pending legislation. By this order we established temporary conservation. So much action, however, created great fury among some of the fishing concerns and some emphatic remarks in the press on my part. I went to Alaska in 1923, and while there made the following statement urging legislation:

. . . There must be strong and immediate restrictions on salmon fishing, if we are to preserve the industry from the same destruction that has ruined many of our national fisheries elsewhere. In fact it should have been undertaken in Alaska years ago. . . .

This is the largest of Alaska's industries. More than half her population and more than half her territorial revenues are dependent upon it. It can in time be built up to much larger dimensions than at present. If nothing is done, it will be lost in a few years. It is of vital importance to the whole American people as a source of national food supply. . . .

Pious statements, scientific discussion, and political oratory will not spawn salmon.

The battle became very bitter and at one time I wrote to the chairman of the Senate Committee on Commerce:

So far as the statement of Delegate Sutherland of Alaska, who is demagoguing for the canners, is concerned, there is no polite answer to him. The real issue is that having fitted a lid on the further destruction of the Alaskan fisheries until Congress acts, I intend to sit on it whether Delegate Sutherland, certain canners, and certain fishermen like it or not.

On June 24, 1924, Congress passed the law as requested, upon which I commented:

The passing of the Alaskan fisheries conservation bill . . . assures the most important step yet accomplished in the preservation of our sea fisheries. I am naturally very much pleased as I have urged this legislation in every session of Congress for the last three years.

I can stand any amount of personal abuse with all the amiability of the winner. . . .

I trust that this is the start of a series of effective measures for the redemption of American sea fisheries. We can, by equally constructive work, yet restore the great lost fisheries of shad, sturgeon, and salmon to the Atlantic and Pacific coast, as the case may be.

After a period of recuperation, the Alaska salmon fisheries under our regulation steadily increased their catch until, for many years, they produced all that the market could take of these species.

After our study of the halibut and herring fisheries in the North Pacific, we initiated, and completed on October 21, 1922, a convention with Canada providing for a joint investigation. Ultimately we made a treaty with our northern neighbor, setting up joint control of these fisheries. While there was some decrease in production of these species during a period of rigid restriction, in a few years they were yielding the highest catches in their history. We tried to arrange similar joint action with Mexico on Pacific fishing grounds. This failed.

In May, 1921, I called a nation-wide conference on pollution of our continental streams and the beaches. The latter originated largely from oil sludge dumped by steamers in harbors and along the coast. It not only had become a great fire hazard to cities, but also was killing fish by the millions and was destroying the pleasure beaches. I said:

Pollution of the coastal waters by industrial wastes is yearly becoming a graver menace to the fisheries, shipping, and use of our pleasure beaches.

Owing to the recent great increase in the use of fuel oil in shipping . . . the pollution of waters . . . in the vicinity of the more important harbors has become particularly flagrant and damaging. Legislation is before Congress in this matter, and unless it is enacted, great and serious damage will ensue.

After much agitation, Congress acted in June, 1924, and that particular pollution ended.

In 1924 I returned to the appeal for conservation of our continental fisheries, saying in the Commerce Report to Congress of that year:

The conservation of our fisheries is a matter of the utmost national importance. Many of them are still threatened with extinction. Our great runs of salmon on the Atlantic coast long ago disappeared as a food supply, and the salmon of Alaska were doomed until we recently called a halt on their destruction. The sturgeon fisheries of the Great Lakes have declined 98 per cent in forty years, and the sturgeon has almost disappeared on the Atlantic coast. Since 1835 the annual catch of shad in the Potomac has dropped from 22,000,000 to 600,000. In ten years the crab fisheries of the Chesapeake and Delaware have been cut in half. Our lobster catch is less than one-third of what it was thirty years ago.

In an address before the Sixth Annual Convention of the United States Fisheries Association at Atlantic City on September 5, 1924, I summarized the work we had accomplished:

First. Congress enacted last winter Federal legislation controlling oil pollution of coastal waters by oil-burning and oil-carrying ships. This measure was vital to the existence of our fisheries and the protection of our shellfish. It is only a beginning at solution of the pollution problem.

Second. We secured by negotiation with Canada the Pacific coast halibut treaty and the enactment of legislation under which the two nations are now able to halt the depletion and destruction of that great fishery and to start its recuperation.

Third. Congress, after three years of controversy, enacted the Alaska salmon fisheries conservation bill, and we have today vigorously stopped destruction and started the rejuvenation of these fisheries.

Fourth. Congress enacted the Upper Mississippi fish and game refuge bill through which the streams of the Upper Mississippi will be preserved for the breeding of fish and game.

Fifth. We have had some success in bringing about cooperation between different states for the protection of fisheries.

These steps have not been accomplished without bitter opposition, part of it venal, part of it innocent, but they have been supported by every true fisherman.

I then enumerated the next steps to be taken, as follows:

1. To cultivate a sense of national responsibility toward the fisheries and their maintenance; to make conservation of those priceless resources a part of the national instinct; to let the whole country understand that we can no more overfish and expect to have sea food than we can overcut the growth of our forests and expect to have timber.

2. To make a vigorous attempt to restore the sturgeon, salmon, shad, lobster, crab, oyster, and clam and other littoral fisheries on the Atlantic coast.

3. To secure the prevention of pollution from sources other than ships both in coastal and inland waters.

4. To undertake the reinforcement of stocks of game fish throughout the United States.

There is constructive joy in the application of science to fisheries. For instance, making "pearl" buttons from fresh-water mussel shells had grown to be an important industry in the Midwest. Then it began to die from exhaustion of the mussels. Investigation revealed that, to mature, the spawn of the mussels must live for some days in the gills of fish. At that time we had established along the Mississippi and its main tributaries a system for the rescue of fish which were marooned and destined to die after the annual floods on these rivers. Every year we put millions of fish back into the streams to go their way rejoicing. It occurred to one of our scientists that we could hatch mussel spawn artificially and then put it into the thousands of buckets of fish gathered during this rescue work. And behold, in a few years the button industry was restored and the danger of buttonless garments averted.

CHESAPEAKE CRAB FISHERIES

One of my unusual experiences in public life occurred when we were trying to bring about an agreement between the states of Virginia and

Maryland to stop the destruction of the crab fisheries in Chesapeake
Bay. The Federal government had no authority in the matter, but I
thought that we could accomplish something by persuasion. Mr.
O'Malley was doubtful and informed me that the quarrel over the Bay
fisheries between the fishermen of the two states dated from the days
when George Washington attempted to settle it. It constituted a feud
with physical battles and annual murders. O'Malley also told me that a
simple method of seasonal restrictions would help solve the problem.
So we waded into the feud.

With the approval of the governors of the two states and the help of
their officials, we called a conference of the fishermen, stipulating that
each of the 50 parishes involved should send two representatives of real
fishermen. When the conference convened, we listed the assembled
delegates. Instead of two delegates, each parish had sent six or more
so that there were over 400 of them. Opening the Conference, I stated
the problem and called upon A for his views. Then came a surprise.
Mr. A delivered an impassioned oration in old-time Methodistic tones,
starting with a description of the division of three powers in the Constitution, and recited George Washington's settlement which, he declared, applied only to fish and that a crab was not a fish. He spoke for
half an hour and wound up with a peroration which called on us to
right the greatest human wrong of the century and to preserve the
division of powers in the Constitution.

While he was speaking I asked O'Malley what it all meant. He said:
"These fishermen have held an oratorical contest in each parish to
choose their champion. If you can stand it, this will be one of the biggest
oratorical finals in all history. The orators are not necessarily fishermen."

Mr. A finished to the loud applause of the delegates from his side
of Chesapeake Bay.

I called up Mr. B and met the same blast of oratory. Being from the
other side of the Bay, he proved that a crab was a fish and that there
was also a stupendous accumulation of wrongs and that any opinion to
the contrary was unconstitutional. His oratorical and peroration tech-
nique was the same, and he sat down in half an hour amidst the same
wild applause—from his side.

We adjourned for lunch and consultation. There were at least forty-eight more orations in store. Wearily O'Malley, Stephen Davis, and I decided to divide the job of presiding and go through with it in shifts. It took three days with evening sessions as late as we dared keep them awake and in full oratorical form.

Late one evening, when they finally had run down, O'Malley and I stated our position briefly and read to the audience a suggested formula of seasonal control as a partial solution. With the feeling that I was only starting another cyclone of oratory, I called on Mr. X, leader of one faction, for his views. To my surprise, he responded, pleasantly and simply, that the arrangement was all right with the delegation from his parish. Mr. Y, who appeared to be chief advocate for the other side, said just as briefly that it suited him and his people perfectly. I sampled a few more parishes. Same result. I put the question to the whole conference. Unanimous approval!

O'Malley laughed.

"They've known for years that this was the only possible direction of solution," he said. "But down in that neck of the woods they admire oratory. This was unprecedented opportunity for an exposition of public speaking." And part of the crabs were saved—for a while.

We tried very hard to arrange a Constitutional interstate compact among the Atlantic seaboard states placing all the fisheries under joint control of the states through a commission representing each state. This proved to be an uphill job, and we did not remain in office long enough to educate all the states up to it. The idea persisted, however, and eighteen years later all but two Atlantic and Gulf states had joined.

CHAPTER 22

AN INTERLUDE—FISHING

Having been elected to the eminent position of President of the Izaak Walton League, I delivered an inaugural address. It has been reprinted as a book, in magazine articles, syndicated by the newspapers, and broadcast in millions of pamphlets of every conceivable form. It has reached at least 15,000,000 readers. The justification for inserting it here is to introduce, for another generation, a gleam of humor into a text composed mostly of grim economics. I said:

As the head of the Department of Commerce and thus charged with such responsibilities for our game fisheries as weigh upon the mind of the Federal government, I wish to state a fact, to observe a condition, to relate an experiment, to lay before you a proposition, to offer a protest, and to give the reasons for all. I shall not discuss the commercial fisheries on this occasion because I wish to be cheerful and philosophical.

The fact I refer to is that our game fishing is decreasing steadily and rapidly. The condition is, that the present method of rehabilitation through hatcheries and distribution of fry and fingerlings is a failure because of high infant mortality. The experiment in the case indicates that artificial hatching can be made successful if the fingerlings are carried through infancy to childhood. The proposition is, further to extend these nurseries in cooperation with this association and all fish clubs. The protest is, that even this is useless unless we can check pollution of our streams. The reason for all is, that fishing is good for the soul of man.

THE FACT

Man and boy, the American is a fisherman. That comprehensive list of human rights, the Declaration of Independence, is firm that all men (and boys) are endowed with certain inalienable rights, including life, liberty, and the pursuit of happiness, which obviously includes the pursuit of fish. America is a well watered country, and the inhabitants know all the fishing holes.

The Americans also produce millions of automobiles. These co-ordinate forces of inalienable right, the automobile and the call of the fishing hole, propel the man and boy to a search of all the water within a radius of 150 miles at week ends alone. He extends it to a radius of 500 miles on his summer holidays. These radii of operations of all these men and boys greatly overlap. All of which has overworked the fishing holes, and the time between bites has become longer and longer, and the fish have become wiser and wiser.

Some millions of fishermen have invented thousands of new lures of seductive order and devised many new and fearful incantations, with a host of new kinds of clothes and labor-saving devices to carry them about.

We have indeed made stupendous progress in physical equipment to overcome the mysteries of fish. We have moved upward from the rude but social conditions of the willow pole with a butcher-string line, fixed with hooks, ten for a dime, whose compelling lure is one segment of an angleworm and whose incantation is spitting on the bait. We have arrived at the high state of tackle, assembled from the steel of Damascus, the bamboos of Siam, the silk of Japan, the lacquer of China, the tin of Penang, the nickel of Canada, the feathers of Brazil, and the silver of Colorado—all compounded by mass production at Chicago, Illinois, and Akron, Ohio. And for magic and incantations we have progressed to application of cosmetics for artificial flies and to wonders in special clothing with pigeonholes for varied lures and liniments and to calling a bite a "strike." Nor do I need to repeat that fishing is not the rich man's sport, though his incantations are more expensive. I have said elsewhere that all men are equal before fishes. But I ask you if, in the

face of all this overwhelming efficiency and progress, there is less time
between bites?

However, our fishermen can put in many joyous hours at home
polishing up the rods, reels, and lures, discussing new flies when the
imponderable forces of spring begin to move their bones. They could
not get such joy out of a collection of live angleworms, and that is all a
part of what we are trying to get at anyway—recreation and soul satisfaction. But I am off the track, because the Department of Commerce
deals not in the beatitudes but in statistics. Moreover, we must also
maintain the economic rather than the biologic method in discussion or
some other department of the government will accuse Commerce of
invading their authority. Nevertheless, I may say, as an aside, that the
fishing beatitudes are much amplified since Izaak Walton, for he did
not spend his major life answering a bell. He never got the jumps from
traffic signals or the price of wheat. The blessings of fishing include not
only Edgar Guest's "wash of the soul" with pure air, but they also now
include discipline in the equality of men, meekness and inspiration
before the works of nature, charity and patience toward tackle makers
and the fish, a mockery of profits and conceits, a quieting of hate and
a hushing to ambition, a rejoicing and gladness that you do not have to
decide a blanked thing until next week.

But to return to the economics of this sport. Having done everything
to improve the tackle, lures, and incantations we must conclude that
the distance between bites has been increased because of rising ratio of
water to fish. In other words, there are less fish. And, to slip back to the
beatific side of fishing a minute, I might mention that there will be
no joy on long winter nights making reinventories of the tackle unless
there be behind it the indelible recollection of having caught a few
bigger ones last summer. But I will say more on the economic importance of the fishing beatitudes later on.

Based upon the number of fishing licenses issued in licensing states,
the Bureau of Fisheries estimates that 10,000,000 people went game
fishing in the year 1926. Any calculation of twenty years ago will show
that not 1,000,000 people went fishing during those years. But I have
no sympathy with attempts at disarmament of the gigantic army which
every year marches against the fish, nor any limitations on its equip-

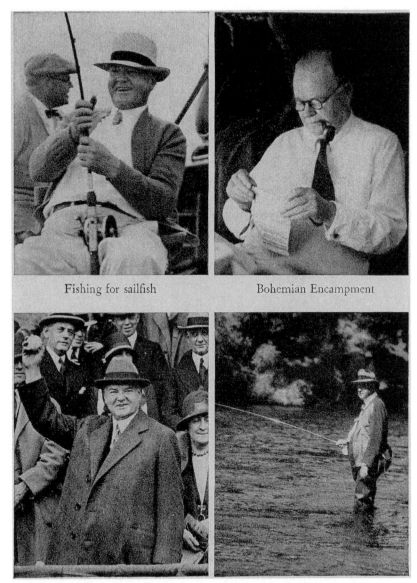

Fishing for sailfish   Bohemian Encampment

Starting the baseball season   Fishing for trout

ment of automobiles, tackle, or incantations. I am for increase in these armies, and more fish.

Despite the statistical efficiency of our department, I do not know how many each one of the army captured last year. Judging by my own experience, it was not so good. I spent several days searching fishing holes at various points between Chesapeake Bay and the Pacific; I tried to find some spot where not more than six automobiles had already camped, or where the campers did not get up before daylight and thus get the two or three fish which were off guard at that time of day. The state of New Jersey secures an accounting from its licensees of the number of game fish they catch. It works out at about 4.5 fish per fisherman per annum. Fishermen are not liars, and therefore I conclude that even in that well organized state it was heavy going.

Now I want to propose to you an idea. I submit to you that each fisherman ought to catch at least fifty during the season. I would like more than that myself, but that ought to be demanded as a minimum under the "rights" as implied in the Declaration, provided it included one big one for purpose of indelible memory, conversation, and historic record.

And at once I come to a powerful statistic—that is, 50 fish times 10,000,000 men and boys—the purpose of which I will establish presently. This minimum ideal of a national catch of 500,000,000 game fish is of the most fundamental importance if we as a nation are to approach a beatific state for even two weeks in the year.

And as we are thinking nationally, 500,000,000 fish divided amongst 120,000,000 people is not so much as you might think at first, for it is only about 4.1 fish per person, and it includes the little ones as well, and each of us eats 1,095 times a year, less whatever meals we miss while fishing.

At this point someone will deny that we have ever taken any 500,-000,000 fish in a year. I agree with him that we have not attained any such ideal per fisherman in long years. If it had been true, the moral state of the nation would have been better maintained during the last calendar year. There were lots of people who committed crimes during the year who would not have done so if they had been fishing, and I assure you that the increase in crime is due to a lack of those qualities of mind and character which impregnate the soul of every fisherman, except those who get no bites. Unless we can promise at least fifty fish per annum, including that occasional big one for recounting and memory purposes, we may despair of keeping the population from further moral turpitude.

THE CONDITION

Nearly fifty years ago the game fishermen in certain localities began to complain bitterly to their Congressmen about all this expanding distance between bites, which in economic terms is called the lag. As an equal opportunity for fishing must be properly considered by any great government as a necessity to public tranquillity, measures were at once taken. The great Government said: "We will now apply artificial means to the natural birth and distribution of fish."

Thereafter the Federal government built 40 game-fish hatcheries. The state governments built 191 hatcheries for game fish, and private enterprise has constructed 60 more. In these mass-production works the maternal carelessness of laying eggs out loose in the water to be eaten by cannibalistic relatives and friends was to be halted and they were thereafter carefully safeguarded in glass jars and troughs and temperatures. The baby fry and fingerlings thus born in security and reared in comfort to half an inch long or so were then placed in special railway cars and distributed back to the streams, being thereupon started on their happy way to be eaten by the same relatives and friends as fresh meat instead of fresh eggs.

We have steadily increased in zeal in all these endeavors to beat the lag between bites until during the last few years these 291 hatcheries working on fifteen species of game fish turn out an average of 1,100,-000,000 infant game fish to be duly launched into life amongst the cannibals.

In addition to these paternal and maternal endeavors on the part of the government, I am aware that Mother Nature has herself been busy also. Private enterprise in the shape of responsible mother fish is working upon the same problem; they are probably doing more than the paternal government, for all I know. Private enterprise usually does. One thing we do know, and that is that it takes a host of fingerlings to provide for the survival of a fish of blessed memory. At a particular control over Alaskan salmon it is estimated that 1,668,750,000 eggs and fry were launched into life and 3,740,000 adult fish came back—and it is thought all who escaped infant mortality did come back—so that the loss was 99.77 per cent. Or, in other words, it took 450 fry to make a fish. And at this rate the annual 1,100,000,000 fry and fingerlings from the whole battery of game fish hatcheries would produce one-third of a fish per fisherman per annum.

I may say parenthetically that I introduce these statistics of birth registration and infant mortality among fish because it will relieve your minds of anxiety as to accuracy. But if anyone feels these figures may be wrong, he has my permission to divide or multiply them by any factor based upon his own experience with the time element in bites, the size of fish, or the special incantations.

In any event, 1,100,000,000 bureaucratic-mothered fry from all our combined government game fish hatcheries was only 2.2 fry for each fish in the modest minimum national ideal which I have insisted upon. And if anybody thinks that it only takes 2.2 fry to make a fish he is mightily mistaken. I conclude statistically from my own experience of the time between bites that the Alaskan figure of mortality should be corrected from 99.77 to 99.99 per cent.

What I am coming to is that it is the solemn fact that only some microscopic per cent of these fry or fingerlings, whether synthetic or natural, ever live to that state of grandeur which will serve as inspiration to polish the tackle or insure the approach to the battle in renewed hope with each oncoming season. And we lose ground every year, sector by sector, as the highways include more fishing holes in the route. We must either multiply the output of our hatcheries by some fearful number or find some other way out.

THE EXPERIMENT

Some four years ago I expressed to Commissioner O'Malley, when inducting him into the headship of the Bureau of Fisheries, my complete skepticism over the effectiveness of our synthetic incubation and its statistical relations to the realistic life of a fish. My general thesis was that those infants did not have a dog's chance to gain that maturity which was required either by public policy or by the fishing beatitudes. He and his able assistant, Mr. Leach, thereupon started experiments to see if we could not apply mass production in nursing infant trout, bass, and other game fish to an age when they could survive traffic accidents or do battle with cannibals or enter the cannibal ranks themselves —and, in any event, hope to survive. It was my aspiration that, if these adolescent youths could not win in open combat, at least some of them reared to three inches long might make a full meal for a cannibal, instead of his requiring 200 fry fresh out of the eggs and then we would save 199 or so. These experiments were seriously successful. And the same authorities, Messrs. O'Malley and Leach, are convinced that by this same means we have improved the fighting chances of these children of fish up to about a 50-50 go, and thereby our 1,100,000,000 governmental fingerlings might serve as a base to produce the national ideal of 500,000,000 big ones. I again refer you to my previous statement on the safety factor in the magic of statistics.

Nor was it so expensive. One hundred bass couples in specially prepared pools produced 200,000 offspring and raised them to three inches long for a total outlay of $500, omitting rent and experts, or four fish for a cent. Likewise, trout were carried along in life under the shelter of hated bureaucracy until they could do battle.

After this preliminary experience I, two years ago, appealed to your chapters and to fish-and-game clubs throughout the country to cooperate with us in establishing more experimental nurseries—the Department of Commerce to furnish free fingerlings, free breeding stock, and free technical supervision. It was one of the conditions that all streams in each neighborhood should be stocked with the product so as to give the boy a chance also. Fifteen chapters of the league, sixteen clubs and private individuals, five states and municipalities have cooperated and established nurseries in nine states. Pennsylvania leads with fourteen stations. Minnesota is next with thirteen stations, every one of the latter being a league chapter whose officers should be taken to the heart of every man and boy who has hopes for the fishing beatitudes. The state of New Jersey, working independently from the same conclusions, has done wonders on its own.

Last year was our first year: 4,667,000 fish were raised up to battling age in these cooperative nurseries and delivered into the streams. The annual capacity of these nurseries when going full blast is probably near 20,000,000 fish. I believe those who have overcome their initial troubles are enthusiastic of success.

Now, the purpose of this speech and these statistics is to demonstrate that we need more nurseries. We ought to have several hundred. They are inexpensive compared to the annual outlay on tackle and the automobile journey to the fishing holes. When you get through at that fishing hole you would have been glad to have paid for several hundred fish at the rate of four to a cent. And by stocking all streams in the neighborhood, they offer a large opportunity for establishing fealty from the small boy to the ideals of the sportsman. He may, for sound reasons of his own, continue to use his worn fly or even a worm, but be assured, brethren, that he will grow up to refined tackle all right later on.

Our government, Federal and state, is today spending nearly $2,000,-000 a year on game-fish hatcheries. We are convinced of their futility unless we can carry their work this one stage further. That stage should be accomplished through local effort and cooperation, and the Federal government is prepared to furnish instruction, advice, breeding stock, and fingerlings free to any chapter or club which will undertake it. If every state in the Union will respond as Minnesota, Pennsylvania, and New Jersey have responded, the job is done.

The hatcheries are the necessary works for mass production of infant fish. That is a technical job requiring large expense, high skill, and training. Clubs cannot well undertake to run them, and we have long since accepted that as a proper function of the Federal and state governments.

But the nurseries require only a few thousand dollars for plant and but a few hundred dollars annually for operation. It is our view that the nurseries are the only agency that will make hatcheries worth while. If our nurseries could turn out 500,000,000 three-inch fish, we could trust the natural mothers to supply the balance.

And I appeal to the fishermen of America to take up and further

expedite this great hope of permanent game fishing in our country. It is
your problem, and the remedy for a departing sport is with you. Not
by demanding that an already maternally and paternally responsible
government do everything on earth, but in the pride of sportsmen to
do their own job. Unless something like this be done, our sons will not
be catching the limit. It is the real hope of triumph over the discourage-
ment between bites.

And there is another phase of all this. Aside from the cannibalistic
enemies of infant, adolescent, and adult fish, acting in lively alliance
with the organized army of 10,000,000 fishermen, we have still another
fish enemy to deal with. That is pollution. Herein is the poison cup
which we give to eggs, fry, fingerlings, adolescent, and adult fish alike.

Now, if we want fish we have to reserve some place for them to live.
They all occur in the water, but it happens that nature adapted them
to clean water. I suppose that was because nature foresaw no fishing
beatitudes along a sewer.

And this question of pollution has a multitude of complications
and lack of understanding.

There are as many opinions about pollution as there are minds concerning it. Those who oppose it are not under the spell of the fishing
lure. Pollution exists in different waters in different degrees—from
ships, factories, coal mines, chemical works in cities and towns—only to
mention a few of them. Many of these things damage public health,
destroy the outdoor appeal of the streams, and all of them damage the
fish.

But after all we are an industrial people. We have to work at least
eight hours a day and all but two or three weeks in the year, and we
cannot abolish our industries and still pay for fishing tackle. So I have
long since come to the conclusion that what we really need in every
state, through our state authorities, is that there should be a survey of
all the streams and a division of them into three categories.

First, to determine the streams that have not yet been polluted, then
give immediate protection to these streams, or parts of them, that they
never shall be polluted; that no industry shall be allowed to settle upon

them unless there is adequate guaranty that there will be no pollution. The second category includes the streams that are polluted to the finish. There are many of these that could never be recovered, as a matter of practical fact, without the displacement of hundreds of thousands of people from their homes through the crushing of their industries. The numbers who would benefit by clearing them would be infinitesimal compared to the suffering and loss implied in such an operation.

Then we should have a third category of streams—those that are perhaps partially polluted, where we could get correction by systematic and sound action and gradually restore them to the first category.

There are also problems of pollution of our coastal waters. I have discussed that before and will not enter upon it now.

The sane handling of our stream pollution is the first game fish conservation measure in our country. For various reasons of states' rights it is but little a Federal problem. But states' rights are state responsibility and the mental complex of some states that their rights extend to passing the buck to the Federal government needs psychopathic treatment by indignant chapters of the Izaak Walton League.

THE REASON FOR IT

Now, the reasons for all this are some of them economic in their nature, some moral, and some spiritual. Our standards of material progress include the notion and the hope that we shall lessen the daily hours of labor on the farm, at the bench, and in the office—except for public servants. We also dream of longer annual holidays and more of them, as scientific routine and mass production do our production job faster and faster. And when they do the job at all they dull the souls of men unless their leisure hours become the period of life's objective—stimulation and fishing.

We are decreasing hours. These same infallible clocks of progress, the humble statistics, tell us that the gainfully employed have steadily decreased in hours of work during the whole of thirty years. The great majority of us (except public officials) really work no more than eight hours a day except during the stress of planting or harvest or elections. Anyway, if we sleep eight hours we have eight hours in which to ruminate and make merry or stir the caldron of evil. This civilization is not going to depend upon what we do when we work so much as what we do in our time off. The moral and spiritual forces of our country do not lose ground in the hours we are busy on our jobs; their battle is the leisure time. We are organizing the production of leisure. We need better organization of its consumption. We devote vast departments of government, the great agencies of commerce and industry, science and invention, to decreasing the hours of work, but we devote comparatively little to improving the hours of recreation. We associate joy with leisure. We have great machinery of joy, some of it destructive, some of it synthetic, some of it mass production. We go to chain theaters and movies; we watch somebody else knock a ball over the fence or kick it over the goal post. I do that and I believe in it. I do, however, insist that no other organized joy has values comparable to the outdoor experience. We gain less from the other forms in moral stature, in renewed purpose in life, in kindness, and in all the fishing beatitudes. We gain none of the constructive, rejuvenating joy that comes from return to the solemnity, the calm and inspiration of primitive nature. The joyous rush of the brook, the contemplation of the eternal flow of the stream, the stretch of forest and mountain all reduce our egotism, soothe our troubles, and shame our wickedness.

And in it we make a physical effort that no sitting on cushions, benches, or side lines provides. To induce people to take its joys they need some stimulant from the hunt, the fish, or the climb. I am for fish. Fishing is not so much getting fish as it is a state of mind and a lure to the human soul into refreshment.

But it is too long between bites; we must have more fish in proportion to the water.[1]

---

[1] My more important statements upon the development of the fisheries while Secretary of Commerce are listed in the Appendix, under the heading Chapter 22.

CHAPTER 23

CURING BAD BUSINESS PRACTICES
AND THE BUSINESS CYCLE

Fixing the boundaries of governmental relations to business perplexed me daily and in innumerable ways during my twelve years as Secretary of Commerce and President. Fundamentally, this problem involved the destiny of the American scheme of life. Although business committed various abuses that were only marginal in an otherwise great productive system, the marginal wrongs had to be cured if the system was to survive—they were abuses of freedom, which grow like a cancer. Also they were the propelling texts of the Socialists, the Communists, and the exponents of the new breed—Fascists. This left-wing cure for all business evil now appeared under the lovely phrase "national planning." It was a mixture of government operation and government dictation of economic life into a free economy.

The real cure of our marginal evils lay in the application, where necessary, of government regulation, which clearly and specifically prohibited an evil practice. But beyond and better than even that was cooperation in the business community to cure its own abuses. I considered it part of the duties of the Secretary of Commerce to help bring business to a realization of its responsibilities and to suggest methods of its own cures.

New marginal abuses were bound to reappear with every step in economic progress so that their cure was a never-ending job in a free system. The American Revolution had formulated its governmental framework mainly to protect political liberty. Those men worked in the mild climate of a comparatively simple economic life. But from the free minds that liberty created sprang a great flowering of scientific discovery and invention. Then initiative, enterprise, and adventure generated by economic freedom transformed these discoveries and inventions into gigantic tools of production, transportation, and communications. With all of them came enormous accumulations of capital. These advances had created the greatest productivity and the greatest rise in standards of living and spread of comfort previously unknown to human history. But every new invention of importance, from railroads to radio, created opportunities for oppression. Moreover, labor relations, restrictions on production and competition could threaten our whole progress.

An economic revolution unique to the United States took place when the Federal government passed the Anti-Trust Act of 1890 to maintain competition in all fields except the various seminatural monopolies, which had been placed under regulation three years before as to rates, profits, and services in transportation and communication. At the time it was not recognized that this was abandonment of the system of *laissez faire*. We had, in fact, departed abruptly from the economic systems of the Old World.

With marginal lapses in individual conduct, the Anti-Trust Acts had preserved fairly well competition and thus the restless pillow of progress. The pressure of maintained competition was to improve methods, improve articles, improve tools, and reduce costs. The European countries pursued a path of governmentally approved cartels, trusts, and trade agreements. The pressures of competition were replaced by fixing prices and restricting distribution. One consequence was that the efficiency of European plant and equipment fell far behind.

The problem before the Department of Commerce could be divided into three parts: first, competition which could be abridged without violation of law; second, competition which could be destructive; and, third, recurrent abuses of the moral code by evil men.

In the first part—abridgment of competition which did not violate the laws—one effort of the Department lay in furnishing information and statistics which would put small business in as favorable a position as big business. The latter was able to provide these services for itself. Another important service in this field was the whole program of improved transportation, electric power, of standards, simplifications, specifications, arbitration of disputes, etc., which I have already described in the chapters on elimination of waste. An effect of these activities was to put all business on a more equal basis.

The second part—destructive competition—was somewhat ameliorated by the elimination-of-waste programs. We tackled some of these practices, together with the third part—violations of the moral code—by securing action through cooperation of business and professional organizations.

Early in my term as Secretary of Commerce, I concluded that there was a form of organization in American business which could be made an instrumentality for all these three categories of action against some of the marginal faults.

Practically our entire American working world was now organized into some form of economic association. We had trade associations and trade institutes embracing practically every industry and occupation. We had chambers of commerce embracing representatives of different industries and commerce. We had the labor unions representing the different crafts. We had associations embracing all the different professions—law, engineering, medicine, banking, real estate, and what not. We had farmers' associations, and we had the enormous growth of farmers' cooperatives for actual dealing in commodities. Each of these associations had officers, paid staff, and annual conventions.

The Department of Justice at this time was insistent that all trade association activities led to violation of the law. It looked with suspicion on their annual meetings and the policies of their officials. Frequent actions in the courts kept the decent business element frightened away from such cooperation where it was obviously in the public interest. In 1922 there were pending in the Supreme Court certain cases by which the Department of Justice sought to stretch the Anti-Trust laws to prohibit what I considered should be constructive cooperation in such associations. That Department had won its cases in the lower courts, and it looked as though this perversion of justice would become the law of the land.

I had the economists of the Department under Dr. Klein make an exhaustive study of the activities of a host of these business associations. The report was published in 1923. It showed that many of their activities were legitimate, and very constructive. But some were cloaks for organized abuses, evasion of the spirit of the law, and violation of primary morals.

We concluded that they could be made instrumental wholly for national benefit if they were given constructive things to do, and in doing it to be free from attack. It seemed to us that instead of keeping them under assault we should define their useful tasks and develop within them definite ethical standards. Therefore, I submitted an informal memorandum on the question to the Department of Justice and the Federal Trade Commission. In this memorandum, I laid out the areas in which trade associations could take constructive action which not only would be of economic benefit, but also would lessen violations of the Anti-Trust laws. The full text will be found in the report of the Secretary of Commerce for 1924. This document was written before the Supreme Court decision upon the cases I have referred to; but it had important consequences and caused much discussion.

Soon after this memorandum was submitted, the Supreme Court overruled the contentions of the Department of Justice and opened the door to reasonable cooperation in matters of public interest.

We had brought the trade groups effectively into our programs for elimination of waste, development of natural resources, and expansion of scientific research for the perfection of their manufacturing methods and products. We defended their right to representation before public bodies.

I made many public addresses and statements upon these subjects in their relation to government and discussed their abuses and moral failures. A typical address was that of May 7, 1924, in which I said:

> The advancement of science and our increasing population require constantly new standards of conduct and breed an increasing multitude of new rules and regulations. The basic principles laid down in the Ten Commandments and the Sermon on the Mount are as applicable today as when they were declared, but they require a host of subsidiary clauses. The ten ways to evil in the time of Moses have increased to ten thousand now.
>
> A whole host of rules and regulations are necessary to maintain human rights with this amazing transformation into an industrial era. Ten people in a whole county, with a plow apiece, did not elbow each other very much.

But when we put 7,000,000 people in a county with the tools of electricity, steam, thirty-floor buildings, telephones, miscellaneous noises, streetcars, railways, motors, stock exchanges, and what not, then we do jostle each other in a multitude of directions. Thereupon our lawmakers supply the demand by the ceaseless piling up of statutes. . . .

The question we need to consider is whether these rules and regulations are to be developed solely by government or whether they cannot be in some large part developed out of voluntary forces in the nation. . . .

National character cannot be built by law. It is the sum of the moral fiber of its individuals. When abuses which rise from our growing system are cured by live individual conscience, by initiative in the creation of voluntary standards, then is the growth of moral perception fertilized in every individual character. . . .

When legislation penetrates the business world it is because there is abuse somewhere. A great deal of this legislation is due rather to the inability of business hitherto to so organize as to correct abuses . . . Sometimes the abuses are more apparent than real, but anything is a handle for demagoguery. In the main, however, the public acts only when it has lost confidence in the ability or willingness of business to correct its own abuses.

Legislative action is always clumsy—it is incapable of adjustment to shifting needs. It often enough produces new economic currents more abusive than those intended to be cured. Government too often becomes the persecutor instead of the regulator. . . .

The problem of business ethics as a prevention of abuse is of two categories: those where the standard must be one of individual moral perceptions, and those where we must have a determination of standards of conduct for a whole group in order that there may be a basis for ethics.

The standards of honesty, of a sense of mutual obligation, and of service, were determined two thousand years ago. . . . Their failure is a blow at the repute of business and at confidence in government itself.

The second field, and the one which I am primarily discussing, is the great area of indirect economic wrong and unethical practices that spring up under the pressures of competition and habit. There is also the great field of economic waste through destructive competition, through strikes, booms and slumps, unemployment, through failure of our different industries to synchronize, and a hundred other causes which directly lower our productivity and employment. Waste may be abstractly unethical, but in any event it can only be remedied by economic action.

If we are to find solution to these collective issues outside of government regulation we must meet two practical problems:

First, there must be organization in such form as can establish the standards of conduct in this vast complex of shifting invention, production, and use. . . . Someone must determine such standards. They must be determined and held flexibly in tune with the intense technology of trade.

Second, there must be some sort of enforcement. There is the perpetual difficulty of a small minority who will not play the game. They too often bring disrepute upon the vast majority; they drive many others to adopt unfair competitive methods which all deplore; their abuses give rise to public indignation and clamor which breed legislative action.

I believe we now for the first time have the method at hand for voluntarily organized determination of standards and their adoption.

I then described the possibilities of using the multitude of associational activities, and their possibilities if directed to public interest, and continued:

Three years of study and intimate contact with associations of economic groups . . . convince me that there lies within them a great moving impulse toward betterment.

If these organizations accept as their primary purpose the lifting of standards, if they will cooperate together for voluntary enforcement of high standards, we shall have proceeded far along the road of the elimination of government from business. . . .

American business needs a lifting purpose greater than the struggle of materialism. Nor can it lie in some evanescent, emotional, dramatic crusade. It lies in the higher pitch of economic life, in a finer regard for the rights of others, a stronger devotion to obligations of citizenship that will assure an improved leadership in every community and the nation; it lies in the organization of the forces of our economic life so that they may produce happier individual lives, more secure in employment and comfort, wider in the possibilities of enjoyment of nature, larger in its opportunities of intellectual life. . . .

In order to bring these ideas to reality we enlisted the different trade associations in creation of codes of business practice and ethics that would eliminate abuses and make for higher standards. I set up a staff in the Department to work them out. After agreement with each association on a "code" we submitted it to the Department of Justice and the Federal Trade Commission; and, to establish confidence in the "code," the Trade Commission promulgated it as a standard of fair practice. No force was attempted or implied. They were solely voluntary. By degrees many standards contained in these codes became embodied in the business custom of the country.

Speaking on the subject November 7, 1924, I said:

The very publication of codes of ethics by many associations . . . the condemnation of specific unfair practices, the insistence upon a higher plane of relationships between employer and employee—all of them are at least indications of improving thought and growing moral perceptions.

All of this is the strong beginning of a new force in the business world.

All this guidance required an enormous number of tiresome conferences with the officers of hundreds of business associations and groups. It was not a universal panacea. It did not squelch the crooks, but it did make life less agreeable for them. It helped to instill in American business a purpose of finding the fields of constructive action and of eliminating abuses. And it contributed to that essential in the development of democracy, cooperative action outside government to eliminate abuses.

These codes should not be confused with the price-fixing device called "Open Price Associations," which we condemned, and which the Department of Justice undertook to suppress after I came to the White House.[1]

GOVERNMENT OPERATION OF BUSINESS

The government of necessity had to engage in some business. My difficulty in practical administration of such enterprises was not the theories of the left wing, but to find the line between proper govern-

[1] The New Deal subsequently declared that the NRA was merely an expansion of my ideas. That is, they made this assertion after the NRA went sour. The fact of the matter is that they were the exact contrary. We were seeking to eliminate combinations in restraint of trade. There was no relation between these ideas except a common use of the word "code." The New Deal set up committees of trade associations to fix prices and limit production in each trade. It gave sanction to wholesale violations of the Anti-Trust laws. This was a long step away from free competition and into sheer economic fascism with all its implications.

mental action and that destructive of individual initiative. For instance, the government alone could build many of the great dams required to conserve water for irrigation, flood control, and navigation. All these dams produce electrical power. The public interest in this power had to be protected. But the distribution of the power by the government was pure Socialism. The practical dividing line, as I have stated in the Colorado River case, was for the government to sell the power at the source to distributing companies or municipalities at prices which would contribute to the cost of the dams and under regulation as to resale prices which would protect the consumers. The "liberals" attacked this by way of demonstrating their liberalism. They wanted the government to operate and distribute the power.

Most of these pseudo liberals also advocated government operation of the railways and no doubt hoped for the growth of Socialism inch by inch. In all this we faced a collectivism which sought to limit and not to expand the freedom of men. Such exponents of these doctrines as Senators Norris, La Follette, and Borah, together with Gifford Pinchot and John Dewey, raised the issue of government operation of utilities in the Presidential campaign of 1924. I, therefore, took a crack at the whole theory in a public address at that time.

Fascism had blossomed in Italy. Its buds were swelling in the United States, with demands from our left wing that government should fix prices, wages, production, and distribution. This was no less an invasion of liberty than Socialism. We had to meet it constantly in direct or indirect attempts at legislation. My colleague, the Secretary of Agriculture, was in truth a fascist, but did not know it, when he proposed his price- and distribution-fixing legislation in the McNary-Haugen bill.

THE STUDY OF THE BUSINESS CYCLE

At the first meeting of the Committee on Business Cycles and Unemployment (appointed by the Business Conference of September 12, 1921), I said:

Booms are times of speculation, overexpansion, wasteful expenditures in industry and commerce, with ·consequent destruction of capital. . . . It is the wastes, the miscalculations and maladjustments, grown rampant during the booms, that make unavoidable the painful processes of liquidation. The obvious way to lessen the losses and miseries of depression is first to check the destructive extremes of booms. Mitigation of depressions is a further task of relief and reconstruction.

In a Report to the Congress I reviewed the investigation we had under way, a summary of which was:

The "business cycle" of course is not based alone upon purely economic forces. It is to some considerable degree the product of waves of confidence or caution—optimism or pessimism. Movements gain much of their acceleration from these causes, and they in turn are often the product of political or other events, both domestic and foreign, and even climatic conditions may play an important part. . . .

We suggested that the first strategic point of attack was that Government construction should be so regulated that it may be deferred in times of intense private construction and expedited in times of unemployment. The effect would be not only to secure more economical construction for the Government but also to stabilize the construction industries and to considerably mitigate unemployment in periods of depression.

The second recommendation is that the Government's statistical services on production, stocks, and consumption of commodities should be vigorously expanded so as to furnish the basic material from which the commercial public may judge the ebb and flow of economic currents.

The Committee also made a report on the use of Federal Reserve credit to stimulate and retard business movements. Both Adolph Miller of the Federal Reserve Board, who was a member of the Committee, and I expressed some doubts as to credit devices being the final answer to the problem; but we thought they could also help.

Our general view was that the irregular tempo of economic movement could never be wholly smoothed out in a free system. It generated its own rhythm which in turn was influenced to some extent by the ebb and flow of optimism and pessimism.

The Committee report created a very large amount of interest and discussion throughout the country. There was favorable editorial comment in more than eight hundred journals, and favorable discussion amongst economic and commercial bodies.

There was one field in which the Department could act positively. That was statistics.

The statistical services had been fragmentary and poorly formulated. Under Director William Steuart of the Census, we immediately made reforms from which we hoped that warnings of economic movements, such as production, inventories, and consumption, would help to make business more certain. We hoped the business world might better detect the approach of booms and slumps. In any event, we believed that business judgment as to supply and demand could be strengthened. We had in mind that small business especially needed such information. Big units provided their own statistics.

We inaugurated a monthly publication entitled *The Survey of Current Business*. Therein, we compiled the statistics of business movement, from old and new governmental services and private sources. We produced figures in the form of index numbers to show the trends in production, stocks of goods, and services, prices, transportation, consumption and employment, together with monetary and credit information of every variety. We did not claim that statistics were the final remedy for booms and slumps.

As I felt the whole subject required more study than this Committee had been able to give it, in 1927, I organized the Committee on Recent Economic Changes with my friend Arch Shaw of Chicago as chairman. The Committee included Adolph Miller; Dr. Julius Klein of the Department of Commerce; William Green of the American Federation of Labor; Professor Max Mason; Daniel Willard, Owen D. Young, and Lewis E. Pierson, businessmen; and Louis J. Taber, Master of the National Grange. They established a strong economic research staff under Frederick C. Mills of the National Bureau of Economic Research, and endeavored to delve much more deeply into the economic problems of the times. I shall have more to say as to the Committee's conclusions in a later volume relating to the Great Depression.[2]

[2] My more important statements upon the study of the business cycle are listed in the Appendix, under the heading Chapter 23.

CHAPTER 24

SOME PART IN FOREIGN AFFAIRS

The Department had of course a considerable contact with foreign affairs in its trade relations. We had a large and able staff in countries abroad from whom we received extensive economic and political information which was placed at the disposal of the Administration and was the subject of constant discussion between myself and Secretaries Hughes and Kellogg. Some special participations in the foreign field outside the normal work of the Department embraced the settlement of World War debts, the Washington Conference for the Limitation of Armaments of 1921–1922, the appointment of the Dawes Commission on German Reparations, and the nonrecognition of Communist Russia.

WORLD WAR DEBT COMMISSION

President Harding in 1922 appointed me to the World War Foreign Debt Commission—a body authorized by the Congress to settle the war debts of our Allies "within their capacity to pay," subject to final Congressional approval. The Commission jointly represented the Senate, the House, and the administration. Its other members were A. W. Mellon, Charles E. Hughes, Reed Smoot, and Theodore E. Burton. The principal and accrued interest on these debts was about $11,000,-000,000, about 40 per cent of which had been loaned after the Armistice for relief and reconstruction.

At one stage in the Commission's work, I proposed that we cancel all the debts incurred before the Armistice and require the payment in full of loans made after the Armistice, with a rate of interest equal to that which we paid on our own bonds. This would have strengthened our moral position, as we should have been asking repayment of advances only for reconstruction and not for war. If the Allies had paid, it would have been as good for the American taxpayer as the method finally adopted; and the probabilities of payment were greater. The British followed this plan and collected more in proportion from their debtors than we did—plus German reparations.

I further proposed that for the small nations, the "liberated countries," whose debts consisted mostly of relief loans, we set up each of these amounts as an educational foundation for the exchange of students and professors, as I had done in the Belgian Relief. It would have resulted in far greater benefits to the United States than even the repayment of the money.

As my colleagues insisted we never could get Congress to approve such settlements, I then proposed that we abandon all claims to interest and spread the principal repayment over reasonable terms of years, adjusted to the debtors' capacity to pay. This would have had sounder moral background and brought just as much to our taxpayers as the ultimate plan. Again my colleagues insisted that we must preserve the appearance of repayment of both principal and interest if we were to get it through the Congress.

The device adopted was payment of principal in installments over sixty years, with interest in some cases as low as $\frac{1}{2}$ per cent for early years.

It looked like the original $11,000,000,000. The concessions by this indirection, however, were very great. For a number of years, the total payments, principal and interest, from all countries did not exceed $250,000,000, whereas the interest alone we were paying on our bonds issued to provide these advances amounted to over $450,000,000 annually.

In the light of the original obligations the settlements actually made, if tested by a compound discount table, showed great reductions. The concession to the British was about 30 per cent, to the Italians about 70 per cent, to the Belgians about 60 per cent, and to the French about 40 per cent. The British and Belgian debts should have been reduced still further. All of us recognized that any settlement would no doubt be revised during a period of sixty years. We, however, did not recog-

.nize with what confidence in further revision the debtors had signed these funding agreements.

The British and French officials, especially, inaugurated at once a propaganda for cancellation. We were Uncle Shylock. Many Americans who loved Europe more and America less took up this cry. Our international bankers agitated for cancellation night and day. They employed economists to prove that the debts never could be paid, that the debtors could not find international exchange to do it, and that anyway payment would hurt us worse than cancellation.

These arguments, false in every particular, got under my economic skin, and repeatedly I delivered myself on all phases of this question.

The fallacy of all the propaganda that these reduced sums could not be remitted was amply proved by experience. Prior to the depression, the total annual payments did not amount to 7 per cent of our imports or exports. They did not amount to 20 per cent of the debtors' expenditures on arms alone. In 1933 the French government repudiated on the ground that it could not find the international exchange to pay their $60,000,000 per annum. At that very moment it had on deposit in New York $500,000,000 which it had accumulated in surplus exchange over a period of four years.

THE WASHINGTON CONFERENCE OF 1921–1922

President Harding appointed me a member of the Advisory Committee of the Naval Arms Conference in 1921. Mr. Hughes urged me to accept in order to keep peace within that Committee. This subsidiary committee was a political repository for some twenty persons who thought they ought to be on the main delegation. They all received seats at public sessions of the Conference. However, some of them were of sufficient importance to rebel when it became obvious to the world that they were only a window dressing. It was difficult to get them back home without their exploding in public.

At various times before and during the Conference Mr. Hughes asked my views on matters connected with it. On one occasion, in October, 1921, he raised the subject of the whole Far Eastern situation, as he had in mind trying at the forthcoming conference to work out by treaty some support to China. He felt it was not enough simply to reaffirm the John Hay Open Door policy. He wished to secure a new and more effective relief to China from threatening foreign encroachments. I told him that our Commerce Department reports indicated that something needed to be done to strengthen the Kuomintang government of Sun Yat-sen against internal as well as foreign pressures. The difficulty was that this government, after overthrowing the Manchu despotism in 1910–1911, had not been strong enough to restore internal order. The external pressures were by no means only Japan, which at that time was in occupation of Shantung. The Russian Communists had penetrated the dreamy government of Sun Yat-sen and even had two Communist officials—Borodin and Blücher—sitting in the government. Combined with these in keeping the country too weak to repel foreign encroachment was the chaos from bandits and war lords.

I stated that Japan certainly had legitimate reasons for complaint because she was seriously dependent for her livelihood upon Chinese raw materials and the Chinese market for her manufactured goods, and that it seemed to me some definitely organized international action was needed to strengthen the rather hazy regime of Sun Yat-sen. I stated that the first necessity of China was a bankers' loan of $250,000,000 to enable her to get on her feet but that, while protecting the Chinese face, it must be conditional upon the elimination of the Communists and the creation of a much stiffer internal administration.

Mr. Hughes asked if I thought there was validity to the Japanese claim that they must have more continental area in Asia. I said that there was no validity to the claim that Japan must have territory. Order and economic stability in China would give her export markets for manufactures and thus imports of food and other supplies in exchange. But that unless order was restored by the Chinese themselves or by united action of all the other nations or both, then Japan was likely to act. He, however, believed the Chinese delegation that if they were given a chance, through agreement to keep hands off, they would restore order. I opined that was fine; but I doubted the capacity of any of the then Chinese leaders to reestablish central power and order without foreign help and suggested that this conference should face the question positively instead of with just a negative hands-off policy.

Two days later Mr. Hughes consulted me on what sort of organization ought to be set up for the Conference. I said Versailles had taught just one thing; simple, broad, direct principles of ultimate action should be agreed upon before the first meeting and announced at the first meeting; that committees of the Conference should be set up to work out details. He laughed and said I would have the Conference before the Conference. I replied, exactly that.

And that was what Mr. Hughes did. Under his leadership the Conference made a great advance in disarmament by limiting battleships and some other major ships. The treaty, however, applied to only 30 per cent of the naval tonnage. The question of the other 70 per cent had to be settled in after years.

Mr. Hughes added to these accomplishments the Nine Power Treaty, which did give China a chance of freedom from external pressures. By the Four Power Treaty Shantung was restored to China. All these accomplishments were made possible by the liberal ministry then dominant in Japan.

After the Conference some negotiations toward internal aid were undertaken along the lines I had suggested. Nothing came of them, largely because the Russian Communists were potent in Sun Yat-sen's government. It was not until five years after these treaties that Chiang Kai-shek put them out of the Kuomintang and forced the Communist leader Mao Tse-tung and his army to retreat to the north.

THE DAWES COMMISSION

I find the following memorandum dated November 5, 1923:

This morning Secretary Hughes asked for a conference of Secretary Mellon and myself over a proposal that an American should sit upon a Commission appointed to advise upon revision of German Reparations. We agreed that as we received no part of the reparations there should be no official participation, but it was desirable, in order to assist in solution, that Americans should sit on the Commission. We canvassed possible membership and agreed upon suggesting General Charles G. Dawes as the head of the Americans, with Henry Robinson and Owen D. Young. Mr. Hughes mentioned that the French demanded that the Commission should not reduce the $33,000,000,000 total of German reparations. He was doubtful whether with this limitation the Commission could be of any service whatever. I suggested that the Commission had better go as they would probably ignore the French demand as preposterous; that the situation in Germany was near breakdown and starvation again imminent; that persistence in these policies would some day bring destruction to France. The French had only one of two courses, to support democratic government in Germany or to face implacable hate and constant danger. In any event the Commission could do something in a desperate situation which was affecting the economic life of the whole world. Hughes said properly that the French policies were totally dominated by fear—and from their experience no wonder—but they had lost all sense of reality.

The Dawes Commission succeeded beyond our hopes. It seemed as though Europe might be on the way to peace and progress.

RECOGNITION OF THE SOVIET GOVERNMENT

The question of recognizing the Soviet government arose periodically during these eight years. It was pressed by pseudo "liberals" and at times by business organizations that believed a lucrative trade could be established with the Communists. Secretaries Hughes and Kellogg and I were in complete agreement that we should have none of it. So were Presidents Harding and Coolidge. I often likened the problem to having a wicked and disgraceful neighbor. We did not attack him, but we did not give him a certificate of character by inviting him into our homes.

We were well aware that the Communists were carrying on underground organization and propaganda for the overthrow of our government by violence. But denial of recognition kept their potency from being serious.

CHAPTER 25

EIGHT YEARS OF ECONOMIC PROGRESS

On August 11, 1928, speaking in the Presidential campaign of that year, I summed up the economic progress of the previous eight years. While I felt that the Department had contributed something, I made no mention of it. The progress was due to the power of a free people. I said in part as to our increase in the standards of living:

. . . To me the test is the security, comfort, and opportunity that have been brought to the average American family. During this less than eight years our population has increased by 8 per cent. Yet our national income has increased by . . . 45 per cent. Our production and . . . consumption of goods . . . increased by over 25 per cent. . . . These increases have been widely spread among our whole people. . . .

While during this period the number of families has increased by about 2,300,000 we have built more than 3,500,000 new and better homes . . . we have equipped nearly 9,000,000 more homes with electricity, and through it drudgery has been lifted from the lives of women.

Many barriers of time and distance have been swept away and life made freer and larger by the installation of 6,000,000 more telephones, 7,000,000 radio sets, and the service of an additional 14,000,000 automobiles. Our cities are growing magnificent with beautiful buildings, parks, and playgrounds. Our countryside has been knit together with splendid roads.

We have doubled the use of electrical power, and with it we have taken sweat from the backs of men.

The purchasing power of wages has steadily increased. The hours of labor have decreased. The twelve-hour day has been abolished. . . .

Most of all, I like to remember what this progress has meant to America's children. The portal of their opportunity has been ever widening. While our population has grown but 8 per cent, we have increased by 11 per cent the number of children in our grade schools, by 66 per cent the number in our high schools, and by 75 per cent the number in our institutions of higher learning.

With all our spending we have doubled savings deposits in our banks and building and loan associations. We have nearly doubled our life insurance. Nor have our people been selfish. . . . The gifts of America to churches, to hospitals and institutions for the care of the afflicted, and to relief from great disasters have surpassed by hundreds of millions any totals for any similar period in all human record.

One of the oldest and perhaps the noblest of human aspirations has been the abolition of poverty. By poverty I mean the grinding by undernourishment, cold, ignorance, and fear of old age by those who have the will to work. We in America today are nearer to the final triumph over poverty than ever before in the history of any land. The poorhouse is vanishing from among us. We have not yet reached the goal, but, given a chance to go forward with the policies of the last eight years, we shall soon with the help of God be in sight of the day when poverty will be banished from this nation. . . .

Economic advancement is not an end in itself. Successful democracy rests upon the moral and spiritual quality of its people. Our growth in spiritual achievements must keep pace with our growth in physical accomplishments. . . . Our government, to match the expectations of our people, must have constant regard for those human values that give dignity and nobility to life. Integrity, generosity of impulse, cultivation of mind, willingness to sacrifice, spaciousness of spirit—those are the qualities whereby we, growing bigger and richer and more powerful, may . . . fulfill the promise of America.

When the European economic hurricane swept over us two years later, we temporarily lost ground. I had this speech often thrown back at me. Nevertheless in time, if free men are again unrestrained, all these advances will be renewed and greatly exceeded.

TO MY ASSOCIATES IN COMMERCE

I should like in this account to pay tribute in detail to my colleagues in the Department but space prevents it. Those were happy years of constructive work. And they were years of cementing and lasting friendships. Seldom has so able and enthusiastic a team worked in government. It would take a directory to name them all. But especially do I owe gratitude to Walter F. Brown, Claudius Huston, Scott Turner, Walter Drake, Stephen Davis, William Lamb, William MacCracken, Henry O'Malley, Ephraim Morgan, Julius Klein, William Mullendore, Christian Herter, Harold Stokes, Lawrence Richey, Paul Clapp, Clarence Young, Thomas Robinson, George Putnam, William Terrell, William Steuart, George Burgess, Arthur Tyrer, Thomas Carson, Frederick Feiker, Edward Libbey, Dickerson Hoover, Lester Jones, and many who occupied less prominent positions. If all men in public service were of their caliber and character, representative government would be perfect.

CHAPTER 26

LIVING IN WASHINGTON AS A
CABINET OFFICER

Prior to joining the Cabinet came an episode which marked for me the final parting of the ways from a further engineering career. In January, 1921, Mr. Daniel Guggenheim had come to see me in New York. He and his brothers had the largest mining and metallurgical firm in the world. He told me that the brothers were getting old; that they wanted a new partner of wide experience; that they had picked me as the man. He made one of the largest offers of remuneration ever paid an engineer. Such a generous offer, so finely made, deserved consideration. Mrs. Hoover and I gave it a week's thought. It meant much more freedom than public service. It meant great wealth. But we decided against it and in favor of the Cabinet appointment, undoubtedly wrongly, from the viewpoint of a comfortable and untroubled life.

Before arriving in Washington, Mrs. Hoover bought a comfortable colonial house with an acre of garden overlooking a large part of the city, at 2300 S Street, which was to be our home for eight years. And again, for the fifth time in our twenty-two years of married life, she was to run a different house with her usual good taste and economy. She soon transformed the garden into charming order. For two-thirds of the year, it was bright with flowers. It contained several great oaks, survivors of the primeval forest which had covered the site of Washington. She built a large porch at the rear of the house where we had meals out-of-doors during the warmer months. The boys attended the Friends' School, the Western High School, and the Palo Alto High School before entering Stanford. Both Mrs. Hoover and I believed that these public schools were a better prelude to American life than many private schools.

Herbert was now eighteen and ready to enter Stanford. During his vacations, he secured jobs at manual labor—an invaluable part of education. Allan was still in the stage of adventure where all sorts of animals must be accumulated. By providing food and water for the birds, he induced scores of them daily to visit us. He also provided them quarters by hanging gourds in the trees. Two dogs and two cats were necessary, and among the transitory possessions were two ducks which he trained to sit on the front porch to the infinite entertainment of passers-by. A selection of land turtles gathered from the woods was all right; but two small alligators, presented to him by Clarence Woolley, were somewhat of a trial, for Allan believed they must be bedded at night in the bathtubs.

During the eight years we lived at 2300 S Street, Mrs. Hoover kept open house. Scarcely a meal, breakfast included, went by without guests. Friends from all parts of the United States, Europe, and Asia were constantly coming to Washington, and to these were added the officialdom of Washington itself. For many years Justice and Mrs. Stone, Mr. and Mrs. Mark Sullivan, and Mr. and Mrs. Ernest I. Lewis were the nucleus of a Sunday evening supper. Every summer we tried to spend a week or ten days at Palo Alto, and every winter I tried to get in a week of deep-sea fishing in Florida. Otherwise there was no idle time from official duties. Two or three times a week I worked at the house evenings with a secretarial staff.

There were contretemps, which gave lasting legends to the family. There was Senator Norbeck, who, in the midst of a powerful political delivery, overlooked the prized small Belgian lace napkin on the dessert plate, placed his ice cream on it, and ate the ice cream and the doily—to Mrs. Hoover's horror. No evil was reported, so that we were assured that the Senator had a good digestion. Then one night the family and a few intimate friends were in the midst of dinner when two Senators and their wives were announced for dinner. I had invited them during the day and had forgotten to notify the house. Mrs. Hoover, with her usual urbanity and humor, was equal to the test. Under her swift orders I steered the new visitors into the library, and she disclosed the situation to our dinner guests, who were temporarily stowed away in another room. In minutes the dining-room table was cleared and the reserve Virginia ham and surplus soup and vegetables were produced by the cook; and we all sat down to another dinner which went around, thanks to the abstemiousness of the prior guests.

Washington up to this time had been rigid in its tiresome social customs and protocol. There was a belief that ladies must call in person on scores of other ladies, or leave their cards. Mrs. Hoover rebelled at spending four or five afternoons a week at this fruitless job and secured an agreement among the Cabinet ladies to an announcement that it would not be done any more. And it ended.

Soon after going to Washington, Mrs. Hoover was elected President of the Girl Scouts, then a feeble organization of fewer than 100,000 girls. She gave a large part of her spare energies to the association during the twelve years we were in Washington and long afterwards. She raised over $2,000,000 of funds and built it up ultimately to nearly a million girls and made it into a potent agency for good.

We never failed to have the boys for the Christmas holidays. But by degrees we lost them, for Herbert insisted he must get married, and Allan grew up and entered Stanford in 1925.

Nomination, Election, and President-Elect

1928–1929

CHAPTER 27

THE REPUBLICAN NOMINATION

On August 2, 1927, Mr. Coolidge issued his cryptic statement, "I do not choose to run for President in nineteen-twenty-eight." At the time, I was attending the annual Bohemian Club encampment in the California redwoods, recuperating from the months of relief work in the Mississippi flood. Within an hour a hundred men—publishers, editors, public officials, and others from all over the country who were at the Grove—came to my camp demanding that I announce my candidacy. Telegrams poured in from all parts of the country in such numbers that the Grove operator had to send for more assistance. Like most other people, I was puzzled by Mr. Coolidge's statement. The word "choose" has various connotations in its New England usage. I determined at once to say nothing until I could have a talk with the President.

We were both back in Washington by September, and at once I called upon him saying that I had received a deluge of urgings from friends to give some indication of my attitude. I said that I felt the country had great confidence in him; I would prefer to continue as a Cabinet officer under him; and that I would appreciate it if he could tell me whether his statement was absolutely conclusive. He made no direct reply. I stated to the press that Mr. Coolidge should be renominated. The President certainly enjoyed the amazing volume of curiosity and the discussion that his statement had evoked and apparently did not want to end it. Nor did he ever do so.

On two occasions I tried again to renew the discussion with him. In February the question was forced by a publicized inquiry by leading citizens of Ohio as to whether I would allow my name to be placed on the Ohio primary ballot. Senator Willis of that state had filed as a "favorite son" candidate, and the predominant groups in Ohio who were opposed to him wished to support me. I informed the President that I was being urged to enter the Ohio primaries by twelve Ohio Congressmen, including former Senator Burton, two former Governors, the Republican State Chairman, and the leading Ohio newspapers, plus a deluge of individuals. The President had often remarked upon Willis's lack of qualifications for the Presidency and knew well that the Senator was no friend of his. I asked if he intended to allow his name to be filed in the Ohio primary. He simply said, "No." As to myself, he said, "Why not?"

Therefore, I accepted the invitation of my Ohio friends on February 12, 1928.

Aside from a short acceptance letter to the Ohio leaders I did not deliver, prior to the convention, a single speech or issue a single press statement having any political connotation. So far as I was concerned, the party should make its decision on the basis of my public record.

I never appointed a "manager," but a group gradually came together and informally took over the pre-convention campaign. The most active were James Good, a former leading Congressman from Iowa, Congressman Burton of Ohio, Senators Sackett and Lenroot, Secretary of the Interior Hubert Work, Odgen Mills, William H. Hill, Ruth Pratt, Edward Anthony, Edgar Rickard, and Alan Fox of New York, Claudius Huston of Tennessee, former Governor Goodrich of Indiana, Walter F. Brown of Ohio, Ferry Heath of Michigan, Mark Requa and Milton Esberg of California. They worked well together. A host of groups sprang up in the various state organizing clubs, fighting in the primaries, and generally advancing their cause. These were led largely by the men and women who had been associated with me over the previous years. The Old Guard dubbed them "Boy and Girl Scouts."

The other leading candidate was Governor Lowden of Illinois. But the active candidate was most of the United States Senate. They wanted neither Lowden nor me. For the first time in many years they had elected one of their members directly from the Senate to the Presidency in the person of Mr. Harding, and they liked the idea. The Senatorial group could not agree upon any one of its members but was resolved to keep control by setting up "favorite sons" in the primaries of various states with the hope of another'stalled convention and a "smoke-filled room." Some pretended that they favored renominating Coolidge. The great majority of the House of Representatives, under the leadership of Congressman Burton, supported me.

Burton had served twelve years in the Senate, was defeated, then elected to the House, and subsequently was reelected to the Senate. A devoted friend, a most able public servant, his death early in my administration was a most serious loss both personally and politically, for he was one of my few bulwarks against the Republican Old Guard.

There were over half a dozen candidates from the Senate. Vice President Dawes, Senators Watson, Curtis, Goff, Steiwer, and Willis were the most active. The favorite among them, if there was one, was Senator Curtis, the Senate Republican leader. Their supporters were united on a deluge of attacks upon me. Their favorite name for me was "Sir Herbert," a reference to my periodic residence in England. They also "found" I had robbed a Chinaman some twenty-six years before and had been convicted in a British court. This latter became so annoying to my friends that they sent Lawrence Richey to England to dig up the record of this ancient litigation in which I had been a witness. Mr. Richey secured a written statement from almost every party to this old lawsuit, and every living lawyer on both sides connected with it. All these statements indignantly denied that there was the remotest truth in the libels and spoke most handsomely of me. Congressman Free and Senator Lenroot took this material, made a digest of it, and introduced it into the *Congressional Record*—and I thought the matter was ended. But I was to hear more of it when we came into the Presidential campaign. Also, a refutation was to come from a surprising quarter.

The Senate created a committee to investigate the pre-convention expenditures of candidates. The committee devoted most of the investigation to my friends. Senator Steiwer of Oregon, himself a "favorite son" candidate, was chairman and sent me a peremptory demand for accounting. I replied that I had no manager, no treasurer, but that I had asked former Congressman James Good of the Washington committee to compile the material and present it to him. Mr. Good appeared and told everything he knew, and the investigation faded out.

One amusing incident of the campaign of the Senators was a speech which they carefully prepared for an Ohio Congressman to deliver in the House. It was a violent attack upon my record of fixing farm prices when I was Food Administrator. They made the mistake of sending advance copies to the press, and thus gave time for Congressman Burton to prepare a reply.

At one time there had been a movement to change me from Secretary of Commerce to Secretary of Agriculture, and President Coolidge had urged me to accept. Among the enthusiasts for this change was this same Congressman. He had sent me copies of his letters to Mr. Coolidge and to farm leaders urging my appointment. They were full of adulatory phrases on my Food Administration record in relation to the farmers. When the Congressman had finished his bombshell speech, Mr. Burton quietly arose and read this correspondence to the House. The Congressman was so discredited that he eventually lost his seat in the House.

By the middle of May, our friends had some 400 sure delegates out of the possible 1,000. I then went to Mr. Coolidge again. I stated this fact, and that I was in a position to influence most of them to vote for him. While some were required by the primary laws to vote for me on the first ballot, I still thought he would be nominated upon the first ballot, and that I should be entirely content to serve under him. He was skeptical as to the 400, saying, "If you have 400 delegates, you better keep them." I could get no more out of him.

The Pennsylvania delegation with a group from New York and Connecticut for some time appeared to be the balance of power. Their action was in doubt almost to the end although there was a minority of delegates for me in each of these states. The Pennsylvania delegation had a meeting late in May and decided to vote as a unit and not to come to any conclusions until they reached the convention. Secretary Mellon dominated the delegation, and I was of course sitting with him in the Cabinet twice a week. I was aware that he was constantly pressing the President to run again and assuring his friends that the Coolidge acceptance was a certainty. Also, Mr. Mellon participated in constant meetings with Charles D. Hilles of New York, who controlled a large part of the New York delegation, and with Henry Roraback, the Connecticut boss, and with others of the opposing groups. These men formed a circle of opposition which collaborated with the Senate in opposing me. But Mellon did not approve of Lowden.

Governor Frank Lowden was a man eminently fitted for the Presidency. He should have been nominated in 1920 instead of Harding. He was unable to secure the support of the Senate group, or he could have been nominated at this time. Although I was not then acquainted with him, he later became one of my most devoted friends.

When the convention began to gather in Kansas City, our supporters found they had 450 sure delegates on the first ballot and enough "second choice" votes to win on the second ballot. There was much conniving of the opposition, much telephoning to the White House, and there was much clatter about "Stop Hoover." But the evening before the convention opened Mr. Mellon telephoned me from Kansas City that the Pennsylvania delegation would meet the following morning, and "I am going to recommend that they vote for you on the first ballot." He asked that nothing be said about it. About two hours later, the press representatives rang me up to say that Senator Vare of Pennsylvania had announced that he and his friends in the Pennsylvania delegation were going to split off from the Mellon group and vote for me. I disliked Vare for adequate reasons, as did Mr. Mellon. It was obvious that he had sensed Mr. Mellon's intentions and wanted to get out in front. As it turned out, I did not need the Pennsylvania delegation anyway.

I have never been able to explain fully Mr. Coolidge's attitude in this matter but I was convinced he was not seeking the nomination either directly or indirectly. On October 10, 1928, Senator Curtis, who was by then my running mate as Vice Presidential candidate, told me that Mr. Coolidge had indicated his favor of Curtis's nomination. If true, it was a natural selection for Mr. Coolidge's type of mind. Some different light came from Senator Butler, who was Mr. Coolidge's most intimate friend and his chairman of the Republican National Committee. A week before the convention the Senator came to see me in New York, and stated that I would be nominated. I asked him about Mr. Coolidge. He replied rather crisply, "I do not know what he wants." A year later (May 22, 1929), Senator Butler told me that in his opinion Mr. Coolidge was convinced up to the last day that the convention would again repeat the deadlock which had produced Harding in 1920, and that at least his views would have weight in the selection.

In any event, it was all over before the convention met—except the noise. The vote on the first ballot was 837 out of 1,084.

Upon receiving notice from the chairman of the convention, Senator Moses, of my nomination, I sent the following message:

Washington, D. C.
June 14, 1928

George H. Moses
Chairman Republican National Convention
Kansas City, Missouri

I have your telegram and I sincerely appreciate the confidence which the party has shown in me and the honor bestowed upon me.

You convey too great a compliment when you say that I have earned the right to the presidential nomination. No man can establish such an obligation upon any part of the American people. My country owes me no debt. It gave me, as it gives every boy and girl, a chance. It gave me schooling, independence of action, opportunity for service and honor. In no other land could a boy from a country village, without inheritance or influential friends, look forward with unbounded hope.

My whole life has taught me what America means. I am indebted to my country beyond any human power to repay. It conferred upon me the mission to administer America's response to the appeal of afflicted nations during the war. It has called me into the cabinets of two Presidents. By these experiences I have observed the burdens and responsibilities of the greatest office in the world. That office touches the happiness of every home. It deals with the peace of nations. No man could think of it except in terms of solemn consecration.

You ask me for a message:

A new era and new forces have come into our economic life and our setting among nations of the world. These forces demand of us constant study and effort if prosperity, peace, and contentment shall be maintained. . . .

This convention, like those which have preceded it for two generations, has affirmed the principles of our party and defined its policies upon the problems which now confront us. I stand upon that platform. At a later date I shall discuss it fully, but in the meantime I may well say that under these principles the victory of the party will assure national defense, maintain economy in the administration of government, protect American workmen, farmers, and business men alike from competition arising out of lower standards of living abroad, foster individual initiative, insure stability of business and employment, promote our foreign commerce, and develop our national resources.

You have manifestly a deep concern in the problems of agriculture. You have pledged the party to support specific and constructive relief upon a nation-wide scale backed by the resources of the Federal government. We must and will find a sound solution that will bring security and contentment to this great section of our people. . . .

Shall the world have peace? Shall prosperity in this nation be more thoroughly distributed? Shall we build steadily toward the ideal of equal opportunity to all our people? Shall there be secured that obedience to law which is essential assurance of life of our institutions? Shall honesty and righteousness in government and in business confirm the confidence of the people in their institutions and their laws?

Government must contribute to leadership in answer to these questions. The government is more than administration; it is power for leadership and cooperation with the forces of business and cultural life in city, town, and country side. The Presidency is more than executive responsibility. It is the inspiring symbol of all that is highest in America's purposes and ideals.

It is vital to the welfare of the United States that the Republican Party should continue to administer the government. It is essential that our party should be continued in organization and in strength in order that it may perpetuate its great principles in our national life.

If elected by my fellow-countrymen I shall give the best within me to advance the moral and material welfare of all our people and uphold the traditions of the Republican Party so effectively exemplified by Calvin Coolidge.   HERBERT HOOVER

CHAPTER 28

THE PRESIDENTIAL CAMPAIGN OF 1928

Anyone who believes that a Presidential campaign includes a luxurious life for the candidate needs further instruction.

The preparation of addresses is a job in itself. And the pneumatic drill on one's brain of personalities, committees, crowds, messages, and incidents never ceases all the eighteen-hour day. Speeches must be spaced in each part of the country. The local committee at every depot must ride to the next station. Hundreds of thousands of people at train stops must have some sort of speech. Thousands of babies must be shaken by their plump fists.

About the most painful thing is to preserve the ego of that part of mankind which expects to be personally remembered by name. In a reception line in Chicago a lady said, "Don't you remember me?" and waited sternly for an answer. I try to be honest, so I replied, "I am sorry, madam, but I would like to and no doubt could, if you will tell me where we met." She said rather indignantly, "Why, I sat on the end of the third row when you spoke in Indianapolis, and you looked right at me." Another trial of campaign life is the autograph. I am convinced that I have half a million in circulation. Certainly there is inflation in these issues.

After the nomination I naturally made an effort to secure unity in action from all groups in the Republican party. I had only a single failure, that being Senator Norris of Nebraska. As I disliked to see any break in our ranks, I related the situation to his friend Senator Borah, who was actively supporting me. To my surprise, Borah broke loose in a tirade against Norris, admonishing me to pay no more attention to him. Norris was, in fact, a devoted socialist; certain left-wing women

furnished funds for his elections and for the maintenance of a publicity
bureau in Washington which constantly eulogized him.

In the campaign I had the strong support of former Secretary of
State Hughes as well as Senator Borah. They traveled over the country
addressing large audiences.

It was obvious, from the beginning of the campaign, that I should
win if we made no mistakes. General Prosperity was on my side. But
the Presidential campaign is a time of education of the people upon the
issues of the day. I felt they had a right to such a discussion even if I did
not need to undertake it. I sought to hold the debate to the decent levels
upon which the election of a President should be conducted.

On October 6 I said:

> Our national officials are chosen in order that they may protect the
> political and economic health of the American people. In a contest such as
> this there is no place for personal bitterness. A great attribute of our political
> life has been the spirit of fair play with which our Presidential contests have
> been waged in former years and the sportsmanlike spirit in which we have
> accepted the result. We prove ourselves worthy of self-government and
> worthy of confidence as officials in proportion as we keep these contests
> free from abuse, free from misrepresentation, and free from words and acts
> which carry regret. Whatever the result, we remain fellow countrymen.

Governor Alfred E. Smith, the Democratic candidate, was a natural
born gentleman. Both of us had come up from the grass roots or the
pavements, and from boyhood had learned the elements of sportsman-
ship. During the campaign he said no word and engaged in no action
that did not comport with the highest levels. I paid a natural tribute to
him when speaking in New York during the campaign, and he did so
to me when speaking in California. In after years, when I was often
associated with him in public matters, we mutually agreed that we had
one deep satisfaction from the battle. No word had been spoken or
misrepresentation made by either of us which prevented sincere friendship the day after election.

I made only seven major addresses during the campaign. I spoke at
Palo Alto, West Branch (Iowa), Elizabethton (Tennessee), Newark

(New Jersey), Boston, New York, and St. Louis, with back-platform remarks along the way. For the first time the radio was in full use in a Presidential election. That invention had made it impossible for Presidential candidates to repeat the same speech with small variations, as had been the practice in those happier speaking times. Then paragraphs could be polished up, epigrams used again and again, and eloquence invented by repeated tryouts. Now every speech had to be original and new. Inasmuch as I have refused all my life to use a ghost writer, I required intervals of two or three weeks to prepare each address.

Robert Moses of New York once told me of an experience in ghost-written speeches. As a young reporter he had been attached to Mr. Hylan's campaign for Mayor of New York. Hylan had only one speech and that advocating a five-cent subway fare. As the campaign went on, the Mayor had repeated it in all parts of the city until it was worn out. Finally he asked Bob to write him a different speech. Bob was greatly flattered and worked diligently. The final sentence of the peroration was, "I call for the spirit of 1776." Hylan stumbled through the strange vocabulary and diction and finally braced himself for the last line— "I call for the spirit of one, seven, seven, six."

While campaign statements are of no great romantic interest, the historian gleans something of economics, ideologies, and politics from them. I shall not cumber this text with a repetition of the arguments. All my addresses have been published in full.[1]

Among the topics debated were: the broad principles of government, various needed reforms, foreign relations and national defense, agricultural policies, labor policies, business regulation, prohibition, use of water resources, the tariff, and the approaches of collectivism.

Concerning many subjects touched upon there was no great difference between Governor Smith and myself. Such were reform of the judicial procedure; the prison system; the promotion of child welfare; better housing; the elimination of national wastes; better organization of the Federal government; control of immigration; development of water resources; and oil conservation.

[1] *The New Day* (Stanford University Press, 1928).

MY DECLARATION OF BROAD PRINCIPLES

In my acceptance address on August 11, 1928, I naturally emphasized
the current prosperity and the successful Republican administration of
the country:

> Our problems of the past seven years have been problems of reconstruc-
> tion; our problems of the future are problems of construction. They are
> problems of progress. New and gigantic forces have come into our national
> life. The Great War released ideas of government in conflict with our prin-
> ciples. We have grown to financial and physical power which compels us
> into a new setting among nations. Science has given us new tools and a
> thousand inventions. Through them have come to each of us wider relation-
> ships, more neighbors, more leisure, broader vision, higher ambitions, greater
> problems. To insure that these tools shall not be used to limit liberty has
> brought a vast array of questions in government.
>
> The points of contact between the government and the people are con-
> stantly multiplying. Every year wise governmental policies become more
> vital in ordinary life. As our problems grow, so do our temptations grow to
> venture away from those principles upon which our republic was founded
> and upon which it has grown to greatness.

Governor Smith made a grave error by advocating the senior Henry
Wallace's agricultural panacea, the McNary-Haugen bill. It was a
scheme of price-fixing for farm produce: a high level for that which
was domestically consumed, and a lower level for that which was exported, permitting it to compete with the cheaper production of
European peasant agriculture and the low wage production of the
Argentine. I dismissed it as a price-fixing scheme which ultimately
meant government control of the farmer's production and distribution.
The Governor may have gained a few votes among radical farmers, but
it cost him much more from other groups in the country. In any event I
carried all the farm states.

PROHIBITION

The prohibition issue was forced into the campaign by Governor
Smith. My innumerable contacts in life had confirmed that alcohol
was one of the curses of the human race. The immediate problem was

whether the widespread devotion to it as an escape or a road to happiness could be controlled by a Federal law. At the time the Eighteenth Amendment was adopted, I was at the Peace Conference in Paris. I had expressed to my friends the reverse of enthusiasm for that method of advancing temperance, saying that I did not believe that the Constitution was the place for sumptuary legislation. I resolved in the campaign not to commit myself to prohibition as a fixture of American life but first to see if the law could be enforced. Already the Harding and Coolidge Administrations had been unable to secure more than poor compliance. I felt that out of more vigorous enforcement some solution might come. I therefore said in my acceptance speech:

I do not favor the repeal of the Eighteenth Amendment. I stand for the efficient enforcement of the laws enacted thereunder. Whoever is chosen President has under his oath the solemn duty to pursue this course.

Our country has deliberately undertaken a great social and economic experiment, noble in motive and far-reaching in purpose. It must be worked out constructively.

Common sense compels us to realize that grave abuses have occurred—abuses which must be remedied. An organized searching investigation of fact and causes can alone determine the wise method of correcting them. Crime and disobedience of law cannot be permitted to break down the Constitution and laws of the United States.

Modification of the enforcement laws which would permit that which the Constitution forbids is nullification. This the American people will not countenance. Change in the Constitution can and must be brought about only by the straightforward methods provided in the Constitution itself. There are those who do not believe in the purposes of several provisions of the Constitution. No one denies their right to seek to amend it. They are not subject to criticism for asserting that right. But the Republican party does deny the right of anyone to seek to destroy the purposes of the Constitution by indirection.

Whoever is elected President takes an oath not only to faithfully execute the office of the President, but that oath provides still further that he will, to the best of his ability, preserve, protect, and defend the Constitution of the United States. I should be untrue to my oath of office, were I to declare otherwise.

This phrase, a great "social experiment noble in motive," was distorted into a "noble experiment" which, of course, was not at all what I said or intended to say. It was an unfortunate phrase because it could be turned into derision. Moreover, to regard the prohibition law as an "experiment" did not please the extreme drys, and to say it was "noble in motive" did not please the extreme wets. However, the prohibition issue did not do Governor Smith any good, for the majority of citizens agreed with me that it must be tried out.

SOME COLOR OF COLLECTIVISM

Under the leadership of William Jennings Bryan, the Democratic party had undertaken to ride the three horses of the extreme conservatism in the Solid South, the radical labor and agrarian groups of the North and the corrupt city machines. Governor Smith inherited this complex and was anxious to retain the support of these Northern groups. While the Governor conscientiously believed in the American system, he was not philosophically very discriminating. Some assurances had been given to Senator Norris and John Dewey's socialist group that the government would go into the power business. Also the Governor had submitted to pressures from the radical agricultural group to advocate price-fixing schemes in farm products. There was certainly a large ideological range in Governor Smith's team of supporters. Aside from the radical groups of the North, and the conservatives of the South, it embraced at the same time such personalities as Pierre DuPont, Senator Norris, and New Jersey boss, Frank Hague.

The United States already was being infected from the revolutionary caldrons of Europe. This had become so evident that I had written a small book on the subject some six years before.[2] In any event, the growing left-wing movement, embracing many of the "intelligentsia," flocked to Governor Smith's support.

I was determined that the Republican party should draw the issue of the American system, as opposed to all forms of collectivism.

Our managers thought that the subject was not of much importance or public interest, and that harping on it carried liabilities. However, I felt that this infection was around, and I dealt with it definitely in an

[2] *American Individualism* (New York, Doubleday, Page & Co., 1922).

address in New York on October 22, 1928. A few paragraphs have some interest in view of later events:

There has been revived in this campaign, however, a series of proposals which, if adopted, would be a long step toward the abandonment of our American system and a surrender to the destructive operation of governmental conduct of commercial business. . . .

You cannot extend the mastery of the government over the daily working life of a people without at the same time making it the master of the people's souls and thoughts. Every expansion of government in business means that government in order to protect itself from the political consequences of its errors and wrongs is driven irresistibly without peace to greater and greater control of the nation's press and platform. Free speech does not live many hours after free industry and free commerce die.

It is a false liberalism that interprets itself into the government operation of commercial business. Every step of bureaucratizing of the business of our country poisons the very roots of liberalism—that is, political equality, free speech, free assembly, free press, and equality of opportunity. It is the road not to more liberty, but to less liberty. Liberalism should be found not striving to spread bureaucracy but striving to set bounds to it. True liberalism seeks all legitimate freedom first in the confident belief that without such freedom the pursuit of all other blessings and benefits is vain. That belief is the foundation of all American progress, political as well as economic.

Liberalism is a force truly of the spirit, a force proceeding from the deep realization that economic freedom cannot be sacrificed if political freedom is to be preserved. Even if governmental conduct of business could give us more efficiency instead of less efficiency, the fundamental objection to it would remain unaltered and unabated. It would destroy political equality. It would increase rather than decrease abuse and corruption. It would stifle initiative and invention. It would undermine the development of leadership. It would cramp and cripple the mental and spiritual energies of our people. It would extinguish equality of opportunity. It would dry up the spirit of liberty and progress. For these reasons primarily it must be resisted. For a hundred and fifty years liberalism has found its true spirit in the American system, not in the European systems.

I do not wish to be misunderstood in this statement. I am defining a general policy. It does not mean that our government is to part with one iota of its national resources without complete protection to the public in-

-terest. I have already stated that where the government is engaged in public works for purposes of flood control, of navigation, of irrigation, of scientific research or national defense, or in pioneering a new art, it will at times necessarily produce power or commodities as a by-product. But they must be a by-product of the major purpose, not the purpose itself.

Nor do I wish to be misinterpreted as believing that the United States is free-for-all and devil-take-the-hindmost. The very essence of equality of opportunity and of American individualism is that there shall be no domination by any group or combination in this republic, whether it be business or political. On the contrary, it demands economic justice as well as political and social justice. It is no system of laissez faire.

I feel deeply on this subject because during the war I had some practical experience with governmental operation and control. I have witnessed not only at home but abroad the many failures of government in business. I have seen its tyrannies, its injustices, its destructions of self-government, its undermining of the very instincts which carry our people forward to prog-ress. I have witnessed the lack of advance, the lowered standards of living, the depressed spirits of people working under such a system. My objection is based not upon theory or upon a failure to recognize wrong or abuse, but I know the adoption of such methods would strike at the very roots of American life and would destroy the very basis of American progress. . . .

The American people from bitter experience have a rightful fear that great business units might be used to dominate our industrial life and by illegal and unethical practices destroy equality of opportunity.

Years ago the Republican administration established the principle that such evils could be corrected by regulation. It developed methods by which abuses could be prevented while the full value of industrial progress could be retained for the public. It insisted upon the principle that when great public utilities were clothed with the security of partial monopoly, whether it be railways, power plants, telephones, or what not, then there must be the fullest and most complete control of rates, services, and finances by government or local agencies. It declared that these businesses must be conducted with glass pockets. . . .

The Republican party insisted upon the enactment of laws that not only would maintain competition but would destroy conspiracies to destroy the smaller units or dominate and limit the equality of opportunity amongst our people. . . .

Nor am I setting up the contention that our institutions are perfect. No human ideal is ever perfectly attained, since humanity itself is not perfect. . . .

And what have been the results of our American system? Our country has become the land of opportunity to those born without inheritance, not merely because of the wealth of its resources and industry but because of this freedom of initiative and enterprise. Russia has natural resources equal to ours. Her people are equally industrious, but she has not had the blessings of one hundred and fifty years of our form of government and of our social system. . . .

CAMPAIGN DIRT

The lower rank and file of party workers on both sides did not show the elevation of spirit one could desire.

The Democratic underworld made a finished job at these low levels with several favorite libels. Again the litigation in London, wherein I was supposed to have robbed a Chinaman, was exploited. However, that gave rise to a boomerang from an unexpected quarter. The principal Chinese owner of the properties in question was Tong Shao-yi, to whom I have referred in the preceding volume of these memoirs. He had now risen to be Prime Minister of his country. Suddenly Tong appeared in the American press with an indignant statement from China that this story was "dastardly," that his family were the principal owners, that he had been enormously benefited by my services on that occasion. He otherwise expressed himself warmly.

Another attack was laid on with a defter touch. Some years before, I had taken an interest in a group of young men to enable them to buy a ranch near Bakersfield, California. From overdevotion, they had named it the "Hoover Ranch" and had painted the name on the gatepost. Agents of the Democratic County Committee painted a sign "No White Help Wanted" and, hanging it on the gate below the name, had it photographed and distributed the prints all over the country. The reference was to the employment of Asiatics. The ranch never had employed any such help. Through my friend Samuel Gompers, I at once secured an investigation by the Kern County labor union leaders. Their report was an indignant denial, but we were never able to catch up with the lie. This smear was used for years afterwards.[3]

Another elaborately engineered attack collapsed miserably. A clerk in the Kensington Borough (London) municipal office wrote to some Democratic campaign agency that he could prove that I was a naturalized British subject and had voted twice in British elections. He offered to produce the proof for a consideration which was ultimately settled at $250 by a Democratic agent sent to England to interview him. In England every householder, whether owner or tenant, must pay local rates (taxes), and under the electoral system every ratepayer of whatever nationality is automatically placed on the voting register. It appeared that without my knowledge my name was thus twice on the register of voters, during a period when we lived in a rented house in Kensington. The Democratic agents photographed the register, took sworn statements from the clerk, prepared full-page advertisements for the American press, and contracted for space in newspapers for the following week.

It was at this stage that the Republican Committee learned of it and went to Secretary of State Kellogg. He instructed an official of the Embassy in London to investigate at once. The Embassy secured certification from the British naturalization authorities that I had never been naturalized, had never applied for naturalization. They also stated that during the war the British government had required me to register as an alien. The Embassy obtained a statement from the British Home Office explaining the system of registration, certifying that I had never voted, that if I had done so I should have received as an alien six months in jail. The Embassy also found I had been regularly registered at the American Consulate as an American. This whole story, being released to the press by the Secretary of State, squashed the advertisement; but with the usual curious reaction of voters who had learned of it from advance "leaks" many, especially among the Irish Americans, concluded that I was an Englishman anyway.

The Democratic propagandists naturally made much ado about the

---

[3] Now, twenty years later, letters or press notices are repeating this smear. It is constantly repeated in labor meetings.

corruption in the Harding administration. This was hard to bear, especially coming from Tammany Hall. In my acceptance speech I answered:

In the past years there has been corruption participated in by individual officials and members of both political parties in national, state, and municipal affairs. Too often this corruption has been viewed with indifference by a great number of our people. It would seem unnecessary to state the elemental requirement that government must inspire confidence not only in its ability but in its integrity. Dishonesty in government, whether national, state, or municipal, is a double wrong. It is treason to the state. It is destructive of self-government. Government in the United States rests not only upon the consent of the governed but upon the conscience of the nation. Government weakens the moment that its integrity is even doubted. Moral incompetency by those entrusted with government is a blighting wind upon private integrity. There must be no place for cynicism in the creed of America.

These were merely run-of-mine incidents typical of any American political campaign. Any man entering public life knows that gremlins of this sort will eventually tear at his public reputation. Because he is smeared at home is the probable reason why "a prophet is not without honor, save in his own country."

RELIGIOUS BIGOTRY

The worst plague in the campaign was the religious issue. Governor Smith was the first Presidential candidate of Catholic faith, and for that matter I was the first Quaker. Religion is a difficult matter to handle politically. Even to mention religious questions was enough to fan the flames of bigotry. I tried to stamp out the issue in my acceptance speech on August 11, 1928, by a forthright reference:

In this land, dedicated to tolerance, we still find outbreaks of intolerance. I come of Quaker stock. My ancestors were persecuted for their beliefs. Here they sought and found religious freedom. By blood and conviction I stand for religious tolerance both in act and in spirit. The glory of our American ideals is the right of every man to worship God according to the dictates of his own conscience.

Governor Smith unwittingly fanned the flame in an address in Oklahoma against intolerance. He insisted that religious faith did not disqualify any man from public office. He was right. But up to that moment it had been an underground issue. The Governor thought that he would gain by bringing it out into the open. The result, however, was to embattle the bigoted Protestants in the open, particularly in the South. I reprimanded many of those who agitated this question. On the occasion of a violent letter sent out from a Virginia organization, I issued the following public statement:

Whether this letter is authentic or a forgery, it does violence to every instinct that I possess. I resent and repudiate it. Such an attitude is entirely opposed to every principle of the Republican party. I made my position clear in my acceptance speech. I meant that then and I mean it now.

Later in the campaign I said on September 28, with reference to circulars in other parts of the country:

I cannot fully express my indignation at any such circulars. Nor can I reiterate too strongly that religious questions have no part in this campaign. I have repeatedly stated that neither I nor the Republican party want support on that basis.

There are important and vital reasons for the return of the Republican administration, but this is not one of them.

Governor Smith was a prominent member of Tammany. During the campaign he made a speech at the Hall eulogizing the organization, apparently believing that he could whitewash it. In so doing he certainly made it fair game for grass-roots debate. I never referred to it.

The issues which defeated the Governor were general prosperity, prohibition, the farm tariffs, Tammany, and the "snuggling" up of the Socialists. Had he been a Protestant, he would certainly have lost and might even have had a smaller vote. An indication of the small importance of the religious issue in final results was the vote in New York State. Here Governor Smith, a Catholic, had been twice elected Governor, and therefore no great amount of religious bigotry could have existed. It was for other reasons than his Catholicism that his own state rejected him for President.

In fact, the religious issue had no weight in the final result. I carried all but eight states. In four or five Southern states it may have had weight on my side, although the prohibition and Tammany issues were of far more influence there. As against this the Catholic votes in all states no doubt went preponderantly for Governor Smith, as evidenced by the fact that he carried Massachusetts, traditionally a Republican state, where the Catholics were stronger than in any other state in the Union.

CHAPTER 29

ELECTION AND PRESIDENT-ELECT

I left Washington for Palo Alto to vote on November 1, making one important address en route at St. Louis. I was elected by 21,392,000 votes against 15,016,000 for Governor Smith. I had carried forty states and secured 444 votes in the Electoral College, against 87 for the Governor.

During the four months between election and inauguration, I undertook three major tasks.

Mrs. Hoover and I made a journey of about six weeks to the Latin-American countries.

I assembled my administrative staff.

I formulated, so far as I could see ahead, our major policies for the next few years.

As Secretary of Commerce I had developed an increasing dissatisfaction with our policies toward Latin America. I was convinced that unless we displayed an entirely different attitude we should never dispel the suspicions and fears of the "Colossus of the North" nor win the respect of those nations. An interpretation of the Monroe Doctrine to the effect that we had the right to maintain order in those states by military force, in order not to give excuse for European intervention, created antagonisms and suspicions which dominated the politics of much of the Latin area. The German-, Italian-, and British-subsidized South American press constantly encouraged this antagonism as part of their trade propaganda. Moreover, our "dollar diplomacy," by threats and intimidation on behalf of our speculative citizens when their investments went wrong, added fuel to the fire. The policy of military intervention practiced by the Wilson Administration had been continued by Harding and Coolidge. At this time, we had troops in Haiti and

Nicaragua. The United States, to put it mildly, was not popular in the rest of the Hemisphere.

I regarded an improvement in these relations as especially vital, for it seemed to me that in the future outlook of the world, we in the Western Hemisphere not only shared mutual interests, but common threats to those interests.

I asked Mr. Coolidge for a battleship on which to make the journey. He suggested that I take a cruiser—"it would not cost so much." However, since battleships as well as cruisers always must keep steam up and their crews aboard, that did not worry me much. I wanted room enough to take Mrs. Hoover, whose California upbringing enabled her to speak considerable Spanish. Also I wanted a diplomatic staff and representatives of the press, so as not only to evidence great interest in these countries but to educate the American people a little on our neighbors to the south. Finally Mr. Coolidge put the battleship *Maryland* at my disposal going south; and the battleship *Utah* met us at Montevideo and brought us home.

We were accompanied by Henry P. Fletcher, former Under Secretary of State, and John Mott, a leading California lawyer, as a special interpreter and some of our best press correspondents—about twenty of them, including my old friends Mark Sullivan and Will Irwin.

We visited Honduras, Salvador, Nicaragua, Costa Rica, Ecuador, Peru, Chile, Argentina, Uruguay, and Brazil. I met with the President of Bolivia and I had intended to visit Mexico and Cuba later on.

We had a real welcome accompanied by parades, banquets, receptions, and speeches. Our Latin neighbors have an exquisite politeness and hospitality. Their leaders are usually understanding and eloquent men.

Some incidents added interest to the journey. In Nicaragua Mr. Coolidge had indirectly imposed a presidential election to stop a civil war, and had it conducted by our Marines. When the Marines registered the voters, they required each registrant to dip a finger in a chemical solution which stained it yellow. At election a few days later only the yellow fingers might vote, and as they left the polls on election day voters were required to dip another finger in a red solution. Thus repeaters were eliminated. I asked the Marine officer in charge where he got that idea. He replied, "I lived once in Tammany New York and proposed it as a cure for one of Tammany's bad habits, but everybody said it would be insulting."

As a result of the election the incumbent President had been defeated. Our diplomatic representatives informed me that he was not going to give up his office peaceably. Therefore, I invited the President-elect and the outgoing President to lunch on the *Maryland*. Neither President wanted to refuse the invitation, but as one of the naval officers observed in mixed metaphor, "They stepped around like fighting cocks making dog-eyes at each other." I found they were both delightful and intellectual men. I did not assume any friction, but we talked at length upon the problems of their country and the need of a reputation for orderly government. I announced that we were going to withdraw our troops and invited them both to visit the United States. In any event, there was no further revolution, for a while.

President Gonzalez Viquez of Costa Rica possessed a fine sense of humor. We were reviewing a parade of the military and civic bodies when he pointed to the 150 soldiers and a military band of 150 pieces and remarked: "That is our total armed force except for another military band. You will observe the variety and expressiveness of the uniforms. But we have 1,800 schoolteachers. They are much more important in maintaining public order."

Arriving by train at Buenos Aires from Santiago, we were met by President Irigoyen. To prevent Communist outbreaks and to hold back the large crowd of civilians, three lines of protection had been provided along the station platform—police, soldiers, and firemen, one behind another, apparently under separate command. After we had alighted and shaken hands with the President and important officials something went wrong, for the whole platform turned into a seething jam with civilians crowding among the guards. President Irigoyen was pushed about, and his coat ripped up the back, at which he became properly excited. Our naval aides kept Mrs. Hoover and me from being crushed. When we arrived at the American Embassy one of our Secret Service

PRESIDENT COOLIDGE'S CABINET

Left to right, sitting: Harry S. New, Postmaster General; John W. Weeks, Secretary of War; Charles Evans Hughes, Secretary of State; President Coolidge; Andrew W. Mellon, Secretary of the Treasury; Harry M. Daugherty, Attorney General; Edwin Denby, Secretary of the Navy.

Standing: Herbert Hoover, Secretary of Commerce; Hubert Work, Secretary of the Interior; Henry C. Wallace, Secretary of Agriculture; James J. Davis, Secretary of Labor.

PRESIDENT HOOVER'S CABINET

Sitting: Patrick J. Hurley, Secretary of War; Charles Curtis, Vice President; President Hoover; Henry L. Stimson, Secretary of State; Andrew W. Mellon, Secretary of the Treasury.

Standing: Robert P. Lamont, Secretary of Commerce; Ray Lyman Wilbur, Secretary of the Interior; Walter F. Brown, Postmaster General; William D. Mitchell, Attorney General; Arthur M. Hyde, Secretary of Agriculture; Charles F. Adams, Secretary of the Navy; William N. Doak, Secretary of Labor.

men complained to the Buenos Aires Chief of Police that he had been robbed of his pocketbook in the melee. The Chief replied, "Well, they got my wrist watch."

The formal banquet tendered us by President Irigoyen developed protocol trouble. He informed us that he did not make speeches and would ask the Argentine Secretary of State to speak for him. The American Ambassador replied that this was perfectly agreeable, and that Mr. Fletcher would reply for me. Whereupon the President decided to make a speech after all, and the Ambassador replied that, in that case, I would reply personally to this special honor. Nevertheless, the program was changed two or three times, so Mr. Fletcher and I went to the banquet each with a speech, waiting to see who was the lead-off for Argentina. President Irigoyen spoke, and spoke well. He afterwards remarked to me that he did not find it as terrible as he had anticipated.

I made fourteen short addresses during the journey and emphasized several different themes. These were later published in English, Spanish, and Portuguese. Some paragraphs from addresses at the different capitals indicate the nature of those addresses:

I come to pay a call of friendship. In a sense I represent on this occasion the people of the United States extending a friendly greeting to our fellow democracies on the American continent. I would wish to symbolize the friendly visit of one *good neighbor* to another. In our daily life, *good neighbors* call upon each other as the evidence of solicitude for the common welfare and to learn of the circumstances and point of view of each, so that there may come both understanding and respect which are the cementing forces of all enduring society. This should be equally true amongst nations. We have a desire to maintain not only the cordial relations of governments with each other but the relations of *good neighbors.*

I have come on a visit as a neighbor. I have thought that perhaps I might symbolize the good-will which I know my country holds toward your own. My hope and my purpose and my aspiration are that better acquaintance, larger knowledge of our sister republics of Latin America, and the personal contact of government may enable me to better execute the task which lies before me. And a large part of that task is the cooperation with other nations for the common upbuilding of prosperity and of progress throughout the world. . . .

. . . Democracy is more than a form of political organization; it is a human faith. True democracy is not and cannot be imperialistic. The brotherhood of this faith is the guarantee of good will.

We who are public servants can do but little in our time. Our minute part of a few years is soon forgotten. But if we can contribute to diminish destructive forces, if we can strengthen the forces of material and spiritual progress, if we can upbuild the institutions of government which assure liberty and freedom we shall have served our part.

. . . There is abundant reason why friendship and understanding between us should be deeply rooted in the hearts of the people of both our nations. We have on both sides a history of common labor, of building in the new world a new form of government founded upon a new conception of human rights; the supreme experience of rebellion from the political and social systems of the Old World; the subjugation of the wilderness; of developments of economic life through the application of the great discoveries of science; the effort to lift the moral and cultural levels of our countries.

Generally the theme stressed a "good neighbor." I suggested immediate measures for development of our relations—one of them was a better organization of intellectual exchanges such as students and professors.

The other theme, more materialistic, was the development of inter-American aviation and determination of the basis of aviation rights. In each country I discussed this question with the President and officials. Having learned in each country the basis upon which common airways could be established, I was able upon my return home to advance the matter rapidly. From this initiative came Pan American Airways to which I refer later.

One result of the journey was the settlement of the long-standing Tacna-Arica dispute between Peru and Bolivia. The United States had some time before been asked by the two countries to arbitrate the matter. The attempts hitherto had failed. By cautious inquiry I learned from the officials of the two governments the approximate limits of concession that both sides would make. Putting these together upon my return to Washington, I was able to offer a compromise which settled the controversy.

Another result was the withdrawal of all American troops from Latin-American countries.

During my journey I had opportunity to observe the character of our Ministers and representatives. Some of them were "career" men doing magnificent service. But some were political appointees who were eyesores both to the countries to which they were accredited and to us. I determined that we must reorganize the whole service.

ORGANIZATION OF THE ADMINISTRATION

The nature of the Presidential office as it has evolved through the history of the Republic is somewhat puzzling. Since the Founding Fathers, we had grown from 3,000,000 population to 135,000,000 and from thirteen to forty-eight states. We had grown from an agricultural country to a complex industrial nation. We had risen in power to the first stature among nations. The original constitutional concept of the President's office had certainly been enlarged. He had become a broader policy-maker in legislation, foreign affairs, economic and social life than the Founding Fathers ever contemplated.

The President is, by his oath, one of the protectors of the Constitution. As "Chief Executive" he is administrator of the government. As "Commander-in-Chief" he has a responsibility in national defense. As "Chief Magistrate" he is the chief Federal law enforcement officer. Through his responsibility for foreign relations, he must keep the peace in a world of increasing perplexities. With the growth of the two-party system, he has become the leader of his party, bearing the responsibility to carry out the platform on which he was elected and to keep the party in power. As adviser to the Congress on the state of the nation, he must demonstrate constant leadership by proposing social and economic reforms made necessary by the increasing complexity of American life. He must be the conserver of national resources, and he must carry forward the great public works in pace with public need. He must encourage all good causes. Presidents have given different emphasis to these functions, depending upon the man and the times. In the end the President has become increasingly the depository of all national ills, especially if things go wrong.

There has been an increasing ascendancy of the Executive over the Legislative arm, which has run to great excesses. The President's veto was not often used in the first seventy years of the Republic as legislative power but was held as a safeguard of constitutionality of legislation. Gradually this power of the veto has expanded until he possesses one-third of the legislative authority. Far from merely advising Congress, he is expected to blast reforms out of it. With the growth of the Federal expenditure the Congress has lost much of its control of the purse, the original citadel of parliamentary power.

I felt deeply that the independence of the legislative arm must be respected and strengthened. I had little taste for forcing Congressional action or engaging in battles of criticism. However, this could not be avoided two years later when I had to deal with a Democratic Congress bent on the ruin of the administration.

It is a handicap to any man to succeed a member of his own party as President. He has little patronage with which to reward his personal supporters. This was especially true in my case as Mr. Coolidge had with few exceptions left me a most able body of public servants. Also a new President cannot blame his predecessor for inevitable mistakes, and therefore he must keep quiet and inherit responsibility for them. I had a further internal difficulty. The older Republican elements of the party in Congress never forgave my elevation to the Presidency and at times occupied themselves politically. However, they were too good politicians to do much beyond surreptitious encouragement to the opposition and refusal to come to the defense of the administration. I had also to deal with those perpetual members of my own party who wished to demonstrate publicly by grasshopper bites that they had greater liberal minds than the President, and that they did not wear his collar.

After the Harding experience, I was especially concerned that we give an administration of rigid integrity and avoid the slightest color of yielding to special influence; I therefore felt it necessary to give much attention to the housekeeping of government, to assure these ends and its general efficiency.

Each President must have his own major policy-making officials sympathetic with his ideas, irrespective of the appointments of his predecessors. But Cabinet making has become more difficult since smearing and irresponsible attack became so much a part of American political life. Moreover, greater incomes are available in private life than the government can pay for demonstrated executive ability. Thus, for many reasons citizens of the right quality must make great personal sacrifices to accept Cabinet positions.

I had to choose ten men who represented different parts of the country, who were men of public esteem, and who had proved by their success as administrators that they could conduct a great department in the greatest business on earth. My first disappointment was the refusal of four most desirable men to accept Cabinet positions, including Charles Evans Hughes, Justice Harlan Stone, Governor Frank Lowden, and Henry Robinson.

The Cabinet members whom I selected were: Secretary of State, Frank B. Kellogg, who consented to remain through June, 1929—thereafter Henry L. Stimson of New York; Attorney General, William D. Mitchell of Minnesota; Secretary of the Treasury, Andrew Mellon until 1932—thereafter Ogden L. Mills of New York; Secretary of War, James W. Good of Iowa, who died in 1929—thereafter Patrick J. Hurley of Oklahoma; Secretary of the Navy, Charles Francis Adams of Massachusetts; Postmaster General, Walter F. Brown of Ohio; Secretary of Agriculture, Arthur M. Hyde of Missouri; Secretary of the Interior, Ray Lyman Wilbur of California; Secretary of Commerce, Robert P. Lamont of Illinois until 1932—thereafter Roy D. Chapin; Secretary of Labor, James J. Davis until 1930—thereafter William N. Doak of Virginia.

The Assistant Secretaries are appointed by the President and, as they are policy-making officials, they necessarily must be in accord with his views on major questions. As to Bureau heads, I made one departure from general practice by appointing all heads of scientific bureaus by promotion from the Civil Service.

I was fortunate in securing Congressman Walter Newton as Secretary to the President, with Lawrence Richey, French Strother, George Akerson, and later Theodore Joslin, Ann Shankey and Myra McGrath as special secretaries. Mr. Newton attended to appointments, and to legislative and Cabinet relations. Mr. Strother was assigned to questions of reform in the social system; Mr. Akerson, to the press; and Mr. Richey, to correspondence.

Among the more important members of the administration, I have already given some account of Secretary Mellon. Secretary Stimson had a long background of public service. An eminent lawyer, he had been Secretary of War in Mr. Taft's Cabinet; he was a colonel in the World War; he had been entrusted with many important missions for our country, including the Governor Generalship of the Philippines. Instinctively, Mr. Stimson's first love was the law; and his second, the military field. Mentally, he was a mixture of a soldier and an advocate. His integrity of character, his loyalties, and his long experience in public affairs were a contribution to American life in its best sense.

Attorney General Mitchell was a Democrat by registration but a Republican in ideas. He had served as Solicitor General in Mr. Coolidge's administration. There never was an Attorney General more able or more devoted to the uplift of the judiciary or more diligent in his primary function of law enforcement.

Ogden Mills, who ultimately succeeded Mr. Mellon, possessed one of the best and most reliable intellects of our generation. His economic sense was uncanny. His courage and administrative ability were of the first order. His long background of public service in New York State and in the Congress had reenforced his natural qualities. He had only one fault. He could not stand discussion with those he called "dumb" or "boll weevils." He was not content with their easy dismissal but felt a duty to correct them effectively.

Secretary Good was a lawyer by training who had served for many years in the House, rising to the chairmanship of the Appropriations Committee. His knowledge of the government was complete. He possessed not only great abilities but fine qualities as an administrator. His death early in the administration was a great loss.

Secretary Hurley, his successor, was a fighting Irishman with all the loyalties and the great personal charm of that inheritance; and, likewise, he was a fine administrator.

Secretary Adams was our generation's distinguished representative of that great family which has contributed so much to American life. In personal appearance he was the image of his great ancestor, John Quincy Adams. He was a man of high cultivation, fine integrity, full knowledge of American life, and was able in the conduct of public affairs. Had I known him better earlier, I should have made him Secretary of State.

Postmaster General Brown had come from a long experience in political life, having first emerged as one of the managers of Theodore Roosevelt's campaign in 1912. He conducted the tangled skein of politics and business inherent in the Post Office with ability and courage.

Secretary Hyde had been a reform Governor of Missouri and had a long experience in the agricultural world. He possessed an extraordinary wit and ability at eloquent presentation. I have known no Secretary of Agriculture before or since who was his equal.

Secretary Wilbur had been my constant friend of nearly forty years from my college boyhood. He was President of Stanford University, and his long background in public phases of the medical profession prior to his university presidency gave him a fine insight into social and educational forces so much needed by the Interior Department at that period. He was a great outdoor man and knew the West and its resources above most men.

Secretaries Lamont, Davis, Doak, and Chapin were all men of ability in their fields—and of high personal character.

Of the "No. 2" string of Under Secretaries or Assistant Secretaries, Joseph Cotton, William R. Castle, Jr., Trubee Davison, Julius Klein, Harvey Bundy, James Grafton Rogers, Henry Fletcher, Walter Hope, Francis White, Alexander Legge, G. Aaron Youngquist, Charles E. Hughes, Jr., Thomas Thacher, John Lord O'Brian, Clarence M. Young, David Ingalls, Frederick Payne, Ernest Lee Jahncke, Monte Appel, Arthur Ballantine, Arch Coleman, Frederic A. Tilton, John Jay Hopkins, James H. Douglas, Joseph Dixon, Charles Rugg, were all promising future Cabinet timber.

And to all these should be added Chief of Staff Douglas MacArthur, Chief of Naval Operations Admiral William V. Pratt and such distinguished Bureau or Agency heads as J. Edgar Hoover, Henry O'Malley,

INAUGURATION, 1929

Sanford Bates, John W. Philp, Edward C. Finney, Hugh S. Cumming, Robert Grant, Horace M. Albright, Charles J. Rhoads, Elwood Mead, George Otis Smith, Walter C. Mendenhall, Mabel Walker Willebrandt, Grace Abbott, Mary Anderson, John R. Alpine, R. Y. Stuart, Thomas E. Campbell, John Lee Coulter, and Charles M. Saltzman. I doubt if any President was ever surrounded by men and women of more personal loyalty or devotion to public service than this group. Had the Republican party remained in power, they were the young men who could have carried the highest traditions of public service. We of course did not always agree, but we searched out solutions without public battles or rancor.

There are three tributes that can be given to them all: First, there has never been substantiated challenge to the integrity of any one of them; we had no scandals, no misfeasance whatever in the administration. Second, no one of them in whom I imposed trust and confidence has ever defamed my actions or even criticized them in after life. Third, every man or woman in the group has given me ever afterwards lasting friendship and loyalty. For all of which I owe them an unpayable debt.

When I formed the Cabinet, I came under strong pressure to appoint John L. Lewis Secretary of Labor. He was the ablest man in the labor world. In view, however, of a disgraceful incident at Herndon, Illinois, which had been greatly used against him, it seemed impossible. He, however, maintained a friendly attitude. As he stated publicly in later years, "I at times disagreed with the President but he always told me what he would or would not do." Lewis is a complex character. He is a man of superior intelligence with the equivalent of a higher education, which he had won by reading of the widest range. He could repeat, literally, long passages from Shakespeare, Milton, and the Bible. His word was always good. He was blunt and even brutal in his methods of negotiation, and he assumed and asserted that employers were cut from the same cloth. His loyalty to his men was beyond question. He was not a socialist. He believed in "free enterprise." One of his favorite monologues had for its burden: "I don't want government ownership of the mines or business; no labor leader can deal with bureaucracy and the government, and lick them. I want these economic royalists on the job; they are the only people who have learned the know-how; they work eighteen hours a day, seven days a week; my only quarrel with them is over our share in the productive pie."

If Lewis's great abilities could have been turned onto the side of the government, they would have produced a great public servant.

In my inaugural address on March 4, 1929, I was somewhat hampered by the fact that I was succeeding a President of my own party, a man for whom I had the warmest of personal feeling, for whose integrity I had the highest respect, and to whom I was indebted for many kindnesses. I paid tribute to Mr. Coolidge in my address, and I could not in good taste say anything that indicated certain differences in our points of view. I therefore confined myself mostly to American ideals and aspirations.

I spoke upon better law enforcement, upon the relations of government to business, upon world peace and disarmament, and concluded:

... The government must, so far as lies within its proper powers, give leadership to the realization of these ideals and to the fruition of these aspirations. No one can adequately reduce these things of the spirit to phrases or to a catalogue of definitions. We do know what the attainments of these ideals should be: the preservation of self-government and its full foundations in local government; the perfection of justice whether in economic or in social fields; the maintenance of ordered liberty; the denial of domination by any group or class; the building up and preservation of equality of opportunity; the stimulation of initiative and individuality; absolute integrity in public affairs; the choice of officials for fitness to office; the direction of economic progress toward prosperity and the further lessening of poverty; the freedom of public opinion; the sustaining of education and of the advancement of knowledge; the growth of religious spirit and the tolerance of all faiths; the strengthening of the home; the advancement of peace.

There is no short road to the realization of these aspirations. Ill-considered remedies for our faults bring only penalties after them. But if we hold the faith of the men in our mighty past who created these ideals, we shall leave them heightened and strengthened for our children.

Inauguration Day was, as usual, cold and rainy. American tradition still insisted upon an outdoor ceremonial at the Capitol, and by the time we arrived at the White House both Mrs. Hoover and I were thoroughly soaked.

I came to the White House with a program of vigorous policies in three directions.

I was determined to carry forward the reconstruction and development measures in which I had participated as Secretary of Commerce.

There was urgent need for reforms in our social and business life. A virile people with a constant output of new ideas, new scientific discoveries, and new inventions makes its own changing world. Its government is continually confronted by problems involving protection of liberty against misuse or abuse. The prolific soil of individual liberty produces not only magnificent blossoms but also noxious weeds. We had our share of thistles and many sprouting weeds.

Little had been done by the Federal government in the fields of reform or progress during the fourteen years before my time. After 1914 the Wilson administration had been absorbed mostly in problems of war. The Harding and Coolidge administrations had been concerned with economic reconstruction after the war. Mr. Coolidge was reluctant to undertake much that either was new or cost money. And by 1929 many things were already fourteen years overdue. I not only was convinced of the necessity for easing these strains of growth and giving impulse to progress but had high hopes that I might lead in performing the task.

The third field was to reorient our foreign relations into a greater cooperation for advancement of peace and international progress.

But instead of being able to devote my four years wholly to these purposes I was to be overtaken by the economic hurricane which sprang from the delayed consequences of the World War. Then the first need was economic recovery and employment. And some actions otherwise possible would have retarded recovery.

I am so immodest as to believe that had we been continued in office we would have quickly overcome the depression and approached economic and social problems from the point of view of correcting marginal abuse and not of inflicting a collectivist economy on the country. We would have better preserved the personal liberty to which the nation was dedicated. As I have stated the next volume of these memoirs will be devoted mostly to "The Great Depression."

Development and Reform

CHAPTER 31

WATER RESOURCES

The reconstruction and development policies carried over to the Presidency from the Secretaryship of Commerce fell into several categories: (a) development of our water resources; (b) conservation of our oil, minerals, fisheries, ranges, and forests; (c) better organization of our aviation, merchant marine, and radio; (d) improvement of our highways, public buildings, and parks; (e) better housing; (f) better protection of our children; (g) expanded scientific research.

PUTTING OUR WATER RESOURCES TO WORK

Putting our water resources to work had been greatly delayed. Mr. Wilson had to suspend action during 1917 to 1920. Messrs. Harding and Coolidge were ultraconservative as to Federal expenditures in these directions.

As President, I carried forward the changes in Federal policies that I had previously advocated: (1) that we must determine the advantageous development of each drainage system as a whole; (2) that we must advance the dimensions of irrigation, navigation, and flood control by construction of great multiple-purpose storage dams; (3) that we must develop our inland water transportation by major interconnected systems instead of isolated local improvements.

WATER STORAGE

The Reclamation Service had been established to build storage dams suitable to irrigate government-owned lands, to sell these lands to settlers and, from the sale of lands, water, and power, to return the cost to the government. The easy irrigation projects already had been largely completed. The idea of finance by the farmers was a failure because the costs were greater than the farmers could bear; moreover, the government-owned lands were largely exhausted. That the farmers could not carry the whole load was evidenced by repeated relief bills passed by the Congress for practically every district; the villages and towns which grew up in consequence of these developments should have borne a substantial part of the costs, which they did not do. This initial plan was now outmoded.

Moreover, Federal administration of the projects two thousand miles away by a bureaucracy in Washington was not only an encroachment on state responsibilities but a source of great evils. I therefore proposed to carry forward my ideas from the Department of Commerce that the Reclamation Service be reoriented to include the construction of great multiple purpose water storage dams which in irrigation would serve both private and public lands, and at the same time give protection from floods and, in many cases, improve navigation—all with a by-product of hydroelectric power.

I proposed to initiate these policies with the cooperation of the governors of the states concerned. We set up joint commissions of representatives of the Federal and state agencies to work out the engineering plans, and we made progress in the following major projects during my administration.

The Colorado River Dam

I have already told about a joint Federal and state commission for the Colorado River on which I served as chairman.

After years of labor we had untangled the legal, legislative, engineering, and financial delays to this development by the Colorado River Compact. The last remaining step to enable us to initiate work on this, the first of the great multiple purpose dams, was to secure the Federal ratification of the Compact. On June 25, 1929, after I came to the White House, the last formality was completed, and I issued the proclamation making the Compact between the states effective, saying:

I have a particular interest in its consummation not only because of its great intrinsic importance but because I was the Chairman of the Colorado River Commission that formulated the Compact. The Compact itself relates entirely to the distribution of water rights between the seven states in the Basin. . . .

It is the final settlement of disputes that have extended over twenty-five years and which have stopped the development of the river. . . . It has an interest also in that it is the most extensive action ever taken by a group of states under the provisions of the Constitution permitting compacts between states. . . . It opens the avenue for some hope of the settlement of other regional questions as between the states rather than the imposition of these problems on the Federal Government.

Under the legislation authorizing the construction of the dam which I had helped to draft during the Coolidge administration, we had first to sell the power to be produced. This was the largest power contract in history. It was negotiated with great skill by Secretary Wilbur and signed in April, 1930. It provided, in effect, for the sale of the falling water, measured as electric power at the bus bar, to municipalities and private companies in such fashion as to protect the public and to return the entire cost of the works to the government. This method kept the Federal government out of the business of generating and distributing power.

The municipalities of southern California having organized themselves into a water district, I secured for them in 1932 a loan from the RFC with which to construct their gigantic system bringing Colorado River water as far as Los Angeles. The over-all cost of the dam and collateral improvements amounted to more than $400,000,000, of which the Federal government will recover its contribution with interest. This dam was the largest and most comprehensive structure of its kind built until then. The total power from the dam and collateral development exceeds 1,000,000 electric horsepower. The dam is over 700 feet high, thus exceeding the Washington Monument. We were able to complete about three-quarters of the construction during my administration.

Following the national custom of naming large Federal reservoirs for the Presidents, Secretary Wilbur named this the Hoover Dam when on September 8, 1930, he started work on the railway to the site. The Roosevelt Dam had previously been named for Theodore Roosevelt; the Wilson Dam, for Woodrow Wilson; the Coolidge Dam, for Calvin

Coolidge. None of the Presidents had taken more than a casual interest in establishing these great works. Following precedent, Congress legalized the name, through appropriations, for the "Hoover Dam."

On my trip back to Washington after my defeat in the election of 1932, I stopped on November 12 to inspect, by night, the progress of construction. At that time I made a short review of the work and its purpose, saying:

It does give me extraordinary pleasure to see the great dream I have so long held taking form in actual reality of stone and cement.

It is now ten years since I became chairman of the Colorado River Commission. . . .

This dam is the greatest engineering work of its character ever attempted by the hand of man. . . .

Its first purpose was to stabilize the flow of the river from these gigantic annual floods, thus preventing destruction of the great Imperial Valley and the agriculture which has grown up in neighboring states and in Mexico. . . . This danger is forever removed by the construction of this dam.

[Its] second [purpose was] to provide a supply of domestic water accessible to Southern California and parts of Arizona. . . .

The third purpose was to provide an adequate supply of irrigation water to the large areas of Arizona, the Imperial Valley and other valleys of Southern California.

Its fourth purpose is to generate a vast supply of cheap power.

The waters of this great river, instead of being wasted in the sea, will now be brought into use by man. . . .

The whole of this will translate itself . . . into millions of happy homes . . . out under the blue sky of the West. It will . . . assure livelihood to a new population nearly as great as that of the state of Maryland. . . .

I hope to be present at its final completion as a bystander. Even so I shall feel a special personal satisfaction.[1]

[1] Responding to a suggestion from Hiram Johnson, and with his characteristic attitude, Secretary Ickes changed the name of the dam.

The hint in the above address that I should like to be present did not secure me an invitation to the dedication ceremonies conducted by President Roosevelt. I have never regarded the name as important. The important thing is a gigantic engineering accomplishment that will bring happiness to millions of people.

In 1947 the Congress, by practically unanimous action, restored the name Hoover Dam—to Mr. Ickes's intense indignation.

The Grand Coulee Dam

At once upon coming into the Presidency, I directed the Reclamation Service to prepare the engineering plans for the Columbia River projects. The Grand Coulee project was a most intricate and immense engineering job, second only to the Hoover Dam. Years of work were required to make the detailed surveys, borings, and plans. This engineering work was begun in 1930, and on January 7, 1932, the Director of the Reclamation Service made his report to me as to feasibility and desirability with the broad engineering plans completed. I approved the plans and directed the further detailed plans be completed as rapidly as possible.

The dam was to be 450 feet high, containing, with the appurtenant structures, about 11,000,000 cubic yards of concrete. It would make a lake over 100 miles long. It could generate about 800,000 "firm" horsepower and a large amount more of seasonal ("secondary") power, which could be used for pumping into large reservoirs and would supply about 1,200,000 acres of land. Construction cost was estimated at about $210,000,000, which could be largely recovered, with interest, from irrigation and power.

The plans were so near completion at the end of my administration that the Roosevelt administration was able to begin construction almost immediately.

The Central Valley of California

I have set forth the preliminary steps which I had taken while Secretary of Commerce to advance the great valley of California water storage and flood control project. Because Mr. Coolidge did not approve of the expenditure implied, I had to wait until I came into the White House. On August 13, 1929, I proposed to Governor Young of California that we appoint a joint commission to examine the engineering and economic phases of the project. The joint commission comprised Lieutenant Colonel Thomas M. Robins, Frank E. Bonner (Federal Power Commission), Dr. Elwood Mead (Director of Reclamation), and the following as Federal members and state representatives: George Pardee, William Durbrow, B. A. Etcheverry, Alfred Harrell, W. B.

Mathews, Judge Warren Olney, Jr., Frank E. Weymouth, B. B. Meek, and W. J. Carr.

At the time I stated to the press:

Some years ago I advocated the coordination of the multitude of activities, governmental and otherwise, engaged in direct and indirect control and development of California water supply and the provision of some definite policies instead of the haphazard and often conflicting action of different agencies. Governor Young has forwarded this idea by enactment of state legislation which now enables us to bring about a larger measure of such coordination. The first step is the creation of a commission to supervise an exhaustive investigation of the engineering facts and to determine the policies which should be pursued in the long-view development of the state, as to irrigation, flood control, navigation, and power.

The joint commission fifteen months later submitted its report, proposing a comprehensive basis for the development and conservation of the whole Central Valley. They recommended the work be undertaken under a joint commission representing Federal, state, and private agencies. The report exerted considerable influence in advancing the great project. In the meantime, I directed the Reclamation Service to undertake detailed engineering work on the necessary dams.

In 1932 the engineering work was sufficiently advanced to determine the location, feasibility, and much of the essential information for construction of the great dams on the Sacramento, the Kings, the San Joaquin, and the American River.[2]

The Tennessee River

The engineering work in preparation for the Cove Creek Dam was undertaken at my instructions in 1930. This dam, subsequently named the Norris Dam, was a major undertaking.

On March 3, 1931, I stated:

The Federal government should, as in the case of Boulder Canyon, construct Cove Creek Dam as a regulatory measure for the flood protection of the Tennessee Valley and the development of its water resources, but on the same bases as those imposed at Boulder Canyon—that is, that construction should be undertaken at such time as the proposed commission is able to

[2] It was a great satisfaction to me to visit these completed works some years later.

secure contracts for use of the increased water supply to power users or the lease of the power produced as a by-product from such a dam on terms that will return to the government interest upon its outlay with amortization. On this basis the Federal government will have cooperated to place the question in the hands of the people primarily concerned. They can lease as their wisdom dictates and for the industries that they deem best in their own interest. It would get a war relic out of politics and into the realm of service.

A storm blew up over the Wilson Dam and works, built as a war measure in 1918 at Muscle Shoals. On March 3, 1931, I stated that, together with the Governors of Alabama and Tennessee, I was appointing a joint commission to study the whole problem of the Tennessee drainage. On November 19 I announced that the commission had reported on the development. It also recommended a lease of the Muscle Shoals power and fertilizer plants to private operation under government regulations of rates and restrictions on the uses.

We were unable to get authority from the Democratic Congress then in power to proceed with Cove Creek Dam on the lines I recommended because Senator Norris and others wanted to turn it into a Federal power distribution and fertilizer scheme, to which piece of socialism I would not agree. I vetoed their bills for this reason.

The Mississippi System

Coming into the White House enabled me to realize many of my dreams as Secretary of Commerce. On December 3, 1929, I outlined to the Congress my views on a real trunk-line system of interior waterways with a uniform depth of nine feet. By systematic development of the Mississippi, Ohio, Missouri, Allegheny, Illinois, and Tennessee rivers and certain canals, we would create a north-south trunk waterway 1,500 miles long and, with various branches, an east-west trunk waterway of 1,600 miles. The network was to be connected with the North Atlantic by the Great Lakes and St. Lawrence System. Thus we would give water transport between such great cities as Chicago, St. Louis, Kansas City, Omaha, Louisville, Cincinnati, Pittsburgh, Memphis, Chattanooga, Minneapolis, St. Paul, and New Orleans. It would cost about $55,000,000 per annum for about five years.

The canalization of the Ohio to a depth of nine feet had been under construction for some years, and I dedicated its completion at Louisville, Kentucky, on October 23, 1929.

In order to secure efficient construction I had reorganized the Corps of Army Engineers into decentralized districts more nearly approximating the various river basins. Congress upon my recommendation authorized, in an act signed July 4, 1930, a large program of river and harbor works, and gave us authority to coordinate the systems into a general national plan.

In a public statement concerning this legislation, I said:

It was with particular satisfaction that I signed the Rivers and Harbors Bill . . . which I have advocated for over five years. . . .

We can now build the many remaining segments of a definite canalization of our river systems through which modern barge trains of 10,000 to 15,000 tons of burden can operate systematically through the Midwest and to the Gulf of Mexico, and through the Lakes to the Atlantic . . . we shall support the present commerce of the Great Lakes and make preparations for ocean shipping by the ultimate deepening of the St. Lawrence. It authorizes numerous improvements in our harbors.

It is a long-view plan for the future. It will require many years to complete its construction. I do not propose that we should proceed in a haphazard manner, but that we should approach the problem on sound engineering lines, completing the main trunk systems and gradually extending the work outward along the lateral rivers. . . .

. . . It will provide employment for thousands of men. It should be fruitful of decreased transportation charges on bulk goods, should bring great benefits to our farms and to our industries. It should result in a better distribution of population away from the congested centers.

As unemployment increased during the depression, increased appropriations were made available by the Congress and we were enabled to speed up the works.

In my report to the Congress of December 8, 1931, I said:

These improvements are now proceeding upon an unprecedented scale . . . during the current year over 380,000,000 cubic yards of material have been moved—an amount equal to the entire removal in the construction of the Panama Canal. The Mississippi waterway system . . . will be in full operation during 1933. Substantial progress is being made upon the projects of the upper Missouri, the upper Mississippi, and others.

Negotiations are now in progress with Canada for the construction of the St. Lawrence Waterway.

We practically completed the great flood control plan for the thousand miles below Cairo on the Mississippi River, with which I had been closely identified years before.[3]

In addition, we constructed the deep waterway between San Francisco Bay and Stockton and completed the flood control of the Sacramento. We deepened the lower Hudson so that ocean-going steamers could reach Albany. We extended the intercoastal canal system on a large scale and initiated systematic improvements on the Columbia, Tennessee and Cumberland rivers.

A total of over $700,000,000 was expended during my four years in river projects, advancing them further during my four years than in the thirty years preceding.

As the result of this work the annual inland water-borne traffic (outside the Great Lakes) increased in thirteen years from about 130,000,000 tons to more than 340,000,000 tons.[4]

The St. Lawrence Waterway

As already related, during my term as Secretary of Commerce I was Chairman of the St. Lawrence Waterway Commission. Jointly with Canada we had completed the economic studies preliminary to this important project, and most of the engineering studies.

When I entered the White House I was able to plane out the remaining engineering differences. At once I directed the State Department to begin negotiations for a treaty with Canada providing for the construction. These negotiations were most difficult because of the conflict between ourselves and Canada over the division of the electric power to be generated. Canada raised the question of the Chicago

---

[3] This system proved so sound and so substantial that when the unprecedented Ohio flood of 1937 poured into the Mississippi basin there was no loss of life or consequential loss of property.

[4] When World War II came on, our whole war transportation would have broken down if we had not had this completed waterway system.

Drainage Canal diverting water from the Lakes and thus diminishing her possibilities of electric power. We were agreed with Canada on the principle of compensations for this factor. The negotiation over the exact amount delayed the treaty and it was not until July 18, 1932, that all differences were planed out and a treaty signed. I made a public statement, saying in part:

The signing of the Great Lakes-St. Lawrence Waterway Treaty marks another step forward in this the greatest internal improvement yet undertaken on the North American continent. The treaty must yet be ratified by the legislative bodies of the two governments and is not effective unless this is done.

The treaty represents to me the redemption of a promise which I made to the people of the Midwest. It provides for the construction of a twenty-seven-foot waterway from the sea to all Canadian and American points on the Great Lakes. Such a depth will admit practically 90 per cent of ocean shipping of the world to our lake cities in the states of New York, Ohio, Michigan, Indiana, Illinois, Wisconsin, and Minnesota. Its influence in cheapening transportation of oversea goods will stretch widely into the interior from these points. Its completion will have a profoundly favorable effect upon the development of agriculture and industry throughout the Midwest. The large by-product of power will benefit the Northeast. These benefits are mutual with the great Dominion to the north.

The waterway will probably require ten years for completion, during which time normal growth of traffic in the nation will far more than compensate for any diversions from American railways and other American port facilities. The economic gains from improved transportation have always benefited the whole people. . . .

When the Senate assembled on December 6, 1932, I submitted the Treaty. It was shelved by my defeat in the election of 1932.[5]

Incidentally arising out of the work of the St. Lawrence Commission under my chairmanship were the measures for saving the scenic values of Niagara Falls. A great cave of rock in the center of the falls threatened to turn it into a rapids instead of that gorgeous cataract so sacred to all honeymooning couples. I had secured in 1926 the appointment of

[5] Mr. Roosevelt recommended the Treaty to Congress, but for some reason did not push it although he had a large majority of his party in both houses. Now, eighteen years later, this great resource lies dormant.

a joint American-Canadian Niagara Falls board, with Mr. Horace
McFarland as the American chairman. On coming to the White House
I initiated a treaty with Canada on the subject which we completed
on April 9, 1930. It provided for such joint conservation work as was
necessary to preserve the beauties of the Falls, and was approved by
the Senate.

CHAPTER 32

CONSERVATION

OIL RESERVES

I had served for some years as a member of the Federal Oil Conservation Board which had been appointed by President Coolidge to pick up the pieces after the Fall-Doheny-Sinclair scandals of the Harding administration. The Board had done good work but was not as vigorous as I thought it should be in conserving possible oil areas on public lands. These lands were then open to oil operators under a system of permits which had been greatly abused.

On March 12, 1929, eight days after coming into the White House, I announced there would be no leases or disposal of government oil lands, except those which might be mandatory by Congressional acts. In other words, there would be complete conservation of government oil in this administration.

On March 15 I amplified this statement, pointing out that 20,000 permits had been issued on public lands under which there had been no compliance with the law requiring active drilling, and they were held simply for speculation. Under my order, permits over hundreds of thousands of acres were canceled, and the rights were returned to the government.

Another question of oil conservation had been under investigation by the Oil Board. That was the overdrilling of new oil pools and consequent waste of gas pressure which, in turn, diminished the total production from a given pool. Under my direction Secretary Wilbur on June 10, 1929, called a meeting of the governors of oil states and executives of the leading oil companies at Colorado Springs. Mark Requa of California was chosen chairman of the meeting. Secretary

Wilbur laid before them a plan I had prepared (following the precedent of the Colorado River Compact) providing for an Interstate Compact by which each of the oil states would agree to set up regulation to repress excessive drilling and waste in collaboration with the others.

I sent a message to the conference, stating that there were only six oil-producing states of consequence. I insisted that the job would be done more effectively, and in a manner consonant with local responsibility, if the states undertook this service themselves. After several days of debate, the conference rejected my plan and recommended direct Federal control of production. The real objection to my proposal was the fact that it was a conservation measure, and not the production control and price-fixing measure that the oil companies really wanted. One of the stupidest actions of big business was this demand for collectivism by Federal action to pull themselves out of a hole of overproduction.

Secretary Wilbur and I nevertheless proceeded in two directions: (a) we secured state conservation legislation; (b) we secured conservation agreements among owners of larger oil pools where the government also held land.

In time the state legislatures of California, Wyoming, New Mexico, Oklahoma, and Kansas established state conservation controls. Each of them prorated and restrained production and volume of each oil well in new fields so as to conserve gas pressure.

Texas would not undertake these measures and great wastes were going on. On August 7, 1931, we issued a statement to the effect that all the great producing states except Texas had acted, saying:

> Except for the failure of the Texas authorities and legislature so far to cooperate by controlling their big new oil pool in east Texas, the whole oil situation would have been corrected months ago. The waste in total production of this pool will be enormous due to unlimited release of the gas.

The governor of Texas blew off much steam, but the state ultimately acted after I left the White House.

As to coordination in pools where there were government holdings, I stated, on March 13, 1931, in a review of progress, that Secretary

Wilbur had brought about a control of production from the newly discovered great oil pool at Kettleman Hills, California, a large part of which is the property of the Federal government. The result saved the California industry from the demoralization which would have been inevitable had this great pool been subject to the usual uncontrolled exploitation. Of more importance, under the old hit-and-miss drilling system the total yield of this enormous pool would have been greatly reduced.[1]

THE WESTERN RANGES

A conference of western governors was taking place in August, 1929. To get cattle and sheep range conservation on government lands under way and to deal generally with western conservation measures, I addressed a message to them on August 21 proposing a joint commission to study the problems of the public domain. I concluded:

... It is my desire to work out more constructive policies for conservation in our grazing lands, our water storage, and our mineral resources, at the same time check the growth of Federal bureaucracy, reduce Federal interference in affairs of essentially local interest, and thereby increase the opportunity of the states to govern themselves, and in all obtain better government.

The governors warmly approved such a joint commission, and, on October 18, 1929, I announced its members—representatives appointed by the governors, together with Federal and public members appointed by me, and including as chairman James R. Garfield, who had been Secretary of the Interior during Theodore Roosevelt's administration. Among the other members were George H. Lorimer, James P. Goodrich, Col. W. B. Greeley, Gardner Cowles, Perry W. Jenkins, Huntley N. Spaulding, E. C. Van Petten, Wallace Townsend, Francis C. Wilson, and Mary Roberts Rinehart.

[1] It is of interest to note that the Federal oil control wanted by the oil companies was adopted by the New Deal as part of the NRA and lasted eighteen months. The Supreme Court declared the law unconstitutional. Then, after this taste of collectivism, the same men who had led the opposition to my proposal at Colorado Springs themselves advanced the "Hoover principle" (by name), and it was almost unanimously supported by the industry—sitting in sackcloth and ashes. This was accomplished by the state governments and has served the nation well.

At the commission's initial meeting, I stated:

The purpose of the Commission is to study the whole question of the public domain particularly the unreserved lands. We have within it three outstanding problems:

First, there has been overgrazing throughout these lands, the value of the ranges having diminished as much as 80–90 per cent in some localities. The major disaster, however, is that destruction of the natural cover of the land imperils the water supply. The problem therefore in this sense is really a problem of water conservation.

Second, the question as to what is the best method of applying a reclamation service to the West in order to gain real and enlarged conservation of water resources.

Third, the Commission is to consider the questions of conservation of oil, coal, and other problems that arise in connection with the Domain.

The Garfield Commission made an exhaustive examination and published a report on September 29, 1931. The sum of its recommendations was:

That additional reserves from public lands should be set up, including all possible oil and coal lands, reclamation areas, forests, parks, bird refuges, and national defense areas;

That the remaining areas (i.e., grazing lands) should be granted to the states—the areas in those states which did not accept to be put under definite Federal administration in the Department of Agriculture.

The Commission pointed out the urgent need behind its recommendations—that the grazing lands were being ruined and should be regulated by the states themselves in conjunction with the "School lands," which years before had been granted to the states by the Federal government and were also largely leased for grazing purposes. Most of the states expressed their desire to undertake the task.

The necessary legislation was introduced and favorably reported by the House committee. It had to give way to depression legislation and never became a reality. The ventilation of the destruction of grazing areas, however, brought legislation later on, although it did not include state responsibility.

My recommendations to the western governors had also included that when water storage dams were completed the states should administer the irrigation projects and take all revenues except those from the sale of power. The major reason was that the states had the authority to create irrigation districts covering both private and public lands, with village participation in costs. Further, the states, through their local governments, could give better administration and get the Federal government out of the business except for water storage and the sale of electric power to existing agencies under proper regulation to protect the public. Most of the governors were favorable, but the Congressional committees were loath to give up their authority.

Also one of the reasons for these proposals was the necessity of relieving the farmers of an undue burden since they alone were carrying the major cost of reclamation as required under the Reclamation Act. A long series of Congressional relief bills, bankrupt farmers, and abandoned farms was ample proof of the need for change.

FORESTS

The major national forests already had been established by previous administrations. Our forest policies were direct and simple: to transfer to the national forests any remaining real forest lands among the public lands and to purchase additional areas. These policies were pushed vigorously by Secretary of Agriculture Arthur Hyde during my administration. The total acreage of the national forests was increased over 2,250,000 acres.

In order further to conserve this important resource, I directed on May 14, 1931, that all leasing of the Federal forests for new lumbering operations should cease for a while.

NATIONAL PARKS

Our policies for the parks were very direct: to create worth-while new parks and enlarge the existing ones by transfer from public lands and by purchase or gift.

Under Secretary Wilbur, we made extensions to sixteen of the national parks and monuments and created new parks and monuments at Bandelier and Carlsbad, New Mexico; Arches in Utah; Canyon de Chelly in Arizona; the Great Smokies in North Carolina and Ten-

nessee; Shenandoah Park, George Washington's Birthplace, and Colonial National Historical Park in Virginia; the Great Sand Dunes in
Colorado; and Death Valley in California. The area of parks and
monuments was extended by some 3,000,000 acres, or more than 40 per
cent, during our administration.

Under my predecessors the National Park Service, by its effective,
non-political administration, had won high favor with the public. For
many years Stephen Mather had given extraordinary service in building
up the parks for public use. Upon his death we placed his principal
assistant, Horace Albright, in charge. He maintained its high ideals and
expanded this service to the people.

CHAPTER 33

DEVELOPMENT OF AVIATION, RADIO,
AND MERCHANT MARINE

Another of the uncompleted tasks in government, which had been under my direction as Secretary of Commerce, was the development of commercial aviation. Owing to the nature of the contracts made by the preceding Postmaster General, the air transport industry was rapidly developing complete chaos as to the routes, character of planes, and public service rendered. Postmaster General New had his eye on mail transport alone. After Walter Brown became Postmaster General in 1929, I recommended to the Congress revision of the postal contracts and the aviation laws which would insure more order in the industry. I stated at the time that, when the mail contracts were let,

the commercial air transport industry was young and experimental. There was but little experience upon which to fix the rates in the contracts, or the routes which should be developed or the conditions which should be required to stimulate traffic or serve best in national defense.

Experience had proved that the early rates were excessive. Exorbitant profits had been made, some mail contracts running as high as $3 per mile. Great speculation in the securities of aviation companies had taken place in expectation of continuance of such bonanza rates. The conditions in the contracts had resulted in most companies' operating purely mail-carrying types of planes, with no great speed, and without adequate passenger and express accommodation. Some thirty companies had engaged in air traffic, and, in consequence, the long routes were served by a series of discontinuous flights. As a result of our recommendations to Congress I was able, on April 29, 1930, to approve the Watres Act which gave authority to revise generally the set-up.

In a conference with the Postmaster General, the Secretaries of Commerce, Navy, and War, I added to their expert knowledge some familiarity of my own with the problems. We laid out as a preliminary ideal four major east-west transcontinental lines and eight major north-south continental lines with certain secondary adjuncts. I instructed the Postmaster General to call a conference of the transport companies and to propose a revision of contracts (*a*) to reduce the exorbitant rates; (*b*) to require in new contracts the use of planes of passenger and express carrying capacity; and (*c*) to induce the consolidation of the operating concerns, so as to give continuous flights. We stated that alternatively we would let new contracts to other concerns, in such fashion as to give continuous transcontinental services, east to west and north to south.

Some years later Secretaries Wilbur and Hyde accurately pointed out the results, saying:

As a result of the amended law and the able administration of Postmaster General Brown, the rates were greatly reduced, the routes were consolidated into a carefully planned national system of commercial airways, the type of plane was entirely changed to passenger and express service, which promised to reduce greatly the volume of subsidy required. The speed, safety and reliability of planes were greatly enhanced. The nation was saved from a hodge-podge of airways similar to the tangle that had grown up in rail transportation and, above all, a great arm of national defense was created.

In the fiscal year ending June 30, 1929, before the act went into effect, commercial aviation companies had flown the mail 10,200,000 miles and the contractors had been paid $14,600,000, or $1.43 per mile. The air mail receipts were estimated at about $1,700,000, bringing the net cost to the government down to about $1.26 per mile.

In the fiscal year ending June 30, 1933, under the revised legislation, the contractors flew the mail 35,900,000 miles and were paid $19,400,000, or about 54 cents per mile. Due to the greatly improved service, however, airmail receipts increased to about $10,000,000, which resulted in a net cost to the government of about 26 cents per mile. The reduction in costs of transportation by the reform had been over 60 per cent on the gross cost per mile and about 80 per cent on the net cost per mile. Of equal importance, the subsidies had been so directed that the whole service was transformed into large passenger- and express-carrying planes, from which the revenues outside the government were growing steadily and with the growth of the air mail traffic bade fair soon to reduce the subsidies to the amount of the mail receipts. Passengers had increased from 165,200 in 1929 to 550,000 in 1933. The manufacturing capacity for planes had increased enormously, and furnished the largest capacity in case of war of any country in the world. The planes had so much improved in character and quality that the mail time between the two seaboards had been reduced from forty-eight hours to twenty-one hours. The number of people directly employed had increased from 15,000 to 35,000, every one of whom in some capacity was a highly trained reserve of personnel in time of war. In military values alone the government would have needed to expend five times the annual sum involved to build up the same organization that had been accomplished.[1]

PAN-AMERICAN AIR POLICIES

I have already recorded my discussions on aviation with South American officials during my journey to those countries when President-elect. These conversations furnished the foundation for the establishment of the Pan American Airways. We obtained the necessary support of the different governments and on March 15, 1930, the Postmaster General announced mail contracts for a new aviation service to South America, to include Cuba, Honduras, Nicaragua, Costa Rica, Panama, Colombia, Ecuador, and Peru, three times a week. This service saved, for instance, from six to nine days in mail transit to Peru.

On October 11, 1930, the first air mail to Brazil and Argentina carried a letter from me congratulating those governments on the early and happy result of our conversations prior to my inauguration. By October 9 of that year Uruguay had been added to the service.

---

[1] Ray L. Wilbur and A. M. Hyde, *The Hoover Policies,* Charles Scribner's Sons, 1937, p. 221. After I left the White House, the New Deal, bent on making an appearance by any method, honest or dishonest, that corruption or malfeasance marked my administration, picked upon the negotiations of Postmaster Brown which had brought about order in the aviation companies. They canceled all contracts, killed a number of Army airmen trying to fly the mails, and in the end had to restore the contracts to the same operators and, in several cases, pay heavy damages. They were unable to find an atom of corruption.

RADIO

Another task which I carried over from my post of Secretary of Commerce was radio. I have already outlined the development of government regulation under my direction. The regional division of the members of the Radio Commission proved unworkable, and on December 3, 1929, I so advised the Congress and the law was amended.

The maintenance of freedom in this age of radio waves, kilowatts, and chemical synthesis keeps the lovers of liberty fighting off those who would have government ownership and monopoly on the one hand, and preventing private enterprise from creating monopoly on the other. The price of liberty thus becomes not only a matter of eternal vigilance, but of a good Attorney General.

On May 13, 1930, following a thorough investigation, and after an unsuccessful attempt at solving the problem by moral suasion, the administration started legal action to dissolve the "radio manufacturing trust." Attorney General Mitchell had laid before me the methods employed by the major manufacturers of radio apparatus to control patents, manufacture, the use of radio apparatus, and even broadcasting. I suggested to Mr. Mitchell that we place former Judge Olney of California in charge of the case. I directed the Attorney General to let them have both barrels. It took Mr. Mitchell and Judge Olney a year, but within that time they made the concerns willing to accept a "consent" decree which, translated from legal terminology into plain English, was a complete admission of violation of law. Naturally I found some of these men, possibly for other reasons, publicly opposing my reelection in 1932.

MERCHANT MARINE

From long observation of the merchant marine while Secretary of Commerce, I knew when I came to the White House that the whole set-up of the government Shipping Board threatened public scandal because of its general inefficiency and wrongly based mail contracts, which subsidized secondary southern ports. The real vice was that Congress had used mail contracts as ship subsidies instead of frank and open subsidies directed toward the creation of a real merchant marine.

The previous administration of the Post Office had relied entirely upon the Shipping Board for advice on marine mail contracts. On June 1, 1929, I appointed an interdepartmental committee consisting of Postmaster General Brown, Secretary of Commerce Lamont, and Secretary of the Navy Adams, to report upon necessary reforms in ocean-mail contracts to be let in the future.

Six months later, I directed the Postmaster General to let no mail contracts unless approved by himself and the Secretary of Commerce, and unless they included provisions which assured new and modern ship construction instead of serving only to subsidize old ships from unprofitable ports.

In my first annual message on December 3, 1929, I recounted the appointment of this committee of investigation and stated in part:

In review of the mail contracts already awarded it was found that they aggregated twenty-five separate awards imposing a governmental obligation of a little over $12,000,000 per annum. Provision had been imposed in five of the contracts for construction of new vessels with which to replace and expand services. These requirements resulted in a total of twelve vessels in the ten-year period, aggregating 122,000 tons. The committee at this time is recommending the advertising of fourteen additional routes, making substantial requirements for the construction of new vessels during the life of each contract. A total of forty new vessels will be required under the contracts proposed, about half of which will be required to be built during the next three years. The capital cost of this new construction will be approximately $250,000,000, involving approximately 460,000 gross tons . . . it will be necessary to recommend an increase in the authorized expenditure by the Post Office of about $5,500,000 annually.

On several occasions actions by the Shipping Board gave rise to much public criticism. Although by special provisions in the Act I had no direct authority over the Board, I protested on June 6, 1930, at certain contracts they were about to enter into; and on July 9 I appointed Ira A. Campbell of New York chairman of a commission to investigate. As a result of their report, the contracts were substantially changed in favor of the government.

Using the great wastes of the Shipping Board as an argument, time and again I urged upon Congress its abolition and recommended that its administrative functions be placed under the control of the Secretary of Commerce.[2] The record shows that I made these recommendations December 3, 1929; December 8, 1931; February 17, 1932; April 1, 1932; December, 1932; and January, 1933.

But the southern senators were an immovable obstacle. They had made a trade. The Board maintained the unprofitable lines and the decrepit ships running from southern ports, and in return these senators stuck to the Board through thick and thin.

My action in directing the Postmaster General not to accept proposals of the Shipping Board for further mail contracts unless they meant new ships and honest contracts brought results. Aside from curing the southern port scandal, this action resulted in good ships. Whereas only 128,000 tons of efficient merchant ships had been built in the previous administrations, we built 254,000 tons in 1930, 386,000 tons in 1931, and 213,000 tons in 1932. Some 30,000 additional men were given jobs in the shipyards.[3] And a modern merchant marine was started—an economic and military necessity.

[2] Eighteen years later the Commission on Organization of the Executive Branch, under my chairmanship, renewed this recommendation, and at last it was carried out.

[3] That the new tonnage of American shipping under the New Deal fell to 66,000 in 1934 and 63,000 in 1935 is a fact which calls for no comment.

CHAPTER 34

PUBLIC BUILDINGS—SAN FRANCISCO BAY BRIDGE—HIGHWAYS

When I came to the Presidency we were far behind in the development of many vital public works (besides water development) which a growing country required.

That the housing of government agencies was entirely inadequate was indicated by several thousand buildings rented by the Federal government in all parts of the country, some of them even condemned by the local authorities as unsafe and unhealthful.

In the thirty years prior to my administration the government had spent a total of less than $250,000,000 on public buildings. To provide employment, to give more efficient housing to Federal agencies, and to beautify our cities, including the National Capital, we pushed building vigorously.

I was deeply interested in improving the city of Washington. Speaking on April 25, 1929, I said:

I am glad that the opportunity has come to me as President to contribute to impulse and leadership in the improvement of the National Capital. This is more than merely the making of a beautiful city. Washington is not only the Nation's capital, it is the symbol of America. By its dignity and architectural inspiration we stimulate pride in our country, we encourage that elevation of thought and character which comes from great architecture. . . .

It is our primary duty to do more than erect offices. We must fit that program into the traditions and the symbolism of the capital. Our forefathers had a great vision of the capital for America, unique from its birth in its inspired conception, flexibility, and wonderful beauty. No one in one hundred and fifty years has been able to improve upon it.

The founders of the Republic also gave us a great tradition in architecture. In after years we have held to it in some periods, and in others we have fallen sadly away from it. . . . I do hope to live to see the day when we shall remove from Washington the evidences of those falls from the high standards . . . [of] the founders of our Republic [and] that have been deplored by the citizens of good taste ever since. . . .

The program for the city envisaged a great departmental "triangle," the beautification of the city approaches by providing a system of parks on the Potomac River side from Great Falls to Mount Vernon, building the Arlington Memorial Bridge, and landscaping Capitol Hill from the Union Station southward. The constructions which either were completed or were started during my administration were the clearance of slum buildings around the Capitol area, a new Supreme Court building, additions to the House and Senate office buildings, an extension of the Library of Congress, and a new civic center for the Washington municipal government. In the great triangle of the buildings, the Departments of Commerce, Labor, Post Office, and Justice, the Interstate Commerce Commission and Archives were either wholly or largely completed. In addition we completed or started scores of buildings outside Washington.

As an indication of the expansion of our building program, I said in a progress statement in mid-term, November 4, 1931:

That portion of the Federal program of aid to unemployment comprised in the great expansion of public buildings under the Treasury Department shows the following progress since the report of September 1. There is a total of 817 projects which have so far been specifically authorized. . . .

A total of 131 buildings have been completed at a total cost of $41,934,-569. . . .

There were 270 buildings in construction at the first of November by contract, at an estimated cost of $229,772,700. . . .

There are 64 projects in which sites have been arranged, drawings are completed, for which construction contracts have been invited, of a total estimated cost of $19,970,500.

There are 240 projects in which sites have been selected, and on which plans are now under way of a total estimated cost of $141,947,923. . . .

It is estimated that the number of men now directly and indirectly em-

ployed on this program is 50,000. It is estimated by the Treasury Department
that the number that will be directly and indirectly employed on January 1st
is 100,000.

By the end of my administration 360 buildings of the national program had been completed and about 460 more were under contract,
or at an advanced stage of preparation, in some 400 towns and cities.
The total expenditures and obligations for buildings amounted to about
$700,000,000. The saving in rents and added efficiency of better de-
signed buildings alone justified this construction in addition to the
employment in construction they gave.

SAN FRANCISCO BAY BRIDGE

As Secretary of Commerce I had interested myself in the possibility
of a bridge across San Francisco Bay and had persuaded President
Harding to obtain a report upon the project by the Army Engineers.
Their report did not favor the Goat Island route but one much less
serviceable. The Navy had opposed any bridge on a usable spot as a
danger to fleet mobilization in time of war. I attempted to conciliate
the military and engineering conflicts; but my authority, without the
backing of the President, was insufficient. Also, opinion in the Bay
cities concerning the proper and feasible route was divided, and much
acrimonious debate was going on. At that time there seemed to be no
way of financing a project so ambitious as this.

Soon after assuming the Presidency, I announced the appointment
of a committee, jointly with Governor Young, to solve the problem
of locating the bridge and designing it. The joint commission comprised Mark L. Requa, chairman, George T. Cameron, Rear Admiral
L. E. Gregory, W. H. Stanley, General G. B. Pillsbury, Colonel E. L.
Daley, Arthur H. Breed, Charles D. Marx, and C. H. Purcell.

I instructed the Federal agencies to come to an understanding with
those of the state. They did. On August 12, 1930, I announced the
decision of the commission. Its report was the result of the first really
open-minded, comprehensive engineering survey for the project. It
recommended the Rincon Hill and Goat Island route, and the Navy
admitted it was high enough to do no harm to defense.

Meantime, the depression had arrived and to finance the bridge with local funds was impossible. I, however, had this project in mind among several others when I proposed that the powers of the Reconstruction Finance Corporation should include loans for reproductive public works, and I recommended the San Francisco Bridge as the type of public improvement which should be undertaken; I used it as an example of constructive remedy for unemployment. When this authority was granted in June, 1932, I suggested that San Francisco should send representatives to Washington to negotiate with the RFC. I advised both of them and the RFC and finally brought to successful conclusion the necessary loans of more than $75,000,000.

Thus, the greatest bridge in the world was built. Its tolls have repaid the RFC loan with interest.

HIGHWAYS

At the beginning of my administration there were more than 3,000,000 miles of roads, of which about 600,000 were state highway systems, the remainder being county and other local roads. Of the state highway system about 102,000 miles, and of the local roads about 8 per cent, were hard-surfaced.

Partly for employment, with the support of Congress, we increased Federal aid to the states from $105,000,000 per annum to over $260,-000,000. The number of men given work was increased from 110,000 to 280,000. The annual rate of construction of major modern highways was raised from 7,400 miles in 1929 to 16,000 miles in 1932. During my administration we increased the length of such highways by 37,000 miles, equal to one and one-half times around the world. We also greatly improved secondary highways and forest roads.

CHAPTER 35

DEVELOPMENT OF AGRICULTURE

Agriculture had been out of balance with the rest of the economic system for some years. The farmer was still overproducing ground crops from war-expanded acreage. The improvements in seed, in food animals, and in mechanization had been added to the large expansion inherited from the war. We were importing large quantities of food from countries of lower living standards.

The Republican platform of 1928 had promised increased agricultural tariffs, which are discussed in Chapter 41.

THE FEDERAL FARM BOARD

The Republican platform had also promised the creation of a Federal Farm Board with a large capital to aid agriculture and, particularly, to build up the cooperatives so as to decrease destructive competition between farmers.

I had called a session of Congress with the objective, among others, of making good on our promises. In my message of April 16, 1929, I said on this subject:

The difficulties of the agricultural industry arise out of a multitude of causes. A heavy indebtedness was inherited by the industry from the deflation processes of 1920. Disorderly and wasteful methods of marketing have developed. The growing specialization in the industry has for years been increasing the proportion of products that now leave the farm and, in consequence, prices have been unduly depressed by congested marketing at the harvest or by the occasional climatic surpluses. Railway rates have necessarily increased. There has been a growth of competition in the world markets from countries that enjoy cheaper labor or more nearly virgin soils. There was a great expansion of production from our marginal lands during the war, and, upon these, profitable enterprise under normal conditions cannot be maintained. Meanwhile their continued output tends to aggravate the situation. Local taxes have doubled and in some cases trebled. Work animals have been steadily replaced by mechanical appliances, thereby decreasing the consumption of farm products. There are many other contributing causes.

The general result has been that our agricultural industry has not kept pace in prosperity or standards of living with other lines of industry. . . .

Because agriculture is not one industry but a score of industries, we are confronted not with a single problem alone but a great number of problems. Therefore there is no single plan or principle that can be generally applied. Some of the forces working to the detriment of agriculture can be greatly mitigated by improving our waterway transportation; some of them by readjustment of the tariff; some by better understanding and adjustment of production needs; and some by improvement in the methods of marketing. . . .

The Government has a special mandate from the recent election . . . to extend systematic relief. . . .

I have long held that the multiplicity of causes of agricultural depression could only be met by the creation of a great instrumentality clothed with sufficient authority and resources to assist our farmers to meet these problems, each upon its own merits. . . .

No activities should be set in motion that will result in increasing the surplus production, as such will defeat any plans of relief.

The most progressive movement in all agriculture has been the upbuilding of the farmer's own marketing organizations, which now embrace nearly two million farmers in membership, and annually distribute nearly $2,500,-000,000 worth of farm products. These organizations have acquired experience in virtually every branch of their industry, and furnish a substantial basis upon which to build further organization. . . .

Senator McNary on April 20 proposed in the Senate the old McNary-Haugen price-fixing subsidy scheme as an amendment to this legislation. In a public memorandum of April 21 I analyzed it fore and aft, exposing its consequences. As the Democrats had advocated it in the campaign of 1928, they mostly voted for it and had the support of the Republican "Progressives." They carried it twice in the Senate, but the House killed it each time. After delays caused by this action, Congress passed the bill for the Farm Board which I signed in July, 1929. It provided $500,000,000 capital to the Board and granted it substantial authority.

I announced that I would canvass the several hundred farmers' organizations and the agricultural colleges to get their views: first, as to whether some outstanding businessman should be placed upon the Board; second, as to the persons whom those organizations favored for appointment to the Board as representatives of the major branches of agriculture. As a result of this canvass, carried out by Secretary of Agriculture Hyde, the farm organizations recommended that a businessman of wide experience be appointed chairman. On their recommendation I appointed to the chairmanship Alexander Legge of Chicago, president of the International Harvester Company, and selected the following from the names submitted in the canvass: James C. Stone, Kentucky, founder and former president of the Burley Tobacco Growers Cooperative Association; Carl Williams, Oklahoma, of the Farmers Cotton Cooperative Marketing Association; C. B. Denman, Missouri, of the National Live Stock Producers Association; Charles S. Wilson, New York, former professor of agriculture, Cornell University; William F. Schilling, Minnesota, of the National Dairy Association; former Governor Samuel McKelvie, Nebraska, publisher of the *Nebraska Farmer*; and C. C. Teague, California, of the California Fruit Growers Exchange.

Later on I describe the "over-all" reform which we proposed for the farmers. That was for the Farm Board to withdraw the excessive acreage of marginal lands which had been brought into cultivation during the war. I felt the farmer deserved the same treatment that had been extended to manufacturers in compensation for overexpansion.

The Farm Board was no more than under way when the Stock Exchange crash at the end of October, 1929, struck us, followed by the European financial panic of 1931. To solve these difficulties we turned the Board into a depression remedy. During that period we took many other steps in emergency aids to agriculture, discussed in the next volume of these memoirs.

CHAPTER 36

DEVELOPMENT OF BETTER HOMES

As Secretary of Commerce I had carried on varied activities bearing on better housing and rebuilding slums. I continued to carry on the private organization "Better Homes in America" while I was in the White House.

After coming to the Presidency I arranged a White House conference on the whole problem of housing. And again, as I did not believe in haphazard public conferences, I announced it fifteen months in advance and in the meantime appointed Secretary of Commerce Lamont as chairman of a program committee, with Dr. John M. Gries as executive secretary. Some years before, I had appointed Dr. Gries head of the then newly created Housing Division of the Department of Commerce. We requested twenty national associations and several mayors of large cities interested in housing to designate members of the program committee, which we divided into thirty groups for reports on the different segments of the problem. When the conference met, more than 400 experienced persons had already taken part in this nation-wide research and preparation of ideas. I met personally and frequently with different committees.

On December 2, 1931, I opened the conference of over a thousand delegates of governors and voluntary associations, saying:

You have come from every state in the Union. . . . Your purpose . . . is the long view. . . . Next to food and clothing the housing of a nation is its most vital social and economic problem. . . .

The conference also has before it that other great segment of housing; that is, the standards of tenement and apartment dwellings. . . . I hope we may subject the question of city housing to more definitely organized national intelligence . . . which will give impetus to public understanding and public action to . . . blighted areas and slums. . . .

While the purpose of this conference is to study and advise upon the very practical questions . . . every one of you here is impelled by the high ideal and aspiration that each family may pass their days in the home which they own; that they may nurture it as theirs; that it may be their castle in all that exquisite sentiment which it surrounds with the sweetness of family life. This aspiration penetrates the heart of our national well-being. It makes for happier married life, it makes for better children, it makes for confidence and security, it makes for courage to meet the battle of life, it makes for better citizenship. There can be no fear for a democracy or self-government or for liberty or freedom from homeowners no matter how humble they may be.

There is a wide distinction between homes and mere housing. Those immortal ballads "Home, Sweet Home," "My Old Kentucky Home," and the "Little Gray Home in the West" were not written about tenements or apartments. They are the expressions of racial longing which find outlet in the living poetry and songs of our people. They . . . are alive with the tender associations of childhood, the family life at the fireside, the free out of doors, the independence, the security, and the pride in possession of the family's own home—the very seat of its being.

. . . We know that as yet it is not universally possible to all. We know that many of our people must at all times live under other conditions. But they never sing songs about a pile of rent receipts. To own one's own home is a physical expression of individualism, of enterprise, of independence, and of the freedom of spirit. We do not in our imagination attach to a transitory place that expression about a man's home being his castle, no matter what its constitutional rights may be.

I then outlined the major problems involved and especially emphasized the problem of securing credit to build homes and clear slums. As to home building credits, I said:

It has long been my opinion that we have fairly creditably solved every other segment of our credit structure more effectively than we have solved that of housing.

· We have in normal times, through the savings banks, insurance companies, the building and loan associations, and others, provided abundant and mobile finance for 50 per cent of the cost of a home through the first mortgage.

But the definite problem is not presented by those who can find 50 per cent of the cost of a home. Our chief problem in finances relates to those who have an earnest desire for a home, who have a job and therefore possess sound character credit, but whose initial resources run to only 10 or 20 per cent. . . . We can make a home available for installment purchase on terms that dignify the name credit and not . . . the credit extended by a pawnbroker. . . . I recently made a public proposal for the creation of a system of mortgage discount banks.

The conference presented a definite program of national action, with exhaustive reports giving the reason for every recommendation and the facts behind it. It established new standards, new methods for community cooperation. It gave nation-wide and renewed interest in community action.

Its special studies entitled "Planning Residential Districts," "Slums and Decentralization," "Home Finance and Taxation," "Home Ownership," "House Design and Equipment," "Negro Housing," "Farm Housing," "Home Furnishing," "Housing Objectives" were sold by tens of thousands. These publications furnish today standards for individual, municipal, and state action over the whole Union.

Later in these memoirs I discuss more fully the creation of the Federal Home Loan Banking System and its purposes. I secured financial backing for slum clearance through the Reconstruction Finance Corporation by loans for such undertakings. To handle the problem efficiently, I arranged, on September 18, 1932, in conference with Chairman Pomerene of the RFC, to set up a committee of leading architects to consider and recommend plans for these activities. Such a double service to public health and welfare, and to employment, formed a part of my original RFC proposals of the year before, but action was delayed by Democratic leaders for over eight months.

I may add an observation on slum clearance. There is scarcely a city where, if the health and building laws were adequately enforced, a large part of the slums would not be empty of tenants. There is no provision in morals or freedom or the Constitution that building owners be allowed to collect income from the pollution of public health and morals in the name of private property.

CHAPTER 37

DEVELOPMENT OF CHILD WELFARE

While in the White House, I carried on the work of the American Child Health Association, which I had founded ten years before. I requested Secretary Wilbur to undertake its active Chairmanship, and I was elevated to Honorary Chairman. I continued to raise private funds for its support.

In order to further expand this activity I issued on July 2, 1929, a call for a national conference on health and protection of children. In accord with my policy of first determining the facts, and at the same time creating public understanding, I invited delegates from each state government, from the larger municipalities, and from the great voluntary associations concerned with the problem to form a preliminary committee. I appointed Secretary Wilbur to head this committee. I raised $500,000 from private sources to pay expenses generally and meet the cost of its publications.

Secretary Wilbur, on July 29, 1929, called a meeting of the preliminary committee which laid out a searching program and appointed special committees from over the country to report upon problems which ranged over every phase of child life. Fifteen months later, the research committees being ready, I called the full national conference for November 19, 1930.

In opening the conference of more than 1,200 delegates, appointed by the governors and mayors and the great voluntary associations, I said in part:

I am satisfied that . . . your conference here will result in . . . benefits which will be felt for a full generation.

The reward that accrues to you is the consciousness of something done unselfishly to lighten the burdens of children, to set their feet upon surer paths to health, well-being and happiness. For many years I have hoped for such a national consideration as this. . . .

I am mindful also of the unseen millions listening in their homes, who likewise are truly members of this conference, for these problems are theirs— it is their children whose welfare is involved, its helpful services are for them.

We approach all problems of childhood with affection. Theirs is the province of joy and good humor. They are the most wholesome part of the race, the sweetest, for they are fresher from the hands of God. Whimsical, ingenious, mischievous, we live a life of apprehension as to what their opinion may be of us; a life of defense against their terrifying energy; we put them to bed with a sense of relief and a lingering of devotion. We envy them the freshness of adventure and discovery of life; we mourn over the disappointments they will meet. . . .

The fundamental purpose of this conference is to set forth an understanding of those safeguards which will assure to them health in mind and body. . . . Our purpose here today is to consider and give our mite of help to strengthen mother's hand that her boy and girl may have a fair chance.

Let no one believe that these are questions which should not stir a nation; that they are below the dignity of statesmen or governments. If we could have but one generation of properly born, trained, educated, and healthy children, a thousand other problems of government would vanish. Moreover one good community nurse will save a dozen future policemen.

Our problem falls into three groups: first, the protection and stimulation of the normal child; second, aid to the physically defective and handicapped child; third, the problems of the delinquent child.

Statistics can well be used to give emphasis to our problem. One of your committees reports that out of 45,000,000 children—

35,000,000 are reasonably normal.	342,000 have impaired hearing.
6,000,000 are improperly nourished.	18,000 are totally deaf.
1,000,000 have defective speech.	300,000 are crippled.
1,000,000 have weak or damaged hearts.	50,000 are partially blind.
675,000 present behavior problems.	14,000 are wholly blind.
450,000 are mentally retarded.	200,000 are delinquent.
382,000 are tubercular.	500,000 are dependent.

I stated that, of the total of 10,000,000 deficients, probably 3,000,000 were not receiving the necessary attention, though our knowledge and experience showed that these deficiencies could be prevented and remedied. I continued:

But that we be not discouraged let us bear in mind that there are 35,000,000 reasonably normal, cheerful human electrons radiating joy and mischief and hope and faith. Their faces are turned toward the light—theirs is the life of great adventure. These are the vivid, romping, everyday children, our own and our neighbors' with all their strongly marked differences—and the more differences, the better. The more they charge us with their separate problems, the more we know they are vitally and humanly alive.

From what we know of foreign countries I am convinced that we have a right to assume that we have a larger proportion of happy, normal children than any other country in the world. And also, on the bright side, your reports show that we have 1,500,000 specially gifted children. There lies the future leadership of the nation if we devote ourselves to their guidance. . . .

There has not been before the summation of knowledge and experience such as lies before this conference. . . . It will rest with you to light the fires of that inspiration in the general public conscience, and from conscience lead it into action. . . .

The conference prepared a wealth of technical reports and recommendations on twoscore phases of the problem. These we subsequently published in separate volumes, copies of which we placed in the hands of every official, public and private, to whom they could be of use. In closing the conference, however, I felt that the reports, owing to their technical character, would not develop popular understanding or make that impression on the country at large which I sought as a support to official action. Therefore, jointly with Dr. Wilbur, I revised what I had some years before stated as the "Children's Charter" and secured its adoption by the conference. This document, which has been reprinted to the extent of several million copies and has had a wide influence, reads as follows:

I

For every child spiritual and moral training to help him to stand firm under the pressure of life.

II

For every child understanding and the guarding of his personality as his most precious right.

III

For every child a home and that love and security which a home provides; and for that child who must receive foster care, the nearest substitute for his own home.

IV

For every child full preparation for his birth, his mother receiving prenatal and postnatal care; and the establishment of such protective measures as will make childbearing safer.

V

For every child health protection from birth through adolescence including: periodical health examinations and, where needed, care of specialists and hospital treatment; regular dental examinations and care of the teeth; protective and preventive measures against communicable diseases; the insuring of pure food, pure milk, and pure water.

VI

For every child from birth, through adolescence, promotion of health, including health instruction and a health program, wholesome physical and mental recreation, with teachers and leaders adequately trained.

VII

For every child a dwelling place safe, sanitary, and wholesome, with reasonable provisions for privacy, free from conditions which tend to thwart his development; and a home environment harmonious and enriching.

VIII

For every child a school which is safe from hazards, sanitary, properly equipped, lighted, and ventilated. For younger children nursery schools and kindergartens to supplement home care.

IX

For every child a community which recognizes and plans for his needs, protects him against physical dangers, moral hazards, and disease; provides him with safe and wholesome places for play and recreation; and makes provision for his cultural and social needs.

X

For every child an education which, through the discovery and development of his individual abilities, prepares him for life; and through training and vocational guidance prepares him for a living which will yield him the maximum of satisfaction.

XI

For every child such teaching and training as will prepare him for successful parenthood, homemaking, and the rights of citizenship; and, for parents, supplementary training to fit them to deal wisely with the problems of parenthood.

XII

For every child education for safety and protection against accidents to which modern conditions subject him—those to which he is directly exposed and those which, through loss or maiming of his parents, affect him indirectly.

XIII

For every child who is blind, deaf, crippled, or otherwise physically handicapped, and for the child who is mentally handicaped, such measures as will early discover and diagnose his handicap, provide care and treatment, and so train him that he may become an asset to society rather than a liability. Expenses of these services should be borne publicly where they cannot be privately met.

XIV

For every child who is in conflict with society the right to be dealt with intelligently as society's charge, not society's outcast; with the home, the school, the church, the court, and the institution when needed, shaped to return him whenever possible to the normal stream of life.

XV

For every child the right to grow up in a family with an adequate standard of living and the security of a stable income as the surest safeguard against social handicaps.

XVI

For every child protection against labor that stunts growth either physical or mental, that limits education, that deprives children of the right to comradeship, of play, and of joy.

XVII

For every rural child a satisfactory schooling and health services as for the city child, and an extension to rural families of social, recreational, and cultural facilities.

XVIII

To supplement the home and the school in the training of youth, and to return to them those interests of which modern life tends to cheat children, every stimulation and encouragement should be given to the extension and development of the voluntary youth organizations.

XIX

To make everywhere available these minimum protections of the health and welfare of children, there should be a district, county, or community organization for health, education, and welfare, with full-time officials, coordinating with a state-wide program which will be responsive to a nation-wide service of general information, statistics, and scientific research. This should include: (a) trained full-time public health officials, with public health nurses, sanitary inspection and laboratory workers; (b) available hospital beds; (c) full-time public welfare service for the relief, aid, and guidance of children in special need due to poverty, misfortune, or behavior difficulties, and for the protection of children from abuse, neglect, exploitation, or moral hazard.

FOR EVERY CHILD THESE RIGHTS, REGARDLESS OF RACE, OR COLOR, OR SITUATION, WHEREVER HE MAY LIVE UNDER THE PROTECTION OF THE AMERICAN FLAG.

The work for protection of children did not end with the conference. A permanent staff of the conference was set up. Steadily we stimulated public opinion for continued and concrete action. State child protection conferences of the national delegates and others were held in twenty states, under the patronage of the governors. A large amount of state and municipal action flowed steadily from the movement. Scores of states and municipalities improved their laws and ordinances.

In order to stimulate this work, I increased the appropriations for the Children's and Women's bureaus in the Department of Labor every year despite the falling revenues.

One of the delegates to the conference was Mr. W. K. Kellogg of Battle Creek, Michigan. He later informed me that it was this conference that inspired him to create the great W. K. Kellogg Child Welfare Foundation.

From the conference conclusions and our experience in the Mississippi flood (Chapter 18), I was particularly desirous of providing Federal grants to the states and the states to the counties, conditional upon similar grants from the state governments for the purpose of building up rural health agencies for children.

I strongly urged such aid to the session of Congress of December, 1929, and again in December, 1930. At this session, Secretary Wilbur and I drafted a bill for the committees. The measure passed the House but was killed in a filibuster organized by Democratic Senator Elmer Thomas of Oklahoma. I returned to the subject in the session of December, 1931; but this time the Congress was Democratic, and the committees refused even to report out the bill.

In a message to Congress on February 29, 1932, I recommended legislation in respect to the many juveniles charged with violation of law who fall into the custody of Federal authorities. I asked for authority to the Attorney General to forgo prosecution of children in the Federal courts and to return them to state authorities to be dealt with by juvenile courts and other state agencies equipped to deal with such delinquents. We secured the passage of this legislation.

On September 29, 1932, in an address to the *New York Herald Tribune*'s Woman's Conference on Current Problems, I gave a review of the results, saying: "In this depression as never before the American people have responded with a high sense of responsibility to safeguard and protect the children." [1]

[1] The subject of depression relief for children is discussed later in these memoirs, but I may note here that our system of local responsibility and administration of relief, with especial emphasis upon the needs of children, resulted in even more and better care of children than in normal years. The statistics of infant mortality indicate this accomplishment.

1928	6,880 deaths per 100,000	1931	6,170 deaths per 100,000
1929	6,730 deaths per 100,000	1932	5,760 deaths per 100,000
1930	6,460 deaths per 100,000		

The Roosevelt administration, having a majority of its own party in both houses, was able to get legislation for Federal aid for the health and protection of children. No one will say that our years of public agitation for these policies did not greatly contribute to bring this about. I rejoiced at their action.

CHAPTER 38

REFORM IN LAW ENFORCEMENT

In my Inaugural Address on March 4, 1929, I said:

The most malign of all these dangers today is disregard and disobedience of law. Crime is increasing. Confidence in rigid and speedy justice is decreasing. I am not prepared to believe that this indicates any decay in the moral fiber of the American people. I am not prepared to believe that it indicates an impotence of the Federal government to enforce the laws. . . .

But the system which its officers are called upon to administer is in many respects ill adapted to present-day conditions. Its intricate and involved rules of procedure have become the refuge of both big and little criminals. There is a belief abroad that, by invoking technicalities, subterfuge, and delay, the ends of justice may be thwarted by those who can pay the cost.

Reform, reorganization, and strengthening of our whole judicial and enforcement system, both in civil and criminal sides, have been advocated for years by statesmen, judges, and bar associations. First steps toward that end should not longer be delayed. Rigid and expeditious justice is the first safeguard of freedom, the basis of all ordered liberty, the vital force of progress.

It was to carry out my ideas of reform that I chose Mr. Mitchell as Attorney General. I have already stated his qualifications.

In the hope of interesting the press in the first requirement—change in public attitudes—I made an address to the American Newspaper Publishers Association on April 22, six weeks after entering the White House. I stated in detail the situation in the country and concluded:

The problem of law enforcement is not alone a function or business of government. If law can be upheld only by enforcement officers, then our scheme of government is at an end. Every citizen has a personal duty in it— the duty to order his own actions, to so weigh the effect of his example, that

his conduct shall be a positive force in his community with respect to the
law. . . .

It is unnecessary for me to argue the fact that the very essence of freedom
is obedience to law; that liberty itself has only one sure foundation, and that
is in the law.

The first thing to be done by way of general reform in law enforcement was to raise the standards of judges and prosecuting officers. No
other Attorney General had insisted as zealously upon quality and character on the bench as Mr. Mitchell. He was not only painstaking in
recommending the appointment of judges, but absolutely determined
to lift the quality of the bench beyond any preceding administration. I
overrode his recommendations only once—and that to my sorrow.

Earlier Presidents had considered impartial appointments to the
Supreme Court as a most sacred duty. Little of either politics or social
beliefs had entered into their appointments. Both Republican and
Democratic administrations had always maintained in the Court a
strong minority of their political opponents. Upon the death of Chief
Justice Taft, with the general approval of the country, I nominated
Charles E. Hughes for Chief Justice. Because of some old grudge,
Senator Borah opposed this appointment, but Hughes was confirmed
nevertheless.

For a second vacancy, on April 10, 1930, I nominated Judge John J.
Parker of the Federal Fourth Judicial Circuit. No member of the Court
at that time was from the southern states, and the regional distribution
of justices had always been regarded as of some importance. Parker
was regarded as a nominal Republican. He had been elected to the local
bench by Democratic support and, together with his service on the
Federal bench, he had served some twenty of his adult years as a
judge with great distinction. The Attorney General had studied more
than 125 of Parker's decisions and had found them of high legal com-
petence. The views of judges and lawyers were overwhelmingly favorable. Ten southern Democratic senators and seven Democratic governors urged his appointment. Trouble rose in the Senate over his confirmation. William Green, President of the American Federation of
Labor, denounced him for some decision which labor did not like,
although the Judge had simply followed previous Supreme Court deci-

sions. Their object was not so much to oppose Judge Parker as to publicize their objections to a particular law. He was also denounced by a Negro association upon the wholly fictitious statement that, when twenty-one years old, he had made some remark bearing on white supremacy in the South. Both lobbies threatened to take reprisals on senators who dared vote for him. Immediately a number of our Republican senators ran like white mice. I soon found that even with the ten Democratic senators who favored him I was one vote short of confirmation. I sent for Senators Deneen and Glenn, men of eminence in the legal profession, and for Senator Vandenberg, who had often spoken about the sacredness of the bench from group pressures. They refused to support Judge Parker on the ground that to vote for him would raise opposition to their reelection. I was beaten. No senator who supported me lost his election on this account. Most of those who ran out were subsequently defeated. This failure of my party to support me greatly lowered the prestige of my administration. I nominated Owen J. Roberts of Philadelphia, and he was confirmed.

On February 15, 1932, when a third vacancy occurred, I nominated Chief Justice Benjamin N. Cardozo of the New York Court of Appeals, a Democrat. The appointment met with Senate approval.

APPOINTMENTS TO THE BENCH, AND THE SENATORS

Appointments of district and circuit judges, district attorneys and marshals offer a special problem in political pressures to all Presidents. As the Senate must confirm these officials, the senators over the years had assumed that they could make unofficial nominations. If the President did not accept their views, then, because of the common interest among senators, anyone not of their selection stood little chance of securing confirmation. With this club the judicial appointments below the Supreme Court had become practically a perquisite of the senators. And conversely the custom of the President asking the senators for suggestions as to such appointments had become a basis of amity.

All this led to some intolerable situations. Senator Vare of Pennsylvania and Senator Schall of Minnesota, for instance, proposed to me certain men who were wholly unfitted for the bench. Those senators refused my alternative selections and held up confirmations for years, thus leaving the bench short of judges. I never did appoint their men. The fact that only a minority of senators were of this class was all that had hitherto saved the bench.

The Attorney General and I finally evolved a method which avoided most of these conflicts. Mr. Mitchell was usually apprised in advance when a vacancy was coming. He then canvassed the situation for proper material. As soon as the event occurred, and before the senator involved was put on the spot by local politicians and others, we submitted to him a small list of men whom we could approve. The senator could thereupon take credit both with the appointee and with the appointee's friends for his support. In most cases this smoothed out opposition and restored the President's authority.

In the general clean-up of the Department of Justice, upon recommendation of the Attorney General, I retired eighteen district attorneys and two Federal judges—the latter accepting resignation as the alternative to impeachment.

The problems of law enforcement required much legislation for their solution. I stated the general needs in this field in my first message to the Congress on December 3, 1929, again in my second message of December 2, 1930, and in my third message on December 8, 1931. I give our detailed proposals under various headings.

REFORMS IN JUDICIAL PROCEDURE

Mr. Mitchell developed the precise legislative reforms needed on judicial procedure and laid them before the Congressional committees. The economic problems of the depression so engrossed Congress that progress was slow. However, on February 29, 1932, it seemed possible to advance our legislative program, and I sent an urgent message to the Congress upon this subject, with a mass of data and specific recommendations. They were of highly technical character, covering relief of congestion in the courts, changes in procedure, in indictments, in appeals, treatment of juvenile offenders and jurisdiction of the courts.

On June 29, 1932, I signed the enactments carrying out our reforms of procedure in criminal cases. On February 24, 1933, the Congress passed further legislation which had been drafted by the Attorney General.

Upon the importance of this measure, Mr. Mitchell wrote to me:

This is the most important measure directed at the reform of criminal procedure in the Federal courts that has been enacted for many years. . . . Convicted persons supplied with ample funds and resourceful lawyers have been able to delay final judgment and the commencement of their sentences from one to four years after juries have returned verdicts of guilty. There have been innumerable instances of this kind. . . . This bill, which allows the Supreme Court of the United States to regulate all these proceedings, opens the way to throwing overboard the entire system of proceedings in Federal criminal cases after verdicts of guilty and to substitute new rules which will compel speedy disposition of these cases. . . .

One class of cases in which these abuses have been greatest is that including prosecutions for use of the mails to defraud. We have had many instances where thousands of persons have been defrauded out of their savings and robbed of vast sums by unscrupulous operators in worthless securities and where the malefactors, finally convicted by juries in Federal courts of using the mails to defraud, have gone at large on bail for years before their cases were finally disposed of in the intermediate courts of appeals. . . .

We have here the means of putting an end to practices after verdicts of guilty which have tended to make people lose confidence in the administration of criminal law.

REFORM OF THE BANKRUPTCY LAWS

Reform in the bankruptcy laws was equally urgent. It was not alone a problem in fraud and crime; it had the widest economic importance.

The Constitution itself recognized its national importance by making supervision of bankruptcy a Federal function. On July 29, 1930, I directed the Departments of Justice and Commerce to make a joint investigation of the whole subject.

The social desirability was to keep every honest, producing unit operating whether individual or corporate. Often enough in ordinary times bankruptcy is the result of bad management, and dispossession is a necessity if the unit is to be kept producing. But with the depression thousands of cases of competent management were submerged in unsupportable debt. The operation of the bankruptcy laws gave very little opportunity to save those who were efficient or interested in making a fight for recovery. Dispossession was indeed a doubly bitter experience during the depression. Business failures from the pressures of the times affected a host of farms and homes through no fault of their own.

Our reforms provided for (a) elimination of fraud in bankruptcy practice; (b) conciliation and adjustment of debt with the aid of the courts; (c) protection during the period of negotiation; (d) creation of a system of conciliators under the courts for farmers, home owners, and small debtors; (e) provision against speculators buying up debt in order to seize property; (f) provision for a two-thirds rule to bind security holders in corporations under protection of the courts—the latter to safeguard against the current hold-ups by minorities and a forced sale of property, usually to speculators.

In December, 1931, I urged these reforms on the Congress, and on February 27, 1932, I transmitted an exhaustive report with recommendations and with draft legislation for consideration by the committees of Congress. I said:

The Federal Government is charged under the Constitution with the responsibility of providing the country with an adequate system for the administration of bankrupt estates. . . . The number of cases in bankruptcy has steadily increased from 23,000 in the fiscal year 1921 to 53,000 in 1928 and to 65,000 in 1931. The liabilities involved have increased from $171,000,000 in 1921 to $830,000,000 in 1928 [before the depression] and to $1,008,000,000 in 1931, and the losses to creditors have increased from $144,000,000 in 1921 to $740,000,000 in 1928 and to $911,000,000 in 1931. The increases are therefore obviously not due to the economic situation, but to deeper causes.

A sound bankruptcy system should operate, first, to relieve honest but unfortunate debtors of an overwhelming burden of debt; second, to effect a prompt and economical liquidation and distribution of insolvent estates; and, third, to discourage fraud and needless waste of assets by withholding relief from debtors in proper cases. . . .

After describing the exhaustive methods of investigation from court records, experience of foreign countries, and with opinions of judges and students, I urged immediate action. On account of Democratic opposition, we did not succeed in getting the bill further than committees in the winter session of 1931–1932.

I returned to the charge, however, on January 11, 1933, in a special message to Congress. The House passed a bill, but it was held up in the

Senate. I addressed yet another message to Congress on February 20, in which I again urged its passage.

To my great surprise the Senate passed the bill on March 3, the day I went out of office. But the Senate excluded the provisions for general corporate reorganization while retaining the provision for individual adjustment and railway reorganization.[1] The year before, I had canvassed many leading insurance and mortgage companies and received assurance that if such a bill were passed they would immediately undertake cooperation with their home and farm debtors for wide-scale and rapid readjustments. Had the unamended bill become law the year before, it would have alleviated a great deal of hardship by readjusting the oppressive debts of farm and home owners due to the depression. It would have offered a method for readjustment of impossible railroad and other corporate debt structure. It would have eliminated much of the waste and fraud permissible under the old bankruptcy processes. It would have kept thousands of concerns out of bankruptcy, and prevented much of that destruction of public confidence when business houses are closing and home owners are being dispossessed. And the hundreds of thousands of readjustments made possible for small businessmen, farmers, and others would have conferred lasting values on the country.

REORGANIZATION OF THE FEDERAL BUREAU OF INVESTIGATION

I have mentioned that I had been somewhat responsible for the appointment of J. Edgar Hoover to head the Federal Bureau of Investigation through my recommendation to Attorney General Stone. J. Edgar Hoover was a lawyer of uncommon ability and character. He served throughout my administration and assisted greatly in building up the Bureau. We secured legislation which steadily strengthened that agency with a personnel of legally trained men and set in motion more scientific crime detection. Among these actions we established the division of fingerprint and other methods of identification and information. The Bureau became a national clearinghouse for state and local peace officers.

[1] These provisions were restored early in the Roosevelt administration.

LINDBERGH KIDNAPING LAW

A wave of kidnaping for ransom had swept over the country. Organized gangs, employing automobiles to move quickly into other states, made suppression by local authorities almost impossible. The kidnaping and murder of the Lindbergh baby in March, 1932, brought public recognition of the necessity for Federal action. I was able to secure vigorous authority from Congress in the following June and July by two acts allowing the Federal government to pursue and prosecute when the kidnapers crossed state lines. The efficiency and courage of the F.B.I. under J. Edgar Hoover finally stamped out this particular crime wave. The fears in the hearts of millions of mothers were lifted.

PRISON REFORM

A part of the improvement in criminal procedure was prison reform. As a start I appointed Sanford Bates Director of Prisons. He had made a distinguished reputation by his reform of the Massachusetts penal system. In my Congressional message of December 3, 1929, I said:

> Closely related to crime conditions is the administration of the Federal prison system. Our Federal penal institutions are overcrowded, and this condition is daily becoming worse. The parole and probation systems are inadequate. These conditions make it impossible to perform the work of personal reconstruction of prisoners so as to prepare them for return to the duties of citizenship. . . .
>
> We need some new Federal prisons and a reorganization of our probation and parole systems; and there should be established in the Department of Justice a Bureau of Prisons, with a sufficient force to deal adequately with the growing activities of our prison institutions. Authorization for the improvements should be given speedily, with initial appropriations to allow the construction of the new institutions to be undertaken at once.

On April 28, 1930, I sent a further message to the Congress:

> There must be extension of Federal prisons with a more adequate parole system and other modern treatment of prisoners. We have already 11,985 prisoners in Federal establishments built for 6,946. The number of Federal prisoners in Federal and state institutions increased 6,277 in the nine months

from June 30, 1929, to April 1, 1930. . . . The overcrowding of the prisons themselves is inhumane and accentuates criminal tendencies.

On May 13, 1930, I signed the first of a series of acts which we had drafted for the committees of Congress covering the Federal prison reforms. These acts provided (1) the creation of a Bureau of Federal Prisons in the Department of Justice, under a director appointed by the Attorney General with complete authority over all United States prisons and prisoners; (2) a National Board of Parole; (3) medical services in all prisons were placed under the Public Health Service; (4) the establishment of a boys' reformatory; (5) special reformatory prisons for women; (6) establishment of a separate prison for vicious offenders; (7) a declaration of policy of classification and segregation of prisoners according to character, offense, etc.; (8) provision for instruction and industrial employment in prisons, the latter to be of noncompetitive type; (9) the creation of temporary camps for prisoners engaged in outside government projects, with reduction in sentences for faithful work; and (10) establishment of a probation system in the United States courts with probation officers under the direction of the Department of Justice.

No such extensive or enlightened reform in dealing with criminals had been accomplished heretofore in the entire history of the Federal government.

Under these authorities and some improving amendments, we constructed reformatories to separate juveniles and the less vicious from hardened criminals. We divided adult prisoners into two classes which we assigned to different prisons—on the one hand, those whose character gave hope of reform and parole and, on the other, the hardened impossibles. Alcatraz Island was selected for the latter, although its occupation was not completed until the succeeding administration.

PROHIBITION

Prohibition cast a cloud over all our problems of law enforcement and was generally a constant worry. I should have been glad to have humanity forget all about strong alcoholic drinks. They are moral, physical, and economic curses to the race. But in the present stage of human progress, this vehicle of joy could not be generally suppressed by Federal law.

The first hard practical fault was in the concept of enforcement. The Federal law assumed that state and local officials would look after violations within the state, and that the Federal government would simply stop the interstate traffic. During the nine years of the law prior to my administration, the officials of the states most clamorous for national prohibition, including Iowa, Kansas, Ohio, Indiana, Alabama, and Georgia, steadily abandoned their responsibilities and loaded them upon the Federal government. Practically nowhere in the country did the local police forces even take notice of violations, except as a basis of graft. The Federal government could not have come anywhere near enforcement with a police force of fewer than 250,000 men. In the meantime, the bootleg business had grown to such dimensions as to be able to corrupt or mislead the Federal enforcement officers all over the country.

However, under my oath of office, the very core of the Presidency was enforcement of the laws. I therefore gave prohibition enforcement the utmost organization that the Federal government could summon. We secured legislative authority to reorganize, consolidate, and greatly expand the Federal agencies. Under Mrs. Mabel Walker Willebrandt's direction we certainly locked up or otherwise punished a horde of bootleggers. During my four years we increased the number of bootlegging citizens resident in Federal jails, or on parole, from an average of about 22,000 to about 53,000. These did not include the vast number of cases resulting in fines, padlockings, confiscations, and other suppression devices. The number of prohibition convictions rose to about 80,000 in 1932, and finally demonstrated the futility of the whole business.

However, prohibition was not the only law to be enforced. This was indicated by the steady increase of Federal convictions for other crimes from 9,600 in 1929 to 13,800 in 1932.

One of the notable triumphs in law enforcement was the conviction of Al Capone. This action represented much more than just sending a gangster to jail. In March, 1929, a committee of prominent Chicago citizens, under the leadership of Walter Strong, the publisher of the *Daily News,* and Judge Frank Loesch, president of the Chicago Crime

Commission, called upon me to reveal the situation in that city. They gave chapter and verse for their statement that Chicago was in the hands of the gangsters, that the police and magistrates were completely under their control, that the governor of the state was futile, that the Federal government was the only force by which the city's ability to govern itself could be restored. At once I directed that all the Federal agencies concentrate upon Mr. Capone and his allies. Our authority was limited to violations of income-tax and prohibition laws. It was ironic that a man guilty of inciting hundreds of murders, in some of which he took a personal hand, had to be punished merely for failure to pay taxes on the money he had made by murder. The Attorney General set up a special Deputy Attorney General and equipped him with the best men from every bureau of investigation in the government. It required two years to assemble the evidence and conduct the trials, but in the end we restored the freedom of Chicago.

In the subsequent Presidential campaign Vice President Curtis informed me he had been approached by an important lawyer who said he was in a position to deliver the bootleg vote in the large cities if I would agree to pardon Capone. I asked the Vice President what answer he made. He said: "I told him he really could think up a better joke than that."

THE WICKERSHAM COMMISSION

On May 28, 1929, I announced the appointment of a commission to investigate and recommend action upon the whole crime and prohibition question, under the chairmanship of former Attorney General George W. Wickersham.

The commission, in addition to Mr. Wickersham, consisted of former Secretary of War Newton D. Baker, United States Circuit Judge William S. Kenyon, United States District Judges Paul McCormick and William Grubb, former Chief Justice Kenneth Mackintosh of the Washington (State) Supreme Court, Dean Roscoe Pound of Harvard, Dr. Ada Comstock, President of Radcliffe College, and Messrs. Henry Anderson, Monte Lemann, and Frank Loesch. Rarely has a more impressive or open-minded commission been appointed.

This body made an exhaustive investigation of every phase of the problem. On the Prohibition Amendment it was mentally divided, and the recommendations were conflicting. On January 20, 1931, the commission brought in a preliminary report opposing repeal of the Amendment—and then made a long report demonstrating the futility of the law. Therefore, its investigations failed to prove of any great use so far as prohibition was concerned, although it made recommendations for other legal reforms that were of lasting value. My personal difficulty was something that did not appear upon the surface.

Former Secretary of State Elihu Root had once been my guest at the White House; and I had used the opportunity to describe the tremendous difficulty of this problem and seek his advice as to whether I should not at once recommend repeal. Without trying to quote his exact language, my note of the time indicates that his reply was as follows:

This amendment should never have been put in the Constitution. But it is there. You are under the most sacred of all oaths to uphold the Constitution. The Constitution does not contemplate any relation of the President to its amendment. You can veto any other form of legislative action but you do not have that power in relation to Constitutional amendments. That distinction was made for the definite purpose of holding alterations of the Constitution away from the President, who is solely an enforcement officer in this relation. Furthermore, this law expresses itself in criminal proceedings. If you were to recommend repeal you would be nullifying the Constitution because from that day no jury and no judge would convict. You must not do that. Your sacred duty is to enforce the law with every power you can exert. Daily the futility will become more evident, and the people will demand its repeal.

The Wickersham Commission had experienced this same difficulty. The nullification problem accounts partly for their indirect damnation of the law and, at the same time, their recommendation against repeal. There can be no doubt that the prohibition law brought economic benefits, but those benefits were more than offset by the spirit of corruption and defiance of law. Until about the winter of 1932, I was convinced that major public opinion was in favor of retaining the Amendment; but, as is often the case in American attitudes toward long contentious issues and impractical reforms, the country suddenly jelled against it. The whole question loomed up large in the 1932 Presidential campaign, in which relation I deal with the subject in the next volume.

CHAPTER 39

REFORMS IN THE EXECUTIVE BRANCH

Immediately upon entering the White House, I attacked the rotten Republican patronage system in the southern states. I set up independent committees of leading citizens in most of these states to make all recommendations for appointments, saying publicly: "Such conditions are intolerable to public service, are repugnant to the ideals and purposes of the Republican party, are unjust to the people of the South and must be ended." I placed a definite responsibility on the Department of Justice to investigate every suspicion of a Federal employee. Several were removed from office.[1]

I was convinced that efficient, honest administration of the vast machine of the Federal government would appeal to all citizens. I have since learned that efficient government does not interest the people so much as dramatics. Holding to this conviction, I was a strong sup-

---

[1] We must have been pretty honest, for the Roosevelt administration created a special section in the Department of Justice under a special prosecutor and a large staff to rake the highways and byways for some crookedness of ours which they could hold up to public opprobrium. Although we had spent some $16,000,000,000 in four years, they ultimately gave up the task as futile. At one moment they believed they had laid hold of a gigantic scandal. The law prescribes that no Cabinet or other officer may be interested as a stockholder or otherwise in any concern doing business with his specific branch of the government. The muckrakers had developed that a Charles F. Adams was a stockholder in ten concerns doing business with the Navy. I had word that this "scandal" was going to be exposed amidst loud thunder by the Democratic member of the House committee concerned—in ten sequent segments lasting ten consecutive days so as to make the act most impressive. I called the former Secretary of the Navy on the telephone and asked him what it was all about. He promptly replied that this stockholder was another Charles F. Adams, no relative of his. We decided to let them spring the first day's attack. Thereupon Secretary Adams hit them a humiliating blow by telling the fact. The nine other exposures were canceled.

porter of the Civil Service. I started off on August 11, 1928, with the statement:

Our Civil Service has proved a great national boon. Appointive office, North, South, East, and West, must be based solely on merit, character, and reputation in the community in which the appointee is to serve, as it is essential for the proper performance of their duties that officials shall enjoy the confidence and respect of the people whom they serve.

Congress for years had failed to meet the recommendations of one President after another to place first-, second-, and third-class post-masters and Internal Revenue collectors within the merit system of the Civil Service Commission. These Federal appointments were the only large groups outside the merit system. They had been universally used for Congressional patronage. I had some power, however, in that I could refuse to submit appointments to the Senate unless I was satisfied with the merit of the applicants. President Harding had installed an imperfect system of examination of postmasters. I took the animal by the horns and issued an order on May 1, 1929, stating that all candidates for these appointments must pass a Civil Service merit examination before I would recommend them to the Senate.

In addition I extended the area of the merit system by executive orders of July 8 and November 18, 1930, bringing other small groups under these requirements. At the close of my administration, 81 per cent of the Federal employees were directly included in the merit system; and with my device requiring the "certification" of postmasters by the Civil Service Commission in effect I had brought the total up to 95 per cent. The remaining Federal officeholders were mostly policy-making officials and transient employees. After fifty years of struggle by disciples of good government, the principle of selection on a basis of merit was made effective.[2]

[2] The merit system of selection was excluded by actual provisions in the law from many New Deal agencies and abolished in some others. At one time under the New Deal the proportion of government employees under merit selection decreased to 57 per cent. Andrew Jackson's "invisible presence" was on the spot in more than one way.

Despite our need to create such emergency agencies as the RFC, Unemployment and Agricultural relief, we succeeded in decreasing the number of government employ-ees in other departments so that while the Civil Service Commission reported 573,000 civilian employees at the end of the Coolidge administration, there were 565,000, or 8,000 fewer, at the end of mine. There were more than 1,000,000 in 1939.

COMMISSIONS AND COMMITTEES

There was a great deal of clatter from the Democrats about the "committees and commissions" with which I was supposed to have deluged the country. As to this "dreadful plague," I seem to have been fairly moderate. Such bodies are of two kinds: those set up at government expense, and those informal groups of experienced, public-spirited citizens called by the President to advise him on special questions, who pay their own expenses. I created thirty-eight such committees, of which only seven received any appropriations, and four were permanent. Theodore Roosevelt, Woodrow Wilson, and Calvin Coolidge all showed a far larger score in their first four years.

Like some of my predecessors, I can claim to be a much misunderstood man on this question of committees and commissions. There is no more dangerous citizen than the person with a gift of gab, a crusading complex and a determination "to pass a law" as the antidote for all human ills. The most effective diversion of such an individual to constructive action and the greatest silencer on earth for foolishness is to associate him on a research committee with a few persons who have a passion for truth—especially if they pay their own expenses. I can now disclose the secret that I created a dozen committees for that precise purpose.

REORGANIZATION OF THE EXECUTIVE DEPARTMENTS

When I first came to Washington as Food Administrator, new to government but experienced in administration, the executive organization of the Federal government appalled me. Early in my period as Secretary of Commerce I studied this chaos and made speeches about it. I was not the discoverer of it. Presidents Taft, Wilson, Harding, and Coolidge struggled with the problem, and with Congress, in an effort to do something about it. The real remedy was to get all the executive agencies related to the same major purpose under one hat—one administrator whom the people could put their finger on, who could trim away the overlaps and obtain unity on policies. Further, we needed to separate the quasi-judicial and quasi-legislative functions from executive functions. In connection with disunited policies, I pointed out:

Under the present system we have different bureau policies, department policies, board policies, and commission policies. We have a bundle of divergent ideas without focus; lumber piled together does not make a house. The treatment of our national resources furnishes a good instance. If anything is certain, it is that the government should have a continuous, definite, and consistent policy directed to intelligent conservation and use of national resources. But it can have no such policy so long as responsibility is split up among half a dozen different departments. The recent occurrences in oil leases are a fair example of what may happen by the lack of single-headed responsibility in such matters. No policy of real guardianship of our reserve resources will exist until we put all conservation business in the hands of an Under Secretary for Conservation, with the spotlight of public opinion continuously focused upon him.

The same is true of our deplorable lack of a definite and organized merchant marine policy.

There were fourteen different agencies engaged in water conservation and other public works under nine different departments; eight engaged in other forms of conservation under five departments; fourteen different bureaus engaged in helping the merchant marine in six different departments; and four helping veterans in four different departments; and so on and on. Worse still was the confusion of executive functions with quasi-judicial, quasi-legislative functions. Quasi-legislative and quasi-judicial matters can well be decided by several minds and therefore can be entrusted to boards and commissions; but executive functions must be exercised by a single, responsible head. Yet there were boards with vast executive functions, making a perpetual mess, and there were executive officials with judicial powers, as great as those of a Federal court, without the safeguards that surround courts.

The waste and inefficiency of the system were enormous. All healthy things grow; and bureaucratic cells proliferate faster than vegetables, for on their growth beams the sunshine of power and prestige, and, of course, it is "all for our good." Any time some proposal for the public good is set on foot, one can be sure that half a dozen bureaus will declare a participation in it, berate one another, and demand more employees and larger appropriations.

The hidden rock to reform was the "gang-up," "log-rolling" tactics of the bureaus and their organized pressure groups, which, over the years, they had polished to beautiful perfection.

Having witnessed failures of all previous Presidents, I determined to make a frontal assault and see if we could scrape off a few barnacles. To keep the enemy busy, I bombarded Congress with messages urging general reorganization. In the meantime, on May 27, 1930, we got authority to consolidate all the agencies dealing with Prohibition and place them in the Department of Justice and, on the following July 8, authority was granted to consolidate all veteran agencies under an Administrator of Veterans' Affairs.

Finally the Democratic Congress made a show of reorganization by passing an act on June 30, 1932. My recommendation had been to give authority to the President to reorganize the bureaus by executive orders which were to lie before Congress for sixty days and, if not expressly denied by joint resolution, to become law. Instead of accepting the recommendation, the Democratic House introduced a joker by which the executive orders were to become effective only if the Congress, by joint resolution, confirmed them. This made the orders amount to no more than a message recommending something. As, however, even such limited authority of recommendation was not operative except when Congress was in session, I could do nothing until after the December, 1932, session of Congress.

In my message to the Congress on that December 6, I said:

I shall issue such executive orders within a few days, grouping or consolidating over fifty executive and administrative agencies, including a large number of commissions and "independent" agencies.

The second step, of course, remains that after these various bureaus and agencies are placed cheek by jowl into such groups, the administrative officers in charge of the groups shall eliminate their overlap and still further consolidate these activities. Therein lie large economies.

The Congress must be warned that a host of interested persons inside and outside the Government whose vision is concentrated on some particular function will at once protest against these proposals. These same sorts of activities have prevented reorganization of the government for over a quarter of a century. They must be disregarded if the task is to be accomplished.

Promptly on the convening of the Congress, I sent up a score of executive orders consolidating fifty-eight separate agencies into nine divisions, each under a separate head. This was intended only as a first installment.

On January 3, 1933, I stated to the press that the reorganization of the government Departments had been blocked by the Democratic leaders in Congress:

The proposals of Democratic leaders in Congress to stop the reorganization of government functions which I have made are a backward step. The same opposition has now arisen which has defeated every effort at reorganization for twenty-five years. . . . Statements that I have made over ten years as to the opposition which has always thwarted reorganization have come true. . . .

Either Congress must keep its hands off now or they must give to my successor much larger powers of independent action than given to any President if there is ever to be reorganization. . . . Otherwise it will, as is now being demonstrated in the present law, again be merely make believe.

And again in a statement to the press on January 20 I expressed regret at the nullification by Congress of the plan for governmental reorganization, saying:

I regret, of course, that the consolidation of fifty-eight bureaus and commissions into a few divisions which I had directed by Executive Orders, has been nullified by the action of the House of Representatives. There was apparently no examination of the merits . . . if they were investigated at all, the majority of them would have been passed. . . .

It is a certainty that great economies would have been made if the program had been carried out. It would have been a contribution to lessening taxation in the forthcoming fiscal year.[3]

[3] Fifteen years later I was called upon to head a bipartisan committee set up by the Congress entitled, Commission on Organization of the Executive Branch of the Government. I devoted two years to the problem. We brought in twenty major and some two hundred secondary recommendations. We showed at that time the waste in duplication and lack of organization exceeded four billion dollars annually. About half of our recommendations were accepted, estimated to save about two billion dollars annually.

CHAPTER 40

REFORM OF VETERANS' AFFAIRS

I had spent four years of my own life in a war. I had seen the dangers, the heroism, the sufferings of our men, with my own eyes. I held to the firm conviction that the nation owed unlimited devotion for that service. I had often expressed my convictions in public addresses, as for instance on November 11, 1929, and October 6, 1930.

We did a great deal for the veterans. We built twenty-five new, free government hospitals for their sick and disabled. We increased the accommodation from 26,000 beds at the beginning of my administration to 45,000 at the end and had hospitals under construction to accommodate 7,000 more.

I initiated an entire revolution in veterans' care, because I felt that a disabled veteran in need of medical care should be a charge on the Federal government no matter how he got that way. I brushed aside a lot of subterfuges disguised as "presumption of war-caused disability" and said that if a veteran was destitute, had disability from any source, even forty years after the war, the nation had an obligation to him. We carried this proposal in the Congress, and by the end of my administration, 853,000 disabled, sick, and destitute veterans or their widows and orphans were on the Federal pay rolls compared with 376,000 at the beginning.[1]

But it was my misfortune to have a clash with the professional money-hunting veterans over other demands to which there was no right or justice in yielding. Their organizations maintained large staffs of paid lobbyists in Washington. The lobbyists and the officers drew

[1] This legislation was repealed by the New Deal, and 200,000 sick or disabled veterans were removed from the government rolls.

large salaries for one major mission. That was to bring home annually some "bacon" from the Treasury.

On May 28, 1930, the Congress under such pressures passed some most objectionable increases in pensions to Spanish War veterans. The act allowed pensions to persons not in need of them; it legalized disabilities arising out of venereal disease and gave pensions to men who had served only one day in the army.

In a press statement I said:

Rich men, or men having substantial incomes, should not draw pensions from the government. . . .

I do not believe we should alter the principles which have been held for Civil War veterans all these seventy years, requiring that men claiming pensions should have at least ninety days' service.

. . . I do not believe it is right to . . . call upon the nation to pay disability allowances to men who have or who may tomorrow destroy their health by vicious habits.

I have received numerous communications from veterans supporting these views.

However, the legislation was passed over my veto. Some years afterwards the stench became so strong that it was amended.

We soon were in difficulties over what was called the "bonus." During the Harding administration the veterans had demanded bonuses to compensate for their small soldier's pay compared to that of the "stay-at-homes." Their demand amounted to about $3,400,000,000 spread over more than 3,500,000 veterans. Someone thought up a trick to avoid facing the issue. That was to give this sum at the end of about twenty-five years and, in the meantime, issue a "bonus certificate" for it. The Federal Treasury was to pay an annual contribution (about $112,000,000) into the fund and thus make it a sort of endowment insurance policy, the government paying the annual premiums.

In 1931, Democratic leaders catering to the veteran vote proposed to lend 50 per cent to the men as an advance upon their bonus certificates. As a measure of relief, I favored the loans if they were limited to the men who were unemployed and destitute—less than 15 per cent of the whole number. Congress, however, insisted on including all the veterans, which implied a drain on the Treasury of $1,700,000,000. I sent a protest to the Senate on February 18, 1931, saying:

I have supported, and the nation should maintain, the important principle that when men have been called into jeopardy of their very lives in protection of the nation, then the nation as a whole incurs a special obligation beyond that to any other groups of its citizens. . . . Protection [should] be given to them when in ill health, distress and in need. Over 700,000 World War veterans or their dependents are today receiving monthly allowances for these reasons. The country should not be called upon, however, either directly or indirectly, to support or make loans to those who can by their own efforts support themselves. . . .

The bill nevertheless was passed, and on February 26, 1931, I analyzed its vicious effects and vetoed it.

Congress passed the bill over my veto. That action helped to deepen the depression. I said at the time:

. . . Although I have been greatly opposed to the passage of . . . loans . . . to people not in need, now that it is a law we propose to facilitate the working of it in every way possible.

Inasmuch as the physical task of making loans to 3,500,000 veterans . . . will require many months, even with the most intensive organization, I have requested General Hines to give complete priority to applications from veterans who are in need. . . .

In the following fall Senator Robinson and Speaker Garner, Democratic leaders of the Congress, again for political purposes, proposed to pay at once the whole bonus in cash ($3,400,000,000). Less than half had accumulated in the fund, and therefore the proposal was not only a discharge of the previous loans but another raid of $1,700,000,000. A resolution supporting the idea was to come up at the annual meeting of the American Legion in Detroit on September 21, 1931. I took the train to Detroit, remaining there an hour, and delivered an appeal to the Legion not to support it. I said, in part:

. . . The world is passing through a great depression fraught with grueling daily emergencies alike to men and to governments. This depression today flows largely from Europe through the fundamental dislocations of economic and political forces caused by the Great War in which your service brought bloodshed to an end and gave hope of reconstruction to the world. Our economic strength is such that we would have recovered long since but for these forces from abroad. Recovery of the world now rests and awaits in no small degree upon our country, the United States of America. Some individuals may have lost their nerve and faith, but the real American people are digging themselves out with industry and courage. We have the self-containment, the resources, the manhood, the intelligence, and by united action we will lead the world in recovery. . . .

Today the National Government is faced with another large deficit in its budget. There is a decrease in the annual yield of income taxes alone from $2,400,000,000 in the years of prosperity to only $1,200,000,000 today. Simultaneously we are carrying a high and necessary extra burden of public works in aid to the unemployed, of aids to agriculture and of increased benefits and services to veterans. . . . Make no mistake. In these circumstances it is those who work in the fields, at the bench and desk who would be forced to carry an added burden for every added cent to our expenditures. . . .

We can carry our present expenditures without jeopardy to national stability. We can carry no more without grave risks. . . .

Today a great service to our country is the determined opposition by you to additional demands upon the Nation until we have won this war against world depression. I am not speaking alone of veterans' legislation which has been urged for action at this convention, but I am speaking equally of demands for every other project proposed in the country which would require increased Federal expenditure. . . .

You would not have the President of the United States plead with any citizen or any group of citizens for any course of action. I make no plea to you. But you would have your President point out the path of service in this nation. That I am doing now. My mind goes back to the days of the war where you and I served in our appointed tasks. At the end of those years of heart sickness over the misery of it all, when the peace came, you and I knew that the wounds of the world were unhealed, and that there would be further emergencies still before our country and the world when self-denial and courageous service must be given. Your organization was born at that time and dedicated to that service by the very preamble to its constitution. No man can doubt the character and idealism of men who have gone into the trenches in defense of their country. I have that faith. This is an emergency, and these are the times for service to which we must put full heart and purpose to help and not retard the return of the happy days we know are ahead of your country and mine.

The Legion refused to endorse the legislation; yet the politicians still persisted, and on March 29, 1932, I issued a further warning. Action was stopped temporarily.

I was deluged with Congressional acts voting pensions to special cases which were barred under the provisions of the Civil and Spanish War pension legislation. I vetoed more of such bills than even President Cleveland, and by describing them to the country succeeded in having my vetoes upheld. I give some specimens of these public statements justifying vetoes:

A pension for a man who was court-martialed for drunkenness and conduct prejudicial to good order, sentenced to six months' confinement, and whose conduct during confinement was so bad that he was finally discharged without honor for the good of the service.

A pension to a man who was discharged without honor because of chronic alcoholism.

A pension to a widow whose claim was filed five years after the death of the veteran, and who upon call for evidence of legal widowhood abandoned her claim for a period of 25 years. A recent investigation indicates claimant was never the wife of the soldier.

A pension to a man guilty of desertion and dishonorably discharged.

A pension to a man shown to have been a deserter, to have been punished by confinement and discharged without honor.

A pension to a man for self-inflicted injuries incurred in attempted suicide.

A pension for a widow whose husband gave eight days' service, with no disability relating to the service.

A pension to a man who still suffers from a wound in the throat self-inflicted with a razor; with no disability relating to the service.

A pension for loss of a leg as the result of being struck by the fender of a streetcar while claimant was lying on the track in a completely intoxicated condition.

A pension to a widow whose husband had only nine days' service in a state militia, for which reimbursement was made by the United States; no disability relating to service being found.

A pension to a man who spent most of his service in the hospital and was discharged without honor because of disease not contracted in line of duty; was shown to have been guilty of malingering by taking soap pills to aid him in appearing anemic. His physical condition was not the result of service.

A pension to a man discharged without honor because of diseases not contracted in the service in line of duty. His condition not being one upon which Federal benefits should be based.

The Congress should not be wholly blamed for such vicious actions. A band of pension lawyers lobbied and logrolled them with great unity. Hard-worked men had no time to investigate all these bills. Often they were innocently voted for as a favor to a fellow Congressman.

By April, 1932, I asked the Veterans' Bureau for a searching examination of wasteful and undue payments arising from technical interpretations of the older veterans' acts. The Bureau reported a growth of something more than $120,000,000 a year in payments to able-bodied, self-supporting, and even rich men as a result of such interpretations or of mistakes in legislation. We had a fierce battle in attempting to reach this evil. I did not remain in office long enough to get the vice cured.

In the spring of 1932 I was compelled to again stop a Democratic Veterans' Bonus bill for $2,400,000,000 which was to be paid in greenbacks. I relate the "Bonus March" which took place at this time in the next volume.

CHAPTER 41

REFORM OF THE TARIFF

The tariff question is complicated by deep-seated tradition, by politics, and privilege. It has been an issue ever since George Washington's first piece of legislation, which was a tariff act. It long has been one of our campaign sources of emotion, eloquence, distortion, and exaggeration. One part of this hocus-pocus lay in the fact that about 63 per cent of all our imports were free of any duty. Most raw materials were thus free as were thousands of other items. Of the group of dutiable goods, nearly half were agricultural products where the tariff was supported by both political parties. About a quarter were luxury goods taxed for revenue only, over which there was no political dispute. There was left about 10 or 11 per cent of the total imports, primarily manufactured goods, over which the debate and the emotion soared. The real issue thus boiled down to tariffs on the items in this 11 per cent of our imports. And even here there were areas of agreement between the political parties.

The Republican platform of 1928 called for revision of the tariff upward on farm products and some readjustment in industrial schedules to meet economic shifts since the last revision. But I may mention here that later statements implying that the passage of the Smoot-Hawley bill was the cause of the depression seem somewhat overdrawn, as it was not passed until nine months after the crash. Moreover it was not, as later statements suggested, the beginning of a world movement to increase tariffs. In fact, the American increase took place only after nearly thirty other countries had imposed higher tariffs. This world-wide tariff movement was largely an outcome of World War I. The world generally was seeking "self-sufficiency" as a measure of national defense in an era of international fear. Furthermore, many nations were seeking to prevent recurrence of the hardships imposed by inability to import necessary supplies from abroad, resulting from the export restrictions and blockades during the war. As an example, Argentina had been compelled during the war to close many schools because the usual children's shoes could not be obtained from abroad. After its war experience, that country changed violently to the theory of protected and expanded domestic industry.

Partly on Senator Borah's insistence (he was then giving me strong support) I had agreed to call a special session for the purpose of increasing agricultural tariffs. I approved of the idea of a special session because I wished, if elected, to get the tariff out of the way of the work I anticipated proposing to the regular session. Congress assembled on April 15, 1929, and the portion of my message relating to the tariff was:

An effective tariff upon agricultural products . . . has a dual purpose. Such a tariff not only protects the farmer in our domestic market, but also stimulates him to diversify his crops and to grow products that he could not otherwise produce, and thus lessens his dependence upon exports to foreign markets. . . .

In considering the tariff for other industries than agriculture, we find that there have been economic shifts necessitating a readjustment of some of the tariff schedules. . . .

It would seem to me that the test of necessity for revision is, in the main, whether there has been a substantial slackening of activity in an industry during the past few years, and a consequent decrease of employment due to insurmountable competition in the products of that industry. . . .

In determining changes in our tariff, we must not fail to take into account the broad interests of the country as a whole, and such interests include our trade relations with other countries.

I was especially insistent on enlarging the powers of the old Tariff Commission, which was mainly a statistical agency. An ineffective step had been taken in this direction some years before, and I determined to go on from there. I believed that the only way to get the tariff out of Congressional logrolling was through empowering this bipartisan commission to adjust the different rates on dutiable goods upon the basis of the differences in cost of production at home and abroad, and to make these readjustments after objective examination and public hearings. We could avoid excessive and privileged protection by thus holding imports to reasonably competitive levels with domestic products. This plan was known as the "flexible tariff."

Any tariff passed by the logrolling process, inevitable in the Congress, is bound to be very bad in spots. The object of the flexible tariff was to secure, in addition to more equitable rates, a hope that Congressional tariff making could be ended.

The House Ways and Means Committee reported the new tariff bill on May 9, 1929. Not liking some of its features, I asked the Republicans of the committee to meet with me at the White House, where I insisted that there should be agricultural increases but a more limited revision of industrial schedules than they proposed, together with the authority to the Tariff Commission to operate the flexible tariff. Chairman Hawley supported me, but the older protectionists under the leadership of Speaker Nicholas Longworth were discontented. Mr. Hawley having reported to me that there were difficulties with certain Republicans on my flexible tariff, I again called in the leaders of the House on May 22 and went over the ground, stating that I could not accept any bill unless the flexible tariff were incorporated. On May 28, the House passed its tariff bill. The provisions were not satisfactory.

The battle was now transferred to the Senate, and I at once held a series of conferences with the Republican senators urging modifications of the House bill. Senator Borah, however, suddenly convinced himself that the flexible tariff deprived Congress of its constitutional authority and persuaded the "Progressive" wing to oppose it as "reactionary." As a matter of fact it was the most progressive step in tariff reform ever proposed to Congress. I had him in to dinner but was unable to overcome his opposition. He was only looking for an opportunity to go into his traditional attitude of opposition to the current administration. The Supreme Court subsequently ruled that the idea was entirely constitutional.

On August 20 the Senate committee reported the bill with wholly inadequate provisions for the flexible tariff. It did "reduce" the House increases on industrial items to an average increase of about 8 per cent.

As the flexible tariff was getting a beating in the Senate, I made a public statement on the subject on September 24, 1929, saying:

> . . . The essential of the flexible tariff is that with respect to a particular commodity, after exhaustive determination of the facts as to differences of cost of production at home and abroad by a Tariff Commission, comprised of one-half of its members from each political party, whose selection is approved by the Senate, then the President should, upon recommendation of the Commission, promulgate changes in the tariff on that commodity not to exceed 50 per cent of the rates fixed by Congress. . . .
>
> The reasons for the continued incorporation of such provisions are even more cogent today than ever before. No tariff bill ever enacted has been or ever will be perfect. It will contain injustices. . . . It could not be otherwise. Furthermore, if a perfect tariff bill were enacted the rapidity of our changing economic conditions and the constant shifting of our relations with economic life abroad would render some items in such an act imperfect in some particular within a year. . . .
>
> The flexible provision is one of the most progressive steps taken in tariff making in all our history. . . .

On September 27 the Progressive senators made a mass attack on the flexible tariff. Many of the Republican regulars were opposed to it under the cover of Republican Senate leader Watson. The Democrats likewise assailed it. I sent word to Senator Smoot, who was convoying the bill, "No flexible tariff, no tariff bill." I was convinced that there was little hope of securing just and equitable rates out of the eternal sectional and group interests, and that any mistakes and injustices would have to be corrected later by the flexible tariff.

On October 2, the Senate, by a coalition vote of Democrats, Progressives, and Old Guard Republicans of 47 to 42, defeated the flexible tariff provisions.

On October 5, the Progressives in the Senate proposed various forms of flexible tariff, just short of my requirements, as a "tryout." I advised the Republican leaders to allow them to put any form of flexible tariff into the bill that they liked, as the principle once in the bill from both houses would enable the conferees to write an adequate flexible tariff provision. Then I could present them the alternative of a veto.

On November 22 Congress concluded its special session, which had begun April 19, but without finishing the bill.

In the meanwhile, I had my difficulties with some of the Old Guard. They again urged that I drop the flexible provision. On January 31, 1930, a vacancy occurring in the Senate from Pennsylvania, Governor Fisher had appointed Joseph R. Grundy. The new senator was universally known as an extreme protectionist. During the 1928 campaign I had definitely disagreed with him. Shortly after his appointment, Grundy made his maiden speech in severe opposition to my views, flexible tariff and all. On February 21, 1930, Democratic Senator Pat Harrison of Mississippi made a characteristic speech on the subject of my differences with Senator Grundy. He accused Grundy of having appealed to his Old Guard colleagues to fight the President because of my more moderate protection views. Grundy found himself allied for the time being with low-tariff Democrats and Progressives against the bill.

On February 24 I invited the Republican Senate leaders to breakfast, where I again stated my views. The position at this time was that four-fifths of the Democratic senators had placed in the bill some increase in industrial duties which their backers or constituents wanted. Most of them hoped that the bill would be enacted, but most of them were also creating a public impression of opposition.

On March 24, after about ten months' deliberation, the Senate finally passed a tariff bill by a vote of 53 to 31. Most of the Progressive Republicans voted for it. So did seven Democrats. It now went to conference with a very weak flexible tariff—so weak as to be useless. The rates in the Senate bill, generally speaking, proved to be higher than they had been in the bill as reported out of committee. Indicating the difference between cloakroom action and public posture, individual Democrats and Progressives during the passage of the bill voted a total of more than a thousand times for increases of their particular pet items, or against decreases in them.

I learned on May 24 that the conferees had overridden Senator Smoot and Congressman Hawley and had watered the flexible provision down to about nothing. I wrote out the provision I wanted. I sent word that unless my formula was adopted, the bill would be vetoed. The result was a complete victory for the flexible tariff in the conference report.

On June 5 Senator Watson, the Republican leader, informed me that Senator Grundy would not vote for the conference report, but that several on the Democratic side, who were making an appearance of opposition, had stated they would vote for the bill if necessary.

On June 7 Senator Steiwer of Oregon issued an effective public statement pointing out that Democratic senators who voted for increasing almost every individual item were at the same time violently condemning the bill. On June 12 Senator Grundy publicly condemned the tariff bill. Again, he denounced the flexible provisions. I recite all these actions of the Senator inasmuch as Mr. Roosevelt later constantly referred to the bill as the "Grundy Tariff."

On June 13 the Senate finally passed the conference report on the bill by virtue of seven Democratic votes. Some of its proponents had exaggerated its benefits. At the same time most of its opponents, both in and out of Congress, had grossly misrepresented its schedules and rates. None of them gave credit for taking tariff making out of Congressional logrolling by the "Flexible Tariff."

I was deluged with a mass of recommendations as to approval or veto from representatives of a diversity of interests. Among those registering opposition to the bill were Albert H. Wiggin, chairman of the Chase National Bank; Charles H. Sabin, chairman of the Guaranty Trust Company; Charles E. Mitchell, chairman of the National City Bank; Thomas W. Lamont of J. P. Morgan Co.; Oswald Garrison Villard, editor of the *Nation*; Henry Morgenthau the elder; Roy Howard of the Scripps-Howard newspapers; John J. Raskob and Jouett Shouse, respectively chairman of the Democratic National Committee and chairman of its executive committee, and a whole group of college professors.

Approval of the bill was urged by the directors of the American Farm Bureau Federation, by the National Grange, the Farmers' Union, the American Federation of Labor, and a smaller group of college professors.

On June 15, 1930, I issued a detailed analysis of the legislation, saying:

I shall approve the Tariff Bill. . . . It was undertaken as the result of pledges given by the Republican party at Kansas City. . . .

Platform promises must not be empty gestures. In my message of April 16, 1929 . . . I recommended . . . the flexible provisions.

A statistical estimate of the bill by the Federal Tariff Commission (bipartisan) shows that the average duties collected under the 1922 law were about 13.8 per cent of the value of all imports, both free and dutiable, while if the new law had been applied it would have increased this percentage to about 16.0 per cent.

This compares with the average level of the tariff under

The McKinley Law (Republican, 1890)..................... 23.0%
The Wilson Law (Democratic, 1894)........................ 20.9
The Dingley Law (Republican, 1897)....................... 25.8
The Payne-Aldrich Law (Republican, 1909)................ 19.3
The Fordney-McCumber Law (Republican, 1922)........... 13.83

Under the Underwood Law of 1913 the amounts were disturbed by the war conditions varying 6 per cent to 14.8 per cent.

The proportion of imports which will be free of duty under the new law compares with averages under

The McKinley Law (Republican, 1890).................. 52.4%
The Wilson Law (Democratic, 1894)..................... 49.4
The Dingley Law (Republican, 1897)................... 45.2
The Payne-Aldrich Law (Republican, 1909).............. 52.5
The Fordney-McCumber Law (Republican, 1922)........ 63.8
The Smoot-Hawley Law (Republican, 1930).............. 62.0

Under the Underwood Law of 1913 disturbed conditions varied the free list from 60 per cent to 73 per cent, averaging 66.3 per cent.

The increases in tariff are largely directed to the interest of the farmer. Of the increases, it is stated by the Tariff Commission that 93.73 per cent are upon products of agricultural origin measured in value, as distinguished from 6.25 per cent upon commodities of strictly non-agricultural origin. . . .

The extent of rate revision [is] indicated by the Tariff Commission. . . . By number of the dutiable items mentioned in the bill, out of the total of about 3,300 there were about 890 increased, 235 decreased, and 2,170 untouched. The number of items increased was, therefore, 27 per cent of all dutiable items, and compares with 83 per cent 'of the number of items which were increased in the 1922 revision.

This tariff law is like all other tariff legislation, whether framed primarily upon a protective or a revenue basis. It contains many compromises between sectional interests and between different industries. No tariff bill has ever been enacted or ever will be enacted under the present system, that will be perfect. A large portion of the items are always adjusted with good judgment, but it is bound to contain some inequalities and inequitable compromises. There are items upon which duties will prove too high and others upon which duties will prove to be too low.

Certainly no President, with his other duties, can pretend to make that exhaustive determination of the complex facts which surround each of those 3,300 items, and which has required the attention of hundreds of men in Congress for nearly a year and a third. That responsibility must rest upon the Congress in a legislative rate revision.

On the administrative side I have insisted, however, that there should be created a new basis for the flexible tariff and it has been incorporated in this law; a form which should render it possible to secure prompt and scientific adjustment of serious inequities and inequalities which may prove to have been incorporated in the bill.

This new provision has even a larger importance. If a perfect tariff bill were enacted today, the increased rapidity of economic change and the constant shifting of our relations to industries abroad will create a continuous stream of items which would work hardship upon some segment of the American people except for the provision of this relief. Without a workable flexible provision we would require even more frequent Congressional tariff revision than during the past. With it the country should be freed from further general revision for many years to come. Congressional revisions are not only disturbing to business but, with all their necessary collateral surroundings in lobbies, logrolling, and the activities of group interests, are disturbing to public confidence. . . .

The new flexible provision established the responsibility for revisions upon a reorganized tariff commission, composed of members equally of both parties as a definite rate-making body acting through semi-judicial methods of open hearings and investigations by which items can be taken up one by one upon direction or upon application of aggrieved parties. Recommendations are to be made to the President, he being given authority to promulgate or veto the conclusions of the commission. Such revisions can

*be accomplished without disturbance to business, as they concern but one
item at a time, and the principles laid down assure a protective basis. . . .*

*As I have said, I do not assume the rate structure in this or any other
tariff bill is perfect, but I am convinced that the disposal of the whole question is urgent. I believe that the flexible provisions can within reasonable
time remedy inequalities; that this provision is a progressive advance and
gives great hope of taking the tariff away from politics, lobbying, and log-
rolling; that the bill gives protection to agriculture for the marketing of its
products and to several industries in need of such protection for the wage
of their labor; that with returning normal conditions our foreign trade will
continue to expand.*

Subsequent reports of the Tariff Commission confirmed that the
increase of total duties applied to total imports was from 13.8 per cent
to about 16 per cent, which was lower than the laws of 1890, 1894, 1897,
and 1909, and but little higher than the laws of 1913 and 1922.

The history of the flexible tariff during the remaining two years of
my administration was that 250 industrial items were reviewed by the
commission, and the rates changed in about 75 of them, mostly down-
ward. More would have been changed but for the depression trade war
engendered by the general abandonment of the gold standard abroad
with consequent currency fluctuations which made costs of production
constantly variable.

In the next volume of these memoirs, I shall refer again to the tariff
in discussing the debate during the campaign of 1932.[1] But I may say
here that raising the tariff from its sleep was a political liability despite
the virtues of its reform.

[1] One of the cynicisms of the times was Mr. Roosevelt's violent attacks and misrepresentation of the tariff at the beginning of the campaign of 1932. Before the campaign
was over he had completely reversed himself. After taking office, he increased the tariffs
on several items. The three-year period from 1936 to 1938 should be representative of
the effects of New Deal tariffs. Whereas the Republican duties represented probably
15 per cent of the total value of the goods imported, the New Deal duties represented
17 per cent. The devaluation of the currency also had the effect of increasing tariffs
which I discuss in the next volume.

CHAPTER 42

REFORMS IN REGULATION OF BUSINESS

In the account of my period as Secretary of Commerce, I have given my views upon the relation of business and industry to the governmental, the social, and the economic life of the nation. Here I deal only with the practical problems of regulation that confronted us during my period in the White House.

Those who contended that during the period of my administration our economic system was one of *laissez faire* have little knowledge of the extent of government regulation. The economic philosophy of *laissez faire*, or "dog eat dog," had died in the United States forty years before, when Congress passed the Interstate Commerce Commission and the Sherman Anti-Trust Acts.

By my time the banks were regulated by the Federal government as well as by state governments. Railway rates, profits, capital structures, and services were regulated by the Federal government and to some extent by the state governments. The telephone and telegraph and radio were regulated by the Federal government, and the telephone and telegraph were also regulated by the states. Electric power companies were regulated in part by the Federal government and in part by the states. The states or municipalities regulated water supply, streetcars, busses, toll bridges, and other utilities. The states regulated the sale of securities. The Anti-Trust Acts, both Federal and state, were in effect regulatory on competitive business. The Federal and state governments regulated many avenues of commerce as to unfair practices, standards of quality, and purity of products. The Federal government regulated the stock yards and the grain exchanges.

I may state at this point that the enactment of the Anti-Trust Acts and of the regulatory powers over banking, railways, telephones, telegraphs, radio, navigation, aviation, fisheries, pure food, and grain exchanges was mostly of Republican origin.

We were a system of "regulated individualism." These regulatory acts required periodic revision with the advance of technology and ingenuity in violations. The problems which confronted me were the weak spots in existing regulations and the socialistic drive to put the government into business.

We needed reforms (a) in the anti-trust laws, (b) in the regulation of some of the natural resources industries, (c) in the regulation of electric power, (d) in the regulation of the railways, (e) in banking, (f) in the regulation of security sales, promotions, and the stock exchange.

THE ANTI-TRUST LAWS

The business world always fretted over the anti-trust laws. I believed that the preservation of our competitive system was the only way to progress. I had long since seen the backwardness of European industry because of the absence of laws against the restraint of trade. Theirs was a constant degeneration in productive efficiency due to monopolies and cartels on every side which sought profits from fixing prices and controlling distribution. The greater competition in our system created constant pressure to make profits by reducing costs of production. Our laws did, at times, have destructive effects. I had pointed out some of the defects and the remedies that should be employed, while I was Secretary of Commerce. In my second annual message to Congress, on December 2, 1930, I requested Congress to investigate the anti-trust law problems in this connection.

A problem inherent in our anti-trust laws arose from the blanket exemption of the labor unions. This was justifiable except in certain particulars. The unions should not have been allowed—any more than business conspiracies—to build monopolies which could wring their ends from the anguish of the public, or to act in collusion with employers for these evil ends, or to use their funds for political purposes. I felt the whole featherbedding process prevented competition and should be abolished. By such evil practices the building trades unions

were increasing the cost of homes 25 to 30 per cent with no benefit to
themselves in wage rates or hours. But we were too much involved in
the depression for constructive action in these directions.

Together with Attorney General Mitchell, I chose John Lord
O'Brian as Assistant Attorney General, to head the Anti-Trust Division
of the Department of Justice, and gave him instructions to enforce the
law without flinching. He investigated and stopped a number of
notable infractions. In the earlier period of my administration, some
business journals complained that the number of prosecutions exceeded
those of the same period in any other administration. However, the
oncoming depression, by its pressure on competition, effectively ended
most violations of the anti-trust laws.

CREATION OF FEDERAL POWER COMMISSION

Through an interdepartmental committee the Federal government
for a number of years had imposed some regulation upon water-gen-
erated power through its control of navigable streams. When I took
office, this covered an infinitesimal part of the power being generated.
At an earlier period I had believed that the states could exercise the
necessary control of the power companies and their rates. But later
on I decided that the time had come for Federal regulation, because
of the development of long transmissions with interconnection and the
consequent increasing volume of interstate electric power, together
with the building up of huge holding companies doing business in
several states.

In my first message to Congress on December 3, 1929, I requested
the creation of a real Federal Power Commission, with teeth. My view
was that this commission should be interlocked with the regulating
commissions of the states as a kind of extension of their powers. I said
to the Congressional committee chairman:

. . . The nature of the electric utilities industry is such that about 60 per
cent of all power generation and distribution is intrastate in character, and
most of the states have developed their own regulatory systems as to certificates of convenience, rates, and profits of such utilities. To encroach upon their
authorities and responsibilities would be an encroachment upon the rights
of the states. There are cases, however, of interstate character beyond the

jurisdiction of the states. To meet these cases it would be most desirable if a method could be worked out by which initial action may be taken between the commissions of the states whose joint action should be made effective by the Federal Power Commission with a reserve power to act on its own motion in case of disagreement or nonaction by the states.

Draft bills for such regulation were furnished to the chairmen of the committees concerned. The power interests and radical members of Congress ganged up in opposition for exactly opposite reasons. However, Congress finally passed, on June 3, 1930, the portion of the act creating the Federal Power Commission, transferring to it only the authorities of the old interdepartmental committee over water powers on navigable rivers. The Congressional committees refused to follow my request that the Commission be given authority to regulate interstate rates in cooperation with the state commissions and to regulate the accounting and financing of companies engaged in interstate power distribution as was done in the case of the railways. I was very indignant at Senator Norris, and other so-called Progressives whose opposition was born of desire to force the government into operation of power. Their theory was apparently to oppose adequate control of private operation in the hope that public resentment of unrestrained, greedy action would forward their cause. That in a nutshell was the American system of regulation running squarely against socialism.

In my second Annual Message to Congress on December 2, 1930, I urged again "effective regulation of interstate electrical power. Such regulation should preserve the independence and responsibility of the states."

I repeatedly urged the matter upon Congress with little hope of overcoming the Radical-Democratic combination, but with the firm purpose to keep aloft the banner of free men protected by law against economic oppression.

We soon had an acute example of all this in connection with the government hydroelectric power plant, which had been erected for war purposes in 1917–1918 at Muscle Shoals on the Tennessee River. On March 3, 1931, Congress passed the Norris bill, which I vetoed. The bill proposed to expand this plant to sell power to the public and to go into the business of making fertilizers. As my veto statement indi-

cates my economic and social views on this subject, I quote it extensively:

I am firmly opposed to the Government entering into any business the
major purpose of which is competition with our citizens. There are national
emergencies which require that the Government should temporarily enter
the field of business, but they must be emergency actions and in matters
where the cost of the project is secondary to much higher considerations.
Also there are many localities where the Federal government is justified in
the construction of great dams and reservoirs, where navigation, flood control,
reclamation, and stream regulation are of dominant importance, and where
they are beyond the capacity or purpose of private or local government
capital to construct. In these cases power is often a by-product and should
be disposed of by contract or lease. But for the Federal government deliberately to go out to build up and expand such an occasion to the major
purpose of a power and manufacturing business is to break down the
initiative and enterprise of the American people; it is destruction of equality
of opportunity amongst our people; it is the negation of the ideals upon
which our civilization has been based.

This bill raises one of the important issues confronting our people. That
is squarely the issue of Federal government ownership and operation of
power and manufacturing business not as a minor by-product but as a
major purpose. Involved in this question is the agitation against the conduct of the power industry. The power problem is not to be solved by the
Federal government going into the power business, nor is it to be solved
by the project in this bill. The remedy for abuses in the conduct of that
industry lies in regulation and not by the Federal government entering upon
the business itself. I have recommended to the Congress on various occasions
that action should be taken to establish Federal regulation of interstate
power in cooperation with state authorities. . . .

I hesitate to contemplate the future of our institutions, of our government,
and of our country if the preoccupation of its officials is to be no longer the
promotion of justice and equal opportunity but is to be devoted to barter
in the markets. That is not liberalism, it is degeneration. . . .

The Federal government should, as in the case of Boulder Canyon, construct Cove Creek Dam as a regulatory measure for the flood protection
of the Tennessee Valley and the development of its water resources, but on
the same bases as those imposed at Boulder Canyon—that is, that construction should be undertaken at such time as the proposed commission is able

to secure contracts for use of the increased water supply to power users or the lease of the power produced as a by-product from such a dam on terms that will return to the government interest upon its outlay with amortization. . . .

The Radical bloc in Congress was determined to paint me as a tool of the power companies. I had appointed George Otis Smith, the Director of the Geological Survey, as Chairman of the new Power Commission. He was a civil servant of thirty years' high standing. He was opposed to government operation of business. He was confirmed by the Senate and on the same day promptly dismissed a Socialist employee of the old interdepartmental committee, who spent all his time doing publicity work for the Radical group in Congress. Senator Norris at once demanded and secured a Senate resolution recalling the confirmation of Mr. Smith. I promptly notified the Senate on March 10, 1931, that they had no power to do anything of the kind, saying:

. . . These appointments were constitutionally made, are not subject to recall. . . . The objective of the Senate constitutes an attempt to dictate to an administrative agency upon the appointment of subordinates and an attempted invasion of the authority of the Executive. These, as President, I am bound to resist.

I cannot, however, allow a false issue to be placed before the country. There is no issue for or against power companies. . . .

The resolution of the Senate may have the attractive political merit of giving rise to a legend that those who voted for it are "enemies of the power interests," and, inferentially, those who voted against it are "friends of the power interests." It may contain a hope of symbolizing me as the defender of power interests if I refuse to sacrifice three outstanding public servants.

During 1932, under the economic strains of the depression, several castles of the electric holding companies began to crumble, with great losses to investors and great indignation of the public. Had the Democratic-Radical bloc in Congress acted upon my recommendations, at least some of these losses might have been prevented. For instance, the fantastic Insull "empire" of holding companies which collapsed in Chicago with such dire results was largely built after my recommendations for regulation had been defeated.

The Cabinet and the Presidency

Upon the refusal of Congress to act on electric power regulation, I commented in a letter of February 17, 1933, to Arch W. Shaw of Chicago, which was published:

There is a phase of all this that must cause anxiety to every American. Democracy cannot survive unless it is master in its own house. The economic system cannot survive unless there are real restraints upon unbridled greed or dishonest reach for power. Greed and dishonesty are not attributes solely of our system—they are human and will infect socialism or any ism. But if our production and distribution systems are to function we must have effective restraints on manipulation, greed, and dishonesty. Our Democracy has proved its ability to put its unruly occupants under control, but never until their conduct has been a public scandal and a stench. For instance, you will recollect my own opposition to government operation of electric power, for that is a violation of the very fundamentals of our system; but parallel with it I asked and preached for regulation of it to protect the public from its financial manipulation. We gained the Power Commission, but Congress refused it the regulatory authority we asked. . . . The inertia of the Democracy is never more marked than in promotion of what seems abstract or indirect ideas. The recent scandals are the result. Democracy, always lagging, will no doubt now act and may act destructively to the system, for it is mad. It is this lag, the failure to act in time for prevention, which I fear most in the sane advancement of economic life. For an outraged people may destroy the whole economic system rather than reconstruct and control the segment which has failed in its function. I trust the new administration will recognize the difference between crime and economic functioning; between constructive prevention and organization as contrasted with destruction.

We ordered the arrest of Insull.[1]

RAILROADS AND THEIR REORGANIZATION

The Transportation Act of 1920 contemplated consolidation of the hundred-odd separate major railway companies into about twenty larger systems as the way to financial stability and more economical operation. The Act granted no powers of compulsion. Divided in its mind about details, the Interstate Commerce Commission had been unable to bring about any action. Certainly the railways desperately

[1] But after years of legal technicalities, including a refuge in Greece, he won freedom.

needed something. In 1930 I called in the railway presidents in the "trunk-line territory" (approximately north of the Mason and Dixon line and east of the Mississippi) and urged them to cooperate with the Commission in setting up a voluntary consolidation into four or five systems. They worked earnestly for several months and consulted me many times. Finally on December 31, 1930, I was able to announce a successful agreement, which would be approved by the I.C.C. But Senator Couzens, chairman of the Senate committee concerned, for reasons which he did not truly explain, led against us an obstructionist group comprising the Radical bloc despite the fact that most of them had voted for the law authorizing this action. The object was, of course, to keep the railways demoralized in the hope of government operation. The group for political reasons was supported by the Democrats as usual. Our plan fell through—as did every attempt of the Commission with my support to carry out the purpose of the law.

The pressures of the depression upon the railways were acute. Their inability to finance renewals and improvements deepened the depression. Receiverships and defaults of interest on bonds were imminent on much of the country's mileage. The shock to insurance companies, savings banks, colleges, and hospitals which held railroad bonds and securities would have brought disaster of immeasurable dimensions. The inevitable curtailment of railway operations in receivership would have increased unemployment. The situation was one of the most serious with which I was confronted.

We resolved this crisis by forming the Reconstruction Finance Corporation, which I discuss later. That operation included railway finance among its other functions. The total loans to railroads were at no one time greater than $300,000,000, and the very existence of this reserve power made possible much private financing otherwise impossible.[2]

It seemed obvious to me not only that the financial structure of the railways required reorganization, but also that, with the development of the airplane, the bus, the pipe line, and motor transport, their future must be more and more a matter of handling heavy freight. Moreover, the great duplication of trackage and terminals ought to be eliminated —partly because of decreasing participation in total traffic. I had given

[2] The government recovered practically every penny loaned, with interest.

much thought and investigation to the subject when Secretary of Commerce. I now cooperated with a number of independent experts with such eminent railway men as Daniel Willard, and with leading members of the Interstate Commerce Commission, and finally evolved a plan of wholesale reorganization. By this time we were on the eve of the election, and I laid it away, since nothing could be done unless we were returned to office. My memorandum covering the plan was not made public, but I give it at the end of the chapter for the benefit of students of economics—the railways have not yet been efficiently organized.

Many thoughtful students were well aware of the wholly inadequate banking and credit organization of the country prior to the depression, yet no one could know its full weakness or where its worst weakness was until after it was put under strain. When I came to the White House, there were 24,000 institutions under forty-nine different systems of regulation; all of them used demand-deposit money not only to make commercial loans but to make long-term mortgages and buy bonds. Many of them, as will be seen, engaged in stock promotion and manipulation.

The establishment of the Federal Reserve System by the Wilson administration had been a valuable reform step; but under strain it wholly failed to bring its anticipated results of stopping booms and panics.

Inasmuch as the mold of our financial system was a creature of our Federal and state laws, the remedy must therefore lie in reform of those laws. But the task was not easy. With a vested interest of some 25,000 banks and deposit institutions in a country where almost everybody believed he had the capacity to go into the banking business, any change was faced by a formidable opposition. And the opposition was the more vigorous in that thousands of the weak sisters wanted to make sure they would be allowed to go on doing business as before.

The battle over banking reform will be taken up at length in my treatment of the depression in the next volume of these memoirs. I may state here that I urged this vital reform in messages to the Congress on

December 3, 1929, December 2, 1930, December 8, 1931, January 4 and December 6, 1932, and February 20, 1933. It became part of the whole depression recovery issue.

Stock dealing and stock promotion reform also will come up in my treatment of the depression, as a side battle connected with that period. In desperation at my failure to persuade the stock exchanges to undertake the reform of their own members, I secured a Senate investigation of the whole matter. The legislation was not completed in my term, but the exposures made it inevitable.

TEXT OF THE 1932 MEMORANDUM ON RAILWAY REORGANIZATION [a]

1. The nominal par value of securities issued by the railways is about 14 billion dollars in bonds and 10 billions in stock. Of which about 11 billion dollars in bonds and 8 billions in stocks are held by the public, the remainder being held by railways themselves. The Interstate Commerce Commission replacement valuation is about 24 billion dollars. More and more roads will go into receivership, improvements and maintenance are falling behind.

Any plan which will place the railways in a sound position for public service must embrace seven principles:

    a. Private ownership and operation.

    b. Consolidation into a lesser number of systems and into terminal companies so as to effect reduction in costs.

    c. Reduction of fixed charges.

    d. Further capital for improvements.

    e. Such a capital structure as will secure future capital.

    f. Recognition that the railways have been rendered partly obsolescent by other forms of transportation, and that the public cannot be expected to support returns upon this obsolescence.

    g. No hardship imposed upon employees.

2. A temporary Reorganization Commission to be set up by Congress with powers to reorganize the railways. The powers in this field now possessed by the Interstate Commerce Commission to be transferred to the Reorganization Commission, and such amended or other powers as are necessary to work out the plan to be granted.

3. Consolidations to be effected by the Reorganization Commission into a lesser number of systems and certain terminal companies. The point of view of consolidations authorized in the present transportation act is to maintain competitive service. The competitive principle is already largely destroyed by rate fixing, and while the competitive principle does not need to be wholly abandoned as a spur to service, it should now yield to the greater principle of reducing operating costs. There are many communities served by two railways where one is ample for the railway transportation now extant. And if consolidation is carried out from this point of view, there is considerable trackage in

---

[a] See p. 308.

the country that could be abandoned and the traffic thus consolidated on the lines where it can be operated at much less cost to the public and the companies.

4. The Reorganization Commission to establish a "system corporation" for each of these new consolidations with as nearly as possible a simple structure of one kind of bonds and one kind of common stock. Bonds and common stock of each "system corporation" to be exchanged directly with the individual holders of securities of the component railways, not with the companies.

5. As a method of determining both the value of the component railways in a "system corporation" and the ratio of exchanges, the following general formula to be used. The quoted market value, averaged over say six months, of each issue of bonds or common or other stock of component railways at some previous period to be determined by the Reorganization Commission. The Commission to choose some past period which represents neither boom nor depression prices.

6. The new "system corporation" bonds and stocks to be exchanged to public holders of the component railways in ratio of these average market values. That is, for a bond having an average market value of par to receive par in the "system corporation" bonds, and a bond having an average value of say 30 to receive 30 in the "system corporation" bonds. That for the deficiency between par of the bonds and the figure at which they are exchanged, a bonus of say 20 per cent (or such rule as may be determined) of the deficiency in common stock shall be given to the bondholder. That is, for a bond standing at 30, the deficiency would be 70, and 20 per cent would be $14 in common stock. This bonus being a compensation for possible equity value of the depreciated bond. The stocks to be exchanged in the same manner. If possible, preferred stocks to be wiped out by some combination of bonds and common stocks.

7. The bonds to be guaranteed by the Federal government and issued at some low rate made possible with such a guarantee, say 3½ per cent. The authorized "system corporation" bonds to exceed the original issue by say 25 per cent in order that, having also the government guarantee, they may be marketed for purposes of immediate improvement. A heavy amortization charge should be established with a view to getting the government out of these guaranteed loans.

8. While exchanges of new "system corporation" securities to public holders of securities of component roads would solve the major consolidations, a problem will arise as to exchanges to cover cross securities and rents which may arise between "systems." This problem is one of detail and is solvable.

9. Systematic consolidation of the railways and terminals should result in savings up to 15 or 20 per cent in operating costs. The reduced interest on bonds, due to government guarantee, should represent a very considerable saving in interest itself—theoretically about $120,000,000 per annum. A calculation of these benefits would appear to put the railways in position to pay a reasonable dividend over average years on the new common stock at present railway rates. The capital structure of the railways, after such a reorganization, would probably not exceed 10 billion dollars in bonds and 7 billions in stock, a reduction of some 7 billions. The reduction might turn out to be even greater.

10. The Interstate Commerce Commission to be required to fix rates such as would earn for the nation as a whole in average years a minimum of 6 per cent per annum, so that future finance can be secured by stock rather than bonds. Any earnings of a given "system" in excess of 6 per cent on the stock to be used for retirement of bonds, thus paving the way to more flexible rates.

11. Reduction of the personnel of the railways to be taken care of by an undertaking not to reduce employees except through the normal retirement and normal death. This

natural wastage in the personnel would cover any needed reduction in personnel in a few years without hardship upon the existing employees.

12. As the public is taking a responsibility for the guarantee of the new bonds, the regulatory commissions in the various states where the "system corporations" have their major business to appoint an aggregate of one-third of its total Board of Directors, to represent this public interest.

There are, of course, other methods of valuing component railways in any given consolidation (such as density of traffic per mile or replacement value), but it is thought that the relative quotation of publicly held securities represents more closely the relative values and is a more facile and quicker method than any other that could be undertaken. It avoids the infinite difficulties of negotiation or physical valuation or density of traffic estimates. It avoids the infinite difficulties of determining the prior lien rights of different securities. It preserves an interest to every holder of securities.

It is believed that at least 66 per cent of the security holders in any given railway would willingly exchange in such a rehabilitation measure when recommended by the Reorganization Commission. Such a percentage could be made to bind the whole or, at least, would put the "system corporation" into possession.

If desirable, it should be possible to work out a method for the "system corporation" to take over the operation of component roads at once by some sort of temporary agreement pending determination of market values and exchange of securities.

*   *   *

[By 1951 inflation and the shifts in traffic had altered the relative values of securities. But the great savings by consolidations into larger systems were still unrealized. The Diesel motor had made great savings in operation, but other increases in expenses had about eaten up the benefits of these improvements. The Diesel, the lighter metals in passenger equipment, and the higher speeds had held more of the passenger traffic than had been expected—but the competition of pipe lines, automobiles, busses, trucks, and planes had constantly reduced the proportionate load carried by the railways. The savings and stronger finance by consolidation were as imperative as ever.]

CHAPTER 43

DEVELOPMENT OF SOCIAL REFORMS

The country was in need of more action in the social field. During the first months of my administration, I took steps to develop ideas in old-age pensions, insurance against irregular employment, better housing, and care of children.

I felt that our first need was a competent survey of the facts in the social field. On September 19, 1929, I appointed a committee of leading economists and sociologists to undertake an exhaustive examination and report. The directing members of the inquiry, Wesley C. Mitchell, Charles E. Merriam, Alice Hamilton, William F. Ogburn, Howard W. Odum, and Shelby M. Harrison, with Edward Eyre Hunt as secretary, made an able team; and French Strother was the liaison with myself. The committee's own statement of instructions was:

In September, 1929, the Chief Executive of the Nation called upon the members of this Committee to examine and to report upon recent social trends in the United States with a view to providing such a review as might supply the basis for the formulation of large national policies looking to the next phase of the national development. The summons was unique in our history. . . . The first third of the Twentieth Century has been filled with epoch-making events and crowded with problems urgently demanding attention on many fronts.

The committee secured the cooperation of several hundred specialists in different fields. The survey required three years. It formulated the first thorough statement of social fact ever presented as a guide to public policy. The loss of the election prevented me, as President, from offering a program of practical action based upon the facts.

Moreover, the depression, beginning a year after my inauguration, required devotion of every energy to the immediate problem of restoration of economic life and recovery. We made progress in some directions, but the financial and unemployment situations compelled the suspension of others.

In issuing the report of this Research Committee on Social Trends after my defeat I said on January 2, 1933:

The significance of this report lies primarily in the fact that it is a cooperative effort on a very broad scale to project into the field of social thought the scientific mood and the scientific method as correctives to undiscriminating emotional approach and to secure factual basis in seeking for constructive remedies of great social problems. The second significance of the undertaking is that, so far as I can learn, it is the first attempt ever made to study simultaneously all of the fundamental social facts which underlie all our social problems. Much ineffective thinking and many impracticable proposals of remedy have in the past been due to unfamiliarity with facts in fields related to that in which a given problem lies. The effort here has been to relate all the facts and present them under a common standard of measurement.

The work cost several hundred thousand dollars, which I raised by private subscription. The reports embrace two volumes of summary and a number of special monographs.

The fact that the report was carried as first-page news through the country indicated the great public interest in the subjects. It has had a profound effect upon national thinking.

OLD-AGE ASSISTANCE

The organization of old-age assistance under some Federal scheme was an inevitability for two reasons:

Medical science and work in public health controls had so prolonged the average life of the population that, instead of the 2 or 3 per cent living beyond 60 years of age a century earlier, we now had 10 or 12 per cent. The burden of the destitute and old people was too great to be met by the old-fashioned county commissioners with their "poorhouses." Some part of the people could not, even with thrift, provide for old age; and another part, through shiftlessness, would not. In consequence, many of the states had already initiated old-age assistance several years before—including California, where I had supported the measure.

In discussing various plans with my colleagues while I was in the Department of Commerce and the Presidency, I wrote out and circulated among them certain principles which I thought should underlie any practical provision for old-age assistance. The memorandum has only academic interest but, I believe, was a better basis than those later adopted:

First. By every device we should encourage private action in savings and private insurance.

Second. No governmental pension should exceed a bare subsistence, in order that we should not weaken the incentives to work and save; anything more than subsistence should be the product of the individual's own effort.

Third. This subsistence level, whether it be $30 or $50 a month per individual, or higher, should be readjusted from time to time according to the purchasing value of money.

Fourth. The same sum should be payable to everybody except income taxpayers (who can look after themselves) and the recipients of pensions from other sources.

Fifth. Federal participation should be limited to collecting a certain percentage from the pay of wage earners with an equivalent contribution from the employers; levying a certain percentage upon the gross income of non-wage-earners such as farmers and small business men, so that they could be included; these sums to be supplemented from the tax income of the government.

Sixth. The whole of such funds should be distributed as grants to the states with the requirement that the states assume part of the load. The states should have entire responsibility for administration.

Seventh. A nation's income is daily or annual. Therefore, all schemes should be based upon making an annual approximation of the cost against the annual outlay, paying it out by appropriation, and closing the books at the end of each year. If the income is insufficient during one year, the rate of collections should be increased the next year.

The height of the world's greatest depression was no time to introduce such ideas, even had we possessed the leisure time to formulate the plans. Our first job was recovery of employment, and any such widespread action was bound to produce some shocks to the economic system. Nevertheless, I was determined that the problem must be met, and for this reason I set up the Committee on Social Trends.

Meanwhile, September 28, 1929, in the hope of securing information from experience and at the same time expanding private action, I invited the heads of the leading mutual insurance companies to have luncheon with me at the White House. I reminded them that they all sold annuities based upon their investments. Could they not, in a special set-up, devise a direct old-age insurance policy with pensions beginning at sixty-five years of age: this policy to be based upon either lump-sum payments or annual premiums starting at any age from one year up, the cost to be lessened by forfeiture of all payments by those who died before sixty-five? I also suggested that they consider selling such insurance to business and industry on a group basis, thus making it easier for such enterprises to provide old-age insurance for their employees. I asked them to give me some computations on lump payments or annual premiums necessary for different ages in order to secure a unit of, say, $50 a month after sixty-five years of age. The companies were greatly interested. They reported that the lump-premium payments that would secure such a pension, if begun at two years of age, would be only a fraction of $500. Some of the mutual companies agreed to issue such policies, and we proposed to launch the idea at Christmas, 1929, by my purchasing a policy for my grandchildren at a lump cost for the two of about $500. This one payment would give them each $50 a month after they reached sixty-five years of age. The cost was so small that we hoped it would attract many parents to provide an old-age pension for their children in this manner. We had gone so far as to set up a publicity organization under Mr. Samuel Crowther. The slump, however, caused the companies to withdraw from this project and await a more favorable moment to launch it.

I had suggested to the companies that if the idea was attractive to the public, we might consider some form of Federal grants to them as an aid to lowering the cost to the beginners in the older groups whose premiums would necessarily be high. I regretted greatly that the depression made it impossible to launch this project, as it might have given us great experience and made it possible to reduce the extent of governmental action.

UNEMPLOYMENT INSURANCE

My suggestion of unemployment insurance by private agencies while I was in the Department of Commerce has already been mentioned.

I believed that with proper safeguards it was feasible. But our people, having had practically full employment from 1914 to 1930 with only one short slump, were not interested in the subject. It required a great depression to awaken interest in the idea.

Moreover, I felt the burdens of the depression had to be removed before we could take the shocks of so widespread a Federal action.

EDUCATION

The Federal government touches the educational system in many directions. Presidents are interested in its problems and its advancement as the very basis of successful freedom. The Federal government maintained a Bureau of Education for the primary purpose of distributing information as to methods and progress.

Certain very vocal educational associations were constantly demanding Federal support to the whole school system of the nation. There were no doubt some states and communities that lagged in their responsibilities, either from neglect or from economic weakness. These areas did infest the whole nation by their failures.

I was not opposed to Federal aid to backward areas where there was genuine need. But this was not the objective of the demands. The associations wanted the Federal head under every state and county tent.

The most successful accomplishment of our system of local government has been the building of free and effective public education over the greater part of the nation. The United States was the first country to make education a public responsibility.

Presidents had long since been kept busy repelling these attempts to shift the schools out from under local and state control and hand them over to the more easily lobbied Federal government. The pressure flared up during my administration in demands for a Federal Department of Education, and many bills were introduced into Congress for direct subsidies.

Doubting that these various guises of Federal control had the approval of the thinking educators, Secretary Wilbur and I appointed a committee of leading educators and laymen on June 6, 1929, to report on the question. The committee reported on November 16, 1931. The members were unanimous on one thing—the Federal government should not encroach upon the public school systems.

On November 17, 1929, I appointed a committee of distinguished membership under Secretary Wilbur to cooperate with the Department of the Interior in developing a nation-wide voluntary movement to abolish illiteracy through immediate informal organization of adult education. This committee set up vigorous action with important results. An interim report on April 8, 1931, stated that national illiteracy amounted to 4.3 per cent of the population. It announced that it had established organization in forty-three states, and that a nation-wide formation of adult educational classes was in progress through cooperation with state authorities or civic organizations.

The existing services of the Federal government to education were scattered through five departments. On February 17, 1932, I recommended to the Congress that we appoint an Assistant Secretary for Education in the Department of the Interior and consolidate all the agencies under him. The Democratic majority, however, refused to approve this measure.

THE INDIANS

I have had a particular interest in Indians from the time when, as a boy, I lived on the Osage Reservation with my uncle Major Laban Miles, who was then the Agent.

The American Indian has been a problem ever since white men landed at Jamestown. That problem is a mixture of national conscience, of agriculture, education, health, poverty, shiftlessness, and ideology. Among the whites a fervid anxiety was felt for the Indians' moral and spiritual welfare, and a twinge of conscience demanded that they be compensated periodically for the "deprival of their land," mixed with a firm determination to civilize them whether they liked it or not. And at the same time the Indian tribes were infested with human

lice in the shape of white men who sold them hard liquor in violation
of the law, married the young squaws in order to get their land in-
heritances and oil rights, or conjured up fictitious claims and pushed
them through Congress with profit-sharing lawyers. Like most of my
predecessors, I had to repulse many such raids. A certain amount of
the time of every President every week, from George Washington
down, has had to be devoted to "Indian Affairs." Certainly, our
400,000 Indians consume more official attention than any twenty cities
of 400,000 white people.

The annual appropriations of the Federal government for Indian
care, education, health, interest on land · purchases and the like
amounted to about $400 a family which, added to their other resources,
gave a higher average income to some tribes than that of the white
population. Others had practically nothing.

Federal policies vibrated from a yearning at one pole to perpetuate
the tribal organization and customs to a desire at the other pole to
make industrious citizens of them and thus fuse them with the general
population. The former proposals were advocated by all left wingers,
who saw in the Indian scheme of society a "true communal life." Such
policies were also supported by the cynical who hoped the Indians
would drink themselves to death or otherwise perish happily.

Secretary Wilbur and I belonged to the "fusion" school of thought.
We chose Mr. Charles Rhoads and Mr. Henry Scattergood, eminent
Philadelphia Quakers, to administer the Indian Bureau. We had in
mind not only their individual abilities, but the fact that Quakers
had always been the defenders of the Indians since the beginning of
American history. Messrs. Wilbur, Rhoads, and Scattergood made an
exhaustive reexamination of the whole question. They reported that
the objective of the administration must be to make the Indians self-
supporting and self-respecting. They were to be viewed no longer as
wards of the nation, but as potential citizens. I secured from Congress
additional appropriations of about $3,000,000 per annum to finance a
vigorous program directed to this end.

At our request Congress amended many of the laws governing the
Indians and their property. We gave them better protection from

exploitation and improved their health and educational services. They were on the way toward wider citizenship and self-support when the believers in the communal pole of thought came in with the New Deal. The Indian problem is still with us, and Presidents are still vetoing phony claim bills.[1]

---

[1] In 1947–1948 I was Chairman of a Congressionally established Commission on Organization of the Executive Branch of the Government. Our investigation found the Indians in just as bad a state as they had been fifteen years before.

CHAPTER 44

AN INTERLUDE—LIVING IN THE WHITE HOUSE

Some account of a family living in the White House may be of interest.

The White House is a structure of singular dignity and beauty. When originally built, it looked like a barn, but the subsequent addition of the North and South Porticoes and the one-story wings corrected its architectural deficiencies. The original fault was due to the fact that it was simply the middle section of an Irish nobleman's palace, the blueprints of which had been accepted from a young Irish architect without material change in either exterior or interior design.

It is far more than a beautiful building. Its rooms and halls are alive with the invisible presence of the great leaders of our country. Here all our Presidents since John Adams had worked and striven for the public good. Here the great conferences with the leaders of the Congress and the nation have worked out measures for the welfare of our country. The spiritual winds which blow through these halls are a constant call to rightness and devotion for service to our people.

Tradition and history recall some incident in every room. They began when Abigail Adams hung her washing in the then unfinished East Room and do not end with the great sideboard bought by the dimes of the "Bands of Hope" and presented to Mrs. Hayes, then the First Lady. She first made the White House "dry." The Theodore Roosevelts in refurnishing the dining room had the sideboard sold at auction. It is said to have been bought by a Pennsylvania Avenue saloonkeeper who installed it as his bar. But these are the trivialities.

The upstairs room which Presidents from Adams down to McKinley used for a study was transformed into a bedroom by the Theodore Roosevelts to accommodate that large tribe. Here Lincoln had worked and suffered. Here the Emancipation Proclamation and the Freedom of Cuba had been signed. Many great national decisions had been taken within its walls. I reestablished it as the President's study. Mrs. Hoover, after examination of the great painting of the signing of the Emancipation, discovered some of the identical furniture in the garret and placed it in the room.

The upstairs where the family lives was as bleak as a New England barn. It was filled with dreary furniture and had not been much lightened over the years. Mrs. Hoover brought in our own household gods and by other arrangements gave it a more livable feeling.

The lower floors contain two noble rooms, the East Room and the Dining Room. The house had to be entirely furnished by President Monroe after the British burned it in 1812. He secured much of the furniture through the American Minister in Paris—rather garish and ponderous Empire. Many pieces survived but were scattered from the garret to the basement. Mrs. Hoover gathered them together, had them refurbished and was able with them to completely furnish the East Room, the huge formal reception room, thus giving it character again. A costly table ornament had been acquired in Monroe's time. Several pages of invective over this extravagance appear in the *Congressional Record*. Nevertheless, it has been used for state dinners for more than a century.

We kept all the White House servants. They had many years' service and great devotion to their positions. Catherine, the head cook, was an honest Irishwoman who at once informed Mrs. Hoover that she did not expect to be kept on, for she had voted for Governor Smith and she was a Catholic. Mrs. Hoover told her that she was not interested in her religion or political faith but in her cooking, which was superlative. She remained during our four years but lost out when the Democratic party came in. She retired to Ireland and for years sent us a magnificent ham every Christmas.

Another servant of long duration was Ike Hoover (no relative). He was chief "usher" and presided over all visitors and social functions. He had been a faithful employee of the White House for over thirty years,

since the Harrison administration. One day after we moved in Ike
called some store to give an order for supplies, saying, "This is Hoover,
calling from the White House." The merchant's phone girl replied:
"Indeed and I am Queen of Sheba."

The publication of "memoirs" by White House attendants has become a publisher's gossip-book feature during the last forty years. As
Presidents do not impart state secrets to servants or clerical staffs, and
as First Ladies do not allow scandal to foul the White House rooms,
these "memoirs" have had need to be jazzed up by peeping Tom
imagination or by some ghost writer who imparted great confidences.
Otherwise the product of such literary and intellectual persons might
not be saleable. To one familiar with White House personnel or routine,
these imaginative additions and tidbits are strange additions. Those
relating to the Theodore Roosevelts, the Tafts, the Wilsons, the Hard-
ings, and the Coolidges, as well as my own, were highly imaginative at
times. Historians should reject all of them.

Washington's exhausting summer heat is known to several million
people from acute experience. Eggs have been fried on the pavements.
In search for relief I sent Lawrence Richey, one of my secretaries since
Food Administration days, together with Colonel Earl Long of the
Marines, on an exploration of the Blue Ridge in Virginia for a summer
camp. They found a delightful location at the headwaters of the Rapidan with an elevation of about 1,500 feet. Mrs. Hoover laid out and
superintended the erection of a series of log cabins furnishing accommodations for twelve to fifteen guests. It was exactly a hundred miles
from the White House, and we connected it by direct telephone. The
week ends with cool nights were a great relief.

That area of the Blue Ridge was incorporated by my administration
into the Shenandoah National Park. At the end of my term, I presented
the land and the camp to the Park for the future use of the White
House or alternatively to the Boy and Girl Scouts organizations. As the
Democratic National Committee charged that it had been bought and
erected with public funds, we were compelled to get out a formal denial
stating the fact that I had paid for the land, buildings, and furniture.

The upper Rapidan bubbled through the camp and, by building a

MRS. HOOVER, IN THE WHITE HOUSE

number of pools along its canyon, we managed to turn it into a fair trout stream.

The social routines of the White House were at times a burden. The nine or ten great annual receptions amounted to a rapidly moving assembly line of thousands of hand shakes. The smiling good wishes of the guests were an encouragement, but after a few thousand the experience was somewhat exhausting. Especially after a hard day in the office it is difficult to continuously reach out a friendly attitude and greeting to these thousands. And often enough my hand would be so swollen for days after that I could not write with it. On one occasion a husky westerner with a turned-in diamond ring gave me such a warm grasp as to cut my hand badly, and we had to terminate the ceremony in a trickle of blood.

President Adams had inaugurated the idea of a New Year's reception at the White House, open to all comers. Except for war periods it had apparently never been interrupted. The report was that 135 people attended the first reception to wish Mr. and Mrs. Adams a Happy New Year.

On New Year's morning, 1930, I was informed that a long line had been waiting since midnight. Not to keep the people waiting, Mrs. Hoover suggested we begin at once. Before the day was over I had shaken hands with over 9,000 people—some three times the usual number. I had sent Mrs. Hoover away for a rest at intervals, but she insisted on going through with most of the day. I concluded that that custom might have properly originated with Adams, but that he did not know that the population would increase from 3,000,000 to 130,000,000 nor what changes there would be in transportation for visitors into Washington.

I thought, and said, that the whole performance of this reception was preposterous. I wanted to abolish it. We did manage to avoid any more New Year's ordeals by going out of town. But Mrs. Hoover's rigid sense of duty would not permit abolishing the other formal receptions. To her it was a part of the job. She felt thousands of people would be disappointed if they could not come to the White House—and she felt also that we might be considered snobbish if we limited our contacts to our family and official friends.

She received a great wound from this conscientious adherence to duty. During my administration there was a Negro Congressman. He had a wife. In giving the usual teas for Congressmen's wives, Mrs. Hoover insisted upon inviting the Negro's wife equally with the others. She was warned by some of her Congressional lady friends not to do it. The Negro Congressman did not particularly help matters by announcing to the press that his wife had received such an invitation. In consequence the southern press denounced this "defiling" of the White House and the southern reporters lined up to watch the colored lady come and go, hoping to witness their prophecy that some Congressman's wife would flop out. Mrs. Hoover had more sense than to give any such occasion for affront to her guest or to the White House. Nor did she wish to offend ladies from the South. Therefore, she divided her Congressional tea into different days and placed the Negro lady on the first day with ladies who had been previously tested as to their feelings. The speeches of the southern Senators and Congressmen, the editorials in the southern press, and a denunciatory resolution by the Texas Legislature wounded her deeply. Her tears, however, did not melt her indomitable determination. I sought to divert the lightning by at once inviting Dr. Moton of Tuskegee to lunch with me. The White House was thus "defiled" several times during my term.

To Mrs. Hoover, her position must be the symbol of everything wholesome in American life. She was oversensitive, and the stabs of political life which, no doubt, were deserved by me hurt her greatly. She was deeply religious, and to her such actions were just plain wickedness. Her only departures from sweet urbanity were in outrage at some unfairness in our opponents—and that in private. I suggested to her one time that a good reason for holding to orthodox religious faith was that it included a hot hell, and that she could console herself that this kind of politician and writer who escaped retribution in this world would find special facilities in the world to come. But she was too gentle a soul to see any humor in my idea.

She had a warm intuition, and she instinctively studied every new person who came into our orbit. Of those who were likely to be more than casual passers-by, she unobtrusively collected a great deal of background. Except where she felt it imperative, she never volunteered her judgments. However, I could tell them from her expression. To her, moral standards were infinitely more important than intellectual qualifications. But Presidents cannot always kick evil-minded persons out of the front door. Such persons are often selected by the electors to represent them. She used to worry a good deal privately as to the devilment they might do to me. Loyalty to a cause, to a party, to a leader were part of her moral standards, and her judgment on these inherent qualities in persons at times proved uncanny.

During this period Herbert became ailing, and the doctors at once determined that he had tuberculosis and must spend a year in bed in some sanitarium under rigorous control if he was to recover. We brought Margaret and the two babies, Peggy-Ann and Herbert III, to the White House. Herbert sorrowfully gave up his job and accepted his sentence to Asheville, North Carolina.

I was able to visit him only once, but Mrs. Hoover and Margaret visited him every few weeks. Being an engineer, he had a radio rigged at his bedside through which he could listen not only to the broadcasts but to the conversations over the transatlantic telephone, which were not "scrambled" at that time. He collected many amusing and startling conversations.

We had a Belgian police dog that was much attached to him and took on the duties of nurse by bringing in the cod-liver-oil bottle at the appropriate times. It was a dreary experience; but his resolution thrilled us with pride, and in ten months he was discharged and restored to the husky health he has enjoyed ever since. Having Margaret and the children at the White House was a continuous joy.

There are some valuable privileges attached to being President— among them the duty and right to terminate all interviews, conferences, social parties, and receptions. Therefore, he can go to bed whenever he likes. I liked ten o'clock, as I had to rise at seven and read a great deal during the night.

The White House office was sorely afflicted with time-consuming and nerve-racking customs. From employees who had held over since the Harrison administration, I learned that up to the beginning of the First World War the Presidents had spent only about two hours daily on office work. They spent another two or three hours a day seeing people and reporters. The rest of the time, I suppose, was devoted to heavy thinking. President Wilson, of course, had the strain of a gigantic war and rid himself of the social activities during that period—and he worked twelve hours a day.

Harding and Coolidge seemed to be bent on restoring the "old customs"—of a host of public callers. One of these ordeals was a noon reception at the White House office six days in the week, where any citizen might shake hands with the President if he passed the Secret Service inspection for respectability and harmlessness. Many were children, whom it was a joy to see. But the average of 30 to 40 persons per day at Theodore Roosevelt's receptions had increased to between 300 and 400 per day under Coolidge. And I soon found myself wasting a whole hour every day shaking hands with 1,000 to 1,200 people.

I tried various expedients to reduce the number. One was to require the caller to have a card from some administration official or member of the Congress. Promptly the Congressmen availed themselves of it as an entertainment feature for their visiting constituents, and it got worse. I finally suppressed it altogether, giving that hour to special appointments with people from out of town who were in Washington on matters of importance.

Another of these useless exhaustions, which had always plagued Presidents, was signing routine papers. No man could read them even on a twenty-four-hour shift. They comprised all military officers' commissions, many appointments of civil servants, Treasury orders, documents relating to the guardianship of individual Indians, pension authorities, etc., all of which the President could only sign on the dotted line and trust to Heaven and his Cabinet officers that they were all right. The Cabinet officers, in turn, trusted to Bureau heads. The number of these documents had increased enormously since the expansion of the government due to the war. During George Washington's administrations, both the President and the Secretary of State found time even to sign all ships' manifests of cargo. I never did learn how this particular activity died. For my relief the Attorney General suggested that a delegation of power to Cabinet officers to do much of the "signing" was proper; and a great relief it was.

With the depression the demands upon the White House increased to war dimensions. Telephone calls, telegrams, and mail were a sort of index. They quadrupled Mr. Coolidge's stint. Telephone calls often ran to more than 1,200 a day, and mail to more than 10,000 letters or telegrams. The staff had to be increased. Congress authorized three White House secretaries instead of one, and we had to borrow aid from the Departments as well. Incidentally, Mr. Coolidge (and I think also his predecessors) did not tolerate a telephone in the President's own office and went into another room when such conversation was imperative. Of course the President is not open to everyone's call. However, I instituted a special telephone switchboard in the building which connected my desk with the desks of all the prominent members of the administration. Scores of small items were cleared by a telephone call which otherwise would have required bringing the people to the White House.

Getting daily exercise to keep physically fit is always a problem for Presidents. Once the day's work starts there is little chance to walk, to ride, or to take part in a game. Taking walks or rides early in the morning is a lonesome business, and the inevitable secret service guard when the President leaves the White House grounds is not enlivening company. I therefore suggested to some of my colleagues that we start a medicine-ball game for seven-thirty in the morning on the White House lawn. The attendance varied from six to eighteen and continued without a break, except Sundays and absences, for the whole four years. The game was played by passing an eight-pound medicine ball over a ten-foot net on a court laid out as for tennis and scored the same way. It required less skill than tennis, was faster and more vigorous, and therefore gave more exercise in a short time. The most regular of attendants were Justice Stone, Attorney General Mitchell, Secretaries Wilbur and Hyde, Assistant Secretaries Hope, Ballantine, and Jahncke, Solicitors General Thacher and Hughes, Walter Newton, Dr. Boone, Mark Sullivan, Larry Richey, and Alexander Legge.

After the game we assembled a few moments for fruit juice and coffee. It was no kitchen cabinet. By common consent the conversation was kept off official matters and on the light side. The morning star shells of humor from the trenches often illuminated the dreary no-man's-land of the depression. It started the day with good cheer. Even on the morning of March 4, 1933, Secretary Hyde produced an account of two bankers involved in the depression. He recounted that one of them, unshaven, hungry, his shirt gone, approached a circus manager for a job, saying he would do anything just for something to eat. The manager told him that he was not even able to feed his present employees, and that he had already killed the lion to feed the tigers. Just then an employee approached and said the gorilla had died of starvation, upon which the manager exclaimed in despair, "This is the finish." Thereupon, the unquenchable, enterprising spirit of the banker came into action, and he proposed they skin the gorilla; he would get into the skin and perform provided he had a square meal and a cut in on the receipts. While he was performing in his cage, the lion in the next compartment pulled open the bars between and made for him ferociously. The gorilla cried desperately for help. Whereupon the lion whispered in his ear, "Shut up, you fool, you are not the only banker out of a job."

Secretary Wilbur pessimistically observed that no doubt the New Deal would end these evils by passing a measure subsidizing circuses.

Foreign Affairs

CHAPTER 45

GENERAL PEACE POLICIES

My ambition in our foreign policies was to lead the United States in full cooperation with world moral forces to preserve peace.

The United States was still under the spell of reaction from the war. That was due in part to heated nationalism, which is the inevitable result of such conflicts. It was also due in part to a sense of frustration over the results of the war, and to disgust at the continual spectacle of European power politics and imperialism since the Armistice. Wilson's idealism, which America had shared deeply, had been mostly rejected at Versailles. The League of Nations, in the American mind, had been made an instrument for enforcing a bad treaty instead of an instrument for amending and revising it as Wilson had hoped. The home-coming soldiers had brought no good reports of "foreigners," and the stigma from Europe of "Uncle Shylock" in the effort to avoid the payment of debts seemed to confirm the views "against."

When I took office America was so isolationist that our proper responsibilities were neglected. Congress was adamant against the World Court, and even to suggest that we would collaborate with the League of Nations in its many nonpolitical activities brought storms of protest.

Secretary of State Hughes had been unable to secure ratification of our participation in the World Court. He made substantial contributions to world stability through the limitations on the larger warships, the return by Japan of Shantung to China and the Nine Power Treaty which gave China a chance to recover her full sovereignty. Secretary Kellogg, through the Kellogg-Briand Pact, had established a promising moral instrument which stands as a monument to his idealism. The acceptance of the Pact, however, was obtained upon the argument that it contained no commitments to action.

At my inauguration the whole world was at peace—at least there were no consequential wars going on. War-provoking social movements were confined to fumes from the Communist caldron in Russia and Fascism in Italy. At this time Fascism was attracting more public attention than Communism, although it was equally a despotism with a police state wholly denying most freedoms. Mussolini rattled his tin saber periodically but without worrying anybody much. Fascism had not yet been transformed into consuming fire by the militaristic castes of Germany and Japan. Indeed, the military party was not to seize control in Japan until three years later, and Hitler was not to come into power until after my defeat in 1932. Germany was still limited in arms except in the hearts of the military caste. The leaders of the democratic regime in Germany were earnestly striving to maintain peace.

But Europe was infested with age-old hates and fears, with their offspring of military alliances and increasing armament. Its rival imperialisms continued as smoldering fires which were the principal source of dangerous wars. Power politics was both the consequence and the cause. I had no desire to see the United States involved. From the beginning I believed that the hope of peace lay in the maintenance of representative government over the world, and I felt there was still some security in the recoil of horror from the war. But I desired that we might contribute to more solid foundations of peace. I believed fervently that we should collaborate with every sincere movement to reinforce peaceful processes.

My special concern that we should take larger responsibilities in world affairs is shown by the many addresses and messages on these subjects.[1]

[1] See *The State Papers and Other Public Writings of Herbert Hoover*, ed. by William Starr Myers, 2 vols., Doubleday, Doran & Co., 1934; *The Foreign Policies of Herbert Hoover, 1929–1933*, by William Starr Myers, Charles Scribner's Sons, 1940; *Herbert Hoover's Latin-American Policy*, by Alexander DeConde, Stanford University Press, 1951.

Based upon broad policies of cooperation with other nations in the moral field as distinguished from the force field, I made specific proposals in many directions during the four years of my administration. They included:

1. Change in attitudes between ourselves and the Latin American states.

2. Reorganization of our diplomatic service in those nations.

3. For advancement of pacific methods of settling controversies between nations, I urged:

    a. Adherence to the World Court.

    b. Increasing the number of direct treaties calling for arbitration and conciliation.

    c. Expansion of the Kellogg Pact.

    d. Full cooperation with the League of Nations in its non-force activities.

4. Elimination of friction with Great Britain.

    a. By ending naval competition.

    b. By ending British expansion of naval and air bases in the Western Hemisphere.

    c. By settling one major conflict over freedom of the seas by immunizing food ships from submarine attack in time of war.

5. Efforts to sustain representative government in Germany.

6. Cooperation with other nations in pacific means to restrain Japanese aggression in China.

7. Limitation of naval arms.

8. Reduction in land armies.

9. International cooperation in the economic field to ameliorate the depression and lessen the dangers of internal revolutions. I deal with these latter measures among those undertaken to ameliorate the depression. They are mainly:

    a. The moratorium on intergovernmental debts.

    b. The "stand-still" agreement upon German private debts.

    c. Revision of war debts.

    d. A world economic conference to stabilize currencies and reduce trade barriers.

I have already described my journey to Latin America as President-Elect.

In an address on April 13, 1929, referring to this journey I repeated an idea that I had expressed many times on the trip, saying:

I mention one sinister notion as to policies of the United States upon our relationships with our Latin-American neighbors. That is, fear of an era of the mistakenly called dollar diplomacy. The implications that have been conveyed by that expression are not a part of my conception of international relations. I can say at once that it ought not to be the policy of the United States to intervene *by force* to secure or maintain contracts between our citizens and foreign states or their citizens. Confidence in that attitude is the only basis upon which the economic cooperation of our citizens can be welcomed abroad. It is the only basis that prevents cupidity encroaching upon the weakness of nations—but, far more than this, it is the true expression of the moral rectitude of the United States.

To give proof of my determination to end force interventions, I directed the withdrawal of American Marines from Nicaragua, which began on June 3, 1931. On December 7, 1929, I requested authority from the Congress for an official commission to examine the situation in Haiti and advise when and how we were to withdraw—in effect, how to extricate ourselves from the mess into which we had been plunged by the Wilson administration. Immediately upon receiving the report of the commission, I began the withdrawal of American forces and the building up of a substantial government in Haiti.

On my return from South America I set up a plan for exchange of students and professors between our own and their universities. I arranged for Mr. Clarence Woolley to head a committee for that purpose and to raise the necessary funds. The depression caused its postponement. The project could not be revived during my administration because of the continued economic stress.

In summary of my term in the White House I did seven things in respect to Latin America:

(a) Arranged the withdrawal of our troops from Haiti and Nicaragua;

(b) Stated that there would be no more military interventions except actually to save American lives;

(c) Declared that American citizens venturing their capital and energies in these states were doing so at their own risk, and that our interventions on their behalf if they were unjustly treated would be purely moral representations;

(d) Set up regular air communications;

(e) Settled the Tacna-Arica dispute between Chile and Peru;

(f) Directed that the State Department publicize a revised interpretation of the Monroe Doctrine which had been prepared by Under-Secretary J. Reuben Clark, eliminating the idea that we were concerned with the domestic affairs of the other American Republics.

(g) Removed political appointees as ministers or ambassadors, sending to each post a career man or otherwise independent person who had a background of experience in the country and a familiarity with the people, their language, customs, and culture.

As a result of these policies, carried on throughout my administration, the interventions which had been the source of so much bitterness and fear in Latin America were ended. We established a good will in Latin America not hitherto known for many years, under the specific term "good neighbors."

LATIN AMERICAN AND OTHER FOREIGN LOANS

As indicated in the chapters covering my term as Secretary of Commerce, I had great anxiety over the character of private loans by our bankers to foreign governments. Some of those in Latin American states had been particularly bad.

As President, I made a public statement on this subject on October 8, 1931, saying:

Such loans . . . are helpful in world development, provided always one essential principle dominates these transactions. That is, that no nation as a government should borrow or no government lend and nations should discourage their citizens from borrowing or lending unless this money is to be devoted to productive enterprise.

Out of the wealth and the higher standards of living created from enterprise itself must come to the borrowing country the ability to repay the capital. Any other course of action creates obligations impossible of repayment except by a direct subtraction from the standards of living of the borrowing country and the impoverishment of its people.

In fact, if this principle could be adopted between nations of the world—that is, if nations would do away with the lending of money for the balancing of budgets, for purposes of military equipment or war purposes, or even that type of public works which does not bring some direct or indirect productive return—a great number of blessings would follow to the entire world.

REORGANIZATION OF OUR FOREIGN SERVICE

The importance of able and experienced American diplomatic representation abroad had been neglected as a factor in preserving peace. Under conditions prior to the World War we did not need much effort in this direction. But it was my conviction that we must now be much better equipped if we were to meet the changed needs of the times. I felt our ambassadors to the five or six great countries should be chosen from outstanding citizens whose public service and personal distinction carried additional weight. I therefore appointed to Britain, France, Germany, Italy, and Japan such men as former Vice President Charles G. Dawes, former Senators Walter Edge and Frederic Sackett, former Governor W. Cameron Forbes, John W. Garrett, William R. Castle, and former Secretary of the Treasury Andrew Mellon. Men of this type could not be obtained for the lesser posts. In the nineteen Latin American states fifteen of our appointments had been political rewards. Before my administration was over we were represented in eighteen out of the nineteen of these nations by career men. I promoted career men to these positions in thirteen other countries and established the idea of an "Ambassador at Large" in Europe for special purposes by appointing Hugh Gibson, Ambassador to Belgium, to such work.

THE KELLOGG-BRIAND PACT

Secretary of State Stimson did not take office until some months after my inauguration in 1929. Mr. Kellogg had consented to remain in office until that time. During his period we formally signed the Kellogg-Briand Pact of the Coolidge administration.

The Pact provided:

Article I. The High Contracting Parties solemnly declare . . . they condemn recourse to war for the solution of international controversies, and renounce it as an instrument of national policy in their relations with one another.

Article II. The High Contracting Parties agree that the settlement or solution of all disputes or conflicts of whatever nature or of whatever origin they may be, which may arise among them, shall never be sought except by pacific means.

I proposed to Secretary Kellogg that we devise some stronger diplomatic teeth for the Pact by the addition of an "Article III" which would make it more potent and make it possible to include nations outside the League in such action. In these proposals we were greatly aided by Professor James T. Shotwell. In the end I drafted two possible paragraphs:

(a) That, in case of violation of the Pact, the other powers should have a right to intervene by setting up an impartial commission to investigate, conciliate, propose a settlement, publish the facts, and withdraw diplomatic recognition from the recalcitrant party.

(b) A declaration by the nations that they would not recognize any territorial or other gains of any nation from aggression and the withdrawal of diplomatic recognition in such cases.

A suggestion somewhat similar to the second had been made by Secretary Bryan early in the Wilson administration. Secretary Kellogg, however, finally concluded that any "Article III" would be too much of a parallel to the pacific steps already authorized to the League and would be resented by the League members.

ADVANCEMENT OF OTHER PACIFIC METHODS FOR SETTLING CONTROVERSIES

Secretary Stimson at this time was not in good health, but he was well supported by such men as Joseph Cotton, William Castle, and Harvey Bundy, who had worked with me before. I was obliged to take over more duties in this field than otherwise would have been the case. The Secretary was a man of integrity, sagacity, loyalty, and patriotism, as befitted that office.

A study of the Senate gave promise that we might get that body to accept membership in the World Court if we could eliminate certain specific criticisms of its protocol. At least the necessary number of senators stated to Secretary Stimson that they would vote for it if this were done. I was suspicious that some of them were practicing avoidance but resolved to try.

Therefore we asked former Secretary of State Elihu Root to canvass these Senate objections and determine whether he could find a formula to which they would agree, and then himself visit Europe to ascertain whether certain reservations by us as to the protocols would be accepted. Mr. Root performed this task with skill and devotion. His great prestige won his points in Europe, and I hoped that the same prestige would help us to prevail in the Senate.

I submitted the amended protocol on December 10, 1930. I presented it again at the next session on December 10, 1931, but many Democratic members joined the Republican isolationists, Hiram Johnson, Norris, Moses, and others, in keeping it bottled up.

Secretary Stimson had much greater success in developing treaties of arbitration and conciliation and securing their confirmation by the Senate. During my four years treaties of arbitration were signed with twenty-five nations, and treaties of conciliation with seventeen. We were jointly obligated with practically every country in the world to refer to these processes any differences which we could not settle by negotiation.

COOPERATION WITH THE LEAGUE OF NATIONS IN NON-FORCE FIELDS

The League was doing splendid work in advancing a wide range of international action outside the force field. Through our Minister in Switzerland we joined in these efforts, and in such particulars as international trade in narcotics, expansion of marine law, and radio regulation, we took the lead. As a consequence we became parties to several score of treaties covering such matters as commerce, aviation, merchant marine, protection of intellectual property, control of international traffic in narcotics, black and white slavery, and disease. Aside from their high importance in developing a civilized world, these treaties served to bring a better realization of world responsibility to our people.

CHAPTER 46

NATIONAL DEFENSE AND WORLD DISARMAMENT

My policies in national defense and world disarmament had one simple objective. That was to insure freedom from war to the American people.

The size of naval and military forces required to insure our country against aggression rests partly upon our foreign policies and partly upon the relative strength of possible enemies. The American concept had always been arms for defense, not for aggression. Our defense required that we defend the whole Western Hemisphere. We needed to have such strength that European and Asiatic aggressors would not even look in this direction.

I had expressed these ideas in my acceptance speech at Palo Alto on August 11, 1928; in my Inaugural Address on March 4, 1929; in a speech from the White House on September 18, 1929; in an Armistice Day address on November 11, 1929; in messages to the Congress on December 3, 1929, and in subsequent years.

Manifestly, with great ocean moats between us and possible enemies, our principal military needs at this time were naval and air forces. With such assurance against foreign armies landing on this hemisphere, we could rely upon a small skeleton Army capable of quick expansion.

Early in my administration, I put the question to the Navy and Army staffs: "Are our defenses strong enough to prevent a successful landing of foreign soldiers on the continental United States and ultimately on the Western Hemisphere?" The reply was emphatically "Yes."

To maintain the Navy under the strong administration of Secretary Charles Francis Adams, we completed the construction of 80,000 tons of new war vessels, largely completed 100,000 more tons, modernized four battleships wholly and three partially.

We improved the efficiency of the Army under the able administrations of Secretaries of War James Good and Patrick Hurley. I had long held that the choice of Chiefs of Staff by seniority led only to dead ends. I therefore searched the Army for younger blood and finally determined upon General Douglas MacArthur. His brilliant abilities and his sterling character need no exposition from me. With the new leadership in the Department we further improved the regular Army, as a skeleton force which could at once furnish general and technical direction to guide the National Guard if it were called into action. The combined regulars and Guard would give us an immediate force of about 650,000 men. We supported various Civilian Training Corps with a view to strengthening these forces. During my administration we insisted upon two changes in the major Army policy. The first was the conversion of the cavalry to a mechanized corps. This was a painful job because a horse was a pet as well as a tradition. There is no body of men so effectively conservative and obstinate of change as the run-of-mine military man. The cavalrymen honestly believed three things: battles could not be won without horses; defeated enemies could not be pursued; and the breeds of horses would deteriorate without the cavalry.

Our second problem was the Air Force, where we had to meet the same conservative attitudes as from cavalry. Aside from building up commercial aviation as a reserve of manufacture and training of personnel, we placed what we called "educational orders," through which we subsidized commercial plane manufacturers so that they would be ready for quick expansion with gauges, blue prints, and trained personnel. The Army and Navy provided them with constantly improved models.

We increased the active air forces by 40 per cent to about 2,800 planes with the necessary expansion of ground services.

Living quarters on Army posts were greatly improved. The Coast Defense was greatly strengthened.

LIMITATION OF WORLD NAVIES

The two problems of naval and land disarmament were very different for America from those of other great powers. We had the second-size Navy in the world. Our regular Army included only 140,000 men. The active Army was less, in proportion to our civil population, than that allowed to supposedly disarmed Germany under the Treaty of Versailles. Thus, while we could deal with other nations for proportional reduction on navies, we could only persuade on armies.

Britain and Japan were engaged in competitive naval building with us, and, as the whole question was one of relative strength, it seemed to me simple common sense to see if we could not come to an agreement to limit further expansion and ratios with other nations. The international naval limitation inaugurated by Secretary Hughes in 1921 covered mainly capital ships and left out other tonnage which was 70 per cent of the whole Navy. President Coolidge in 1927 inspired a conference to extend limitations to cruisers, destroyers, submarines and other craft. That conference had failed because of the refusal of the British to accept parity with the United States. I took up the problem.

Before my inauguration I availed myself of the opportunity of Ambassador Gibson's presence in Washington to draft with him a speech which he would deliver as our Ambassador at Large at a forthcoming meeting of a League of Nations Committee on Disarmament which I instructed him to attend. The League had never seriously dealt with this question, and I thought to inject life into its discussions by having Mr. Gibson deliver a bold and unexpected proposal. He did so at Geneva on April 22, 1929. The British had denied that there was any practicable basis upon which parity could be based. In this speech he dealt with "yardsticks" which might be used. I followed it up by a public statement on May 30.

We proposed that another Naval Conference be called, this time in London, to extend the limitation to all warships. I had seen too many international conferences fail from lack of preparation. I therefore insisted that the conference not be convened until there was agreement upon major principles by the major powers.

General Charles G. Dawes, our Ambassador, being in Washington, I requested him upon his arrival in London to ascertain whether Prime Minister MacDonald would agree to carry on preliminary negotiations with me through diplomatic channels instead of appointing the usual preliminary committees of technicians who would inevitably bog down in such mazes as gun calibers, tons, and dates of construction. We would, of course, consult our naval experts. I proposed that we should keep the Japanese fully informed as we went along, having previously found that their then liberal government would be agreeable to any reasonable proposal.

General Dawes opened the discussions on this line with Mr. Mac-Donald on June 24, 1929, and found him fully receptive. We early agreed to extend the battleship formula of a ratio of 5 for Britain, 5 for the United States, and 3 for Japan for all craft except submarines. Beyond that point, however, the negotiations repeatedly came near breaking through the activities of the British Admiralty. The same old difficulty was raised as to assessing the comparative power of different ships and agreeing as to dates of new construction for replacement.

The Prime Minister was not very good at figures; and what one of his secretaries called "the He-men, old salt-sea dogs" of the Admiralty, tangled him all up in technicalities. They were naturally suspicious that the "two welfare workers"—MacDonald and myself—were in a conspiracy to injure "that greatest safeguard of world peace and world stability," the British Navy. I had no such difficulties. Admirals Pratt, Hepburn, and Jones genuinely supported what we were trying to do. They believed that it was the road to peace and that a limited, well-rounded Navy would be more efficient in defense of the Western Hemisphere. After five weeks of interminable negotiations through the State Department we were getting nowhere.

I finally sent a personal cable through the Department to General Dawes expressing my disappointment at the British proposals as they did not provide real parity or a decrease in British construction. I carefully outlined the only basis we could accept, with the necessary technical details covering the whole problem. General Dawes wrote in his Journal on August 1:

Hoover's telegram seemed unanswerable, for, without mistake, it was from his own hand chiefly. I shot it into MacDonald with full force for the necessity of the moment is a precipitation of the real issues between us, in order to determine whether we can proceed further or not. He took it pleasantly and like a thoroughbred.[1]

This cable cleared the air and by early September we had narrowed down our differences greatly. On September 17, to further narrow the gap, I dictated a long letter to the Prime Minister again covering all open points and making some suggestions. Formalism required that I change the pronouns and address it to our Secretary of State, who forwarded it to General Dawes for Mr. MacDonald to read. Mr. MacDonald was less formalistic in an acknowledgment to General Dawes which started off: "What I take as a personal letter from your President to myself . . ." This correspondence is too lengthy and technical for reproduction here. It is given in full in General Dawes's Journal.[2] It narrowed differences to a point that I was sure we could settle in personal interview. Throughout, we fully informed the Japanese Ministry, and they were in general agreement.

THE MACDONALD VISIT

My immediate purpose in extending an invitation to Prime Minister MacDonald to visit the United States was of course to settle the remaining questions as to the naval limitations. I, however, had in mind broader questions as to the relations between Britain and the United States.

Believing that elimination of friction with Great Britain must be one of the foundation stones of our foreign policies, I sought ways to end the various gnawing differences between us. The most dangerous of these frictions was of course competitive naval building. There were other sources of ill will, such as the action of the British in preparing to strengthen their naval and air bases in the Western Hemisphere, the World War debt, and the old dispute over freedom of the

[1] Charles G. Dawes, *Journal as Ambassador to Great Britain,* The Macmillan Company, 1939, p. 45.
[2] *Ibid.,* pp. 75–82.

seas in wartime. I felt that MacDonald's winning personality, the fact
that he represented the British Labor Party, and his oratorical abilities
on a visit would prove beneficial to the relations between our two
countries. He arrived on October 4, 1929, leaving ten days later.

Shortly after his arrival I motored him to the Rapidan Camp, and
during the ride had an opportunity to discuss freely the subjects I had
in mind. He seemed receptive upon many of them. At one moment
he queried, "How would you express these matters to the public of
the two countries?" I stated I would make a draft covering my ideas.
I hurriedly extended some memoranda I had already prepared into the
sort of statement we might make. Its purpose was largely to reduce
the discussion to definite points. The text, never published, was as
follows:

In the field of reduction of international friction we have examined the
broad problems of naval reduction and limitation. We have further examined
the question of limitation upon construction of military bases and we have
examined the question usually referred to under the heading of "freedom
of the seas."

We have engaged in an examination of the broad questions of reenforcing
the peace of the world. The situation in the world has been importantly
altered in consequence of the Pact of Paris. The declaration of that pact,
"that the world has renounced war as an instrument of national policy"
and its undertaking that settlement or solution of disputes and conflicts
of whatever origin shall never be sought except by pacific means reorients
all problems of peace.

I

In the furtherance of practical application of these ideas, we have examined the possibility of the extension of the Pact of Paris to strengthen
measures against the outbreak of war and to reenforce the machinery of
pacific settlement of controversies.

We are united in the feeling that an advance step could be taken in
development of pacific means for the settlement of controversies if an article,
to be called "Article 3," could be added to the Pact of Paris to the effect
that, in event of any controversy in which satisfactory settlement is not
made by direct negotiation or agreed reference to arbitration or judicial
decision, such controversy shall be investigated by a commission to be selected

by the parties to the controversy, upon which commission the parties shall be represented together with impartial members; this commission to examine all the facts concerning the controversy, to endeavor to conciliate the difficulties and to publish the facts; that suggestion of the desirability of such action by nations strangers to the controversy would not be considered an unfriendly act.

The state of peace is recognized as normal by the Pact of Paris, and war is outlawed. All nations have a legitimate interest in the preservation of peace, and all are injured by a breach of peace.

The United States, in numerous treaties of conciliation with the leading powers of Europe, in treaties with the Pan American nations, in its adhesion to the Hague treaties, has already accepted these principles. The Covenant of the League of Nations provides that the Council of the League shall make such inquiry among its members. The principles of this suggestion, therefore, have been widely agreed to by the nations of the world.

This proposal, however, differentiates itself from the older agreements in that it would extend the number of nations adhering to these ideas; it undertakes to secure action by initiative of the parties to the controversy themselves; to secure to each nation the right to have the facts determined and an appeal to public opinion, and to arouse world opinion and world conscience that the facts shall be determined.

II

One of the primary necessities of the world for the maintenance of peace is the elimination of the frictions which arise from competitive armament and the further necessity to reduce armament is economic relief to the peoples of the world. The negotiations which have taken place between the United States and Great Britain have been based upon a desire on both sides to find solutions to their peculiar problems which have hitherto stood in the way of world agreement on this question.

The negotiations which have taken place during the past three months have resulted in such an approximation of views as has warranted the calling of a conference of the leading naval powers in the belief that at such a conference all views can be reconciled. (Between ourselves we have agreed upon parity, category by category, as a great instrument for removing the competition between us.) All the reconsideration of capital ship replacement programs provided in the Washington Arms Treaty, the limitation and reduction in the categories of cruisers, destroyers, and submarines, yield strong hope of final agreement, and it has been agreed that we shall continue to mutually examine these questions involved prior to the conference. And we shall continue to exchange views upon questions and concurrently discuss these views with the other naval powers.

III

With further view to reducing friction and minimizing the possibility of conflicts, we believe that we should agree that Great Britain should not establish new or maintain fortified military bases in the Western Hemisphere, such area to be defined as that portion of the globe lying west of, say, the 25° meridian to the 180° meridian, or thereabouts; and that the United States on the other hand should not establish or maintain military bases in the Eastern Hemisphere, except so far as that provided in the Pacific treaties of 1922—the Eastern Hemisphere for this purpose to be defined as that area of the globe lying east of the 25° meridian to the 180° meridian.

IV

We recognize that one of the most troublesome questions in international relations is that of freedom of the seas. Not only does this subject arouse fear and stimulate naval preparation, but it is one of the pregnant causes of expansion of the area of war once it may have broken out, by dragging other nations in as the result of controversies with belligerents.

Misunderstandings arising out of these questions have been the greatest cause of controversies in the past between our two countries. We have resolved therefore that we will examine this question fully and frankly.

The President proposes, and he hopes the American people will support the proposal, that food ships should be declared free from interference during times of war, and thus remove starvation of women and children from the weapons of warfare. That would reduce the necessity for naval arms in protection of avenues of food supplies. Such a proposal goes wider than the rights of neutrals in times of war and would protect from interference all vessels solely laden with food supplies in the same fashion that we now immunize hospital and medical supplies.

Secretary Stimson did not think I would get far with most of these proposals, but I thought they would test MacDonald's views.

I made one other proposal verbally to him which hitherto has not been made public. I suggested that the British consider selling to us

Bermuda, British Honduras, and the island of Trinidad. I told him I
thought we could give them a credit upon the war debt which would
go a long way to settle that issue. I explained that we were not interested in their West Indian possessions generally. I wanted Bermuda and
Trinidad for defense purposes, and I wanted to have British Honduras
as an item to use in trading with Mexico for the use of the mouth of
the Colorado River so as possibly to cure certain frictions between
Mexico and Guatemala. He did not rise to the idea at all. He even excluded British Honduras although, aside from officials, probably fewer
than 1,000 Englishmen got a living out of it. I had a hunch he did not
take the payment of the debt very seriously.

Mr. MacDonald toyed with the idea of a further article to the
Kellogg Pact but finally, as I have said, concluded it would be objected
to by the League of Nations as building up rival instrumentalities. In
the view of both Secretary Stimson and myself, this was not the case
as it was a strengthening of the League provisions and might free the
League of many controversies. Moreover, it would include nations not
in the League.

On the 6th at Rapidan Camp we went down the creek and on a log
threshed out the points as yet unsettled in the naval agreement. We
felt that Japan would go along, but we did not believe we could
secure the agreement of France or Italy. While their naval strength
was much inferior to the three major powers, they were engaged in a
bitter naval competition with each other in which France was demanding an inferior fleet for Italy. We decided that, if they would not
agree, we would make it a tripartite agreement between the United
States, Britain, and Japan anyway.

As to British activity in the improvement of their naval and air bases
in the Western Hemisphere, I pointed out to MacDonald that this
might at any time become a live coal in the American mind. I have
already shown that I proposed to him that we enter into an agreement
defining a line from pole to pole down mid-Atlantic and mid-Pacific
beyond which neither should expand air or naval bases. Our American
admirals under the leadership of Admiral Pratt approved the idea, and
I asked them to draw up the formula, which they did. I submitted it
to the Prime Minister. He stated that he would urge its acceptance

upon the British Admiralty. This he did by cable. He reported to me, with what I felt was genuine regret, that they rejected it absolutely. Made known to the world, it would have contributed to dissolution of many fears on both sides—and it would have been a further guarantee that our navies would not fall into conflict with each other. The proposal had, however, very practical results. The British made no additions to these bases for some years.

The Prime Minister also toyed for some days with the idea of immunizing food ships from attack in a similar fashion to that already established for hospital ships. He was naturally sympathetic to it. After he returned to England he sent word that he could get nowhere with it. I never really expected the British Admiralty to approve it, as its military vision was fixed upon the idea that wars are won by starving people through blockade, and its primary argument for a big navy was the protection of British food supplies. I concluded, however, to make the subject public in the hope that some day, some time, the world might think it worth while. In an Armistice Day address a month later, I stated this proposal and the arguments for it in detail.

The proposal was welcomed by the press of practically all nations of the world except the inspired press of Britain and Japan. The opposition of these nations was so violent that it seemed useless to go on with the plan at that time.[3]

On October 10, 1929, the Prime Minister and I issued a joint statement upon our discussions the gist of which was:

Our conversations have been largely confined to the mutual relations of the two countries in the light of the situation created by the signing of the Peace Pact. Therefore, in a new and reinforced sense the two governments not only declared that war between them is unthinkable. . . . On the assumption that war between us is banished, and that conflicts between our

---

[3] When historians come to write the true history of the Second World War, to explore its causes, to examine the useless slaughter of millions of women and children, and to weigh the minor military advantages of the renewed blockade, they will agree that this proposal would have diminished the causes of war, reduced its horrors, and saved millions from starvation. And had the proposal been in force it would not have changed the outcome of the war one iota as soldiers, officials, and war workers get their food anyway.

military or naval forces cannot take place, these problems have changed
their meaning and character; and their solution, in ways satisfactory to
both countries, has become possible.

The conference of the principal naval powers assembled in London
in January, 1930. Secretary Stimson headed the American delegation
composed of Secretary of the Navy Adams, Ambassadors Dawes and
Gibson, Senators David Reed and Joseph Robinson, and Dwight Morrow. Admiral William V. Pratt was Chief Naval Advisor.

While the conference was sitting in London a New York judge
transmitted to me a claim which had been filed by a well known international "fixer" in his court for some half-million dollars against
certain American armament manufacturers for services in having
destroyed the Naval Conference during the Coolidge Administration.
It disclosed that he had received large sums from them on account. I
exposed the scandalous matter with appropriate remarks, and thus we
had none of this sort of sabotage around our conference. It left some
of our shipbuilders explaining themselves to the American people for
months.

The conference had no difficulty in carrying through along the lines
of our prior arrangements so far as Britain and Japan were concerned;
but France demanded early that some sort of guarantee of her future
security be given by the United States and Great Britain in return for
the limitation of her navy. The demand was finally reduced from a
military guarantee of security to a pact of "consultation" as to measures
to be taken in case of a threatened attack. Secretary Stimson urged me
to accept this proposal. I was compelled to instruct him that we could
not agree: that I had no objection to such pacts *per se,* for we had
already signed many treaties of that import, but that, if France reduced
her fleet in consideration of such a pact, the consequence in case of a
war would be a moral obligation on our part to give her military assistance. I had no belief in such camouflaged obligations. At once a storm
of denunciatory propaganda broke loose in the European dispatches to
the effect that the Americans were wrecking the conference, and our
usual New York associations on foreign policies joined in the howl. I
instructed our delegation that we did not care whether the French

limited their inferior navy or not, and our major purpose of parity with Britain and the extension of the 5–3 ratio with Japan would be accomplished even if France and Italy stayed out of the agreement. As France and Italy could not agree upon their relative strengths, they only partially accepted the final treaty.

I submitted the Naval Limitation Treaty to the Senate on May 1, 1930. That body took no action and proposed to adjourn without doing so. In fact several members under the leadership of Senator Moses joined in a "round robin" demanding that I delay ratification. My reply was to announce a special session of the Senate for July 7.

My message to this session shows the importance of the accomplishment:

In requesting the Senate to convene in session for the special purpose of dealing with the treaty for the limitation and reduction of naval armament signed at London April 22, 1930, it is desirable that I should present my views upon it. This is especially necessary because of misinformation and misrepresentation which have been widespread by those who in reality are opposed to all limitation and reduction in naval arms. We must naturally expect opposition from those groups who believe in unrestricted military strength as an objective of the American nation. Indeed, we find the same type of minds in Great Britain and Japan in parallel opposition to this treaty. Nevertheless, I am convinced that the overwhelming majority of the American people are opposed to the conception of these groups. Our people believe that military strength should be held in conformity with the sole purpose of national defense; they earnestly desire real progress in limitation and reduction of naval arms of the world, and their aspiration is for abolition of competition in the building of arms as a step toward world peace. Such a result can be obtained in no other way than by international agreement.

The present treaty is one which holds these safeguards and advances these ideals. Its ratification is in the interest of the United States. It is fair to the other participating nations. It promotes the cause of good relations.

The only alternative to this treaty is the competitive building of navies with all its flow of suspicion, hate, ill will, and ultimate disaster. History supports those who hold to agreement as the path to peace. Every naval limitation treaty with which we are familiar, from the Rush-Bagot agreement of 1817, limiting vessels of war on the Great Lakes, to the Washington Arms Treaty of 1921, has resulted in a marked growth of good will and confidence between the nations which were parties to it.

It is folly to think that because we are the richest nation in the world we can outbuild all other countries. Other nations will make any sacrifice to maintain their instruments of defense against us, and we shall eventually reap in their hostility and ill will the full measure of the additional burden which we may thus impose upon them. The very entry of the United States into such courses as this would invite the consolidation of the rest of the world against us and bring our peace and independence into jeopardy. We have only to look at the state of Europe in 1914 to find ample evidence of the futility and danger of competition in arms.

It will be remembered that in response to recommendations from the Senate a Conference between the United States, Great Britain and Japan for limitation of those categories of naval arms not covered by the Washington Treaty of 1921 was held at Geneva in 1927. That Conference failed because the United States could not agree to the large size of fleets demanded by other governments. The standards set up at that time would have required an ultimate fleet of about 1,400,000 tons for the United States. As against this the total United States fleet set out under this treaty will be about 1,123,000 tons.

Defense is the primary function of government, and therefore our first concern in examination of any act of this character is the test of its adequacy in defense. No critic has yet asserted that with the navies provided in this agreement, together with our army, our aerial defense, and our national resources, we cannot defend ourselves, and certainly we want no military establishment for the purpose of domination of other nations. Our naval defense position under this treaty is the more clear if we examine our present naval strength in comparison to the present strength of the other nations, and then examine the improvements in this proportion which will result from this treaty. This improvement arises from the anticipation of parity in battleships to be reached ten years hence under the Washington Arms Treaty and the fact that other nations have been building in the classes of ships not limited by that treaty, while we, until lately, lagged behind.

On the 1st of January last the total naval tonnage, disregarding paper fleets and taking only those ships actually built and building, was, for the United States, 1,180,000 tons; for the British Empire, 1,332,000 tons; for

Japan, 768,000 tons. That is, if the United States Navy be taken as 100, then the British Navy equals 113 and the Japanese Navy 65. Under this treaty the United States will have 1,123,000 tons, Great Britain, 1,151,000 tons, and Japan 714,000 tons, or a ratio of 100 for the United States to 102.4 for Great Britain and 63.6 for Japan. The slightly larger tonnage ratio mentioned for Great Britain is due to the fact that her cruiser fleet will be constituted more largely of smaller vessels, weaker in gun power, but the United States has the option to duplicate the exact tonnage and gun caliber of the British cruiser fleet if we desire to exercise it. . . .

To those who seek earnestly and properly for reduction in warships, I would point out that as compared with January 1st of this year, the total aggregate navies of the three powers under this treaty will have been reduced by nearly 300,000 tons. Had a settlement been made at Geneva in 1927 upon the only proposal possible at that time, the fleets of the three powers would have been approximately 680,000 tons greater than under the treaty now in consideration.

The economic burdens and the diversion of taxes from welfare purposes which would be imposed upon ourselves and other nations by failure of this treaty are worth consideration. . . .

If we assume that our present naval program, except for this treaty, is to complete the ships authorized by Congress and those authorized and necessary to be replaced under the Washington Arms Treaty, and to maintain a destroyer fleet of about 225,000 tons and a submarine fleet of 90,000 tons, such a fleet will not reach parity with Great Britain, yet would cost in construction over $500,000,000 more during the next six years than the fleet provided under this treaty. But in addition to this, as stated, there is a very large saving by this treaty in annual operation of the fleet over what would be the case if we even built no more than the present programs.

The more selfish-minded will give little credence to the argument that savings by other parties to the agreement in the limitation of naval construction are of interest to the American people, yet the fundamental economic fact is that if the resources of these other nations are freed for devotion to the welfare of their people and to pacific purposes of reproductive commerce, they will result in blessings to the world, including ourselves. . . . the saving in construction and operation by the treaty is literally billions of dollars. . . .

This treaty does mark an important step in disarmament and in world peace. It is important for many reasons that it should be dealt with at once.

The subject has been under discussion since the Geneva Conference three years ago. The lines of this treaty have been known and under discussion since last summer. The actual document has been before the American people and before the Senate for nearly three months. It has been favorably reported by the Senate Foreign Relations Committee. Every solitary fact which affects judgment upon the treaty is known, and the document itself comprises the sole obligation of the United States. If we fail now the world will be again plunged backward from its progress toward peace.

HERBERT HOOVER

The usual wrangle took place in the Senate, but on July 22, 1930, when the Treaty was ratified and signed, I said:

... With the ratification by the other governments the Treaty will translate an emotion deep in the hearts of millions of men and women into a practical fact of government and international relations. It will renew again the faith of the world in the moral forces of good will and patient negotiation as against the blind forces of suspicion and competitive armament. It will secure the full defense of the United States. It will mark a further long step toward lifting the burden of militarism from the backs of mankind and speed the march forward of world peace. It will lay the foundations upon which further constructive reduction in world arms may be accomplished in the future. We should, by this act of willingness to join with others in limiting armament, have dismissed from the mind of the world any notion that the United States entertains ideas of aggression, imperial power, or exploitation of foreign nations.

REDUCTION OF LAND ARMIES

The Treaty of Versailles called for a reduction of land armament among the Allies. The League of Nations was entrusted with the mission of bringing it about. During the twelve years thereafter nothing was done except for desultory and "preparatory" talks and committee meetings.

Mr. Coolidge's view had been that we should have nothing to do with the League, and, moreover, that the strength of our army had been reduced in proportion to our population below that of any other major power in the world, and nothing could be given or asked of us.

I believed, however, that we had an interest in the matter since the growing armies of Europe could bode no good to the peace of the world. I therefore decided that we should seriously participate in the League efforts, and that I should stir that body into some kind of action. I took advantage of an assembly of delegates from all nations to a meeting of the International Chamber of Commerce in Washington on May 4, 1931, to open fire. The text is important only as indicating the state of armaments at that time:

I wish to give emphasis to . . . the limitation and reduction of armament. The world expenditure on all arms is now nearly five billions of dollars yearly, an increase of about 70 per cent over that previous to the Great War. We stand today with nearly 5,500,000 men actively under arms and 20,000,000 more in reserves. These vast forces greatly exceed those of the prewar period. They still are not demobilized, even though twelve years have passed since the Armistice, because of fear and of inability of nations to cooperate in mutual reductions. Yet we are all signatories to the Kellogg-Briand Pact, by which we have renounced war as an instrument of national policy and agreed to settle all controversies by pacific means. Surely, with this understanding, the self-defense of nations could be assured with proportionately far less military forces than these. This vast armament continues not only a burden upon the economic recuperation of the world but, of even more consequence, the constant threats and fears which arise from it are a serious contribution to all forms of instability, whether social, political, or economic. . . .

We have made considerable progress in the limitation and reduction of naval arms. We have laid the foundations for still further progress in the future. These agreements have contributed greatly to reduce the burden of taxes and to establish confidence and good will among the nations who have been signatory to them.

The League had called one of its conferences on armament to meet at Geneva on February 2, 1932. I determined that the United States should join in full participation despite the anguished cries of our isolationists. I designated Ambassador Hugh Gibson as head of our delegation. The United States not being a major party to calling the conference, I could not use my own tactics of prior preparation as in the case of the Naval Conference. I mentioned my proposed action to the Congress on December 10, 1931.

The Geneva Conference engaged in oratorical futilities for more than four months. The governments primarily concerned offered no constructive plans. Finally, in order that it should stop dawdling and come to realities I instructed Ambassador Gibson as to certain avenues of disarmament which he should first broach privately to leaders of the conference. These proposals were of an entirely new order. They embraced the reduction of armies in excess of the level required to preserve internal order by one-third, together with the abolition of certain "aggressive" arms. These proposals were the most practicable and far-reaching before or since that time. While many members of the conference privately expressed their approval, nothing resulted. Finally, I instructed Ambassador Gibson to make public the memorandum I had sent him in order to summon world public opinion. I had drafted the original in longhand which I still preserve. It reads:

. . . The time has come when we should cut through the brush and adopt some broad and definite method of reducing the overwhelming burden of armament which now lies upon the toilers of the world. This would be the most important world step that could be taken to expedite economic recovery. We must make headway against the mutual fear and friction arising out of war armament which kill human confidence throughout the world. We can still remain practical in maintaining an adequate self-defense among all nations; we can add to the assurances of peace and yet save the people of the world from ten to fifteen billions of wasted dollars during the next ten years.

I propose that the following principles should be our guide:

First: The Kellogg-Briand Pact, to which we are all signatories, can only mean that the nations of the world have agreed that they will use their arms solely for defense.

Second: This reduction should be carried out not only by broad general cuts in armaments but by increasing the comparative power of defense through decreases in the power of the attack.

Third: The armaments of the world have grown up in general mutual relation to each other. And, speaking generally, such relativity should be preserved in making reductions.

Fourth: The reductions must be real and positive. They must effect economic relief.

Fifth: There are three problems to deal with—land forces, air forces, and naval forces. They are all interconnected. No part of the proposals which I make can be dissociated one from the other.

Based on these principles, I propose that the arms of the world should be reduced by nearly one-third.

Land Forces. In order to reduce the offensive character of all land forces as distinguished from their defensive character, I propose . . . the abolition of all tanks, all chemical warfare, and all large mobile guns. This would not prevent the establishment or increase of fixed fortifications of any character for the defense of frontiers and sea-coasts. It would give an increased relative strength to such defenses as compared with the attack.

I propose furthermore that there should be a reduction of one-third in strength of all land armies over and above the police component.

The land armaments of many nations are considered to have two functions. One is the maintenance of internal order in connection with the regular police forces of the country. The strength required for this purpose has been called the "police component." The other function is defense against foreign attack. The additional strength required for this purpose has been called the "defense component." While it is not suggested that these different components should be separated, it is necessary to consider this division as to functions in proposing a practical plan of reduction in land forces. Under the Treaty of Versailles and the other peace treaties, the armies of Germany, Austria, Hungary, and Bulgaria were reduced to a size deemed appropriate for the maintenance of internal order, Germany being assigned 100,000 troops for a population of approximately 65,000,000 people. I propose that we should accept for all nations a basic police component of soldiers proportionate to the average which was thus allowed Germany and these other states. This formula, with necessary corrections for powers having colonial possessions, should be sufficient to provide for the maintenance of internal order by the nations of the world. Having analyzed these two components in this fashion, I propose as stated above that there should be a reduction of one-third in the strength of all land armies over and above the police component.

Air Forces. All bombing planes to be abolished. This will do away with the military possession of types of planes capable of attacks upon civil populations and should be coupled with the total prohibition of all systematic bombardment of civilians from the air.

Naval Forces. I propose that the treaty number and tonnage of battleships shall be reduced one-third; that the treaty tonnage of aircraft carriers, cruisers, and destroyers shall be reduced by one-fourth; that the treaty ton-

nage of submarines shall be reduced by one-third, and that no nation shall
retain a submarine tonnage greater than 35,000.

The relative strength of naval arms in battleships and aircraft carriers,
as between the five leading naval powers, was fixed by the Treaty of Washington. The relative strength in cruisers, destroyers, and submarines was
fixed, as between the United States, Great Britain and Japan, by the Treaty
of London. For the purposes of this proposal, it is suggested that the French
and Italian strength in cruisers and destroyers be calculated as though they
had joined in the Treaty of London on a basis approximating the so-called
accord of March 1, 1931. There are various technical considerations connected
with these naval discussions which will be presented by the delegation.

General. The effect of this plan would be to effect an enormous saving in
cost of new construction and replacements of naval vessels. It would also save
large amounts in the operating expense in all nations of land, sea, and air
forces. It would greatly reduce offensive strength compared to defensive
strength in all nations.

These proposals are simple and direct. They call upon all nations to contribute something. The contribution here proposed will be relative and
mutual. I know of nothing that would give more hope for humanity today
than the acceptance of such a program with such minor changes as might be
necessary. It is folly for the world to go on breaking its back over military
expenditure and the United States is willing to take its share of responsibility
by making definite proposals that will relieve the world.

The publication of this statement gave great satisfaction to those
members of the conference who wished seriously to accomplish something. It certainly excited the British and French who did not want
anything done. I was greatly surprised to hear from Mr. Gibson that
the Army Technical Committee of the conference, which represented
the general staffs of the world, accepted it as the most constructive
proposal that had been put forward and, subject to some secondary
amendments, had voted by a very large majority for its adoption. In
other words, the soldiers were for it. It was supported by some thirty-
eight nations, including Germany and Italy, but opposed by the French,
British, and their dependent satellites. The conference adjourned to
meet again late in the year, by which time I had been defeated in the
election and was without the power to carry on.

It has been said that such a limitation of "aggressive" arms would have had no effect. It is true that nations intent upon war and violation of their various nonaggression pacts might resume the manufacture of these implements. However, no such activity could have been kept secret, and the revelation of these acts would at least have been notice to the world of aggressive intentions.[4]

TRADE IN ARMS

An international treaty for control of trade in arms had been signed by Mr. Coolidge in June, 1925. It had been allowed to sleep in the Senate. In a special message to the Congress on December 10, 1931, I said:

The Convention for the Supervision of the International Trade in Arms and Ammunition and in Implements of War, signed at Geneva, June 17, 1925, represents another of the steps taken in the general field of restriction of armament. It has been ratified unconditionally by some nations, conditionally by others. With the added impetus which ratification by the United States would lend to such a move, it is quite possible that the fourteen ratifications necessary by treaty stipulation would be received to bring the convention into force.

The leaders of the Senate committee made promises of action from time to time. Finally, to draw public attention, I sent a special message to the Congress on January 10, 1933, urging immediate action.

Later on December 5, 1934, in a smearing campaign, members of a committee of the Senate through their attorney, Alger Hiss,[5] made the false charge that I had stimulated international trade in arms while I was Secretary of Commerce. The charge was spread through the press for days. I disliked this charge, since the trade in arms had always been particularly repugnant to me. The story hinged around an informal conference which I had called of arms manufacturers at the request of

[4] Mr. Roosevelt, soon after entering into office, ignoring both the origin of the proposals I had made and the League as the organizing body, made a direct proposal to all heads of states embodying my formula for abolition in offensive land arms, i.e., tanks, bombers, and large mobile guns. The nations apparently ignored the proposal, and I was informed that they considered the League should not be so sidetracked. In any event, all American pressure was discontinued, and all American interest was allowed to die.

[5] Hiss was later convicted of perjury in relation to betrayals to Russia.

Secretary Kellogg. Instead of being military arms, however, it was confined to finding a formula to exempt sporting arms.

During the time these lies were being widely spread in the press, one of my old subordinates in the Department sent me copies of the documents which he said were suppressed in the hearings.

With this information I made the following statement to the press:

The full reports and details of the conference of sporting arms manufacturers which was called by myself as Secretary of Commerce in 1925, yesterday referred to before a Senate committee, are no doubt in the State Department. The conference was called at the written request of the Secretary of State and for the purpose of giving a hearing to the manufacturers' views as to methods of discriminating between sporting arms on one hand and war arms on the other. . . . As a result of the negotiations an international treaty was secured controlling that traffic. . . . During eight years from 1925 to 1933 its ratification was held up by the Senate and probably is yet. As late as January 10, 1933, I called the attention of the Senate to the fact that it had now been ratified by a large number of other nations, and that its failure of adoption in the world was largely because of the failure of the United States. . . .

CHAPTER 47

POLICIES AS TO OUR ISLAND POSSESSIONS

I was not in favor of the United States' permanently holding foreign possessions except those minor areas vital to our defense. Our mission was to free people, not to dominate them.

I took occasion to visit our Caribbean islands, Puerto Rico and the Virgin Islands. In Puerto Rico I found that the success of our government in improving health and perfecting public order had resulted in an increase in population from less than a half-million to more than a million. In consequence the people were more impoverished than before. I did not know any answer except birth control, and that was impossible. However, we did organize a number of relief measures, and I arranged that private agencies should expend as much as a million dollars; also, we made substantial appropriations from Federal funds. I believed then, and do now, that it would be better for Puerto Rico and the United States to give its people independence, merely reserving our naval and air bases.

The Philippines offered a larger problem. I favored independence, provided that it was a complete and absolute separation, and provided that the economic stability of the islands was assured before we agreed to their demand for a divorce. They were dependent upon trade with the United States under the United States customs union. Economic stability had to be assured after that advantage was lost to them. The pressure in Congress for their independence came from Filipino political leaders supported by American sugar producers who wanted to end duty-free sugar from the islands. I sent Secretary of War Hurley for a re-examination of the situation. Upon his return, I said, October 27, 1931:

Independence of the Philippines at some time has been directly or indirectly promised by every President and by the Congress. In accord with those undertakings, the problem is one of time. The economic independence of the Philippines must be attained before political independence can be successful. Independence tomorrow without assured economic stability would result in the collapse of Philippine government revenues and the collapse of all economic life in the islands.

In December, 1932, the Democratic Congress, mostly under pressure from our sugar producers, passed a Philippine bill that pretended to independence. As an alternative, I proposed that we enlarge the authority of the Philippine Legislature to complete cabinet government as a step toward freedom. I vetoed the bill, stating:

The Philippine people have today as great a substance of ordered liberty and human freedom as any people in the world. They lack the form of separate nationality which is indeed their rightful spiritual aspiration. . . .

The period of intermediate government prior to complete independence . . . in this act is too short, too violent. . . .

A large part of the motivation for the passage of this bill is presumed relief to certain American agricultural industries from competition by Philippine products. We are trustees for these people and we must not let our selfish interest dominate that trust. . . .

The income of the Philippine government has never in the past been sufficient to meet, in addition to other expenditures, the cost of supporting even the Filipino Scouts, much less an army or navy. . . .

In the meantime we should develop steadily through an expansion of the organic act a larger importance to their own officials by extension of authority to cabinet government.

We are here dealing with one of the most precious rights of man—national independence interpreted as separate nationality. It is the national independence of 13,000,000 human beings. We have here a specific duty. The ideals under which we undertook this responsibility, our own national instincts, and our institutions which we have implanted on these islands breathe with these desires. It is a goal not to be reached by yielding to selfish interests, to resentments, or to abstractions, but with full recognition of our responsi-

bilities and all their implications and all the forces which would destroy the boon we seek to confer and the dangers to our freedom from entanglements which our actions may bring. Neither our successors nor history will discharge us of responsibility for actions which diminish the liberty we seek to confer nor for dangers which we create for ourselves as a consequence of our acts. This legislation puts both our people and the Philippine people not on the road to liberty and safety, which we desire, but on the path leading to new and enlarged dangers to liberty and freedom itself.

A side light on this whole transaction is shown by the real views of Osmeña and Roxas, the Philippine independence leaders. They came to see me at the White House while this bill was being debated in Congress and stated that they hoped I would veto it; they said the Philippines were not economically prepared for independence, and if they stood alone they would be in jeopardy from either China or Japan. I was utterly astonished and said so. I asked why they were lobbying with Congress to pass the bill and why they were carrying on propaganda to that end in the United States in cooperation with our sugar producers. They replied that independence was their political issue in the Philippines, and that unless they promoted it their leadership would be lost to more dangerous elements. I was disgusted and said that I would call in the entire press at once and repeat their statements. To which they replied blandly that they would say that I had entirely misunderstood their remarks. I told them I hoped they would never come into the White House again. When I discussed this incident with Secretary Hurley, he stated that they had said the same thing to him; but he agreed with me that a dispute unsupported by evidence would only make the situation worse.[1]

[1] Independence was granted to the Philippines in 1934, to take final effect in 1946. The subsequent invasion by the Japanese in 1941 with its terrible hardships and destruction materially obscured their economic and political progress.

CHAPTER 48

THE JAPANESE AGGRESSION IN CHINA
IN 1931–1932, AND A SUMMARY OF
MY FOREIGN POLICIES

Secretary Stimson published [1] in 1936 a painstaking account of the Japanese aggression in Manchuria of 1931 to 1933. I must, however, recount some phases of this crisis in order to point out secondary differences in viewpoint, to illuminate some dark corners, and to emphasize some lessons in the organization of world institutions to preserve peace.[2]

This expansion of the Japanese Empire onto the continent of Asia at the expense of China was no new policy. Japan had taken sections of China at various times but had relinquished them in part under pressure from the other powers. The Manchurian invasion was just one more step. Japan was a late-comer among the nations that seized parts of China. Britain, France, Germany, Russia, and Portugal, all had taken territory from her. Japan's delay was no doubt due to the fact that she was much later than the others in securing modern arms and in understanding the principles of imperialism. In any event, Japan was a faithful follower of the European powers in the dividing of China.

The distinction between her morals and those of the older empires was one of timing. The old empires had held the titles longer and thus

---

[1] *The Far Eastern Crisis* by Henry L. Stimson (Harper & Brothers, New York, 1936).

[2] The episode has a bearing upon the origins of World War II. Also, it has been asserted that America refused to cooperate with the European nations, and that, had we done so, the Japanese would soon have been cured of all evil and there would have been no World War ten years later. The statement of the facts demonstrates that the failure to cooperate came from Europe, not from the United States.

were more sacrosanct. I have often thought that perhaps the Kellogg Pact of 1929 marked a sort of datum point of imperial morals, and titles secured after that date were considered less moral.

To appreciate the problems of Japanese aggression in 1931–1932, it is necessary to give some historical background of both Japan and China.

Japan began her aggression on China as early as 1876. In that year she began her persistent steps to separate Korea from China. Acknowledgment of the "independence" of Korea finally was forced upon China by the Treaty of 1895, which followed an aggressive war on the Chinese in 1894; but Korea was not formally annexed to Japan until 1910. In the Treaty of 1895 with China, Japan also obtained possession of Formosa and of the Liaotung Peninsula of Manchuria. But the European powers, under Russian, British, and German leadership, compelled her to return Liaotung. Later on, Russia "leased" from China these former Japanese holdings and other areas in Manchuria, expanded her Siberian railways to its ice-free ports and built a great naval base at Port Arthur. In 1904 Japan attacked Russia and defeated her within a year. By the Treaty of Portsmouth in 1905, Japan recovered the Liaotung Peninsula from Russia, took over Port Arthur and half of the island of Sakhalin, obtained also the southern railways of Manchuria, together with other footholds in China.

Taking advantage of the European war in 1914, Japan seized the German possessions in Shantung, which she promptly enlarged. In the years 1915 and 1916 she seized other parts of China and made an agreement with Russia which defined their spheres of interest, thus dividing up all that part of Asia. In the Versailles Treaty of 1919, she secured confirmation of her holdings in Shantung and elsewhere. Finally she secured a "mandate" for the German islands in the South Pacific.

In all four major military operations, 1894, 1904, 1914, and 1931, Japan followed the consistent bad habit of attacking without a prior declaration of war.

Aside from the motivations of imperialism, generally there were deeper forces moving in the Japanese people. The nation was overcrowded, steadily becoming more industrial; and the people were in constantly increasing need of foreign raw materials and foreign markets for their products. Asia to the west seemed to them to be their natural economic province. Their militaristic groups naturally drove with this power in their engines. Other forces also aided the militarists in their designs. Russia had built a gigantic naval and air base at Vladivostok—a spear pointed directly at the heart of Japan. The Japanese greatly feared this base and had always been restive about its existence, especially since the development of air power had rendered it a perpetual menace to a wood-housed nation. The desire to outflank Vladivostok by annexation of Manchuria, and the vision of development of the great vacant spaces of Eastern Siberia, were constantly in the mind of militarist Japan.

During the half-century before the events of 1931 the control of the Japanese government had vibrated from the military castes of the two great clans, to the liberal elements who were genuinely and earnestly trying to bring Japan into the family of decent nations. Over the whole period the degree of her aggressive attitudes varied with the group in power. Fortunately, for ten years from 1921 to 1931, the liberal elements were dominant.

Another important factor was the situation in China itself. The revolutionary party—the Kuomintang under Sun Yat-sen—which overthrew the Imperial regime in 1911 had proved too weak to preserve order. Moreover, Sun Yat-sen had come under Communist domination with Russian advisers in his government. The regime had developed strong antiforeign propaganda and action.

Secretary Hughes's Nine Power Treaty, which included the United States, Britain, France, Japan, China, the Netherlands, Italy, Belgium, and Portugal, guaranteed the integrity of China. And the Four Power Treaty of China, Japan, Britain, and the United States restored Shantung province to China among other settlements.

Internal order in China, however, did not substantially improve. In 1927, Chiang Kai-shek led a military rebellion which defeated Mao Tse-tung and other Communist Chinese leaders. The Communist forces withdrew into Kiangsi province and established a Soviet state from which they continued to harass the country. In the meantime, the Chinese took up, as a weapon against foreign encroachments, a series of emotional boycotts of foreign goods. They boycotted the British from

1925 to 1927, and thereby scarcely won British affections. They had begun a boycott of Japanese goods in 1927. Incidentally, I have often wondered whether these boycotts did not originate in the Chinese mind from the "economic sanctions" provisions in the League of Nations Covenant. They were futile weapons in both cases.

Finally in 1931, taking advantage of a Western World weakened by the depression, and a China split among several warring war lords and torn by Chiang's war against Mao Tse-tung's Communists, the Japanese military party seized the opportunity to renew their slumbering imperial policies. Chiang did not have the military strength to undertake successful action against the Japanese aggression and fight the Communists at the same time.

In September of that year, without even consulting the liberal Konoye Ministry then in power, and on the slim excuse of a Chinese killing of a Japanese guard on the Japanese South Manchurian Railway, these militarist elements seized various cities along the railway and then went still farther afield on the pretext of "putting down bandits."

It was an act of rank aggression. It was a direct violation of the Nine-Power Treaty of 1922, by which Japan had joined in guaranteeing the integrity of China. It was a gross violation of the John Hay agreement of the Open Door in China. It was a cynical violation of the Covenant of the League of Nations of which Japan was a member. It was an impudent violation of the Kellogg Pact to which Japan was a signatory.

I fully realized the great seriousness of the situation and determined that we must do everything possible to uphold the moral foundations of international life. With my experience at Versailles, and having lived in the Orient, I was not without some knowledge of the problem.

At once I agreed with the Secretary of State that we must protest to the Japanese government, which he did on September 24. When, on September 21, China appealed to the League of Nations, I authorized the Secretary to cooperate fully with the League as it furnished a central point for coordination of action with the European nations. I insisted that we encourage the League to take the lead, and that we would cooperate with them. We directed our representative in Geneva to sit with the Council of the League. The Council passed a resolution of disapproval of the Japanese, and we approved their action. We also agreed to attend the Council at its next meeting on October 14.

At this time, early in October, Secretary Stimson laid before me two alternative courses of action, stated in his own words:

(1) Some form of collective economic sanctions against Japan, or in default of that,

(2) The exercise of diplomatic pressure and the power of world public opinion, to try to get as fair play as possible for the weaker power, China, in the eventual negotiated settlement. By a vigorous judgment against Japan backed by the public opinion of the world, to save as much respect as possible for the great peace treaties which had been publicly flouted by Japan's action.

I was fully in favor of the second proposal but was greatly disturbed over the first and told Mr. Stimson so. I was soon to realize that my able Secretary was at times more of a warrior than a diplomat. To him the phrase "economic sanctions" (boycott) was the magic wand of force by which all peace could be summoned from the vasty deep. On that point we developed a difference. Ever since Versailles I had held that "economic sanctions" meant war when applied to any large nation. I urged upon him that no nation of spirit would submit to having her whole economy totally demoralized and her people thrown out of employment and into starvation. It meant all the penalties of war except shooting. Sanctions or the threat of them also meant rising emotions, the development of incurable hatreds, and an insensate opposition to any remedial action.

The sanctions question fell into two phases: first, should the United States impose them alone? and second, would the members of the League join and thus all the important nations take part? The Secretary was prepared to go it alone. He argued that the sanctions, if applied by the United States alone, were "only pressure" and Japan would give away under them. I insisted that if we were to apply them alone, it would lead to war; and therefore we must examine our willingness and preparedness in the frame of war if we adopted this course. I was willing to go to war for the preservation of America, but I believed we should not go around alone sticking pins in tigers, or alone impose futile sanctions.

The Secretary believed that we could induce the League members to join in general sanctions. I argued that Britain, France, and Italy would not go along for various reasons. I stated that Britain and France had imperialistic titles to parts of China, exactly like what Japan was trying to establish; that there was a trade-union sentiment among empires; that the others had few moral grounds for complaint against the Japanese action; that the importance of their trade with Japan, ill will in Britain from the recent Chinese boycott, and the distress of the world depression would combine to prevent European nations' ever allowing the League to apply the sanctions or any other form of force, and that in the circumstances the only weapon was moral pressure. The Secretary felt sure the European nations would maintain their fidelities to the League Covenant and its economic sanctions, to which they were signatories. He never would admit that those sanctions inevitably meant war.

In order to get all the factors in hand and to avoid any public communications and any hurt feelings, I asked Secretary Mills to telephone a friend in London and ask him to find out personally and confidentially the real attitude of the British Ministry. Would the British join the United States in sanctions? If so, and if such action involved military danger, would their fleet join with ours? If this resulted in war, would they go along? The reply came quickly: "The answer to the first question will be certainly and emphatically 'No,' and therefore no replies to the other questions are necessary." I did not feel out the French, but later it was confirmed that they held the same view.

However, in order to explore the matter fully, I sent at this time for my military advisers and asked them what our situation would be in case we got into a war with Japan alone. They agreed that we should be victorious, but that the job would take from four to six years. They pointed out that our fleet was in the ratio of 5 to 3 to the Japanese, but that the naval reserves we must keep elsewhere would greatly reduce the effective strength which we could apply to Japan in her own waters. We should need time to make great additions to our Navy. We should have to prepare a large army and build a great transport fleet to land it in China or Japan. Our military leaders stated that in case of war we must either withdraw from the Philippines or lose them until victory was won. The looting and sufferings of the millions of Philippine

people would need be set off against the benefits to Manchurians by
change from Japanese to Chinese rulers. Our military advisers agreed
we might do the job in two years if the British would put their entire
fleet under joint command. And in this case we could probably hold the
Philippines. When I stated that the British would not join even in the
economic sanctions they said: "If we want to fight Japan—prepare first
and take five years to do it." An incidental result of these discussions
was that I abandoned some cuts in naval construction which I had
proposed to incorporate in the budget, and this despite our sore need
for reduction in national expenses.

Shortly after the middle of October I laid my formulated ideas before
the Cabinet. Secretary Wilbur had great experience in Pacific relations and was most helpful in all our discussions. After this Cabinet
meeting, at his request and in his presence, I dictated a memorandum
of my Cabinet statement for him to hold as a record. It was subsequently published by Dr. Wilbur and reads as follows:

The whole transaction is immoral. The offense against the comity of
nations and the affront to the United States is outrageous. But the Nine-
Power Treaty and the Kellogg Pact are solely moral instruments based upon
the hope that peace in the world can be held by the rectitude of nations and
enforced solely by the moral reprobation of the world. They are not military
alliances. We are not parties to the League of Nations, the covenant of which
has also been violated.

The problem lies in three parts:

First, this is primarily a controversy between China and Japan. The
United States has never set out to preserve peace among other nations by
force, and so far as this part is concerned we shall confine ourselves to
friendly counsel. In this connection we must remember some essentials of
Asiatic life: time moves more slowly there; political movements are measured
in decades or centuries, not in days or in months; that while Japan has the
military ascendancy today and no doubt could take over parts or all of China,
yet the Chinese people possess transcendent cultural resistance; that the
mores of the race have carried through a dozen foreign dynasties over three
thousand years; that the Chinese are ten to one in population. No matter
what Japan does in time they will not Japanify China and if they stay long
enough they will be absorbed or expelled by the Chinese. For America to

undertake this on behalf of China might expedite it but would not make it more inevitable.

There is something on the side of Japan. Ours has been a long and deep-seated friendship with her, and we should in friendship consider her side also. Suppose Japan had come out boldly and said:

"We can no longer endure these treaties and we must give notice that China has failed to establish the internal order these treaties contemplated. A large part of her area is Bolshevist and cooperating with Russia. The government of Manchuria is in the hands of a military adventurer who ignores the Chinese government, and China makes no effort to assert her will. That territory is in a state of anarchy that is intolerable. The whole living of our people depends upon expanding the sales of our manufactures in China and securing of raw materials from her. We are today almost economically prostrate because there is no order in China. Beyond this with Bolshevist Russia to the north and a possible Bolshevist China on our flank, our independence is in jeopardy. Either the signatories of the Nine-Power Pact must join with us to restore order in China, or we must do it as an act of self-preservation. If you do not join we consider we cannot hold to an obligation around which the whole environment has changed."

America certainly would not join in such a proposal, and we could not raise much objection.

Second, our whole policy in connection with controversies is to exhaust the processes of peaceful negotiation. But in contemplating these we must make up our minds whether we consider war as the ultimate if these efforts fail. Neither our obligation to China, nor our own interest, nor our dignity requires us to go to war over these questions.

These acts do not imperil the freedom of the American people, the economic or moral future of our people. I do not propose ever to sacrifice American life for anything short of this. If that were not enough reason, to go to war means a long struggle at a time when civilization is already weak enough. To win such a war is not solely a naval operation. We must arm and train Chinese. We would find ourselves involved in China in a fashion that would excite the suspicions of the whole world.

Third, we have a moral obligation to use every influence short of war to have the treaties upheld or terminated by mutual agreement. We should cooperate with the rest of the world, we should do so as long as that cooperation remains in the field of moral pressures. As the League of Nations has already taken up the subject, we should cooperate with them in every field of negotiation or conciliation. But that is the limit. We will not go along on war or any of the sanctions either economic or military, for those are the roads to war.[3]

AN EXERCISE IN POWER POLITICS

Secretary Stimson and I agreed to disagree on the sanctions point, and I must say at once that he loyally carried out my policies in his negotiations with the powers. Nevertheless, he constantly returned to this idea, while I held that one who brandishes a pistol must be prepared to shoot.

As a byplay to all this, I had to meet some international intrigue. A sizable and influential group in the United States actively advocated our joining the League. Parallel with them was a considerable coterie of Americans residing in Geneva, interested in the work of the League. They derived great satisfaction from hovering around this international center and feeling they were a part of great events, associated with prominent persons. In addition to these groups, the Chinese government naturally wanted violence against Japan and added to the clamor.

Under the leadership of Viscount Cecil (the British representative on the Council of the League), several members of that organization decided to advocate the economic sanctions to their home governments. At once we began to receive echoes from the Geneva Americans and their collaborators in the United States and the Chinese.

Fortunately these "power events" do not need to rest upon my account alone. Viscount Cecil, in his autobiography,[4] brilliantly illuminates these dark passages. He says that prior to the October 14, 1931, meeting of the League its permanent officials had formed a small committee to consider measures; that this body concluded that economic sanctions might need to be applied; that they could not be applied unless the United States would join and the American position must be first found out.

Cecil and the American groups, both in Geneva and in the United States, were undoubtedly aware of Secretary Stimson's favor of eco-

---

[3] Secretaries Wilbur and Hyde, who had a copy of this memorandum, subsequently published it in *The Hoover Policies* (Charles Scribner's Sons, New York, 1937), p. 600.

[4] Viscount Cecil, *A Great Experiment: An Autobiography* (Jonathan Cape, London, 1941).

nomic sanctions. Pressures on us began. There at once appeared in the
Geneva press and in dispatches to the world press, statements to the
effect that nothing could be done about Japanese aggression unless the
United States would agree to imposing economic sanctions.

The internationalist groups and internationalist press in New York
coincidentally began to support sanctions. President Lowell of Harvard
started a sanctions "movement" which had many important supporters.
They drove at me with all the usual propaganda weapons.

However, all this evaporated when the Geneva pro-sanction groups
began to drive upon their home governments. Promptly and on no
inspiration from us, they were informed by their home authorities that
they would have no part in sanctions. Cecil relates that Lord Reading,
British Foreign Minister, at the meeting of October 13, directed Cecil
to desist his sanctions agitation. The European end of the movement
died out.

The British, French, and Italians were not for war measures—and
the British, as will be shown later, were to some extent sympathizing
with Japan. Thus, irrespective of any views of my own, the problem
resolved itself into moral sanctions by way of protests, negotiation,
and diplomatic pressures.

LEAGUE ACTION

To show our desire to cooperate with the League, we directed our
Consul at Geneva, Prentiss Gilbert, to attend the meeting of the League
Council on the 13th. They asked him to take a seat at the actual Council
table which, with our approval, he did. But instantly the League enthusiasts at Geneva and in the United States welcomed this as the first step
toward America's joining the League. There was a hailstorm of protests from a section of the press which, by stimulating the Senate,
threatened defeat to our every effort at cooperation with the League. So
we had to hoist Gilbert from his seat at the Council table and seat him
at the side of the room so that all America could see that we had not
joined the League.

The League even on moral pressures backed and filled, because of the
uncertainty in the British and French minds. Moreover, the whole
problem was rendered difficult for the League and ourselves because we

all realized that the Liberal Ministry in Tokyo under Prince Konoye was earnestly trying to restrain the militarists. We did not want to embarrass these good men, yet we must show a strong attitude. Now and then the Japanese Ministry even gained some ascendancy, and the militarists were forced temporarily to recede in their activities. At the same time we had to cut a trail through the thickets of American public opinion and the power politics of Europe.

On November 14, the League Council again met in Paris. We sent Ambassador Dawes to represent us with instructions to "sit" at the Council table or "sit" outside as he chose. He chose the latter and conducted his work most ably. The Council sessions continued for ten days during which new resolutions were drawn up for a subsequent meeting to appoint a special commission to investigate the situation on the spot. Again we supported the League and appointed General Frank McCoy to what became later known as the Lytton Commission. The British attitude of leaning toward Japan, however, became even more positive at this November 14 session. Cecil says, "It quickly became clear that Sir John Simon, the Foreign Minister, was not prepared to take any step to compel Japan." [5]

By December 10 Congress had assembled, and in my annual message I set forth the situation and announced my determination to cooperate with the League.

The League Council on the same day formally passed the resolutions prepared at the Paris meeting. Also the same day the liberal Japanese Ministry fell, and the militarists gained greater power. Plots for assassinating the liberal leaders were exposed, and indeed the honesty of these men was proved when later on several of them were assassinated.

ORIGIN OF THE DOCTRINE OF NONRECOGNITION

As stated elsewhere, after taking over the Presidency in 1929 I had discussed with Secretary of State Kellogg the possibility of proposing that the world put some moral teeth in the Kellogg Pact. As stated

[5] The records of the State Department include a conversation between Secretary Stimson and Ambassador Dawes which seems inconsistent with this account. Dawes was new to the problem and was unaware of the real British attitude on sanctions as shown by Cecil. He learned the truth later.

earlier in this section Secretary Kellogg and I considered several ideas for incorporation in it, including the nonrecognition of spoils or territory seized, advanced originally by Secretary of State William Jennings Bryan. We also considered withdrawal of embassies, public denunciation, refusal to admit aggressor nations to membership in world conferences, and other forms of moral deterrents. Secretary Bryan did not have the world-wide foundation for such action against aggression as was afforded by the Kellogg Pact.

Recollecting these ideas, I suggested to Secretary Stimson early in December, 1931, in Cabinet meeting, that we consider proposing to the League that the members refuse to recognize any territory obtained by the Japanese in violation of the Kellogg Pact and emphasize the refusal by withdrawing all legations from the offending nation.

In the latter part of December we took up the elaboration of this idea of nonrecognition. In the interest of accuracy of historic fact, I may mention here that an attempt was made to stamp this as the "Stimson Doctrine" with the implication that I had no part in it, nor Secretary Bryan, either. In consequence of such statements to the press before I left Washington in 1933, Secretaries Hurley and Wilbur wrote me letters of protest, both having been present at Cabinet meetings when I first proposed this idea (originally Bryan's).

IMPLEMENTING THE NONRECOGNITION DOCTRINE

Who originated the nonrecognition doctrine is of little importance. In consequence of our prior discussions, Secretary Stimson formulated the idea in a dispatch to Japan and submitted it to me on January 4, 1932. We agreed that he would endeavor to get the British and French to send identic nonrecognition declarations.

Our dispatch to Japan was sent on January 7 and published on January 8. We had reason to expect that the British and French would join. But the British note did not mention the fundamental question of preserving the integrity of China or nonrecognition. Certain of the press at once interpreted the British note as a slap by the British government at our ideas. The French informed us that in view of the British attitude they could not go along with us. Both had in fact deserted us in even this moral pressure against an outrageous violation of all international law.

In discussing the effect of this British note to Japan, Cecil says:

... [The British note] ignored altogether the mention of the integrity of China. ... This reply ... must have been read in Japan as a clear intimation that we [the British] should not do anything to secure the integrity of China. ...

The truth is that the British Government recognized no duty to take action beyond remonstrance for the maintenance of peace under the Covenant of the League nor did they believe that our treaty obligations to China required us to take any active steps to preserve her integrity.

The Japanese militarists were quick to seize upon this divided attitude. In any event, they at once developed a new and more violent stage of military action.

On January 28, on various excuses and probably in order to force Chinese acquiescence to their actions in Manchuria, they seized Shanghai with large naval and military forces. Their behavior toward the civil population was brutal beyond belief. At once I ordered a strong contingent of American troops and naval forces to Shanghai to protect the lives of Americans. I increased our Pacific fleet. I reenforced our Hawaiian and Philippine bases. There was no bluffing about this. It was indeed a period of added anxiety, for we were in the depths of the great depression and in a battle with a Democratic Congress to secure measures of depression relief.

The crisis had now switched from the rape of Manchuria to the Japanese attack upon Shanghai and central China. It was evident that, with the Japanese trading on the divided attitude of the powers, and with their occupation of Shanghai, something must be done to pull the situation together. I therefore suggested that a joint appeal should be sent directly to the Emperor of Japan who, we had been reliably informed, was opposed to the militarist groups. This message was to be signed by the President of the United States, the King of England, the President of France, the King of Italy, and the heads of all other noncombatant states signatory to the Nine-Power Treaty. The first condition in the note was to stop all military action in its tracks; the second, to set up a conference of the Nine Powers for the consideration of methods for the establishment of stable government in China. I drafted such an appeal. Mr. Stimson believed that it would be a constructive step at least demonstrating unity of action among all the important powers. He called Prime Minister MacDonald on the telephone and asked what he thought of it. Mr. MacDonald agreed to reply later. The reply was in the negative.

Secretary Stimson would not give up his idea of economic sanctions. He returned to the idea of our acting alone in early February, 1932, and still persisted in the belief that such a boycott would not mean war. We, of course, could do nothing of the sort without Congressional approval, and he thought that this could be secured. He had the support of various groups of the war-minded in the United States, and some legislation was introduced into Congress. In his book he states: "I believed that such a measure would have more chance of being adopted by Congress if it were recommended following the invocation of the Nine-Power Treaty than if it had been recommended solely by the League of Nations." [6]

I took no stock in it because it was certain that Congress would never authorize us to go alone and it was also obvious that the British and French would never go along on force measures. I informed the Secretary again in a memorandum of February 23, 1932, that I did not agree. I also refused to recommend any such action to the Congress. Aside from any views of my own it was certain that Congress would refuse, which would leave the situation even more weakened. I stated to the Secretary that if I recommended the use of force it would be a recommendation that Congress should declare war; and that was wholly unjustified.

The Secretary proposed that, in view of the expansion of Japanese military activities to Shanghai, we again test the European willingness to cooperate in other than force measures more fully and more vigorously; and this I approved. We decided to try again, basing action this time on the provisions of the Nine-Power Treaty instead of undertakings in the League or the Kellogg Pact. It gave a new point of departure, and I thought that, in view of the Japanese threats to the

[6] *The Far Eastern Crisis* (Harper and Brothers, New York, 1936). p. 161.

British and French economic "spheres" in Central China, they might now go along on the nonrecognition proposals.

Repeatedly, Mr. Stimson took the matter up with the British Foreign Minister, Sir John Simon, by telephone, pressing him strongly. He sent Simon the draft of a note which should be sent to Japan by the leading signatories of the Nine-Power Treaty. The unanimous verdict of the British Cabinet was adverse. The Secretary and I, however, determined to make our views public, and therefore Mr. Stimson practically repeated this new nonrecognition note in the form of a letter on February 23 (1932) to Senator Borah, chairman of the Senate Foreign Relations Committee.

On March 3, 1932, the Assembly of the League met; and on the 11th, to our surprise, it expressed its adherence to the doctrine of nonrecognition. The British and French voted for it. Their change was no doubt due to increased alarm at the Japanese occupation of Shanghai, which endangered their "spheres of influence."

Our long and earnest negotiations both with Europe and with Japan, and the European acceptance of the nonrecognition declaration, possibly were responsible for halting Japan's attack on Central China and inducing their subsequent withdrawal. But it did not restore Manchuria. The Secretary got some satisfaction at the adoption of the doctrine, hoping it would be of use to the world in the future.

In May, the Secretary being in Europe and an agitation for "economic sanctions" having been renewed by the Chinese and our internationalists, I instructed Under Secretary of State Castle to include in a forthcoming address a statement that the United States would not undertake sanctions, and to give reasons.[7]

---

[7] Subsequent to this Japanese aggression the world had an exhibit of economic sanctions. In October, 1934, Italy outrageously invaded Ethiopia. The League declared her an aggressor and imposed economic sanctions. There was at once a lack of unanimity among European nations in carrying out the League's orders, particularly on the part of France. But more importantly, upon the Italian threat of war, the British practically withdrew. Plainly, in this case, the British believed that to pursue the economic sanctions meant war. In 1937 the Japanese again resumed aggression on China. Secretary Stimson in a well formulated letter to the *New York Times* proposed immediate "economic sanctions." He set up an organization to propagandize the American public in favor of it with himself as chairman. On June 20, 1940, he joined the Roosevelt Cabinet as Secretary of War. The embargoes on certain goods to Japan were gradually

The Lytton Report on Manchuria was signed on September 4, 1932, but was held secret until October 1. It utterly condemned the Japanese action as rank aggression—a violation of the League Covenant—but, like most such documents, recommended a compromise. It made no suggestion of economic sanctions. On December 6, following the Lytton Report, the General Assembly of the League met, and Sir John Simon on behalf of Britain made an address which Cecil describes as so conciliatory to Japan that the Japanese thanked him. Cecil adds: "It was that speech which made it finally impossible to take any effective action on behalf of the central doctrine of the Covenant. . . ."

That central doctrine was force. Four days after this meeting the British embargoed arms to both Japan and China. This curious action could only embarrass China, as Japan had plenty of arms and munitions plants while China had very few. It pleased the Japanese.

On February 24, 1933, the League endorsed the Lytton Report. Nothing came of it. The Japanese at this time withdrew from the League. Our ability to do anything further in the matter had ended with my defeat in the previous November. The Secretary, under my instructions, consulted the President-Elect as to his wishes, but Roosevelt ceased any effort to organize the world for restraint on Japan.

The lessons that I received from this experience confirmed my views as to American policies.

Besides effective defense of the Western Hemisphere, America can take either of two roads in international relations. The one is to develop moral standards of conduct among nations and to support them with moral forces. The other is to use economic and inevitably military force against aggressors. Having seen the wreckage to civilization by World War I, I believed that the long-view contribution to preserving peace would be for America to stand on moral forces alone in support of law between nations. It was not isolationism. It was a

---

increased in intensity during 1941 until, on July 25, full economic sanctions were applied, including seizure of Japanese assets in the United States. Similar action was taken by Britain and Holland. The economic paralysis of Japan was complete with huge unemployment and destitution. She struck back four months later at Pearl Harbor. Here was ample proof that "economic sanctions" not only failed in their purpose to restrain Japan; they probably had some part in precipitating war.

belief that somewhere, somehow, there must be an abiding place for law and a sanctuary for civilization.

From the experience with the League we could have learned something as to the practical results in the use of force to prevent aggression. General commitments of many nations, such as the Covenant, to use force—either economic sanctions or military action—will not hold against the shifting tides in relations between nations and the changing interest of peoples.

Nor can the use of force be directed by a debating society. No amount of signed papers will assure such collaboration.[8]

SUMMARY OF FOREIGN POLICIES—1929–1933

In a later volume of these Memoirs I will discuss other international efforts on our part of great importance, including the moratorium on international debts; the stand-still agreements on German and Central European private obligations; a proposed revision of the war debts, and the calling of a World Economic Conference.

I may here shortly summarize our foreign policies.

Early in the discussion of foreign relations I pointed out that my over-all hope was to pull the people of the United States out of the extreme mental and spiritual isolationism which for years had made impossible a proper American participation in the constructive building of peace in the world. During these four years, however, we traveled a long distance into wider collaboration with other nations through (a) the reorganization of our relations in the Western Hemisphere;

---

[8] I have allowed these views, written prior to World War II, to stand as then stated, for they indicate the general American attitude at that time.

As shown in the earlier chapters of this volume, I supported the American entry into the League of Nations with a minor reservation. The American people rejected it for many reasons which, stated or unstated, revolved around commitments to use force to stop aggression. As time went on, experience showed not only the futility of economic sanctions but the inability of the League to secure the cooperation necessary to conduct measures of force against aggression.

After the hideous experience of World War II, I advocated that the world should try again to organize collective force against military aggression. But doubt has already risen as to whether the United Nations can function against the division of interests among its members. I need cite only the British recognition of, and sending supplies to, Communist China which, as a declared aggressor in Korea, was daily attacking the American army which was acting on behalf of the United Nations.

(b) the advancement of pacific methods of settling controversies by direct treaties; (c) the doctrine of nonrecognition; (d) collaboration with the League of Nations in all non-force fields; (e) elimination of frictions with Britain and ending of naval competition; (f) the moratorium on international debts; (g) the stand-still agreement, which contributed to the sustaining of democratic government in Germany for some time; (h) actively pushing revision of the World War debts; (i) a World Economic Conference to stabilize currencies and lower trade barriers; (j) striving to reduce world armies and aggressive weapons; (k) developing international cooperation to restrain the military aggression of Japan upon China; and (l) urging our membership in the World Court on the Senate.

APPENDIX

Since 1929 all the public addresses and press statements of Mr. Hoover have been published in book form. From 1919 to 1929 they often appeared in the press; but for reference purposes, they are listed here under the chapters relating to that period. They may be consulted at the War Library, Stanford University.

The published books covering the period 1929 to 1933, available in most libraries, are as follows:

The New Day: Campaign Speeches of Herbert Hoover, 1928 (Stanford University Press, 1928).

The State Papers and Other Public Writings of Herbert Hoover, collected and edited by William Starr Myers (Doubleday, Doran & Company, 1934).

Campaign Speeches of 1932, by President Hoover and ex-President Coolidge (Doubleday, Doran & Company, 1933).

Mr. Hoover's addresses and press statements, since 1933, have been published from time to time in book form under the title, *Addresses upon the American Road.*

CHAPTER 6

1919: Oct. 9, address at San Francisco; Dec. 27, article in *Saturday Evening Post.*

1920: Feb. 28, address at Chicago; March 2, Congressional Committee hearings; March 24, address at Boston; April 10, article in *Saturday Evening Post*; Oct. 12, address at St. Louis; Aug. 27, address on public works at Minneapolis; Oct. 9, address at Indianapolis; Nov. 19, address at Washington.

1921: Feb. 14, address at Syracuse, N. Y.

The full texts of all these may be found in the War Library.

CHAPTER 10

On a variety of matters:

1921: May 25, address at Washington; June, Foreword to *Waste in Industry;* Nov. 15, address at Washington.

1922: Jan. 5, address to American Engineering Council; Feb. 3, statement before Interstate Commerce Commission; address to United States Chamber of Com-

merce; March, article in *Nation's Business*; April 29, interview on American Liv-
ing Standards; May 15, 16, addresses at Washington; May 19, address at Atlantic
City; May 22, 24, addresses at Washington; Oct. 5, article in *Hardware Age*;
Oct. 17, address at Detroit.

1923: May 23, 26, addresses at Washington; June 18, press release; Oct. 13,
statement at New York to Super-Power Conference; Dec., article in *Nation's
Business*.

1924: Jan. 9, address to Transportation Conference; Feb. 9, article in *Saturday
Evening Post*; April 9, House Hearings on Railroad Rates; May, statement in
American Food Journal; May 21, Senate Hearings on Railway Consolidation;
May 21, 28, addresses at Washington; June 3, American Engineering Standards
Committee; July 24, International Convention of Weights and Measures; Oct. 1,
Introduction to *Standardization* (published in English and Spanish); Nov. 19,
National Conference on Utilization of Forest Products; Nov. 26, Division of Sim-
plified Practice; Dec. 6, report to President Coolidge on Coordination of Rail and
Water Facilities.

1925: January, article in *Factory*; Jan. 12, 14, 16, addresses at Washington;
April 11, address at New York; May 1, address at Washington; May 15, American
Institute of Electrical Engineers; May 25, address at Washington; Dec. 9, address
at Washington; Dec. 29, interview for *Saturday Evening Post*.

1926: Jan. 12, address at New York; April 12, to International Scientific Management Congress; April 20, to National Lumber Manufacturers Association;
April 28, to National Committee on Wood Utilization; May 27, address at Washington; June 4, on National Highway System; June 21, to National Association
of Building Owners and Managers; July 13, report of Building Code; Sept. 24,
to National Association of Manufacturers; Oct. 19, to American Institute of Steel
Construction; Nov. 29, to Pacific Coast Building Officials Conference; Dec. 17,
meeting of New England Council.

1927: Jan. 14, address at Washington; Feb. 5, to Textile Institute; April 5, to
Atlantic States Regional Advisory Board of Shippers; April 7, to National Lumber
Manufacturers Association; Nov. 9, address at Mt. Carmel, Pa.; Dec. 1, address at
Washington.

1928: Feb. 13, to Chemical Industry; Feb. 15, to Associated Traffic Clubs;
Feb. 21, address at New York; March 22, to *A Century of Individual Progress*.

On the subject of research:
1921: March 13, press statement, Food Research Institute; September, article
in *Industrial and Engineering Chemistry*.

1923: Nov. 13, letter to Stevens Institute on Technical Training.

1924: Oct. 3, address at Troy, N. Y., to Rensselaer Polytechnic Institute Cen-
tennial.

1925: Oct. 21, address to the General Electric Program on the Incandescent Lamp Anniversary; Dec. 1, address at New York to the American Society of Mechanical Engineers; Dec. 16, address at Washington to the National Distribution Conference of the United States Chamber of Commerce.

1926: April 9, address to the Pan-American Congress of Journalists at the Bureau of Standards Laboratories; May 24, address at Tuscaloosa to the University of Alabama; June, article in *Nation's Business*; July 6, press interview on Human Progress and Science; Dec. 4, address at Washington to the Anniversary Dinner of the Bureau of Standards; Dec. 28, address at Philadelphia to the American Association for the Advancement of Science.

1927: April 10, address at Chicago to the Northwestern University; July, message to "new" *Scientific American.*

1928: February 4, article in *Textile World*; March 18, statement on establishment of National Hydraulic Laboratory in the Bureau of Standards.

CHAPTER 11

1921: March 9, on Latin-American Relations; May 18, address at New York; July 12, address at Boston; Sept., article in *Farm and Home*; Oct. 6, address at New York.

1922: Jan. 7, article in *Collier's*; May 6, article in *Export Trade*; May 8, report on Foreign Trade; May 10, 16, addresses at New York; Dec. 13, to Congressman Greene on German Potash Prices.

1923: Jan. 21, on Tariff and Imports; Jan. 25, to Congressman Hutchinson, on German Potash Prices; Feb. 2, to Senator McCormick on Trade Promotion; March 19, press statement on Foreign Buying Power and Tariff; May 8, address at New York; May 11, Sugar Facts; June 11, article in *Commerce and Foreign Trade;* Sept. 14, *The Balance of International Payments of the United States*; Oct. 30, address at Washington; Nov. 8, address at New York.

1924: Jan. 7, article in *Annalist*; Feb. 7, Congressional Hearings on Foreign Commerce; March 6, to Senator Capper on Legislation Against Foreign Monopolies; March 21, to Senator Capper on Foreign Monopolies; Aug. 27, Reparations Settlement and Foreign Trade; Dec. 11, article in *Manufacturers' Record.*

1925: Jan. 5, article in *Annalist*; April, *Balance of International Payments of the United States*; April 28, *Crude Rubber Survey*; June 2, on Reclamation of Rubber; June 10, Synthetic Chemicals; Oct. 31, address at Erie, Pa.; Dec. 10, to Senator Capper on Rubber Price-Fixing; Dec. 22, on Rubber Consumption Reduction.

1926: Jan. 4, 10, on Foreign Monopolies; Jan. 6, 18, House Hearings on Rubber and Coffee; Jan. 26, on Rubber Price Reduction; Feb., article in *American Motorist*; article in *Saturday Evening Post*, Feb. 13; March 16, address at New York; April, *Balance of International Payments of the United States*; April 14, 17, on

Present International Trade Conditions; April 29, House Hearings on Potash; Aug. 21, address at Tacoma, Wash.

1927: May 2, address at Washington to Pan-American Commercial Conference.

CHAPTER 13

1921: April 14, letter to Building and Loan Associations; May 12, address at Washington; July 15, address at Chicago; Oct. 7, address at New York.

1922: April 13, "Own Your Home"; May 10, to the Russell Sage Foundation; Oct., Nov., articles in *Delineator*.

1923: Sept. 7, *How to Own Your Own Home.*

1924: Feb. 1, *Better Homes in America Guidebook*; Feb. 11, to Building Code Committee; Feb. 15, State Zoning Act; April, on Architects' Small House Service Bureau; May 12, on Better Homes Week; Nov., Better Homes in America.

1925: April, article in *Delineator*; May 8, on Survey of Home Equipment; May 11, on Better Homes Week; Aug. 11, on Home Financing; Oct., Better Homes in America Campaign.

1926: July 14, on Better Homes in America Prize; July 20, address at Minneapolis; Oct. 21, address at Columbus, Ohio.

1928: March 5, on Better Homes Movement; March 29, on Home Building and Stability; April 20, on Better Homes Week; Aug., *Present Home Financing Methods.*

CHAPTER 14

1921: Dec. 8, on Child Labor.

1922: June 27, address at Providence, R.I.; Oct. 12, address at Washington to American Child Hygiene Association.

1923: Feb., "Bill of Rights for Children"; June, article in *Good Housekeeping*; Oct. 15, address at Detroit to American Child Health Association.

1924: April 25, American Child Health Association; Dec. 16, American Child Health Association.

1925: Jan., on May Day in *Child Health Magazine*; May, articles in *Delineator, Child Welfare,* and *McClure's*; May 1, broadcast, May Day; May 1, American Child Health Association; May 2, article in *Collier's.*

1926: April, article in *Child Welfare*; May 18, address at Atlantic City to American Child Health Association; Oct., article in *Forum.*

1927: April, article in *Child Welfare*; May 1, "Child's Bill of Rights," in New York *Herald Tribune* Magazine; May 9, address to American Child Health Association; Dec. 31, *Five Years of American Child Health.*

1928: April, article in *Child Welfare.*

CHAPTER 15

1921: April 1, article in *Industrial Management*; Nov. 4, address at New York; statement in *Labor* on strikes.

1922: Feb. 18, statement on Coal Strike; Aug. 7, on Railroad Strike.

1923: Jan. 27, May 8, addresses at New York.

1925: April 11, address at New York; May 19, on the Seven-Day Work Week; Sept. 5, at American Federation of Labor; Dec. 28, on Labor Arbitration.

1926: May 12, address at Washington.

1927: Aug. Foreword to *Year Book on Commercial Arbitration in the United States, 1927* (American Arbitration Association).

1928: Feb. 25, Report to President from Secretaries of State, Commerce, Labor, on immigration.

CHAPTER 16

1921: Sept. 21, article in *Farm and Home*.

1922: March 16, address to Arizona Legislature; March 21, address at Los Angeles; Oct. 21, article in *Country Gentleman*; Dec. 30, Senate Hearings on Rural Credits.

1923: Feb. 23, to Congressman Anderson on Rural Credits; March 7, statement on Agricultural Foreign Markets; April 26, to American Farm Bureau Federation; June, article in *Capper's Farmer*; Oct. 2, address at Washington to World Dairy Congress.

1924: Jan. 14, on Cooperative Marketing; Feb. 4, President's Conference on Northwestern Agriculture; June, article in *Agricultural Projects*; July 11, on Cooperatives; Sept. 18, Wheat Prices; Oct. 1, address at Milwaukee; Nov. 6, address at San Francisco; Nov. 14, address at Sacramento; Dec. 8, report to President's Agricultural Conference; Dec. 19, to American Council of Agriculture.

1925: Jan. 7, address to National Council of Cooperative Marketing; Jan. 16, refusal of Secretaryship of Agriculture; Jan. 19, President's Agricultural Conference; Feb. 10, message in *Modern Miller*; March 23, address at Florence, South Carolina; March, article in *Capper's Farmer*; April 7, address at Washington; Nov. 18, interview for *Commerce and Finance*; Dec., article in *Farm and Fireside*.

1926: Jan. 13, address to New Jersey State Agricultural Convention; March, article in *Country Gentleman*; Aug. 14, on Farm Land Prices; Oct. 9, on Cotton Textile Institute.

CHAPTER 17

On water resources in general:

1922: Jan. 9, Hearings on Cape Cod Canal.

1924: July 3, World Power Conference on Government Policies and Power Development.

1925: Dec. 9, address at Washington to National Rivers and Harbors Congress.

1926: Jan. 30, House Hearings on Inland Waterways; March, article in *Country Gentleman*; March 9, address at Chicago to the John Ericsson League; May 22, article in *Liberty*; July 20, address at Minneapolis; Aug. 14, address at Hammond, Ind.; Sept. 26, article in New York *Herald Tribune*; Sept. 28, address at Mitchell, S.D.; Sept. 30, address at Omaha to Chamber of Commerce; Dec. 8, address at Washington to National Rivers and Harbors Congress.

1927: Nov. 18, address at Springfield, Mass.; Dec. 8, address at Washington to National Rivers and Harbors Congress.

On the Colorado project:

1922: Jan. 26, on the Colorado River Commission; May, article in *Industrial Management*; June 21, House Hearings on Colorado River Development; Aug., article in *Nation's Business*; Nov. 25, signing of the Colorado River Basin Compact; Dec. 1, address at San Francisco; Dec. 5, address at Los Angeles; Dec. 8, address at Phoenix, Ariz.

1923: Jan. 30, House Hearings on Colorado River Compact; March 2, Commission's Report on Colorado River Compact.

1924: Feb. 13, House Hearings on Colorado Basin.

1925: July 13, on Colorado River Dam; Dec. 10, Senate Hearings on Colorado River Basin.

1926: March 3, House Hearings on Colorado River Basin.

1927: Press statement on Dam Legislation.

1928: Aug. 18, address at Los Angeles.

On the Great Valley project:

1925: June 27, addresses at Sacramento and Stockton, Calif.; July 22, address at Oakland, Calif.

1926: Sept. 8, 11, addresses at Los Angeles and Sacramento, Calif.

On the Columbia River development:

1926: Aug. 21, addresses at Tacoma and Seattle, Wash.; Dec. 27, to Representative Sinnott on Columbia River.

On the St. Lawrence Waterway:

1924: June 14–16, addresses at Toronto; Sept. 17, on Progress of St. Lawrence Waterway.

1925: Sept. 7, Albany *Knickerbocker Press*; Dec. 5, Toronto *Daily Star*.

1926: June 4, on Preservation of Niagara Falls; Dec. 27, Report of St. Lawrence Commission.

1927: Jan. 26, Regional Conference of Great Lakes–St. Lawrence Tidewater Association; March 12, address at New Haven; April, article in *Farm Journal*.

CHAPTER 18

On waterway development and Mississippi flood control:

1926: Aug. 4, Missouri River Development; Oct. 20, speech at Louisville, Ky.; Oct. 25, on Mississippi River; Nov. 22, address at St. Louis.

1927: April 22, on Establishment of Mississippi Valley Flood Disaster Committee; April 30, address from Memphis; April 30, on Mississippi Flood Control; May 2, Report to President's Flood Committee; May 5, to House Flood Control Committee; May 7, statement from Baton Rouge; May 8, statement on Flood Control; May 13, to Senator Capper on Negro Flood Sufferers; May 18, statement on Flood; May 23, statement to Louisiana Reconstruction Commission; May 25, Principles of Organization in Flood Relief and Reconstruction; May 28, address at New Orleans; May 31, Railroad Restoration; June 11, Control of Mississippi Flood; June 21, Health Program for Flooded Area; June 25, Address at Little Rock; June 27, Pine Bluff on Negro Program; June 29, New Orleans; July 1, on Flood Rehabilitation; July 2, article in *Editor and Publisher*; July 16, article in *Collier's;* July 20, Report to the President on Flood Control; Sept. 9, address to Louisiana Legislature; Sept. 15, Report to President Coolidge on Flood Relief; Oct. 30, Main Street and Flood Relief; Nov., article in *Magazine of Business*; Nov. 14, address at St. Louis.

1928: Jan. 29, article in New York *Herald Tribune* Magazine on Flood Control; Feb. 24, Senate Hearings on Flood Control.

CHAPTER 19

On aviation:

1924: Dec. 17, House Hearings on Bureau of Civil Air Navigation.

1925: Jan. 10, House Hearings on Operation of the United States Air Services; Sept. 23, statement to President's Aircraft Board.

1926: Aug. 15, statement on Government Plan to Help Airways; Sept. 2, address at San Francisco; Sept. 30, article in *California Journal of Development*.

1927: April 9, interview on Commercial Aviation; June 24, 26, New York *Times* on Air Service; Aug. 7, article in New York *Herald Tribune* Magazine; Sept. 10, on Control of Overseas Flights; Dec. 5, address at Washington; Dec. 19, on Airport Facilities for New York.

1928: April, article in *Aero Digest* on Civil Aviation; April 15, address at Washington; Sept., on National Aeronautics Association.

On the merchant marine:

1923: Nov. 8, address to Merchant Marine Congress.

1924: Nov. 4, House Hearings on Merchant Marine.

1925: Nov. 16, address at Washington.

1926: March 8, House Hearings on Reorganization of Shipping Board; March 16, address at New York; June 26, address at Philadelphia.

CHAPTER 20

On radio:

1921: Aug. 30, Radio Convention.

1922: Feb. 27, address opening first Radio Conference; May 4, article in Boston *Evening Transcript*; July, article in *Popular Science Monthly*; August, article in *Scientific American*.

1923: Jan., article in *Radio Broadcast*; Jan. 2, House Hearings on Radio Act; March 20, address opening second Radio Conference; April 2, on Radio Conference.

1924: March 10, Control of Radio Broadcasting; March 11, House Hearings on Regulating Radio; March 16, article in New York *World*; March 22, article in *Radio Digest*; March 26, broadcast from Washington; May 18, Radio Improvement; Aug. 16, address at San Francisco; Oct., article in *Radio News*; Oct. 6, address to third Radio Conference; Oct. 16, press release on Radio Monopoly; Dec. 4, to Congressman White on Radio Regulation.

1925: Jan., article in *Radio Retailing*; Jan. 1, Radio and the Public; Feb. 8, Radio Situation; May 28, Special Privilege in Radio; Sept. 12, address to Radio Exposition; Nov. 9, address opening fourth Radio Conference; Nov. 12, broadcast from Washington; Dec. 3, message to American Radio Relay League; Dec. 26, Radio Control.

1926: Jan. 6, House Hearings on Radio Regulation; April 20, Radio Legislation; April 30, Radio Manufacturers; July 9, on Radio Legislation.

1927: Feb. 24, Radio Situation; March 6, Radio Legislation; Oct. 4, address opening International Radio Conference; Oct. 15, address at New York; Nov. 25, address at Washington to International Radio Conference.

1928: Jan. 1, International Radio Conference; March 15, letter to Federal Radio Commission.

CHAPTER 22

On the development of fisheries:

1921: Dec. 7, House Hearings on Pollution of Navigable Waters.

1922: Feb. 15, Hearings on Pollution of Navigable Waters; Dec. 21, to Congressman Greene on Alaska Salmon Fisheries.

1923: March 16, to Senator Jones on Alaska Salmon Fisheries; May, article in

Izaak Walton League Monthly; July 9, address at Wrangel, Alaska; July 20, address at Cordova, Alaska; Nov. 20, to Senator King on Alaska Fisheries; Dec., article in *Outdoor America*; Dec. 6, Alaska Sealskin Situation.

1924: Jan. 23, Hearings on Pollution of Navigable Waters; Feb. 7, Hearings on Alaska Fisheries; April 12, address at Chicago; April 27, Alaska Fisheries Conservation Legislation; May 5, to Attorney General on Alaska Salmon Packers; May 28, Alaska Salmon Industries; June 23, Alaska Fisheries Regulations; June 30, Progress in Fisheries Conservation; Sept. 5, address at Atlantic City; Nov. 20, on Game Fishing.

1925: Jan., Nov., articles in *Outdoor America*; April 29, Fish Conservation; May 22, address at Washington; June 20, article in *Liberty* Magazine; Dec. 3, Convention of Izaak Walton League.

1926: Dec. 15, article in *Farm Life*.

1927: April 9, address, "Remedy for Disappearing Game Fish," to Izaak Walton League.

CHAPTER 23

Mr. Hoover's more important statements upon the study of the business cycle were:

1921: June 2, on Federal Trade Commission Law; Oct. 22, American Mining Congress; Oct. 28, Nov. 15, addresses at Washington; Nov. 4, address to Academy of Political Science; Dec., article in *Nation's Business*.

1922: Feb. 17, to Senator Willis on Trade Associations; March 18, on Trade Association Activities; April 12, address at Washington; April 22, article in *World's Work*; May 10, Sept. 12, addresses at New York; Oct. 10, American Mining Congress.

1923: April 11, National and State Trade Associations; May 24, address at Washington.

1924: Jan. 10, to Attorney General on Trade Association Activities; Feb. 16, on Trade Association Statistics; May 7, address at Cleveland; June 1, article in *Open Road*; Nov. 7, address at Del Monte, Calif.; Nov. 11, National Association of Railway and Utilities Commissioners.

1925: Feb. 3, on State Regulation of Electric Utilities; March 10, on Credit Abuse; March 18, address at Washington; April 29, on public relations to utilities; May 11, address at Houston, Texas; June 5, article in *Journal of Commerce*; June 9, address at Washington; June 17, address at San Francisco; Oct., article in *Factory*; Oct. 14, Dec. 9, addresses at Washington; Dec. 10, Washington Conference on Government in Industry.

1926: March 27, article in *Industry*.

1928: Feb. 28, message to National Negro Business League; Sept., article in *Nation's Business*.

CHAPTER 24

Mr. Hoover spoke on foreign debt funding:

1922: Oct. 16, address at Toledo.

1924: Aug. 8, address at San Francisco.

1926: March 16, address in New York; April 20, press statement on the French Debt.

Mr. Hoover made statements on naval arms limitation:

1921: Nov. 4, address at New York; Dec. 25, statement in *Current Affairs*.

1922: Feb. 22, address at Chicago; March 22, address at Los Angeles.

1923: April 11, address at Des Moines, Iowa.

1924: Aug. 8, address at San Francisco; Sept. 12, address at Brooklyn.

1925: Oct. 26, address at Washington.

Mr. Hoover's most important statements on coal and oil were:

1921: May 18, to National Coal Association; July 9, Public Utilities Associations.

1922: Feb. 18, on Coal Strike; May 16, on Coal Prices; May 31, address at Washington Coal Conference; June 2, Report on Coal Strike; June 5, Coal Situation; June 8, National Retail Coal Merchants' Association; letter to Senator Borah on Coal Prices; June 11, to John L. Lewis, United Mine Workers; June 14, to John L. Lewis on Coal Prices; June 15, Special Coal Committee; July 21, to Attorney General on Coal Price Fixing; July 26, to governors of states; July 30, on Coal Distribution; Aug. 18, to Senator Borah on Coal Prices; Aug. 23, to President on Coal Profiteering; Aug. 28, House Hearings on Coal; Sept. 5, on Coal Situation; Sept. 14, on Coal Strike Losses; Nov. 4, to Governor Miller of New York on Coal Situation.

1923: Feb., article in *Industrial Management*.

1924: Jan. 26, to Pittsburgh Coal Producers' Association; Feb. 6, on Jacksonville Coal Conference.

1925: April 14, on Jacksonville Agreement; May 27, in *Coal Trade Journal*.

1926: May 14, House Hearings on Anthracite Coal Situation; May 27, to Senator Copeland on Coal Testimony; May 23, Oil Industry on Standardization; Sept., Report of the Federal Oil Conservation Board; Oct. 28, article in *Oil and Gas Journal*.

1927: Nov. 9, address at Mt. Carmel, Pa.

1928: Jan., Report II of Federal Oil Conservation Board.

Mr. Hoover's more important statements as to reorganization of the Federal government were:

1921: April 16, address at Philadelphia.

1922: Oct. 17, address at Grand Rapids; June 7, address at Dayton, Ohio.

1924: Jan. 22, House Hearings on Reorganization of the Executive Departments; April 9, address at Washington; May 16, press statement.

1925: Jan. 16, May 21, addresses at Washington; July 24, address at San Francisco.

1926: April 8, Joint Recommendation by Secretaries Work, Jardine, and Hoover to Senate and House Committees on Territories.

Mr. Hoover's more important statements on street and highway safety were:

1924: Oct. 27, Convocation of National Conference on Street and Highway Safety; Dec. 15, address to Conference.

1925: Feb. 24, Safety Conference.

1926: March 23, 25, addresses to second Conference on Street and Highway Safety.

1927: March 23, address at Washington.

INDEX

Abbott, Grace, 97, 221
Accidents, reduction of, 72–73
Adams, Charles Francis, Secretary of Navy, 218, 219–220, 247, 339; his double causes him to be suspected of law violation, 279 n.; at London Naval Conference, 348
Adams, John and Abigail, 320, 323
Adult education, 317
Advertising, by radio, 147
Aeronautics, in Commerce Dept., 43, 72, 73, 132, 134
Agriculture, development of, 253–255
Agriculture Department, 83; discord with Commerce Dept., 109–110; offered to H. H., 111, 193
Air Force, 245 n., 339
Air mail, 132, 133, 134, 135, 243, 244, 245 and n.
Aircraft industry, 132, 134, 245, 339
Airports and airways, 132, 133, 134, 135, 244
Akerson, George E., 43; press secretary to President, 218, 219
Alaska, Harding visit to, 48, 49–50; fisheries of, 149–151, 152
Albert, King of the Belgians, visit to California, 6–9
Albright, Horace M., 221, 242
Alcatraz Island, 275
Alien Property Custodian, See Miller, T. W.
Alpine, John R., 221
American Bankers Association, and credits to Europe, 13
American Child Health Association, 32, 97–100, 103; 1930 national conference, 259–265
American Child Hygiene Association, 32
American Communists, fund drive for 1921 Russian famine, 24; defamation of H. H. by, 26; aims of, 27
American Engineering Council, 31

American Engineering Standards Committee, 66
American Farm Bureau Federation, 296
American Federation of Labor, 77, 102, 296
American Friends Service Committee, and A.R.A., 20, 22
American Legion, and 1931 bonus legislation, 287–288
American Red Cross, and A.R.A., 20–22; and 1927 Mississippi flood, 126
American Relief Administration, beginnings of, 18–22; in U.S.S.R., 23–26
American system, 27–30, 202–205, 301, 303, 304
Anderson, Henry W., 277
Anderson, Mary, 221
Andrews, Capt. Adolphus, 52
Anthony, Edward, 191
Anti-trust laws, 168, 169, 170, 173 n., 300; significance of, 301–302
Appel, Monte, 220
Arbitration and conciliation treaties, 332, 337
Argentina, on "good will" journey, 211, 212–213; air mail to, 245; change to protective tariff, 292
Arizona, 84, 115, 116, 117, 229
Armenia, 22
Armies, reduction of, 352–357
Arms, trade in, 357–358
Asheville (N.C.), 325
Austria, 22
Autographs, inflation in, 197
Aviation, development of commercial, 132–135, 243–245, 339; inter-American, 214, 245, 334; treaties on, 337
Aviation Division, 72, 73, 133, 134

Baker, Newton D., 34, 277
Balance of trade, 84
Ballantine, Arthur A., 220, 327
Bankers, as promoters, 107

Banking, reforms in, 308–309
Bankruptcy laws, reform of, 271–273
Barber, Col. Alvin B., 19
Barnes, Julius H., 16; in A.R.A., 18
Baruch, Bernard M., 34
Bates, Sanford, 221, 274
Belgium, U.S. concession on debt from, 178
Bell, James F., 19
Bermuda, 346
Better Homes in America, 92, 93, 256–258
Bigotry, religious, 207–209
Blockade, military use of, 347 and n.
Bohemian Club, 1927 encampment, 190
Bolivia, and Tacna-Arica dispute, 214–215
Bombing planes, abolition proposed, 355
Bonner, Frank E., 230
Bonus certificates, 286–287
Bonus legislation, 286–289
Booms and slumps, study of, 174–176
Boone, Dr. Joel T., and President Harding's final illness, 51; medicine-ball player, 327
Bootlegging, 276
Borah, William Edgar, 36, 174; on Senator Norris, 197–198; in 1928 campaign, 198; opposes C. E. Hughes appointment to Supreme Court, 268; and increase in agricultural tariffs, 292; and flexible tariff, 293
Boston Chamber of Commerce, 31
Boulder Canyon dam, 56, 115, 116, 117
Boyden, Roland W., 19
Brazilian Coffee Valorization, 81, 83, 90
Breed, Arthur H., 251
British Admiralty, 341, 347
British Board of Trade, 78
British Honduras, 346
Brookhart, Smith W., retort of Congressman Cole to, 57
Brown, Walter F., 185, 191; Postmaster General, 218, 220, 243, 244, 245 and n., 247, 248
Brown, Walter Lyman, 23
Bryan, William Jennings, 202, 336, 373
Buenos Aires, reception in, 212–213
Building and Housing Division, 43, 92–93, 256
Building code, adoption of standard, 93, 94
Bundy, Harvey H., 220, 336
Bureau of Education, 316
Bureau of Federal Prisons, 274–275
Bureau of Fisheries, 42, 73; conservation activities of, 149–155; hatcheries, 160, 161–163
Bureau of Foreign and Domestic Commerce, 42, 62, 69; built up, 79–80
Bureau of Mines, 43, 72, 83
Bureau of Navigation, 42, 43, 72
Bureau of Standards, 42, 62, 67, 73, 83, 134
Bureaucracy, swollen, 28; primary reforms

needed, 71; in Agriculture Dept., 109; vs. local responsibility, 114; liberalism and, 203; limitation of Federal, 239; growth of, 282
Burgess, George K., 185
Burton, Theodore E., 177; for H. H. for President, 191, 192; record of, 192; defense of H. H. as Food Administrator, 193
Business, 167–176; 300–311
Business cycle, 63; study of, 174–176
Business ethics, development of a code of, 170, 171–173
Butler, William M., 194
Button industry, 153

C.I.O., 102 n.
Cabinet, making a, 218
Cajuns, in the flood, 127–130
Caldwell, R. E., 116
California, return to (1919), 2–5; King Albert in, 6–9; H. H.'s candidacy against Hiram Johnson in 1920 Presidential primary, 34–35; 1924 Presidential primary, 56; cotton in, 84; water development of Great Valley, 114, 115, 118–119, 230–231; and project for dam at Boulder Canyon, 115–117, 229; oil of, 238, 239; old-age assistance in, 314
Cameron, George T., 251
Campbell, Ira A., 247
Campbell, Thomas E., 221
Canada, and the St. Lawrence shipway, 113, 122, 234–235; joint action with, on fisheries, 151, 152; and Chicago Drainage Canal, 234–235; joint action with, on Niagara Falls, 235–236
Capone, Al, 276–277
Capper, Senator Arthur, 24
Cardozo, Benjamin N., 269
Carnegie Corporation, 76
Carpenter, Delph E., 116
Carr, W. J., 231
Carson, Thomas, 185
Cartels, foreign, against U.S., 81, 83, 84, 90; growth in Europe, 168
Castle, William R., Jr., 220, 335, 336, 376
Catholicism in 1928 election, 208, 209, 210
Cattle and sheep ranges, conservation of, 239–241
Cavalry, mechanization of, 339
Cecil, Robert, Viscount, and pressure for economic sanctions, 370–371; on British attitude toward Japan, 372, 374, 377
Chapin, Roy D., Secretary of Commerce, 218, 220
"Cheerio," 99
Chesapeake Bay, 149, 152; oratorical contest, 153–155

Chiang Kai-shek, 181, 364, 365
Chicago, 1929 crime in, 276–277
Chicago Drainage Canal, 234–235
Chicken, fried, and peas, 57
Child health, 28, 32, 97–100, 259, 260, 262, 264, 265, 266 n.
Child Health Day, 99
Child labor, 31, 32, 99, 102–103, 264
Child welfare, 259–266
"Child's Bill of Rights," 99–100
Children's Bureau, 265
"Children's Charter," 261–264
Children's Relief, 4, 18–22
Chile, nitrates from, 81, 83; Tacna-Arica dispute, 334
China, and Washington Conference for Limitation of Armaments, 179–181; Japanese aggression in, 180, 181, 332, 362–377
Chinaman, the "robbed," campaign smear about, 192, 205
Churchill, Winston L. S., and rubber control, 81
Cities, health survey of eighty-six, 98–99
Civil Service, in Commerce Dept., 42–43, 79; heads of scientific bureaus appointed from, 218; expansion of, 280 and n.
Civil War, recovery from, 61
Civilian Training Corps, 339
Clapp, Paul S., 43, 185
Clark, J. Reuben, 334
Coal industry, ills of, 70–71
Coast Defense, 339
Coffee, 81, 83
Cole, Cyrenus, retort to Senator Brookhart, 57
Coleman, Arch, 220
Collective bargaining, 30, 101
Colorado, 115, 116
Colorado River Commission, 115–118, 227
Colorado River Compact, 115–118, 227–228
Columbia River, water utilization project, 114, 115–120, 174
Combinations, foreign trade, against U.S., 81–84
Commerce Department, H. H. appointed to, 36, 40; and State Dept., 36–37; Enabling Act, 40; building a team spirit in, 41–43, 184; advisory committee to, 41, 44; bureaus of, 42, 43; Civil Service in, 42–43; development under H. H., 44; and 1921–1922 unemployment crisis, 44–46; program for eliminating waste, 61–78; and foreign trade, 79–84; and foreign loans, 85–90; housing activities, 92–96; activities for child health and welfare, 97–100; activities in labor field, 101–108; service to farmers, 109–111;

and utilization of water resources, 112–123; and Mississippi flood control, 123–124; and aviation, 132–135; and merchant marine, 135–138; and radio broadcasting, 139–148; and the fisheries, 149–155, 160, 161–163; relations to business, 167–176; and foreign affairs, 177–182
Commercial arbitration, 63, 68–69
Commission for Conservation and Administration of Public Domain, 239–240
Commission for Relief in Belgium, 15, 17
Commission on Organization of Executive Branch, 248 n., 284 n., 319 n.
Commissions and committees, use of, 281
Committee on Business Cycles and Unemployment, 174–175, 176
Committee on Economic Trends, 77
Committee on Recent Economic Changes, 176
Commonwealth Fund, 22
Communism, 331, 364, 365
"Company unions," 30–31
Competition, 28, 62, 168–169, 171–172, 173 n., 204, 301, 302
Comstock, Ada L., 277
Congress, and the President, 216, 217
Conservation, of water, 29, 56, 112, 115, 240; of oil, 69–70, 237–239, 282; of fisheries, 149–155; of Niagara Falls, 235–236; of cattle and sheep ranges, 239–241; of forests, 241; need for an Under Secretary for, 282
Construction industries, seasonal operation in, 63, 68, 93; and a standard building code, 94; policy toward, in business cycle, 175
Coolidge, Calvin, succession to Presidency, 51, 52; and dedication of Harding tomb, 52; attends Harding burial, 53; handling of government scandals, 53–55; qualities as President, 55–56; as fisherman, 56; and water development projects, 56; H. H.'s services to, in 1924 campaign, 56–57; and Dwight W. Morrow, 57; appoints Oil Conservation Board, 69; and foreign loans, 88; and Agriculture Dept., 111; and water development projects, 115; and Colorado River Compact, 117; and California Great Valley development, 119; and Grand Coulee project, 120; and St. Lawrence shipway, 122; and Mississippi River flood control, 124; and 1927 Mississippi flood, 125; and aviation, 133; and Federal Board of Radio Control, 145; opposed to recognizing U.S.S.R., 182; and 1928 race for Republican nomination, 190–191, 192, 193–195; military intervention policy, 210–211; and H. H.'s "good neighbor" trip, 211; H. H.'s heritage of public servants from, 217; H. H.'s inaugural

Coolidge, Calvin (*continued*)
 tribute to, 221; reluctant to authorize costly
 projects, 226, 230; in White House, 326,
 327; view of League and the U.S. Army,
 352
"Coolidge prosperity," 56
Cooperative marketing, to reduce waste, 63
Cooperative movement, 110
Corruption, political, 206–207, 245 n.
Costa Rica, 211, 212, 245
Cotton, long-staple, 81, 83–84
Cotton, Joseph P., 220, 336
Coulter, John Lee, 221
Couzens, James, 307
Cove Creek Dam, 231, 304
Cowles, Gardner, 239
Crab fisheries, 149, 152, 153–155
Cramer, Charles F., 49, 54
Crane, Clinton, 97
Credit, use of, in business cycle, 175
Crime, and law enforcement, 267, 270–271,
 273–275, 276; under prohibition law, 275–
 277; in Chicago, 276–277; and prohibition,
 Wickersham Commission report, 277–278
Crowther, Samuel, 315
Crumbine, Dr. S. J., 97
Cuba, 83, 245
Cumming, Hugh S., 221
Currency devaluation, 299 n.
Currency stabilization, 332
Curtis, Charles, as Presidential candidate, 192,
 194; receives offer of bootleg vote, 277
Czechoslovakia, 22

Daley, Col. E. L., 251
Daugherty, Harry M., Attorney General, 40,
 48; injunction against railway employees,
 47–48; and Harding Alaska trip, 49; and
 Jesse Smith, 49; sees Harding at Vancouver,
 50; removed, indicted, 54
Davis, Dwight F., Secretary of War, 40
Davis, James J., Secretary of Labor, 40, 41;
 Cabinet relations with, 101, 105; reappointed by H. H., 218, 220
Davis, John W., 56
Davis, Stephen B., Commerce Dept. Solicitor,
 42, 185; on Colorado River Commission,
 116; and broadcasting wave lengths, 141;
 and the oratory contest, 155
Davison, F. Trubee, 220
Dawes, Charles G., 181, 192, 335; and naval
 arms limitation, 341–342; at London Naval
 Conference, 348; at League Council session
 on Japanese aggression against China,
 372
Dawes Commission on German Reparations,
 177, 181–182

Democratic party, H. H. and, to 1920, 33–34;
 in 1928 campaign, 198, 202, 205–206
Denby, Edwin, Secretary of Navy, 40; victim
 of persecution, 54
Deneen, Charles S., 269
Denman, Cyrus B., 255
Depression, 1921–1922, 41–42, 44–46; in
 business cycle, 63, 175; public works ex-
 panded in, 233, 252; debts and bankruptcy
 in, 273; bonus legislation in, 287; and anti-
 trust laws, 302; effect on railways, 307;
 and banking reform, 308–309; interference
 with social reforms, 313–314, 314–315
Dies Committee, 24
Dinwiddie, Courtenay, 97
Diplomatic service, 215, 332, 334, 335
Disarmament. *See* World disarmament
Dixon, Joseph M., 220
Doak, William N., Secretary of Labor, 218,
 220
"Dollar diplomacy," 210, 333
Douglas, James H., 220
Drake, J. Walter, 185
Dubrowsky, Moscow Communist agent, 24
Dunn, Gano, 73
Durbrow, William, 230
Dutch, foreign trade with, 81, 83

Economic Conference (Sept., 1921), 44–46
Economic sanctions, and Japanese aggression
 in China, 366–368, 370–371, 372 n., 375–
 376; against Italy in Ethiopia, 376 n.
Economic trends, committee on, 77
Economy, steps toward, 283, 284 and n. *See
 also* Wastes
Edge, Walter E., 335
Education, 28, 32; by radio, 146; 8-year increase in pupils, 183–184; Federal government and, 316–317
Efficiency, increasing national, 28, 31, 61, 63,
 64, 73, 77
Egypt, cotton from, 81, 84
Elections:
 1912: H. H. for T. Roosevelt in, 33
 1918: H. H.'s support of Woodrow Wilson in, 33
 1920: friends' advocacy of H. H. for
 President in, 33, 34; California Presidential
 primary, 34–35; Republican National Convention, 35; Harding campaign, 35–36
 1924: H. H.'s services to Coolidge in,
 56–57
 1928: economic progress in 8 years preceding, 183–184; pre-convention campaign,
 190–194; nomination of H. H., and acceptance, 194–195; general character of
 election campaign, 197–199; H. H.'s dec-

Elections (*continued*)
laration of broad principles, 200–202; H. H.'s stand against collectivism, 202–205; campaign dirt, 205–207; religious issue, 207–209
1932: evil of foreign loans exaggerated, 90
Electrical power, progress through expansion of, 63, 65–66
Elimination of waste, 28, 29, 112; program of Commerce Dept., 61–78; defined, 62; contributions to foreign trade, 80; essential for high real wage, 108; service to farmers, 110; in the fisheries, 149–155
Emerson, Frank C., 116
Emmett, Richard, 43
Employment, stabilization of, 63, 95
Engineering, H. H.'s 1919 return to profession, 3–4; an offer from the Guggenheims in, 186
Equality of opportunity, 203, 204, 304
Esberg, Milton H., 191
Etcheverry, B. A., 230
Europe, absence from, 2 and n., 3; credits to, 13–14; war atmosphere of, 87; relief in, compared with relief in U.S., 131; loss in industrial efficiency, 168, 301; power politics, 330, 331
European Relief Council, founding of, 20
Evangeline, in the flood, 129
Executive branch, reforms in, 279–284
Executive orders, use for departmental reorganization, 283, 284
Export Council, 15
Exports, increase in, 79, 80, 85; reproductive use of, 87; promotion of farm, 109, 110; of airplanes, 134

Fall, Albert B., Secretary of Interior, 40, 48; resignation, 53, 55; indicted, convicted, 54
Farm products, price-fixing of, 109–110, 111, 174, 200
Farmers, service to, 109–111
Farmers' Union, 296
Fascism, 27, 167, 331
Featherbedding, 101, 301
Federal Board of Radio Control, 145
Federal Bureau of Investigation, 55, 273, 274
Federal Council of Churches, 20
Federal Farm Board, 253–255
Federal Power Commission, 119, 302–306
Federal Reserve Banks, credit of, 175
Federal Reserve System, 308
Federal Trade Commission, 170, 173
Feiker, Frederick M., 62, 185
Field, Charles K., 99
Finney, Edward G., 221

Fish hatcheries and nurseries, 160–163
Fisheries, development of, 149–155; 160–163
Fishing, an essay on, 156–166; in Florida, 187
Flesh, Edward M., 16, 19, 97
Fletcher, Henry P., 220; on "good neighbor" journey, 211, 213
Flexible tariff, 292–299
Flood control, 63, 113, 115, 119, 123–124, 226, 227, 229, 230, 231, 234
Florida, fishing in, 187
Food drafts, 19–20
Food ships, immunizing of, 332, 345, 347
Forbes, Charles R., 48
Forbes, W. Cameron, 73, 335
Foreign affairs, 177–182; 378–379
Foreign Debt Commission, 177–179
Foreign loans, 13–14, 56, 85–91, 334–335
Foreign Relations Committee (Senate), 12
Foreign trade, 79–84
Forests, conservation of, 241
Four Power Treaty, 181, 364
Fourteen Points, 12
Fox, Alan, 191
France, U.S. concession on debt from, 178; Uncle Shylock propaganda and 1933 interest repudiation by, 179; policy on German reparations, 181–182; and naval arms limitation, 346, 348–349; and Japanese aggression in China, 362, 364, 367, 371, 373, 374, 376
Free, Arthur M., 192
Freedom of the seas, 332, 343, 345
Freedoms, interdependence of, 28

Galpin, Perrin C., in A.R.A., 19
Garfield, James R., 239
Garner, John Nance, 287
Garrett, John W., 335
Gary, Judge Elbert H., 103, 104
Geneva Conference for Limitation of Naval Armaments (1927), 340, 348, 350, 351
Germany, 20; potash from, 81, 83; reparations from, 177, 178, 181–182; democratic regime, 331, 332
Gibson, Hugh, an "Ambassador at Large," 335; and "yardsticks" proposal for naval arms limitation, 341; at London Naval Conference, 348; at League 1932 Geneva conference on armament, 353, 354, 356
Gilbert, Charles H., 150
Gilbert, Prentiss B., 371
Gillett, Frederick H., 48, 50
Girl Scouts, 188, 322
Gitlow, Benjamin, his exposures of Communists, 24 n., 26 n.
Glasgow, William A., 19
Glenn, Otis F., 269
Goff, Guy D., 192

Gompers, Samuel, 205
Good, James W., 191, 192; Secretary of War, 218, 219, 339
"Good neighbor" policy, 213–214, 333–334
Goodrich, James P., 23, 191, 239
Gorky, Maxim, and A.R.A., 23, 25
Government operation, of railways, 27, 30, 63–64, 307; of merchant marine, 27, 135–138; issue under Colorado River Compact, 117; of business, 167, 173–174, 203–204, 303–305, 306
Government ownership, 30, 135, 137; of broadcasting systems, 147; of businesses, 303–305
Government regulation, of public markets, 29, 300; of hydroelectric power, 113, 300–306 *passim*; of radio broadcasting, 141, 144, 145; of various businesses, 167, 168, 171, 204, 300–301. *See also* Public utilities; Railways
Grain Corporation, 15, 16, 22–23, 24
Grand Coulee project, 120, 230
Grant, Robert J., 221
Great Britain, foreign debt policy of, 178; U.S. concession on debt from, 178; Uncle Shylock propaganda by, 179; peace policy toward, 332; and naval arms limitation, 341–343, 346, 348–351; and Japanese aggression in China, 362, 364, 367–377 *passim*
Great Lakes, 114, 120–121, 123, 233; and St. Lawrence shipway, 120, 122–123, 232, 233, 234–235; and Mississippi waterway system, 232, 233
Great Lakes–St. Lawrence Waterway Treaty, 234–235 and n.
Greeley, William B., 239
Green, William, 176, 268
Gregory, Luther E., 251
Gries, Dr. John M., 92, 256
Grubb, William I., 277
Grundy, Joseph R., 295, 296
"Grundy Tariff," 296
Guggenheim, Daniel, an offer from, 186

Haiti, 210, 333
Halibut fisheries, 149–150, 151, 152
Hallowell, John W., 19
Hamill, Dr. Samuel, 97
Hamilton, Dr. Alice, 312
Hammond, John Hays, 70
Harding, Warren G., and League of Nations, 13, 35–36; Presidential campaign, 35–36; initial Cabinet, 36, 40; Cabinet changes, 40–41; personality, 47–48; Alaska trip and death, 48–52; funeral journey to Washington, 52; dedication of his tomb at Marion, 52–53; burial, 53; and oil reserves, 69; and

coal industry overexpansion, 70; and foreign loans, 85, 88; and the twelve-hour day, 103–104; and 1922 rail and coal strikes, 105; and his Secretary of Agriculture, 109; and St. Lawrence shipway, 122; and merchant marine, 136; and Alaska fisheries, 150; opposed to recognizing U.S.S.R., 182; military intervention policy, 210; and San Francisco Bay Bridge, 251; and postmasterships, 280; in White House, 326
Harding, Mrs. Warren G., 51
Harrell, Alfred, 230
Harrison, Pat, 295
Harrison, Shelby M., 312
Haskell, Col. William N., 24
Hawley, Willis C., 293, 295
Hays, Will H., on H. H.'s speeches, 35; Postmaster General, 40
Health survey, of 86 cities, 98–99. *See also* Child health; Public health
Heath, Ferry K., 191
Heinz, Howard, in A.R.A., 19
Hepburn, Arthur J., 341
Herring fisheries, North Pacific, 149, 150, 151
Herter, Christian A., 20, 43, 185
Hilles, Charles D., 193
Hines, Gen. Frank T., 287
Hiss, Alger, 357
Hitchcock, Gilbert M., 12
Holding companies, 302, 305
Homes, activities for better, 92–96; 8-year progress in, 183
Hook, Charles R., 103
Hoover, Allan, 2, 8; education of, 186, 188; in Washington, 187
Hoover, Dickerson, 185
Hoover (Herbert) administration: initial program, 223; development of water resources, 226–236, 240–241; conservation steps, 237–241; building up of national parks and monuments, 241–242; development of aviation, 243–245; development of radio and merchant marine, 246–248; achievement in public works, 249–252; development of agriculture, 253–255; achievement in housing, 256–258; work for children, 259–265; reform in law enforcement, 267–278; executive reforms, 279–284; and the veterans, 285–290; handling of tariff question, 291–299; policy toward business and industry, 300–311; general peace policies, 330–337; national defense policy, 338–339; world disarmament policy, 338, 340–358; and U.S. island possessions, 359–361; and Japanese 1931–1932 aggression in China, 362–378; foreign policies summarized, 378–379

Hoover, Mrs. Herbert, 1919 return to California, 2–3; and new house at Stanford, 5; on Harding Alaska trip, 49; at home in Washington, 186–188; work for Girl Scouts, 188; on "good neighbor" journey through Latin America, 210, 211, 212; in the White House, 321, 323–325; and the Rapidan camp, 322

Hoover, Herbert, Jr., education of, 186–187; prospective marriage, 188; at Asheville with tuberculosis, 325

Hoover, Herbert III., 325

Hoover, Ike, 321–322

Hoover, J. Edgar, head of F.B.I., 55, 220, 273, 274

Hoover, Margaret (Mrs. Herbert, Jr.), 325

Hoover, Peggy-Ann, 325

Hoover Dam, 227–229, 230. *See also* Boulder Canyon

"Hoover principle," 239 n.

Hope, Walter E., 220, 327

Hopkins, John Jay, 220

Hospitals, for veterans, 285

Housing, 31; Commerce Dept. and problems of, 43, 92–95; effect of depression on, 96; New Deal and, 96; 1931 White House conference on, 256–258

Houston, David F., 34

Howard, Roy W., 296

Hudson River, 114, 234

Hughes, Charles E., 13; becomes Secretary of State, 36–37, 40; and Daugherty's labor injunction, 47–48; and succession of Coolidge, 51, 52; urges Daugherty's removal, 54; previous unawareness of criminal transactions in government, 55; as a friend and a statesman, 58; and South American oil, 69; and research in abstract science, 73; and foreign loans, 85; discussions with, 177; on Foreign Debt Commission, 177; and Washington Conference for Limitation of Armaments, 179–181; and Dawes Commission, 181–182; opposed to recognizing U.S.S.R., 182; in 1928 campaign, 198; declines Cabinet post under H. H., 218; appointed Chief Justice, 268; contributions as Secretary to world stability, 330

Hughes, Charles E., Jr., 220, 327

Hungary, 22

Hunt, Edward Eyre, 312

Hurley, Patrick J., Secretary of War, 218, 219, 339, 359, 361

Huston, Claudius H., 42, 185, 191

Hyde, Arthur M., Secretary of Agriculture, 218, 220, 241, 255, 327

Hydroelectric power, development of, 62, 65–66, 112–120, 122, 123, 174; from multiple purpose storage dams, 227–232 *passim;* under Great Lakes-St. Lawrence Waterway Treaty, 235, 241; government regulation vs. operation of, 302–306

"I do not choose to run," 190

Ickes, Harold L., renames Hoover Dam, 229 n.

Idaho, 119

Illiteracy, 317

Imperial Valley, 115, 229

Imports, increase in, 80; foreign price fixing of U.S., 81–84; agricultural, 110

Inauguration Day (1929), 222–223

Indianapolis, 13; the lady from, 197

Indians, Federal policies toward, 317–318

Individualism, American, 204, 257

Industrial Conference of 1919, 30, 102

Industrial Conference of 1920, 30–31

Inflation, 31

Ingalls, David S., 220

Insull, Samuel, 305, 306 and n.

Interior Department, 43, 317

Internal Revenue collectors, and merit system, 280

International Radio Conference (1927), 145–146

Interstate Commerce Commission, and reorganization of railways, 306–308, 309, 310

Invisible Guest, banquets to, 21

Irigoyen, Hipólito, reception of H. H. on "good neighbor" journey, 212–213

Irrigation, 112–120 *passim,* 226–231 *passim,* 241

Irwin, Will, 211

Isolationism, 35, 330, 337, 353, 378

Italy, U.S. concession on debt from, 178; rising Fascism, 331; and naval arms limitation, 346, 349; and Japanese aggression in China, 364, 367, 371; economic sanctions against, 376 n.

Izaak Walton League, inaugural address to, 156–166

Jadwin, Gen. Edgar, 124

Jahncke, Ernest Lee, 220, 327

Japan, its aggression in China, 180, 181, 332, 362–377; and limitation of world navies, 340, 341, 342, 346–351 *passim*

Jardine, William M., Secretary of Agriculture, 41, 111

Jenkins, Perry W., 239

Jennings, Malcolm, 49

Johns Hopkins University, 12

Johnson, Hiram, 11; in 1920 California Presidential primary, 34–35; anti-League, 34,

Johnson, Hiram (*continued*)
  36; and President Harding's San Francisco speech, 51; loses in 1924 California Presidential primary, 56; and Colorado River Compact, 117; and renaming of Hoover Dam, 229 n.; against World Court, 337
Joint Distribution Committee, 20, 22
Jones, Hilary P., 341
Jones, Lester, 185
Joslin, Theodore G., 218
Justice Department, scandal in, 49; anti-trust-law prosecutions by, 170–171; and codes of business ethics, 173; and "open price associations," 173; clean-up of, 270; and Federal prisons, 274, 275; to investigate Federal employees under suspicion, 279; under F. D. Roosevelt, special section to look for crookedness in Hoover administration, 279 n.; prohibition agencies consolidated under, 283

Kamenev, Lev B., and A.R.A., 23, 25–26
Kansas, 238, 276
Kellogg, Frank B., Secretary of State, 40, 41, 177, 182; upsets "proof" H. H. was Britisher, 206; reappointed by H. H., 218; and Kellogg-Briand Pact, 330–331, 335–336; asks H. H. to call conference of arms manufacturers, 357–358
Kellogg, Dr. Vernon Lyman, in A.R.A., 19; report on 1921 Russian famine, 23
Kellogg-Briand (Paris) Pact, 330–331, 332, 335–336, 343–344, 346, 353, 354, 363; and Japanese aggression in China, 365, 368, 372–373
Kellogg (W. K.) Child Welfare Foundation, 265
Kenyon, William S., 277
Kettleman Hills (Calif.), oil pool, 239
Kidnaping, 274
King, John T., 54
Klein, Julius, 62, 79, 169, 176, 185, 220
Knights of Columbus, 20
Knox, Philander C., 34
Konoye, Prince, 365, 372
Kuomintang government, 180, 181, 364

Labor relations, H. H.'s general views on, 101–102; in steel industry, 103–105; railway, 105–108
La Follette, Robert Marion (1855–1925), 174
Lamb, William, 185
Lamont, Robert P., Secretary of Commerce, 218, 220, 247, 256
Lamont, Thomas W., 296
Lane, Franklin K., 20, 34

Lane, Gertrude B., 19
Latin America, antagonism of, toward U.S., 210–211, 334; H. H.'s six weeks' journey through, 210, 211–215; creation in, of good will toward U.S., 332, 333–334
Laura Spelman Rockefeller Memorial, 22
Law enforcement, reform in, 267–278
League of Nations, 3; campaign for U.S. membership in, 10–13; factor in 1920 Presidential election, 34–36; Secretary Hughes an advocate, 37; and American isolationism, 330; cooperation with, in non-force activities, 332, 337; and Kellogg-Briand Pact, 336; entrusted with reduction of land armament, 352; 1932 Geneva conference on armament, 353–356; and Japanese aggression in China, 365–378 *passim*
League of Nations Covenant, 10, 11, 12, 37; and Japanese aggression in China, 365, 367, 374, 377, 378
Legge, Alexander, 103, 220, 255, 327
Lemann, Monte M., 277
Lenroot, Irvine L., 102, 191, 192
Lewis, Ernest I., 187
Lewis, John L., remedy for coal industry over-expansion, 70; considered for Secretary of Labor, 221–222
Libbey, Edward, 185
Liberalism, true and false, 203
"Liberals," 174, 182
Liggett, Walter W., 24 and n.
Lindbergh, Charles A., Jr., kidnaping, 274
Litvinov, Maxim, 23
Lobbying, 268–269, 285, 290, 298, 299
Lodge, Henry Cabot (1850–1924), 11, 34, 36
Loesch, Frank J., 276, 277
Logan, Col. James A., Jr., 19
Log-rolling, 282, 290, 292, 293, 296, 298, 299
London Naval Conference (1930), preliminaries, 340–348; meets, concludes Naval Limitation Treaty, 348–349
Long, Col. Earl, 322
Longworth, Nicholas, 293
Lorimer, George H., 239
Los Angeles, 115, 116, 228
Louisiana, flood in, 127–130
Lowden, Frank O., 35; 1928 Presidential candidate, 191, 194; declines Cabinet post under H. H., 218
Lowell, A. Lawrence, and sanctions "movement," 371
Lytton Commission, 372, 377

MacArthur, General Douglas, 220, 339
McClure, W. F., 116
McCormick, Paul J., 277

McCormick, Vance C., 34
McCoy, Frank R., 372
MacCracken, William P., Jr., Asst. Sec. of Commerce for Aeronautics, 134, 185
MacDonald, J. Ramsay, and naval arms limitation, 341–343, 346; H. H. memoranda to, for discussion, 343–345; and idea of selling Bermuda, British Honduras, Trinidad, 345–346; and idea of further article to Kellogg-Briand Pact, 346; and British naval and air bases in Western Hemisphere, 346–347; and immunizing of food ships, 347
McFarland, Horace, 236
McGrath, Myra, 218
McKelvie, Samuel R., 255
Mackintosh, Kenneth, 277
McNary, Charles L., 254
McNary-Haugen bill, 47, 109, 174, 200
McPherson, Aimee Semple, 142
Mail contracts, as ship subsidies, 246–247
Mails, use of, to defraud, 271. *See also* Air mail
Manchuria, Japanese aggression in, 362–377
Mao Tse-tung, 181, 364, 365
Marginal lands, 110–111, 254, 255
Marines, in Nicaragua, 211–212, 333
Marion (Ohio), dedication of Harding tomb at, 52–53
Market Street (San Francisco), a parade up, 7–8
Marx, Charles D., 251
Maryland, 154
Maryland (battleship), 211, 212
Mason, Max, 176
Mass production, 66
Massachusetts, in 1928 election, 209
Mather, Stephen T., 242
Mathews, W. B., 231
Mayer, Raymond S., 20
Mayor, the, and the King, 7–9
Mead, Elwood, 221, 230
Mediation, labor, 105–106, 107
Medicine ball, at White House, 327
Meek, B. B., 231
Meloney, Mrs. William Brown, 92, 97
Mellon, Andrew William, Secretary of Treasury, 36, 40, 41; as a banker, 58, 59; on Mellon family fortune, 58–59; and an inventor, 59; his plans for National Gallery of Art, 59–60; persecution under New Deal, 60; and foreign loans, 85, 88; on Foreign Debt Commission, 177; and Dawes Commission, 181; in 1928 campaign, 193–194; reappointed by H. H., 218; in diplomatic service, 335

Mendenhall, Walter C., 221
Merchant marine, 110, 135–138, 246–248, 282, 337
Merchants' Association of New York, 14
Merit system, 280 and n. *See also* Civil service
Merriam, Charles E., 312
Metropolitan Life Insurance Co., 102
Metropolitan Water District of Southern California, 228
Mexico, 346; sisal from, 81, 83; and the Boulder Canyon dam, 113, 115, 229; and Pacific fisheries, 151
Military interventions, 210–212, 333–334
Miller, Adolph C., 175, 176
Miller, Nathan L., 35; declines Attorney Generalship, 54
Miller, Thomas W., Alien Property Custodian, 48, 53; indicted, convicted, 54
Millikan, Robert A., 73
Mills, Frederick C., 176
Mills, Ogden L., 191; Secretary of Treasury, 218, 219, 367
Mississippi River, projected waterway system, 114, 115, 120–121; flood control of, 123–124, 234; the 1927 flood, 123, 125–131, 190; Upper, fish and game refuge, 152; rescue of flood-marooned fish, 153; waterway development of, 232–234
Mitchell, Charles E., 296
Mitchell, Wesley C., 312
Mitchell, Gen. William, 133
Mitchell, William D., Attorney General, 218, 219, 246, 267, 268, 270, 271, 302, 327
Monroe, James, in White House, 321
Monroe Doctrine, 210, 334
Moratorium on intergovernmental debts, 332
Morgan, Ephraim F., 185
Morgenthau, Henry, Sr., 296
Morrow, Dwight W., 54; public record of, 57; and aviation, 133; at London Naval Conference, 348
Moses, George H., 195, 337, 349
Moses, Robert, ghost writer, 199
Moton, Robert R., at White House, 324
Mott, John G., 211
Mullendore, William C., 43, 185
Muscle Shoals, 232, 303
Mussels, fresh-water, 153
Mussolini, Benito, 331
Mutual insurance companies, 315
"My Redeemer Liveth," 52

NRA, 173 n.
Napoleonic Wars, recovery from, 61
Narcotics, international traffic in, 337
National Academy of Sciences, 74

National Association of Architects, 93
National Board of Parole, 275
National Conference on Street and Highway Safety, 72
National defense, 338–339, 350
National Gallery of Art, and Andrew W. Mellon, 59–60
National Grange, 296
National Guard, 339
National parks and monuments, 241–242
National planning, 167
National Radio Conferences (1922–1925), 140, 141, 142, 143, 145, 147
National Republican Club, 33
National Research Council, 73
Naval Limitation Treaty (1930), 349–352
Naval Reserve oil, scandal over, 53, 54
Navigation, inland waterways and, 113, 119, 120, 123, 232–235
Nevada, 115, 116
New, Harry S., Postmaster General, 40, 135, 243
New Deal, and A. W. Mellon, 60; and home construction, 96; its NRA, 173 n.; cancellation of air-mail contracts, 245 n.; American shipping under, 248 n.; and merit system, 280 n.; and care of disabled, sick, destitute veterans, 285 n.; tariffs, currency devaluation, 299 n.; and the Indians, 319
New Mexico, 83, 115, 116, 238
New York, engineers' 1919 reception to H. H. in, 2; H. H. opens office in, 3, 4; dinner to Invisible Guest, 21
New York Federal Reserve Bank, 86
New York Herald Tribune, Woman's Conference on Current Problems, 265
New York State, vote in 1928 election, 208
New York Times, 1919 poll to select most important Americans, 4
New York Tribune, 106
Newton, Walter H., Secretary to President, 218, 219, 327
Niagara Falls, 235–236
Nicaragua, military intervention in, 211–212, 333–334; two Presidents come to lunch with H. H. in, 212; air mail to, 245
Nine Power Treaty, 181, 364, 365, 368, 369, 374, 375, 376
Nitrates, 81, 83
"No White Help Wanted," 205–206 and n.
Nonrecognition, 372–376
Norbeck, Peter, 187
Norris, George William, 36, 174, 197; and the Cove Creek Dam, 231, 232; and Senate resolution recalling confirmation of an appointment, 305; against World Court, 337

Norris bill, 303–305
Norris Dam, 231
Norviel, W. S., 116

O'Brian, John Lord, 220, 302
Odum, Howard W., 312
Ogburn, William F., 312
Ohio, 1928 Presidential primary, 190–191; and prohibition, 276
Ohio River, canalized, 232–233
Oil, conservation of, 69–70, 237–239, 282
Oil Conservation Board, 69, 237
Oklahoma, 238
Old-age assistance, 313–315
Old-age insurance, 31, 315
Old Guard, Republican, 191, 192, 217, 294, 295
Olney, Warren, Jr., 231, 246
O'Malley, Henry, Bureau of Fisheries Director, 149, 161–162, 185, 220; and Chesapeake Bay crabbers, 154–155
Opelousas (La.), triplets at, 127
Open Door policy, 180, 365
Order of the Crown (Belgian), 7, 8–9
Oregon, 119
Osmeña, Sergio, 361
Overproduction, agricultural, 110–111; of oil, 238

Palmer, Dr. George, 97
Palo Alto (Calif.), visits to, 187, 198, 210
Pan American Airways, 214, 245
Pan-American Commercial Conference (1927), 89
Pardee, George, 230
Paris Pact. *See* Kellogg-Briand Pact
Parker, John J., nomination to U.S. Supreme Court, 268–269
Patronage, Republican, in South, 279; Congressional, Federal appointments used for, 280
Payne, Frederick H., 220
Pearl Harbor, 377 n.
Peace policies, 330–337
Pennsylvania, in 1928 Republican convention, 193–194
Penrose, Boies, 34, 36
Pensions in Civil Service, 43; for war veterans, 285–286, 287, 289–290; old-age, 312, 314, 315
Perishables, marketing of, 64, 110
Pershing, Gen. John J., 21
Peru, and Tacna-Arica dispute, 214–215, 334; air mail to, 245
Philippine Islands, independence for, 359–361; and Japanese aggression in China, 367–368, 377

Philp, John W., 221
Pierson, Lewis E., 176
Pillsbury, Gen. G. B., 251
Pinchot, Gifford, 174
Poker, 48
Poland, 22
Political pressure, 269–270
Pollution, 151–152, 153, 164–165
Pomerene, Atlee, 258
Post Office Department, and air mail, 132, 134, 135, 243, 245; and ocean mail, 247, 248; appointments in, as Congressional patronage, 280
Potash, 81, 83, 90
Pound, Roscoe, 277
Power. *See* Electrical power; Hydroelectric power
Power politics, European, 330, 331; an exercise in, 370–371
Pratt, Mrs. Ruth S. B., 191
Pratt, William V., 220, 341, 346, 348
President, the office of, 216–218
President's Aircraft Board, 133
Pressure groups, 269, 283
Price-fixing, foreign, against U.S., 81–84; under McNary-Haugen bill, 109–110; advocated by Agriculture Dept., 109, 111; in Europe, 168; under New Deal, 173 n.; demands in U.S. for, 174
Prices, movement of, and wages, U.S. and Gt. Britain, 78; and production, 108
Prohibition, in 1928 campaign, 200–202, 209; and law enforcement, 275–277; Wickersham Committee report on, 277–278; agencies dealing with, consolidated, 283
Promoter-bankers, 107
Propaganda, by radio, 146–147
Public health, 97–100, 258, 264, 313
Public Health Service, 275
Public lands, 226–227; oil drilling on, 237; and conservation, 239–241; and national parks, 241–242
Public utilities, unemployment insurance in, 102; government operation of, 174; regulation of, 174, 204, 300, 302–303
Public works, concentration of, 29; by government, 46, 204; progress in Hoover administration, 249–252
Puerto Rico, 359
Purcell, C. H., 251
Putnam, George R., 185

Quakerism, H. H.'s background, 207
Quezon, Manuel L., 361

RFC, loan to Metropolitan Water District of

Southern California, 228; loan for San Francisco Bay Bridge, 252; backing for slum clearance, 258; and the railways, 307
Radio, in Commerce Dept., 43, 73, 139–146; in 1924 campaign, 57; assets and liabilities, 146–148; in 1928 campaign, 199; government suit against "manufacturing trust," 246
Radio broadcasting, 139–148
Railway Association, 64
Railway brotherhoods, 105, 107
Railway Mediation Act, 64, 107–108
Railways, government operation of, 27, 30, 63, 64; elimination of wastes in, 62, 63–64; unemployment insurance in, 102; machinery to obviate strikes, 107–108; and marketing of perishables, 110; increased rates, 114, 123; opposition to St. Lawrence shipway, 123; and 1927 Mississippi flood, 126; plan for reorganization of, 306–308, 309–311
Rapidan River, summer camp on, 322–323; Ramsay MacDonald at, 343–347
Raskob, John J., 296
Reading, Rufus Isaacs, Marquess of, 371
Reclamation, 113, 118, 119, 124, 240, 241
Reclamation Service, 226, 227, 230
Reconstruction Finance Corporation. *See* RFC
Reed, David A., 348
Reid, Mrs. Whitelaw, Sr., 106
Republican party, H. H. and, to 1920, 33–34; in 1920 election, 34–36; 1928 convention, 194–195; in 1928 campaign, 202, 206; patronage system in South, 279
Requa, Mark L., 56, 191, 237
Research, scientific, 28, 63, 73–76, 170; in aeronautics, 132, 134; on the fisheries, 149, 150, 151, 153
Research Committee on Social Trends, 312–313, 315
Rhoads, Charles J., 221, 318
Richey, Lawrence, 55, 185, 192; correspondence secretary to President, 218, 219, 322, 327
Rickard, Edgar, 16; in A.R.A., 19; in American Child Health Assn., 97; for H. H. for President, 191
Rinehart, Mary Roberts, 239
Rio Grande, 114
Rivers and Harbors Bill (1930), 233
Roberts, Owen J., 269
Robins, Thomas M., 230
Robinson, Henry M., 73, 181, 218
Robinson, Joseph T., 287, 348
Robinson, Thomas L., 185
Rockefeller, John D., Jr., 21
Rockefeller Foundation, 126, 130

Rogers, James Grafton, 220
Rolph, James, Jr., at San Francisco reception to King Albert, 7, 8–9; funeral of, 9
Roosevelt, Franklin D., and child labor, 103; at Hoover Dam, 229 n.; and Great Lakes-St. Lawrence Waterway Treaty, 235 n.; and child welfare, 266 n.; search under, for crookedness in preceding administration, 279 n.; and "Grundy Tariff," 296; 1932 tariff misrepresentation, 299 n.; and Japanese aggression in China, 377
Roosevelt, Theodore, 33, 228; in the White House, 320, 321, 326
Root, Aida de Costa, 97
Root, Elihu, 13, 36, 73, 76; on prohibition, 278; and World Court protocol, 337
Roraback, J. Henry, 193
Rosenberg, James N., 20
Rosenwald, Julius, 30 n., 95
Rubber control, British, 81, 82–83
Rugg, Charles B., 220
Russia. *See* U.S.S.R.

Sabin, Charles H., 296
Sackett, Frederic M., Jr., 191, 335
Sacramento River, 118, 119
St. Lawrence Great Lakes Waterways Commission, 122–123, 234
St. Lawrence shipway, 29, 115, 120, 122–123, 232, 233, 234, 235
St. Martinville (La.), in the flood, 129–130
Salmon fisheries, 149–151, 152, 153
Saltzman, Charles M., 221
San Francisco, H. H. opens office in, 3; entertainment of King Albert, 7–9; 1919 address on hope of peace, 11; President Harding's illness and death at, 50, 51; Bay Bridge, 251–252
San Joaquin River, 118
Sanctions, moral vs. economic, 377–378. *See also* Economic sanctions
Santa Barbara (Calif.), entertainment of King Albert, 6–7, 8
Santa Fe (N.M.), 116
Sawyer, Dr. Charles E., White House physician, 50–51
Scattergood, J. Henry, 318
Schall, Thomas D., 269
Schilling, William F., 255
Schools, public vs. private, 187; Federal vs. local and state control of, 316–317
Schwab, Charles M., 103
Scrugham, J. G., 116
Seasonal operation in industry, 68
Seattle, 50
Senate (U.S.), and League and Versailles

Treaty, 10, 11, 12; in 1928 Republican pre-convention campaign, 191–193, 194; and appointments to Federal bench, 268–270; an attempt at dictation by, 305
Shad fisheries, 149, 151, 152, 153
Shanghai, Japanese attack on, 374, 375, 376
Shankey, Ann, 218
Shantung, 180, 181, 363
Shattuck, Edwin, 16
Shaw, Arch W., 176
Shenandoah National Park, 322
Sheriff, the, and the King, 7
Ship subsidies, 246
Shotwell, James T., 336
Shouse, Jouett, 296
Shylock, Uncle, 179, 330
Simon, Sir John, 372, 376, 377
Simplification, to eliminate waste, 63, 64, 66–68; and foreign trade, 80
Sinclair, Harry F., 54
Sisal, 81, 82
Slum clearance, 256, 257, 258
Small business, 168, 176
Smith, Alfred E., Presidential campaign of, 198, 199, 200, 202, 207–209, 210
Smith, George Otis, 221, 305
Smith, Jesse, 48; suicide of, 49, 54
Smoot, Reed, 177, 294, 295
Smoot-Hawley tariff, 291, 293–299
Social reforms, 312–319
South, Republican patronage system in, 279
South America, oil lands in, 69; antagonism toward U.S. in, 210; 1928 journey through, 211, 212–215; air mail to, 245; exchange of students and professors with, 333
Soviet. *See* U.S.S.R.
Spaulding, Huntley N., 239
Specification directory, 67
Specifications, uniform, 63, 66, 67–68
Speeches, in a Presidential campaign, 197, 198–199; on Latin America journey, 213–214
Standardization, to eliminate waste, 63, 64, 66–68; and foreign trade, 80; in building materials, 95
"Standstill" agreement, on German private debts, 332
Stanford Food Research Institute, 76
Stanford University, campus cottage at, 3; H. H.'s new house at, 5; 1919 address supporting League, 10
Stanley, W. H., 251
State Department, appointment of C. E. Hughes to, 36, 40; and Commerce Dept., 36–37; and foreign loans, 85–86
Statistics, business movement, 175, 176

Steel manufacturers, White House dinner conference of, 103
Steiwer, Frederick, 192, 296
Steuart, William M., Director of Census, 176, 185
Stimson, Henry L., Secretary of State, 218, 219, 335; beginnings in office, 336–337; achievement in arbitration and conciliation treaties, 337; and Rapidan discussions with MacDonald, 345; and further article for Kellogg-Briand Pact, 346; at London Naval Conference (1930), 348; and Japanese aggression in China, 365–367, 370, 372 n., 373, 375–376
Stock exchanges, reforms in, 309
Stockton (Calif.), seaway to, 119, 234
Stokes, Harold Phelps, 43, 185
Stone, Harlan F., Attorney General, 40, 41, 54, 55; regular Sunday evening guest, 187; declines Cabinet post under H. H., 218; medicine-ball player, 327
Stone, James C., 255
Stratton, Samuel W., 62
Straus, Oscar S., 42
Strauss, Lewis L., 16; in A.R.A., 19
Strikes, 31; railway, 47–48, 64, 105–106; coal, 70–71, 105
Strong, Benjamin, and foreign loans, 86
Strong, Walter A., 276
Strother, French, administrative asst. to President, 218, 219, 312
Stuart, Robert Young, 221
Sturgeon fisheries, 149, 151, 152, 153
Sugar Equalization Board, 15, 16–17
Sullivan, Mark, 187, 211, 327
Sun Yat-sen, 180, 181, 364
Survey of Current Business, 176
Sutherland, Daniel A., 151

Taber, Louis J., 176
Tacna-Arica dispute, 214–215, 334
Taft, Robert A., 16; in A.R.A., 19
Taft, William Howard, 13, 36, 268
Tammany Hall, 207, 208, 209
Tariff Commission, 292, 293, 294, 297, 299
Tariff question, 110, 291–299
Taussig, Frank William, 16–17, 30 n.
Taxation, a proper system of, 29
Taylor, Dr. Alonzo E., 19, 76
Teague, Charles C., 255
Teapot Dome, 53
Tennessee River, flood control and power development, 231–232, 303–304; improvements, 234
Terrell, William D., 185
Texas, 83, 238

Thacher, Thomas D., 220, 327
Thomas, Elmer, 265
Tilton, Frederic A., 220
Tong Shao-yi, campaign dirt about London lawsuit, 192, 205
Townsend, Wallace, 239
Trade agreements, foreign, against U.S., 81; in Europe, 168
Trade associations, 169–170, 172–173 and n.
Transportation, applying waterways for, 112, 114, 120–123; by air, 243–245
Transportation Act (1920), 306
Treasury, appointment of A. W. Mellon to, 36, 40; and foreign loans, 85, 88
Trinidad, 346
Triplets at Opelousas, 127
Turner, Scott, 185
Twelve-hour day, 28; abolishing of, 103–105, 183
Twelve-Hour Shift in Industry, The (report, Committee on Work-Periods in Continuous Industry, Federated American Engineering Societies), 104
Tyrer, Arthur, 185

U.S.S.R. (Russia), relief by A.R.A. of 1921 famine, 23–26; sale of paintings to A. W. Mellon, 60; nonrecognition of, 177, 182; influence in China, 180, 181; influence toward war, 331
Ukraine, 1921 famine in, 23
Unemployment, 1921–1922 crisis, 41–42, 44–46; in "business cycle," 63; "technological," 77; and loss on foreign loans, 90–91; insurance against, 102, 312, 316; former misuse of, 108; mitigation of, in a depression, 175; 1931 Federal aid to, 250, 251; aid through highway construction, 252; veterans' bonus as a relief for, 286
Unions (labor), after First World War, 28, 29, 30; anti-Socialist and anti-Communist, 102; change in attitude toward jobs, 108; monopolies and featherbedding of, 301–2
United States Army, 338, 339, 340, 352
United States Board of Mediation, 107–108
United States Chamber of Commerce, 77, 126
United States Coal Commission, 70
United States Coast Guard, 125, 127
United States Food Administration, 15 and n., 17, 18, 19, 22, 76, 109; 1928 campaign attack on H. H.'s record in, 193
United States island possessions, 359–361
United States Navy, 338, 339, 340, 350, 351, 367, 377
United States Shipping Board, 135–138, 246–248

United States Supreme Court, Anti-Trust cases in, 169–170; nominations to, 268–269; and reform of criminal procedure, 271; on flexible tariff, 293

United States Veterans' Bureau, 48, 49, 53, 290

Ural Mountains, H. H.'s supposed mines in, 26

Utah, 115, 116

Utah (battleship), 211

Vancouver, B.C., 50

Vandenberg, Arthur H., 269

Vanderlip, Frank A., 54

Van Ingen, Dr. Philip, 97

Van Petten, Edward C., 239

Vare, William S., 194, 269–270

Veto, President's, 217

Versailles Peace Treaty, 3; U.S. campaign for ratification, 10–13; Secretary Hughes and, 36–37; teaching of, 181; American revolt from, 330; and reduction of land armament, 352, 355; Japan under, 363

Veteran agencies, consolidation of, 282, 283

Veterans' affairs, reform of, 285–290

Villard, Oswald Garrison, 296

Viquez, González, President of Costa Rica, 212

Virginia, 153

Volga River, 23

Wages, creation of higher real, 28–29, 66, 108; miners', 70; movement of, and prices, U.S. and Gt. Britain, 78; steadily increasing, 105, 183

Wall Street Journal, 90

Wallace, Henry A., Secretary of Agriculture, 110 n.

Wallace, Henry C., Secretary of Agriculture, 40; on Harding Alaska trip, 48; difficulties with, in Cabinet, 109–110; death, 111; his price-fixing proposals, 174

War debts, revision of, 332; British, balanced against British Western Hemisphere possessions, 345–346. *See also* France; Great Britain; Hughes, Charles E.; Italy

Washington (D.C.), H. H.'s 1919 move to, 4; Cabinet years in, 186–188; improvements in Hoover administration, 249–250

Washington (state), 119

Washington Conference for Limitation of Armaments, 177, 179–181, 350, 351

Waste in Industry, 31 and n.

Wastes, great national, 29; industrial, 31, 63–64, 66–69, 171; in chaos of Federal agencies, 281–282, 284 n. *See also* Elimination of waste

Water, true conservation of, 29, 56, 112, 115, 240; divided responsibility for conservation of, 282

Water resources, development of, 112–123, 226–235

Water rights, 115, 116, 119, 228

Waterways, development of, 110, 112, 114, 120–123, 232–235

Watson, James E., 34, 192, 294, 296

Webb, Harry, 6, 8

Weeks, John W., Secretary of War, 40

West Point, 12

Western ranges, conservation of, 239–241

Weymouth, Frank E., 231

White, Francis, 220

White, John B., 16, 19

White-Jones Merchant Marine Act, 137

White House, living in the, 320–328

Whitmarsh, Theodore F., 16, 19

Wickersham Commission, 277–278

Wiggin, Albert H., 296

Wilbur, Curtis D., Secretary of Navy, 40, 41

Wilbur, Dr. Ray Lyman, and President Harding's final illness, 51; Secretary of Interior, 218, 220; Colorado River power sold by, 228; and tentative interstate oil compact, 237–238; and Kettleman Hills oil pool, 239; and national parks and monuments, 241; and child welfare, 259, 261, 265; and adult education, 317; and Federal policy toward Indians, 318; medicine-ball player, 327; in discussions of Japanese aggression in China, 368

Willard, Daniel, and 1922 rail strike, 105–106; and U.S. Board of Mediation, 107; on Committee on Recent Economic Changes, 176; consulted on reorganizations of railways, 308

Willebrandt, Mrs. Mabel Walker, 221, 276

Williams, Carl, 255

Williams, Dr. Linsly, 97

Willis, Frank B., 190–191, 192

Wilson, Charles S., 255

Wilson, Francis C., 239

Wilson, William B., 30 and n.

Wilson, Woodrow, 1919 illness, 6, 12; and failure of Versailles Treaty ratification, 11–12; failure to acknowledge H. H.'s resignation, 15; orders sugar control ended, 16–17; and A.R.A., 19, 21; calls 1920 Industrial Conference, 30; supported by H. H. in 1918 election, 33; 1912 election of, 34; Secretary Hughes on, 37; military intervention policy, 210, 333; working hours, 326

Wilson Dam, 228, 232

Women's Bureau, 265

Wood, Leonard, 34

Wood, Dr. Thomas, 97
Woolley, Clarence M., 187, 333
Work, Hubert, Cabinet appointments, 40, 41, 53; on Harding Alaska trip, 49, 50; and Harding's final illness, 51; and the Boulder Canyon dam, 56, 117; supports H. H. for President, 191
World Court, 37, 50, 330, 332, 337
World disarmament, 338; naval, 340–352, 355–356; land, 352–355, 356–357; air, 355; and treaty for control of trade in arms, 357–358

Wyoming, 115, 116, 238

Y.M.C.A., 20
Y.W.C.A., 20
Young, Governor C. C., 230, 231, 251
Young, Clarence M., 185, 220
Young, Owen D., 176, 181
Youngquist, G. Aaron, 220

Zabriskie, George, 16
Zoning laws, 92, 94, 95

(Continued from front flap)
welfare, better housing, and improving agriculture. As he sets it down here, it is an impressive record of solid achievement.

These memoirs bear the obvious stamp of Mr. Hoover's personality. His characterizations of Harding and Coolidge, of contemporary industrialists and politicians (foreign and domestic), friends and opponents, are incisive, illuminating, and colorful but never malicious. His comments on controversial topics are frank and straight-from-the-shoulder. He writes with strong feeling, absolute sincerity, and with felicitous touches of humor. His *Memoirs* constitute another public service on the part of one whose contributions, in and out of public office, to his country and fellow men are recognized more widely than ever at their true value.

Praise for Volume I
The Years of Adventure
1874–1920

"It is fascinating reading, this story of the evolution of one of the finest administrators in the history of the world." — ARTHUR SEARS HENNING, *Chicago Tribune.*

"His book is genuinely historic and one which every student of the time must deal with." — *Newsweek.*

Published in part in Collier's

CPSIA information can be obtained
at www.ICGtesting.com
Printed in the USA
BVHW040840140222
628964BV00012B/448

9 781013 542480